Nationalism and Particularity

Nationalism and Particularity is a work of political theory that examines nationalism in two ways. First, it draws out the ideological connections and associations of nationalism by analysing its relation to a series of key political concepts, theories and practices, namely: sovereignty, the nation state, citizenship, liberal theory, patriotism, communitarianism, multiculturalism and cosmopolitanism. Second, it looks at the drift to particularity in political debates by assessing nationalism as a key example of particularity. The central argument is that the notion of the particular in contemporary thought derives its moral and generative force from association with the idea of the personality and individuality. The book concludes that we should treat all forms of particularity with caution and scepticism. It is an original contribution to political theory accessible to students in philosophy, politics and law.

Andrew Vincent is Professor of Political Theory at the University of Sheffield. He is the author of several works including, as editor, *Political Theory: Tradition and Diversity* (Cambridge University Press, 1997).

Nationalism and Particularity

Andrew Vincent
University of Sheffield

PUBLISHED BY THE PRESS SYNDICATE OF THE UNIVERSITY OF CAMBRIDGE
The Pitt Building, Trumpington Street, Cambridge, United Kingdom

CAMBRIDGE UNIVERSITY PRESS
The Edinburgh Building, Cambridge CB2 2RU, UK
40 West 20th Street, New York, NY 10011–4211, USA
477 Williamstown Road, Port Melbourne, VIC 3207, Australia
Ruiz de Alarcón 13, 28014 Madrid, Spain
Dock House, The Waterfront, Cape Town 8001, South Africa

http://www.cambridge.org

First published 2002

Printed in Singapore by Craft Print

Typeface Plantin (*Adobe*) 10/12 pt.   *System* QuarkXPress® [BC]

A catalogue record for this book is available from the British Library

National Library of Australia Cataloguing in Publication data
Vincent, Andrew.
Nationalism and particularity.
Bibliography.
Includes index.
ISBN 0 521 81690 4.
ISBN 0 521 01709 2 (pbk).
1. Nationalism. 2. Patriotism. I. Title.
320.54

ISBN 0 521 81690 4 hardback
ISBN 0 521 01709 2 paperback

Contents

Preface

This book has had a rather long gestation period. It has wended its way in and out of my thoughts over a good many years. Over the last five years, specifically, I have incurred intellectual debts to many colleagues and friends who have discussed, listened patiently and criticized my ideas. Thus, I would like to thank Ed Andrew, David Boucher, Bob Brown, Barry Hindess, John Hoffman, Barry Jones, Rex Martin, Peter Nicholson, Raymond Plant, Vicki Spencer and David West. Some have also read and commented on draft chapters, for which I am deeply grateful. I am certain that none will think that I have fully addressed their criticisms or developed the ideas in ways that they would find satisfactory. Such are the joys of academic life. I can only hope that they will find some of the arguments reasonably developed. I was also fortunate to have a very sympathetic and perceptive editor in Peter Debus, as well as three excellent and very constructive reviewers of the original typescript, who made many helpful suggestions for improving the work.

In practical terms, the final writing and polishing of the book were completed in the very congenial and stimulating surroundings of the Humanities Research Centre in the Australian National University, Canberra, where I was fortunate enough to be a fellow between 2000–2001. I am immensely grateful to the Director of the Centre, Iain McCalman, and Caroline Turner (Deputy Director) for facilitating such a friendly and agreeable period of reflection and extensive writing. For all other arrangements at the Centre, including some excellent social events, my gratitude to Leena Messina. Thanks are also due to my old University at Cardiff for sabbatical leave and also to my politics colleagues in Cardiff for their years of friendship and support.

Chapter three has been adapted from my essay 'Liberalism and Citizenship' in Mark Evans (ed.) *The Edinburgh Companion to Contemporary Liberalism* (2001) by permission of the copyright holders Edinburgh University Press. Chapters four and six have been adapted respectively from my articles in *Political Studies* (vol. 45, no. 2, June 1997: 275–95) and the *Australian Journal of Politics and History* (vol. 3, no. 1, 1997: 14–27) by permision of the copyright holders Blackwell Publishers.

Finally, my deepest thanks go to my wife Mary, my children Lisa, Sara, Jason and Rachael, and their respective spouses Stephane, Steve and Rebekah, my granddaughters Josie and Laura, and my dear friend Diana, who have all kept me very firmly rooted in the most valuable of all particulars.

Introduction:
The Drift to Particularity

One important characteristic of recent political theory has been a gradual but marked shift of interest away from universalist forms of argument towards favouring communities and groups. It is these groups which form the key 'particulars' of this study. The drift to particularity is therefore the drift to group or collective forms of particularity. It is no surprise in this context that the notion of universal characteristics of human nature, universal human needs, values or rights have been viewed with increasing scepticism from many quarters. In this scenario, the idea that the task of political theory is to seek out universal foundations for our social and political judgements is partly in abeyance. For the moment, at least, for many theorists, the only good universal foundation is a dead one. Universalism has been cast into the flames of particularism. Human life appears as one long aporia. In fact, it would not be inappropriate to describe this drift of interest as a slow haemorrhage into group particulars, a haemorrhage which shows little sign of being easily staunched. The consequent anaemic appearance of political theory is thus marked out by the motif of particularity. This appears to be the watchword for this shifting momentum. The idea of a non-aporetic consensual society, characterized by a Kantian, utilitarian or contractarian scheme of universal values, has definitely moved, for the moment, into the background of social and political theory.

Thus, the central aim of this book is a critical engagement with the shifting momentum to the particular. The particulars that are of concern here are the diverse forms of groups and collectivities. The intellectual sources for this stress on group particularity are many and diverse and will be examined throughout the book, but clearly, state theory, nationalism, historical, anthropological and sociological theory, communitarianism, multicultural, postcolonial theory, postmodern and poststructural theory, late Wittgensteinianism, forms of liberal pluralism, and so forth, have all made subtle and significant contributions to the debate concerning particularity.

Yet, it is important to realize that to lay such stress on group particulars changes the dynamics of political theory. If the human individual is no longer seen, necessarily, as of absolutely central moral or political importance, then the way in which we view politics can alter quite radically. A range of fundamental questions therefore underpin this book, for example, what is the relation between the individual and collectivity – be it nation, ethnicity, state or cultural group? Does the right of the group or collective association trump that of the individuals? What is the relation between the various levels and types of group, for example, between nationalism and multiculturalism? What role do particular groups, states, nations, cultures or communities play in shaping the values of their members? What obligations or duties, if any, do individuals owe to their communities, cultures or nations? Are there any universal values which are not tied in some way to particular groups?

Thus, this book aims to take on one of the most singular and important issues of the current era – the drift to group particularity. For many liberal-minded theorists this is a pointless enterprise. Groups are *not* the significant particulars. Yet, in response, it is simply not good enough to try to dismiss groups as irrelevant or incoherent, or, alternatively to only valorize the notion of the human individual, on neo-Kantian, utilitarian, rational choice or contractarian grounds. In fact, what we term contemporary individualism is historically a comparatively recent phenomenon. The background to the significance of individualism lies in certain changes in European thought over the last three hundred years. Individualism is the product of this gradual historical and conceptual development (see Vincent 1989). Although for many individualistically inclined writers terms like 'tribalism' have been more a term of abuse; in fact, the 'tribe' is the more common experience for the great mass of human beings. It is the tribal group which usually takes precedence.[1] In this sense, the general individualistic intuitions and inclinations of liberal theorizing are seriously out of touch with a raw nerve of much contemporary social and political reality. This latter point however should emphatically *not* be taken as an endorsement or attempt to justify or validate tribes or group particulars. It is rather an observation of what is the case.

What is so particular about particularity?

For many liberal theorists, as indicated above, the term particularity implies (in politics or morality) human individuality.[2] Political theory, in this liberal mode, therefore begins with the human individual as the fundamental premise.[3] For proponents, this is the only foundation on which any reasonable account of politics or morality can be built. This understanding of political theory consequently sees communities, cultures and nations as having no fundamental or singular reality or moral status, apart from the individuals that comprise them. Communities or nations are consequently seen as aggregations or collections of individuals. But, the individual is always, minimally, morally prior to any idea of the community or group.

However, as any reader of contemporary political theory over the last two to three decades will be aware, there has been a marked shift of theoretical emphasis. Critics of individualistic theory have argued consistently that such theorizing begins in the wrong place. The group is morally and sociologically prior to the individual. In many ways, this shift has also been, at the same time, a recovery of older themes and ideas present in some eighteenth and nineteenth century thought. The intellectual movement has therefore been towards reversing the priority of the particular individual and group. The primacy – at a foundational level – has shifted towards communities, nations, cultures and ethnic groups. Put plainly, the group is envisaged as a morally complete entity in its own right. It does not need to be explained via individuals. Conversely, the group explains the nature of individuals.[4] This perspective is also reflected, much more obviously, in sociological, anthropological and ethnographic theory, where the social or communal is, quite literally, the key unit of analysis for the discipline. In this sense, the group (community, culture or ethnos) can be viewed as the foundational or significant particular. The group therefore has a definite nature, identity and purpose. In this sense, the 'drift to particularity' is towards diverse forms of communal or group existence.

Many contemporary political theorists, within the liberal perspective, find the latter 'group particular' idea either difficult to grasp or just deeply morally repugnant. One reason for this repugnance is that some contemporary individualist theorists see the human individual as truly universal, that is, wherever one encounters human individuals, they are formally the same, regardless of race, gender, age, ethnicity or nationality. They all possess a fundamental equal dignity and moral value which ought to be respected worldwide, regardless of states or communities. In other words, the individualistic position has a close correlation with traditional articulations of universal human rights. To assert a belief in the community or group as the true particular or individual shifts the whole onus of morality away from human individuals towards groups (of many and various types). This tends immediately to cast doubt on both moral and political individualism and traditional human rights theory. Thus, there is often a deep tension between, on the one hand, universal human rights theory and cosmopolitan accounts of morality, and, on the other hand, communal, state or culturally defined accounts of morality. This broad dichotomy underpins a great deal of the discussion in the book.

The reasons for the intellectual shift of attention (referred to above), in the last few decades, from the individual to the group, are complex and will be touched upon throughout this book. Crudely, there are two very broad sets of reasons focusing on realism and normativism. For some, the emphasis on the nation, community or culture is a matter of realistic resignation with the intransigent realities of world politics. Namely, tribes, indigenous groups, communities or cultures can be viewed as immovable social and political facts, which simply have to be lived with. The communal or tribal fragmentations of, for example, the Balkans, Northern Ireland, Indonesia and Rwanda are not preferable forms of social existence. They are rather stark realities which have to be mediated in some way. Communities and cultures see individuals through the medium of group identification. For many this can be a life or death identity. This often bloody identification is something that many practitioners and theorists think we must find constitutional or pragmatic solutions to. Realism therefore dictates the grudging acceptance of group particularity, even if we feel uneasy with its basic ontology. Another broad response to group particularity is to suggest that fragmentation, difference, and the discovery of one's own customs, law, culture and communal traditions are a valuable and positive political development. Thus, any movement which emphasizes, for example, indigenous or ethnic communities, and which encourages respect for communal or state-based customs, laws, values, or rights to self-determination, is a normatively desirable development. It is the latter set of normative reasons which dominates much of the critical discussion in this book.

The point of stressing this fairly elementary distinction between individual and communal ontologies is to emphasize a neglected point that particularity *can* be viewed from widely different theoretical perspectives. For some, this assumption might seem obvious, to others, it is counter-intuitive. Nonetheless, the key idea is that a group *can* be viewed legitimately as a morally valuable 'particular', in the same way that the human individual is regarded as a valuable particular. It is worth underscoring this point at the very beginning of this book to avoid potential misunderstandings about my use of the term particular. My basic contention is that in the last few decades a strong moral and political emphasis has been given to 'group particulars'. The specific group particular that has had most publicity, in this same period, has been the nation, although it also clearly overlaps with cultures, communities and ethnicities. Nationalism is used as a foil in each chapter, namely, as a way of contrasting different conceptions of group particularity. It follows that the nation is by no means the only significant 'group particular' in political theory. Much of the discussion of this book will, in fact, be taken up with fierce debates *between* group particulars. The only caveat to enter here is that the emphasis on the particularity of the group or community has a much longer and more complex history than most of its more recent adherents appear to be aware of. Thus, in my reading, both state and sovereignty vocabulary have made their own distinctive contributions to the logic of particularity.

Why nationalism?

As mentioned above, one of the more pervasive conceptions of group particularity, in the last two to three decades, has been nationalism. Despite the power of nationalism in practice, political theory – particularly liberal political theory up until comparatively recently – has been deeply troubled by its status. Nationalism has been seen as overly narrow and potentially irrationalist in content. Liberal and socialist theories both consciously developed more internationalist stances during the bulk of the twentieth century. Nationalism was associated with recidivist tribalism – tribalism here being used in a derogatory manner. This post-1945 generation of theorists – which was also the immediate post-war generation involved in setting up the United Nations and formulating the United Nations International Declaration of Human Rights (1948) – had a powerful effect on social and political thought in the English-speaking world, certainly up to the 1980s. Indeed, for those educated in the discipline of political theory, during the period 1950–1980, it can still be regarded as incongruous to enthuse about nations or other such group particulars.

During the twentieth century there have been two broad approaches to nationalism both within political theory and in the apprehensions of ordinary citizens. One approach, as mentioned, has been generally troubled by nationalism – a discomfort which was profoundly affected in most European states (and in some Asian states like Japan) by the events surrounding the world wars. Thus, for many, national socialism, fascism and extreme authoritarianism marked out early to mid-twentieth century nationalism for specific abhorrence. Nationalism was seen as potentially totalitarian, theoretically specious and politically bellicose. The second approach to nationalism dates originally from the early nineteenth century and the first inception of nationalist theory. This sees a positive social, moral, political and economic value in nationalism. Nationalism implies the emancipation of cultures from alien oppression. Although this latter idea went into abeyance during the mid to later twentieth century, since the collapse of the Berlin Wall in 1989 and the changing political landscape of international politics, there has been, once again, a surge of positive interest in nationalism (amongst other forms of group particularity). Many have seen this as a hopeful prospect for the twenty-first century.

Most contemporary theorists, who are interested in nationalism, admit that it has a brutal and unpredictable history, but they are also certain that it does have a moderate face. For such theorists, nationalism plays certain fundamental moral and political roles in the ordinary lives of citizens, which no other form of loyalty can perform. Thus, for its proponents, membership of nations lets individuals transcend the constraints of both time and place. It gives a rich meaning and identity to human beings. It provides a conceptual and moral framework which permits human beings to comprehend their own existence within a community. Further, nations are seen to make up a part of our overt personal identity, that is, we constitute our lives through the rich value structures of nations. For many theorists, all human identity is deserving of respect; thus, the principle of basic respect obliges us to respect that which in others constitutes any part of their own sense of identity. Consequently, there ought to be a fundamental respect for national differences. In addition, for many current nationalist advocates, individual autonomy does not necessarily conflict with national context; in fact, a liberal nation can provide the context for human autonomy. A free society and a free nation can therefore be linked.

However, it is still important to realise that there is still no one overarching consensual nationalist political theory. There are rather a heterogeneous cluster of often mutually hostile perspectives, which can be loosely grouped under the rubric of nationalism. This makes it a profoundly elusive doctrine to deal with. For example, the outline of nationalist functions, offered in the previous paragraph, is basically a late twentieth century *liberal* understanding of nationalism. However, conservative, fascist or authoritarian understandings of nationalism are equally valid. Another way of viewing this point, concerning the 'open texture' of nationalism, is that from its inception in the European political vocabulary it has been wholly parasitic on other host ideologies to make any sense or headway. Nationalism, in itself, has no answers to any substantive political or moral problems (see Vincent in Freeden (ed.) 2001). It is other forms of thought – conservatism, liberalism and fascism – which provide answers or ways of being and acting in the world. Nationalism is therefore in a quandary, namely, that it has no necessary substantive content. Its relation with any moral or political content is purely contingent. Liberalism, during the 1990s, has made considerable headway in forging a connection with nationalism, partly because it has been hegemonic in the contemporary political theory establishment. Consequently, discussion of nationalism in this book usually focuses on the theme of liberal nationalism. But, it is important to stress that this is little more than a contingent connection.

There is one further point to note about the use of the concept of nationalism in this book. Its use as a foil in each chapter is *strategic*. Nationalism is not seen as the only, or, necessarily the most significant form of group particular. Conversely, it is envisaged as a useful device for highlighting and contrasting with other senses of group particularity.

The concept of particularity

There is one further point concerning the use of 'particularity' which can be briefly glossed. This is the philosophical account of the particular – which places the universal and particular relation into a slightly broader framework. It should be noted immediately that no attempt is made here to encompass the philosophical field. This is only a brief sketch. There are *three* broad permutations on the relation between universals and particulars. Each of these permutations contains a complex range of sub-views, which cannot be entered into. The first permutation can be described as the Platonic view. This places its key emphasis on the universal for grasping any particular. The universal is thus always prior to the particular. A second permutation takes the contrary position and emphasizes the significance and reality of particulars over universals. This is the nominalist view. A third position stresses the Hegelian point that the universal and particular interpenetrate, that is, they are not distinct or opposed, but are conversely, correlatives.

In the first perspective, Platonism suggests that knowledge must provide a consistent, objective and unchanging account of reality. However, our sense perceptions are in a process of continual change and flux. Thus, the senses, and what we immediately perceive around us, can never be the basis for knowledge, since they are continually changing. If the senses are in this relativistic flux, how do we gain any unchanging objective knowledge? Something must provide the universal stability which allows all the particular things we experience in the world to cohere. Platonists refer to this 'something' as the universal 'Form'. Unless the universal stable Form (or idea) of each object existed, there would be no way that we could have any knowledge. The Form therefore provides an answer to problems of sensory flux and contingency of meaning. In sum, Forms are universals which allow us to apprehend all the imperfect particulars in the world around us. In other words, the universal takes priority over the particulars. Without universals, particulars would not exist. The heart of the doctrine of the Forms is that ideas are universal, timeless and immutable essences. All particular things relate to Forms. The Forms (universals) are what is ultimately real. Thus, all particular objects or properties are incomplete or imperfect expressions of a universal Form.

The second philosophical permutation sees particulars as the only substantially real things in the world. Universals have no reality or existence, beyond possibly linguistic predicates or simple mental conveniences. For example, there is nothing actually equivalent to a property such as 'redness', or an object such as 'mountain', in the world that we know. We can only know particular cases of what we loosely call red or mountain. This does not mean that over time, through careful induction from many examples of particulars, one cannot make some rough approximations as to what appears to be more general about such properties or objects. Yet, it would still only be an approximation which would always be subject to revision. Particulars are the basis of reality. The most forceful statement of this position has been associated with various forms of nominalist philosophy. In this context, only singular or particular objects or properties exist, universals are fictions. Universals exist, minimally, and somewhat mysteriously, in the human mind. They are psychological props. No universal, as such, has any substantive reality. No one object or property is alike. Each particular is literally unique, unrepeatable, idiosyncratic and individual.

The third philosophical permutation integrates the particular and universal. This perspective can be articulated through Hegelianism. For Hegelians, a purely exclusive particularism, as found for example in the second permutation, undercuts any coherent account of knowledge. This latter perspective provides us with a series of unrelated particulars, with nothing to bring them into any kind of coherent relation or unity. Thus, philosophical particularism sacrifices unity for the sake of maintaining the complexity of particulars. Alternatively, a totally monistic approach to knowledge, which only focuses on the universal, is equally objectionable for the opposite reason. An undifferentiated philosophical universalism sacrifices the immensely complex and rich pattern of particulars for the sake of an undifferentiated unified whole. This was largely Hegel's critical view of Spinoza's and Schelling's philosophies. For Hegelians, the way out of this is a self-differentiated unity – which might be a reasonable description of the whole Hegelian system. Unity and difference, transcendence and immanence, universal and particular, had to be considered in dialectical tandem. Neither aspect should be neglected. The universal could not therefore be separated from particulars. They are interpenetrating terms, that is, an identity in difference. Each particular thus immanently embodies the universal.

If a philosophical label were to be put on the 'drift to particularity' theme, examined in this book, then, in my reading, it would largely be under the rubric of the second philosophical permutation. The drift to particularity is embedded in an implicit form of philosophical nominalism. This philosophical nominalism implies that the particular is always contrasted to the universal – the universal denoting ubiquitous, pervasive, common, applying to all cases or comprehensive. Particularity is therefore the property of being or expressing the particular, as distinct from the universal. Further, when the particular is emphasized, it refers not only to a single definite thing, but implies, by default, one amongst other particulars. Since there are no adequate universals, therefore, there must be a plethora of particulars. Thus, particularity, of necessity, implies a plurality of particulars. In addition, each particular or singular thing is noteworthy. The particular stands out. This 'standing out' is implied in the synonyms for particularity, for example, notable, sole, specific, unique or idiosyncratic. The particular also implies, in this context, that which is most *real*. In addition – although this may not always be the case – it can indicate that which is closest or most familiar. Thus, the only things which are real and can be actually known are the diversity of particulars. Universals are fictional abstractions which we habitually apply to aggregations of real particulars. One possible further inference from this – which again does not have to be made but is quite reasonable – is that because the particular is the most real, immediate and familiar, it might well be the most valuable. In this reading, it is far easier to be familiar with the reality and value of particulars than of universals. The familiar is therefore the particular, whereas the universal, in this perspective, is remote and abstract.

In summary, from this nominalist perspective, particularity denotes a thing which is not universal, is concrete rather than abstract, is one amongst many particulars, is something which is unique (or individual), and is potentially more real, immediate and familiar. From this philosophical nominalist perspective, therefore, the 'drift to particularity' theme implies that the reality of morality and politics can *only* be found within the diversity of group particulars, that is, in states, cultures, nations, communities or ethnicities. Universals, such as abstract reason, cosmopolitan ethics or human rights, do not really exist except as mental fictions. The universal is, in fact, envisaged as a distortion or imaginary unity imposed upon the complex particularity of the world.

Overview

Overall, this book has two interwoven themes. It can thus be read at two levels. The first level involves a series of wide-ranging critical studies of the relation between nationalism and specific concepts, theories and political practices, namely, sovereignty, the nation state, citizenship, liberal political theory, patriotism, communitarianism, multiculturalism and cosmopolitanism. These concepts have not been chosen at random; they rather reveal an intricate web of concepts surrounding, intersecting and interpenetrating nationalism in contemporary political theory. Thus, the basic initial aim of this study is to analyse the implicit or explicit role of nationalism within these various concepts and political practices. The underlying argument is that the role of nationalism, within each of these conceptual domains, is a great deal more problematic, complex and often incoherent than is often admitted or identified in most contemporary discussion. The book critically charts these complexities. The general attitude to nationalism evinced within this study is highly critical and sceptical.

The second major theme is the 'drift to particularity'. All the concepts examined in this book exemplify what I term a drift towards particularity, in one shape or another. Nationalism is but one example of this drift. It is important to note that despite the fact that nationalism is taken as a critical motif throughout the book, it is by no means the only significant particular. Thus, the use of nationalism, as pointed out earlier, is mainly strategic. Other theories and concepts, which will be analysed closely in this study, have their own distinctive rendering of particularity. However, nationalism is taken as a key theme to anchor the overall discussion. In consequence, it figures as the major comparator within each chapter. This also allows more subtle contrasts and similarities to be noted throughout the whole range of the discussion.

In terms of the first two chapters: the most tried and tested manner of discussing nationalism, often in tandem with the virtues of democracy and liberalism, has been through sovereignty and state language. The discourse of both the latter concepts predates nationalism by centuries. Both concepts also embody, implicitly, the logic of particularity. Sovereignty and the state, in contrast to medieval conceptions of empire or universal Christendom, are archetypal particulars, which undermined ideas of universality. Both terms were then filtered through nineteenth and twentieth century nationalist vocabulary. Thus, the sovereignty of the people, or the sovereignty of the state, has frequently been interpreted as 'national sovereignty'. Nationalism also inherits many of the individualizing or particularizing aspects inherent in sovereignty language. Chapter one analyses the relation between sovereignty and nationalism, concluding that nationalism, in effect, plagiarizes a pre-existent sovereignty discourse. Chapter two analyses the compound term, which dominates nineteenth and twentieth century domestic and international politics, namely, the 'nation state'. The relation between the state and the nation – both deeply particularist vocabularies – remains unclear and vague. This chapter critically analyses the complex dynamics of this relation, arguing that the two should be kept distinct.

Another closely related discourse, which focuses on the state and nation from another perspective, is citizenship. This is the theme of chapter three. The state and citizen have often been seen as two sides of the same coin. Citizenship theory can, in fact, be viewed as another way of either giving liberal or constitutionally acceptable shape to nationalism, or, alternatively of avoiding nationalism altogether, whilst retaining a strong sense of allegiance and loyalty. This chapter concentrates on the profound ambiguities of citizenship arguments in relation to the particularity of nationalism. In effect, it sees citizenship as caught between contradictory impulses of, on the one hand, trying to universalize its claims, and, on the other hand, of finding itself caught in the particularist imperatives of both nation and state.

One of the principal ways in which recent political theory has tried to salvage elements of both particular human individuality and universality has been through linking liberalism quite deliberately with nationalist language. Consequently, we have the phenomenon of liberal nationalism. This will be the main focus of chapter four. Liberal nationalism appears, *prima facie*, to preserve all the universal values of liberal individualism, within the domain of the democratic nation. Liberal nationalism has been a very prevalent theoretical construction in recent years. My argument is that liberal nationalism is still not to be relied on, partly because nationalism is so notoriously unstable and unpredictable. It is not a settled or consistent partner for liberalism. The two aspects of the compound – liberal nationalism – are potentially deeply at odds. This chapter is thus a sustained critical reflection on the phenomenon of the particularity of the nation, in relation to the more universalistic claims of liberalism.

A cognate argument to those on liberalism and citizenship is dealt with in chapter five, which focuses on the concept of patriotism, viewed largely through the lens of republican theory. Republican patriotic theory contends that nationalism should not be confused with patriotism. Patriotism is seen as a morally defensible and valuable form of allegiance, which provides a collective or communal fidelity that is morally and politically preferable to nationalism. In effect it still performs the same generic function as nationalism and is yet another manifestation of particularist argument. Rather like liberal nationalism, patriotism trades on being a more acceptable and civilized particularity. Thus, the republican patriot can apparently gain all the advantages of nationalism without the costs. Again, the argument of this chapter views this claim critically and contends that patriotism is often misrepresented and misunderstood. It argues that patriotism may be a different particularist language to nationalism, but it is not necessarily morally or politically preferable.

If a contemporary political theorist has a strong sense of the endemic and deeply rooted problems of both universality and liberal individualism, and senses that a stronger ontological grounding for the individual is needed, then the standard response has been to adopt a communitarian position. Communitarianism has been one of the more prevalent and commonly used discourses in contemporary political theory in the last two decades. Since its rediscovery in the 1980s, the relation between

the two particularist vocabularies, of communitarianism and nationalism, has remained profoundly obscure. This forms the theme of chapter
six. There clearly was something more than fortuitous in the coincidence between, on the one hand, the growing disenchantment with the
liberal individualism and universalism of the 1980s, the collapse of the
communist bloc in 1989, the recrudescence of nationalism in the 1990s,
and, on the other hand, the more general theoretical interest in communitarian political theory. Like patriotism – with which it overlaps –
communitarian particularism also tries to perform functions similar
to nationalism, but without using the overt terminology or structure of
nationalist argument. Communitarianism has served important functions in contemporary theory. However, it has never clearly articulated
its awkward and ambiguous theoretical relation with nationalism. The
present chapter explores this hazardous relationship in more depth.

One major critique of the idea of consensual nationhood and community, over the last decade, lies in another dimension of the particularist
argument. This dimension focuses self-consciously on the themes of
difference and multicultural politics. The particularism of difference
and multicultural theory has a profoundly troubling relationship with
nationalism. On one level, in affirming the importance of difference-
based identity politics, multicultural theory claims to be more sociologically and historically realistic and astute about contemporary politics than
nationalism. It also usually articulates the values of the marginalized
groups in any society. Further, in denying the relevance or reality of overarching nationalist or communitarian claims, multiculturalism acts as a
severe critic of both forms of particularist theory. Yet, appearances can be
deceptive. Both multiculturalist and nationalist expressions of particularism also share many common concerns. They may even be viewed as
part of the same generic pattern of thought about politics. This forms the
central argument of chapter seven.

Finally, if there has been one continuous critique of particularism in its
nationalist, patriotic, statist, communitarian or multicultural shapes, it
has arisen from one key source, namely, cosmopolitanism. The term
cosmopolitanism is often used synonymously with universalism – as in
universal or cosmopolitan human rights. At first glance, cosmopolitanism
appears to contrast itself with all forms of particularity. Consequently,
cosmopolitanism is often seen to be solely related to universalistic concerns. The ultimate appeal of cosmopolitanism is to *all* individual
human persons, regardless of tribe, nation, ethnicity or culture; in other
words, regardless of any particularity. In this sense, it might well be
described as the most articulate critical alternative to the logic of particularity. In recent years, a number of strands of particularist political

theory have argued that cosmopolitanism exemplifies the most extreme and duplicitous form of particularity. The penultimate chapter closely examines these arguments. The concluding chapter places the whole debate of the book into a broader political theory framework and then develops certain critical points against particularist argument.

1   Sovereign Particulars

There are two underlying questions in this chapter: first, if states possess an identity from whence is it derived? The second question is: what is the relation between nationalism and sovereignty? The quick answer to the first question is that state identity has usually been established by utilizing a language of individuality and personality, which was initially filtered through the concept of sovereignty. The answer to the second question is that nationalism is a late addition to an older state and sovereignty vocabulary. Nationalism essentially parasitizes upon and then reinforces themes of particularity and identity which were originally formulated in sovereignty language. The central components of nationalist argument thus use pre-established particularist renderings of the state and sovereignty. The organising questions therefore within this chapter are: first, where does sovereignty derive from? Second, what role does sovereignty play in political discourse? Third, what is the relation of sovereignty to the state? Fourth, the discussion turns to interrogate the sources of the 'identity' implicit within sovereignty theory. Finally, what is the precise relation between sovereignty and nationalism?

Where does sovereignty derive from?

There is no sense here of any attempt at a full-scale history of sovereignty, but rather to note certain important facets of the discourse of sovereignty which have had significant ramifications for nationalism and the state. However, some brief points should be noted in terms of the history of the concept. Sovereignty was not a concept or word familiar to Greek, Roman or early medieval political or legal thought, although there were undoubtedly many attributes, values and concepts, characteristic of these periods, which were subsequently integrated into political and legal discussion of sovereignty. It contributed most to the background of sovereignty theory, specifically after its revival in the twelfth and thirteenth centuries in Europe. It provided a specific vocabulary for speaking of authority and power. For example, *potestas* denoted official legal power, which all magistrates possessed. *Potestas* was distinct from *auctoritas*, the latter implying influence or prestige. *Imperium* was a discretionary power to perform acts in the interests of the whole political organization. It was also a right to command inherent in certain offices. Under the Roman Republic it was more limited. *Imperium* was usually obtained by a consul, and later by the emperor, from the senate, via the doctrine of *lex regia*, which maintained that all powers were derived from the *populus*. With the Roman emperors this idea expanded considerably in scope. During the late Roman Empire, legal and political superiority increasingly centred on the emperor as the linchpin of the whole political and legal structure, the centre of dignity and majesty, an office viewed as the source of law and not subject to it. The emperor, as *Imperator*, thus had *plenitudo potestas* (the fullness of legal powers) and possessed *legibus solutus*, in effect, that the prince was above the law. The emperor became legislator (*legis lator* – the one who lays down the law). Thus, emperors were often referred to as 'living law'. Under later emperors, such as Constantine and Diocletian, as under the later absolute monarchs of Europe, the doctrine of *legibus solutus* was emphasized by lawyers and *lex regia* diminished in significance.[1]

Roman law, in this sense, contributed to the first formulation of a theory of public power, later to be transformed and modified into a theory of sovereignty. For Anthony Black, for example, the early medieval view of sovereignty implied 'independence from legal constraints by outside powers' and 'it was chiefly by appropriating the terms of Roman dignity for rulers that sovereignty was claimed'. Kings thus claimed the powers and insignia of *Imperium*.[2] Frances Yates also noted that 'the [Roman] imperial idea in the Middle Ages and Renaissance ... is a necessary preliminary to the study of the ethos and symbolism of the national monarchies of Europe' (see Yates 1977, 77 and Figgis 1922, 43, n. 3). Despite the fact that papal rule, and indeed the Holy Roman Empire, tried to emulate many of the Roman public law attributes of the emperor, something that secular rulers learned, in turn, from the medieval papacy, the middle ages was not a period of striking development in sovereignty theory. The average feudal rulers in Europe did not really possess *Imperium* or the right of *legibus solutus*. Further, the existence of codes of customary law, feudal relations and the resilience of the many and various estates assemblies, guilds, towns, cities, and the like, did not foster centralization of legal powers. Medieval society was more universalist by inclination (qua religion), and sovereignty resided, if anywhere, ultimately in God. The medieval empire and church were not easily reconciled with the notion of state sovereignty.[3]

Some scholars have connected this lack of a medieval sense of legal and political authority to the particularist cellular and federalized structure of medieval life, although others again have seen this 'cellular theme' as wholly overdone.[4] Nonetheless, it would still be odd to speak of the singular and fully developed 'sovereign state' in the medieval period. Equally, to describe what one writer has called the 'ramshackle structure' of the Holy Roman Empire as sovereign would be equally absurd (Lichtheim 1971, p. 13). Not only was there no systematic concept of sovereignty in the medieval period, but neither emperor nor kings were viewed as possessing absolute *Imperium*. Rulers tended to be seen in more contractual terms. This idea was even fostered within elements of the Catholic church in, for example, the conciliarist movement. However, gradually, almost imperceptibly, the concepts, insignia, symbols and legal axioms of the church and Roman Empire were absorbed and taken up in the quasi-secular authorities of the new states in the 1500s. Coronation rituals and the like also confirmed the quasi-religious character of the state – something much later to be dressed up in the clothes of divine right and patriarchalism. Consequently, as one scholar of sovereignty has commented, 'the concept, symbols and insignia of rulership took on the sempiternal existence as universal' (Bartelson 1995, 98). The state and sovereignty thus acquired a strong aroma of incense – often claiming for themselves the mantle of universal empire in their own bounded, quasi-secular realms.[5]

Thus, the 'thought structure' underpinning sovereignty has an extensive genealogy dating back to Roman thought. However the character of medieval political life did not facilitate its development. The term sovereignty itself was beginning to be utilized in the 1500s; however, virtually all scholars agree that the first self-conscious and highly systematic use of the concept was developed by the French thinker Jean Bodin. France, in the 1500s, was in the throes of religious civil war. The problem of order was the paramount concern. Bodin's *The Six Bookes of the Commonweale* (1576) was designed to meet this problem and sovereignty was the key device. The idea became the linchpin of what became known as the absolutist theory. After Bodin's writing, this idea of sovereignty became more explicit and widespread across Europe. The other major theorist associated with its systematic employment was Thomas Hobbes. In fact, for many international relations writers at the present moment, the concept of sovereignty and the writings of Hobbes encapsulate a whole perspective on politics and the interaction of states up to the twentieth century.

The conventional reading of the modern era, qua sovereignty, usually arises in the context of the Treaty of Westphalia (1648), and the subsequent conferences at Münster and Osnabrück, which, in effect, settled the Thirty Years War (1618–48). Essentially, Westphalia reflected the interests of France, Sweden and Holland. It was focused, at one level, on controlling or thwarting the universalist claims of the universal papacy and the Holy Roman Empire, as well as the dynastic aspirations of Philip II of Spain and the Hapsburgs. Many scholars have though – with hindsight – characteristically seen this treaty as symbolic of a new moment in the political practice of Europe, a moment characterized by the institutionalized acceptance and establishment of the 'state form' and the classical absolutist-inclined theory of sovereignty, across the European continent. Sovereignty was understood as the focus of centralized law-making power and political authority in the prince or executive. Sovereign states now had the monopolistic right to make war and peace, make treaties and to regulate internally their own religious practices. Westphalian sovereignty, in this reading, thus embodied a transformation from a medieval world of larger empires and more plural dispersed authority, to a purportedly modern world, namely, an international society of centralized sovereign states. Each prince or king became an *emperor* in his own realm. The universalist Holy Roman Empire survived until the nineteenth century, but it was a hollow vessel. International society, from Westphalia to the present, was therefore seen to be peopled by roughly equal juridical states with sovereignty. As one recent commentator notes, 'Westphalia remains the most significant revolution in sovereignty to date' (Philpott 1999, 582). He continues that after 1648, the next three hundred years were largely the history of the spread of this Westphalian system of state sovereignty. Another recent commentator has consequently remarked that this classical conception of sovereignty virtually 'defines the modern era and sets it apart from previous eras'. It has thus become part of the very 'grammar' of modern politics (Jackson 1999, 431).

What does sovereignty imply?

As briefly indicated above, the concept of sovereignty formally implies a power that is absolute, perpetual, indivisible, imprescriptible and inalienable. These terms are the so-called 'marks of sovereignty', often indicated by jurists after Bodin. Each mark is vague and contestable. However, in practice, the term implied, firstly, that sovereignty was essentially a legislative concept. In other words, it was the active power to make law. Unlike the medieval conception of law – understood largely as an aggregate of traditional prerogatives, conventions, customs and rights – Bodin particularly saw sovereignty embodying absolute legislative power itself. Thus, sovereignty and the power to make law were regarded as virtually synonymous.

Second, whereas the medieval period tended often to consider rulers as judges and administrators, in Bodin the supreme legislative role became crucial. This freed sovereignty effectively from judicial limitation, unless voluntarily agreed to. The sovereign embodied the ultimate authority and right to command over all other groups, institutions and individuals within a realm. This was the idea which was eventually to translate into the nineteenth and twentieth century legal positivist view that every legal system is a self-sufficient structure of rules, and that such a structure must logically possess a supreme norm – a *Grundnorm* for Hans Kelsen – through which all other rules are identified, legitimized, adjudicated and coordinated (see, for example Kelsen in Stankiewicz (ed.) 1969). Sovereignty thus became an analytical component of any legal order. Delegation of power still implied that the power was the *possession* of the sovereign.

Third, if the sovereign was supreme and the source of law, then law could be considered as the will or imperative of the sovereign. Jean Bodin's own legal training had been in Roman law and he was deeply familiar with its key doctrines. Effective law was the imperative or command of the sovereign. This idea later became known as the 'command theory of law'. Customary, conventional, constitutional and international law became more indeterminate in this scenario. Admittedly, unlike nineteenth and twentieth century legal positivists, Bodin and Hobbes did not draw a distinction between 'law as it is' and 'law as it ought to be', yet, they nonetheless associated effective law with the commands of the sovereign.[6]

Where did sovereignty apply? The answer to this conventionally breaks down into two broad domains. Sovereignty has both *external* and *internal* applications. The *external* refers to the relation between states and indicates whether a state is recognized as a state by other states within an international society. This is the area which has usually been of most interest to international relations scholars. Sovereignty here is a matter of the way states conduct themselves in an international setting. The *internal* conception of sovereignty refers to the state's hegemony, dominance or authority over all citizens, associations and groups within a given bounded territory. This internal conception has traditionally been the main area of interest for political theorists and lawyers.[7] In both contexts, sovereignty is addressed to the state. The question of the location of sovereignty conventionally produces two broad answers. The first answer associates sovereignty with a person, a prince, monarch or supreme executive. The second links it with the whole people, the general will or electorate, qua democracy. In both cases, the sovereignty is still identified with and addressed to the state.

Sovereignty and states

What was the relation between sovereignty and the state? Practically, sovereignty was focused on the self-preservation of the state, initially at a time of profound civil and religious conflict and disorder; further, it focused on the state's independence from external controls and its relative equality with other states. Sovereignty thus conventionally embodied a potential explanation of the international system as an interaction of relatively independent states. All this is fairly well known. However, I wish to turn to another question, namely, is there any deeper conceptual and historical linkage between sovereignty and the state? The gist of my response would be that both sovereignty and statehood articulate a strong sense of particularity, set against any sense of the universal. Admittedly states did often become members of an international society with some recognition in principle of international law, however the idea and practice of the state still represented a fragmented vision of the political world.

Why are states and sovereigns viewed as particulars? To answer this question we need to track back briefly to the origin of the state form in European discourse. In effect, the state was a manifestation of particularity in relation to the universal, or, more concretely, initially, against the international aspirations of both the medieval church and conceptions of empire. The idea of Rome and the legacy of empire provided the vocabulary of universal (what might now be termed) transnational citizenship, namely, 'the notion that all belonged in some sense to a universal "Roman Empire"'. This idea 'remained strong even in the absence of a transnational secular government' (Black 1993, 88). The universal church was also viewed as an overarching moral, spiritual and political unity. All Christians were part of the body of Christ – the *Respublica Christiana*. In addition, the church was a universal juridical unit, of sorts, premised on systems of canon law. Both the universal supra-national church and empire remained important themes in European thought and practice up until the fifteenth century. As Otto von Gierke put it, with regard to the unified ends of church and empire: 'in all the centuries of the Middle Ages Christendom ... is set before us as a single universal Community, founded and governed by God himself. Mankind is one "mystical body"; it is one single and internally connected "people" or "folk"; it is an all embracing corporation (*universitas*) which constitutes the Universal Realm, spiritual and temporal' (Gierke 1900, 10). In more abstract theory, one God, one Pope for spiritual welfare, and one Emperor for temporal concerns. In effect, the gradual breakdown of this universal conception was a precondition and stimulus to the rise of the particular state.[8] Thus, the fragmentation of the Holy Roman Empire into particular states, led initially by France and England, and more specifically the collapse of both the political and religious influence of the papacy (which was integrally connected with the empire *per se*), were viewed as a revolt of the particular against the universal.

However, one of the ironies of the idea of empire and church in the middle ages was that there was little effective overarching *Imperium*, sovereignty or central authority. The empire regularly claimed some form of imperial interstate authority, although it remained, from the tenth century, a power largely in the hands of ruling dynasties in (what we now term) Germany. Political internationalism was ably defended by thinkers such as Dante Alighieri, essentially arguing for one world monarchy and one world *patria* (Black 1993, 93ff). Despite this, the political life of Europe was more generally characterized, on the ground, by cross-cutting domains of authority. Medieval *regna* or kingdoms contained within themselves (and thus even more so within the Holy Roman Empire), what Walter Ullman called a massive sublife of 'numberless associations', including cities, guilds, nobility, estates assemblies and clergy. Power-wielding deliberative assemblies 'were acting at all levels of political life' (Tilley (ed.) 1975, 22). Thus, the empire, papacy, kingdoms, counties, domains, diocese, boroughs, cities, universities, guilds, villages, and so forth, all had powers and rules. There were also cross-cutting federations and confederations across Europe, such as the Hanseatic League of Northern German towns and the Swiss Confederation. Some of these associations and assemblies later melted in parliaments and estates assemblies. Medieval kingdoms (and thus even more so the empire) were therefore criss-crossed with a large number of associations, groups and diverse loyalties. This scenario constituted what some scholars have referred to as the cellular character of medieval society.[9] This cellular character was also reinforced, to some degree, by the practices of feudalism. Feudalism, in its broadest sense, was an intricate structure of often symbiotic contractual and mutual obligations existing within a complex social hierarchy of powers and authorities. This structure included the prince, who was part of and reliant upon the 'community of the realm', and was consequently, as medieval jurists such as Bracton kept emphasizing, also to a large degree under law. Unitary conceptions of sovereignty or statehood were difficult to formulate or conceive of in this context. Coupled with the above points is the problematic issue of a geographical territory with a consistently loyal population, which again appears to be minimally some requirement of statehood. This latter requirement again was more difficult to identify in this period. Thus the Holy Roman Empire remained a composite of many different types of political association.

Law was also another problematic issue with regard to the international empire and church. In early medieval conceptions, firstly, there was a strong tradition which placed princes and emperors under the universal law of God. Second, customary or conventional law preceded and was seen to be declared, not created, by monarchs. This was

McIlwain's thesis concerning the 'High Court of Parliament' (McIlwain 1910). As Gierke put it: 'Medieval doctrine, while it was truly medieval, never surrendered the thought that law is by its origin of equal rank with the state and does not depend upon the state for its existence' (quoted in D'Entreves 1939, 17; see also Black 1984, 60). Third, many powerful associations in the medieval period possessed their own systems of law and courts. The best known of such separate legal systems was church canon law. In this context it is impossible to speak of any one unitary legal conception. The Holy Roman Empire manifestly was constituted by legal pluralism. In one sense, the *prima facie* view of law was that it was part of the universal empire and church. However, the reality of medieval life was more complex, namely, a form of legal plurality. In an important sense, though, the state did not rest easily with either international or universal religious law or internal legal pluralism. Internal legal pluralism, as a form of micro-particularity, has arisen again within nineteenth and twentieth century states, in the form of secession, difference, multiculturalism and group rights theories, and is still an immensely problematic facet of states in the twenty-first century.

The universal loyalty, which transcended diverse localized interests, was the church and this exceeded both the *regnum* and the authority of empire. All citizens across Europe were members of the *Respublica Christiana*. Ultimately, the church was higher than the civil authorities. It was not only higher than civil authorities, but also in some senses incorporated them. This theme was pushed strongly by popes such as Innocent III, Innocent IV and Gregory VII. However, as has been noted, 'it is perhaps one of the ironies of history that the law of the Roman Empire gave to feudal monarchies and Italian communes the rationale of the sovereign, independent state and thus contributed to the dissolution of the noble ideal of Christendom or Holy Roman Empire' (Post 1964, 562). Thomas Hobbes was quite clear – in a more derogatory manner – on the peculiar logic of this point in his *Behemoth*, noting that the Catholic church had always 'encroached upon the rights of kings' and that there 'was never such another cheat in the world' as the Pope. Hobbes continued, 'I wonder that the kings and States of Christendom never perceived it' (Hobbes 1990, 21). The conflict of *imperium* and *sacerdotium* was something that Hobbes saw virtually re-enacted between Charles I and a religiously inspired Parliament. The separation of commonwealths from the papacy and the Holy Roman Empire was a positive benefit and advance to Hobbes, as also to Hegel a century or so later. It is worth noting here also that, ironically, divine right theory, which was gradually developed in a number of nascent states in the sixteenth and seventeenth centuries, was clearly a highly particularist anti-papal or anti-universal church weapon in the armoury of individual states (Figgis

1922, 121). Divine right theory, like patriarchalism, set its face against the empire and papal sovereignty. It was premised on the rejection of external authorities. Churches, as such, became gradually more state-based.

One of the crucial turning points in the growth of the 'particularity' of the state, set against the breakdown of the empire, is the rise of Renaissance Italian city-states and the presiding figure of Machiavelli – although the role of both is debatable.[10] There are commentators, for example, who see a much earlier manifestation of the state, and others again, conversely, who see it as a much later phenomenon. However, if either late medieval or Renaissance political structures embodied the central characteristics of the state, they did it clearly at the expense of the empire's tutelage. Thus, Italian city-based patriotism was often contrasted to the vaguer loyalties of the Holy Roman Empire. Petrarch, for example, set his face against Dante's world monarchy and universalism. As Frances Yates put it: 'patriotism [arose] to take the place of the old vaguely defined universal loyalties'. Thus, the middle ages dominance of the universal church and empire was seen increasingly as a transitional period between the particular polis of classical antiquity and the independent states of Renaissance Humanism. As many have asserted, such as Yates, it was Machiavelli, 'animated by an intense patriotism', who 'wished for the creation of a strong well-organized state in Italy ... This realistic approach of necessity ruled out the old idealist and universalist conceptions. The two foci of medieval history – the Papacy and the Empire – are neither of them conducive, in Machiavelli's view, to the welfare of Italy' (Yates 1977, 13 and 18). This Machiavellian tradition blossomed, as argued by writers such as Pocock and others, into the civic republican perspective, which looked to civic autonomy and the idea of a free non-dominating state, as contrasted to the apparent servitude of rule by princes or monarchies (Pocock 1975). The *res publica* would be a genuine autonomous public power devoted to the 'public welfare' of its citizens.

Not all agree with this Renaissance-based argument. Some have indeed seen the state as a much later product of the seventeenth century, that is, Bodin and Hobbes. Anthony Black, however, rejects both the Renaissance and seventeenth century readings. He comments that much depends on what is meant by the term state. He contends that the basic idea of the state was present in the 1200s – a view he shares with the medievalist historian Gaines Post (Post 1964, 365). There were, in other words, conceptions of sovereignty, connected to law and monopoly of coercion, in this earlier period. For Black, 'the main literary and academic stimulus for concentration of power and the emergence of royal, ducal or civic states came from classical Roman and Greek political thought, especially Cicero and Aristotle'. Aristotle's polis was taken to be the same as medieval associations. In Aristotle's polis, Cicerorian legal theory and Roman law there were 'presented as paradigmatic a kind of state in which all legal and governmental powers were exercised at the centre, whether by one few or many. There was no place for either local immunities or an overarching empire' (Black 1993, 108–9). Thus, Thomas Aquinas ignored the issue of world government and many, such as Cicero, condemned the activities of lesser associations.[11] Black admits that no *word* actually existed in this earlier period for the state (or sovereignty), but he contends that 'to argue that the *idea* was not present because no single word corresponded to it is surely to press the connection between language and thought too far. It is abundantly clear that the meaning of "state" was fully conveyed by a range of terms' (Black 1993, 187). Black sees further evidence of the state's existence in the abstract use of the term 'crown' – indicating continuous authority – in the 1250 to 1450 period. The ruler became the 'public person' or 'office'. The crown, in effect, became a 'metaphor of sovereignty'. Black concludes 'all this shows that the idea of the state was no mere afterthought in the Middle Ages; it was woven into the fabric of political sentiment' (Black 1993, 190).

Black's view, predictably, runs directly counter to Walter Ullman and other notable commentators.[12] Thus, for other scholars, medieval kingdoms and the empire were – as another medievalist commentator has put it – 'not-yet-states' (Cheyette 1978, 146). They did not possess many of the characteristics that we now associate with the state. In fact, for such writers, neither the word nor the recognizable practice of the 'state' existed until the late fifteenth and early sixteenth century. In this sense, as has been remarked, words like state 'cannot appropriately be used to talk about the world before they appeared' (Cheyette 1978, 147). However, whichever way this scholarly dispute swings, it does not substantively affect the present argument, namely, that the state represented a strong sense of 'particularity' or 'individuality' set against the 'universal' empire and church. Thus, the diminution of the empire and church was connected to state development. Black in part agrees with this view. He notes that the period 1250–1450 saw the progressive separating out of religious and secular authority and the growth of the latter in the form of the state. This, for Black, was decisive in the 'development of the state idea'. Essentially, as he notes, 'the withering away of papacy and Empire coincided with the strengthening hold of kings over barons, bishops and towns' (Black 1993, 188–9). It was therefore crucial that the universalist vision of empire and church broke down. After this point, it is a matter of debate whether medieval kingdoms and the empire were interlocking hierarchies with no clearly defined sovereignty, or whether, like Black or Gaines Post, one conceives of the sovereign state as a coherent entity in the 1200s.

Sovereigns, states and identity

States are manifestations of particularity. Each particular has an identity. A society of states, specifically from the 1600s, is seen as a collection of these particular identities. Such particulars are seen as entities with interests, wills and policies. Such particulars also address each other in terms of diplomacy and foreign policy. Yet, if these particular states possess an identity, from whence is it derived?

The issue of the identity of the state was filtered through absolutism and the language of sovereignty. The concept of sovereignty, developed in Bodin, was, as argued, linked to the growth of the state idea. What one finds in writers such as Bodin is the idea that the sovereignty is an analytical implication (or primitive essence) of the state (Skinner 1978, vol 2, 287; Church 1941, 226; Franklin 1973, 23 and 93). Bodin opened his famous *Six Bookes* with the remark that a commonwealth (or state) was 'a lawful government of many families ... with puissant soveraigntie' (Bodin 1606 and 1962, 1). Thus, the concept of the state or commonwealth denoted sovereignty. Sovereignty embodies the entire body of authority necessary to bring the state into existence. In Hobbes, equally, the sovereign is described as a legal person or *persona ficta*. For Hobbes, therefore, 'a Multitude of men are made *One* Person, when they are by one man, or one Person, Represented ... it is the *Unity* of the Representer not the *Unity* of the Represented, that maketh the Person *One*' (Hobbes 1968, 220). A people can become one – in a covenant – and the state can only exist by virtue of one who represents them in the *persona ficta* of the sovereign. Thus, the state exists – has an identity – in the sovereign person. The nineteenth century jurist John Austin followed a similar line of reasoning in his *Lectures on Jurisprudence*, noting that 'The State is usually synonymous with the "sovereign". This is the meaning which I annex to the term' (Austin 1880, part 1, 95). The sovereign, in this sense, embodies all the necessary logical prerequisites or preconditions for there to be a state.[13] Sovereignty might thus be described as the condition of the possibility of the state – the political transcendental unity of apperception of the state and thus the international system. It has no empirical reality as such.

The question is, though, how can sovereignty provide an identity? Behind the above ideas on sovereignty (as indicated in the Hobbes reference) lay a long tradition of legal personality theory. This is an issue of, on the one hand, the location of sovereignty, and, on the other hand, of the legal formulation of identity itself. The sovereign was located in a real or fictional person and the state was embedded in the person of the sovereign. Roman law theory, in Justinian's *Institutes* and *Digest*, had already fully utilized the idea of legal personality. Legal personality implied an activity which transcends or is qualitatively different to the members or 'natural persons' acting individually. As Hobbes noted, the sovereign, as *persona civitatis*, can be conceived as representing the totality of the state. At its apogee, legislative sovereignty became focused (in terms of location) on the monarch or prince, often later underpinned by divine right theory and reason of state doctrine. It is important, however, to grasp here that the more purportedly impersonalized state of the twentieth century originated in the personalized state of the sixteenth century. The apparent unity and more specifically the identity of the state – even in the twenty-first century – is still an imaginative and cognitive leap of sorts. This imaginative act relates closely to underpinning notions of both legal and moral personality theory. It is a short step from the actual human person, to the fictional person, and finally to the abstract personality of the state.[14] Essentially, practically some thing must be supreme in law-making, some person or body of persons, in order for there to be a state. The present use of the term sovereign, qua state, still embodies part of this complex clandestine ancestry concerning legal and moral personality. Although the overt vocabulary of absolutism has long since been abandoned, we still speak of states 'having interests', 'embodying purposes or aims', 'making contacts with other states', 'performing actions', 'prosecuting their policies', 'making war' and 'speaking to each other'. None of this vocabulary would make much sense without the underpinning identity, if only fictional.

There were some variations on the theme of moral and legal personality theory, for example, in the jurisprudential work of Samuel Freiherr von Pufendorf. Unlike Hobbes, Pufendorf developed a sophisticated contractual theory, culminating in the state considered as a *moral* rather than a legal personality. The state was conceptualized by Pufendorf as a *composite* moral person – distinct from what he called simple moral persons – entailing a collection of persons united by a moral bond. For Pufendorf, this composite moral person was neither just a legal nor a fictitious entity. As David Boucher notes, it was a 'real autonomous moral person with the capacity to will, deliberate, and pursue purposes' (Boucher 1998, 237). Thus, the state, for Pufendorf, must be 'conceived as one person, and is separated and distinguished from all particular men by a unique name; and it has its own special rights and property, which no man ... may appropriate apart from him who holds the sovereign power ... hence the state is defined as a composite moral person' (Pufendorf 1991, Bk II, ch. 6, section 10, 137). Sovereignty essentially animates the person of the state, which is free from all external interference, and is only guided by natural law and natural reason. This places moral controls on the behaviour of the composite state person, namely, to look to the safety and welfare of the people. Pufendorf, on one level, offers a much stronger theory of personality than Hobbes' fictional legal theory. However, unlike Hobbes' account, Pufendorf's conception of morality was not associated with expediency or prudential concerns. Morality meant the strictures and imperatives of natural reason and natural law. The state was not a fictional legal person, but a real moral deliberating agent with individual purposes.

Thus, sovereignty in the sixteenth century was initially located in terms of the person of a monarch or an executive body. This might be a real or artificial notion of the person. Gradually, as argued above, this became a more complex 'state person' which implied a power, identity and will embodied in an office, or body of persons or offices. As one more traditional commentator noted, 'the essence of the sovereignty of the state ... is found in the fact that the functions and powers of the body politic are not exercised for their own sake alone, that is, as governmental rights; nor are they the private property of individuals, but they are rooted in the unity of the state itself. In this sense the state is the sovereign personality' (Merriam 1900, 92). In a number of nineteenth and early twentieth century jurists, the real personality – qua sovereignty – of the state became a crucial theme to explicate the state and its identity. Jurists such as Lorenz von Stein, Carl von Gerber, Paul Laband and Georg Jellinek, and many others, thus literally envisaged the state as a real person, in the sense that all its powers were self-derived, qua sovereignty and personality. The state was the personification of sovereignty. This is, in major part, the force and meaning that underpin the concept of 'self-determination' – although in terms of the European political vocabulary self-determination is a very late term, dating from the early twentieth century. Sovereignty, as self-determination, implied 'state person volition'. The term 'self', in self-determination, would be meaningless verbiage unless will and personality were involved.[15] As Lorenz von Stein commented, in a Kantian mode, on the state person, 'it is its essence to have its ground in itself. It can as little be demonstrated or grounded as the [individual human] ego' (quoted in Coker 1910, 68).[16] The state is thus a form of transcendental unity of apperception for politics. Legal personality theory also made the state responsible for the tort of its officials.[17] In this context, sovereignty as personality – as forming the identity of statehood – also takes on the abstract persona of the individual human subject. As one commentator, early in the twentieth century, noted, 'the State is a person because it has a will of its own, that is recognized in the national consciousness in a manner similar to the feelings of an individual organism'. The sovereign state, as the transcendental ground of its own rights, 'is thus independent of its particular powers in the same way that the self-conscious power of volition and determination of the individual person is distinguished from its various faculties or the aggregate of them' (Willoughby 1896, 134 and 195).

Three points are worth noting here from this brief excursus on personality and identity. Firstly, legal and moral personality theory are integral to the development of the state. The state, through sovereignty, becomes an acting person. Sovereignty could be concentrated in the hands of one person or the social body. The potential conflict here between the divisibility of democracy and the indivisibility of sovereignty is only surficial. Second, both sovereignty and personality implied indivisibility of power. Sovereignty is the vehicle of this indivisibility. Indivisibility is individuality, and, in many writers, individuality is synonymous with personality. As one recent study of sovereignty notes therefore, 'whenever sovereignty is used in a theoretical context to confer unity upon the state as an acting subject, all that it conveys is that this entity is an individual by virtue of its indivisibility' (Bartelson 1995, 28). Sovereignty can thus be described as 'a principle of individuation'. In a sense, as mentioned above, the sovereign personality *is* the transcendental condition of the state. As the same author continues, 'sovereignty establishes the transcendental conditions of possibility of the modern state as a *subject*, telling us in the abstract what is a state and what it is not ... Sovereignty [thus] differentiates the state ontologically and ethically from other forms of political life, and furnishes us simultaneously with the condition for knowing the state as such' (Bartelson 1995, 189). Sovereignty consequently provides indivisibility and unity to the state both domestically and internationally. The sovereign state also takes on a corporeal determinate location in space and time in terms of a territory (Bull 1977).[18] Third, nineteenth and early twentieth century theorists began to make a direct link here between the identity of the state person and the phenomenon of national consciousness.

In the context of the above analysis, it is of little surprise that Michel Foucault should have quite correctly commented that political theory in general '*has never ceased to be obsessed with the person of the sovereign* [my italics]'. Foucault continues that 'Such theories still continue today to busy themselves with the problem of sovereignty. What we need, however, is a political philosophy that isn't erected around the problem of sovereignty ... We need to cut off the King's head: in political theory that has still to be done' (Foucault 1980, 121). This perceptive judgement is part of Foucault's more general inversion of questions in political philosophy. Instead of political philosophy trying to formulate authentic arguments on rights, justice or the limits of power, Foucault is concerned with 'what rules of right are implemented by the relations of power in the production of discourses of truth?'(Foucault 1980, 93). The present discussion is not primarily concerned with Foucault's deeper project of identifying a new form of 'biopower', 'micro-power' or 'disciplinary power', subtly replacing the focus on overt 'sovereign power'. The present discussion is rather more concerned to annex this component of Foucault's project to support another contention, namely, that legal sovereignty, legal personality theory and the theory of *de jure* right are and have been central to political philosophy and practice from the late medieval to the modern period, particularly as characterizing the state. Wittingly or unwittingly, this is and has been an 'obsession' of political philosophy. To supplement what Foucault says here, sovereignty theory is also *integral* to the way the *state* has been conceived. Definitionally, it is of little or no concern, in one sense, if the sovereignty is absolute or popular, since the relation of sovereignty to the state is analytical. Further, this indivisibility of the state/sovereign is accounted for in terms of personality and individuality. It may well be, as Foucault insists, that the notion of the individual, person or subject is an 'effect of power' rather than the originator of power (Foucault 1980, 98). However, from the late medieval to the modern period, the particular individual, subject or person became the exemplar of the sovereign and the state.

In summary, sovereignty provided the linchpin of the early and modern theory of the state. Although some scholars have disagreed with this point, its development appears to coincide with the first systematic development of the state, in juridical and political theory and practice. State implied sovereignty. Sovereignty was the source of law. In fact, for many absolutist theorists, the state was literally the property of the sovereign. Yet, sovereignty asserted the unity of the represented in a single power, will or person and this unity was contrasted, as a particular, to things outside itself, namely, other sovereign states. Thus sovereignty existed by proclaiming its unique indivisibility and particularity.

Sovereignty and nationalism

The relation between nationalism and sovereignty is complex. One immediate reason for the concepts being so closely linked lies in the historical claim that the language and practice of both national identity and sovereignty developed contemporaneously in the fifteenth or sixteenth centuries, coinciding with the development of state theory.[19] With regards to national identity, however, this is a deeply contentious and unsubstantiated claim. Scholarship on this issue, although intensive, has come to no clear consensus. Thus, this is not a particularly safe area to begin with.

A second line of enquiry focuses on the issue of identity itself, namely, the supposition that all organizations require some kind of collective identity or social cement. It is not clear why this is the case. However, it would be true that nationalism is focused primarily on identity. As one recent writer has put it, every nation necessarily expresses itself through the 'first person plural', or a 'we saying' (see Scruton in Beiner (ed.) 1999). Thus, nationalism provides a convenient identity for the state. Yet, given that sovereignty is *also* focused on identity, there appears to be a duplication of identities. The conventional and often implicit response to this is to register a distinction between legal and cultural, or, impersonal and personal identity. The suggestion is that sovereignty may provide a form of overt rational legal identity and *modus operandi* to the state, but it is cold, rule-governed, overly theoretical, abstract and impersonal – namely – what is essentially required from a legal order. Nationalism, on the other hand, provides an untheoretical, warm and expressive identity. Nations are thus a ghostly tepid emotive presence within states.

The difficulty with this expressive 'untheoretical' view of nationalism is that it is regarded with considerable unease by many nationalist theoreticians. The recent 1990s liberal nationalist writer, Yael Tamir, for example, is quite insistent on this point (Tamir in Beiner (ed.) 1999, 67). For her, nationalism is abstractly theorizable and rule-governed. Thus, a theory of nationalism, for Tamir, structures itself 'independently of all contingencies. Its basis must be a systematic view of human nature and of the world order, as well as a coherent set of universally applicable values' (Tamir 1993, 82). Tamir's general position is, in fact, shared by the majority of contemporary political theorists who are interested in nationalist theory, such as Brian Barry, David Miller, Neil MacCormick and Kai Nielsen. Even Barry's more lukewarm instrumental and subjectivist view of nationalism nonetheless sees it clearly rooted in a theoretical conception of common history (Barry in Miller and Seidentop (eds) 1983, 121–54). Thus, the distinction between a cold abstract identity in sovereignty and a warm expressive identity in nationalism looks distinctly fuzzy and unhelpful.

A more reasonable solution to this identity question would be that nationalism is undoubtedly focused on identity. The core of identity is selfhood or personality, or more abstractly, indivisibility. Nationalism has no intrinsic explanation of identity. But sovereignty and state theory, qua legal and moral personality theory, are premised on identitarian criteria. If one believes that sovereignty and state vocabulary precede nationalist language – which is indeed historically more accurate – then it would be more reasonable to assume that nationalism surreptitiously appropriated the pre-existent identity established by sovereignty.

A third line of investigation focuses on the analogous 'particularising' aims and functions of both nationalism and sovereignty. First, for both, humanity is understood to be fragmented into groups, each with its own traditions. Second, for both, each group has an identity. Third, nation and sovereignty are both linked with a territory. Fourth, the nation and sovereign are dominant over all individuals or groups within that territory. They both form the ultimate ground of legitimacy and loyalty. Fifth, nations and sovereignty both imply self-determination. The only apparent difference is that, for nationalists, human beings must identify with their national culture for a meaningful existence.[20] This latter theme does not appear in sovereignty argument, although culture frequently remains unexplained in the nationalist position. This argument concerning 'analogous language' can be read in a number of ways. However, what is most likely – as in the previous argument – is that nationalism has arrogated an existing sovereignty and state vocabulary. Sovereignty does have a strong language (whether one believes it or not) of identity. This is the language of real or fictional legal and moral personality. Generations of lawyers and political theorists have used this language from the 1500s, although its origins go back much further. Thus, notions of identity, self, interests, purposes, and so forth, make some sense in sovereignty discourse. However, nationalism has no comparable 'inner structure' or tradition of thought to speak of identity. The theoretical cupboard of nationalism is bare. The conclusion which stands out here is that nationalism is a much later and much fuzzier idea which literally plagiarizes sovereignty discourse.

A fourth line of enquiry, which establishes the more precise conceptual link between nationalism and sovereignty, focuses on two concepts, popular sovereignty and democracy. As argued, sovereignty terminology is comparatively old, in terms of the European political and legal vocabulary. The initial use, deriving from Roman law, was absolutist in character and formed the backbone to the classical theory of sovereignty. Yet, one other crucial sense of sovereignty developed, primarily in the seventeenth century, namely, sovereignty of the people, or more usually, popular sovereignty.[21] The idea of the will of the people arose out of the seedbed of absolutist dynastic sovereignty. Thus, some see it originating in the Glorious Revolution of 1688, as a direct challenge to absolutism (Wight 1977, 159). More often it is seen to become significant in the vocabulary of American and French revolutions of 1776 and 1789. The presiding figure, in this latter perspective, is J. J. Rousseau, whose theory of the general will is often associated with the link between popular sovereignty and nationalism. Summarising this general position, Anthony Smith has observed, 'It was only after the French Revolution that the *populus*, the *peuple* (in fact, the third estate, but theoretically and by precedent the whole body of citizens) was recognized as the sovereign "nation". The total population, and not just the aristocrats and clergy, now constituted the "nation"' (Smith 1971, 7–8). Sovereignty was no longer conceived in terms of the law, the monarch, executive or ruler, but rather in terms of the people (or *Volk*), and the term 'people' became (in some minds) completely synonymous with the nation. Many state policies, in the last two centuries, have intensified this apparent synonymity of the *people* and *nation* by consciously trying to homogenize populations through language uniformity and state-based education policies.[22] Others, again, have linked the development of popular sovereignty more closely to the twentieth century interest in self-determination in the League of Nations, Atlantic Charter and United Nations Charter.

In effect, in all of the above, a people is considered sovereign when it is supreme in terms of law-making and self-governance. Ironically, the United Nations, despite its name, tended, in framing its documents and charters, to use the word 'people', as against 'nation'. Thus, for example, the 1960 UN Declaration on colonial independence remarked that 'all *peoples* [my italics] have the right to self-determination'.[23] James Mayall, commenting on this UN preference for people over nation, remarked that it was 'presumably in an attempt to avoid the destructive confusion that had accompanied the reconstruction of Europe after 1918'. He continues that 'the result was not a huge improvement. Finding objective criteria to define "a people" is not easier, indeed, no different, to defining a nation' (Mayall in Jackson (ed.) 1999, 481). This latter judgement is only too true. There is a key problem here as to who or what are the people? People can denote the population of a territory; the markedly different idea of *whoever* populates a state territory; an electorate (which can vary considerably in size); a racial or ethnic majority, or indeed minority; legal citizens (qua nationality law); a representative assembly; or, finally, some kind of aggregation or compound of any of these. How, or in what manner, any of these senses of people relate to the concept of the nation remains utterly obscure. Thus, the connection that many assume between the nation and the people remains unclear and unsubstantiated.

Despite the above logical conclusion, it is clear that a practical or rhetorical link between nation and sovereignty, over the nineteenth and twentieth centuries, has been established, via the conception of popular sovereignty, mainly through the purported synonymity of nation and people. Nationalists always rest legitimacy within some kind of whole, and the people seems, *prima facie*, the most appropriate whole. Once the legitimacy is focused on the whole people, then it is but a short theoretical step to another concept – democracy.[24] Democracy is seen as the conventional manner in which 'the people' expresses itself. The linkage between democracy and nationalism was also reinforced in the writings of key nineteenth century figures in the nationalist pantheon, such as Ernest Renan and J. S. Mill. Renan had famously described the nation as a 'daily plebiscite', and for Mill, the national will was just another expression of the principle of representative democratic government. Ironically, such 'peoples' democracies' – as the terminology implies – can articulate every dimension of the ideological spectrum from fascist to anarchist. The popular democratic will is an unwieldy vessel which can veer from harmless spectacle to mass chauvinism and xenophobia. Democracy is not an end in itself. It solves certain problems, but when it becomes identical with the ends of nation and state, then it is unpredictable.[25]

However, it is still important to recognize that the link between nationalism, popular sovereignty and democracy is intuitively deep. The Georgian political theorist, Ghia Nodia, writing in 1994, despite noting the obvious deep problems caused by nationalism in Eastern Europe, nonetheless contends that 'the idea of nationalism is impossible – indeed unthinkable – without the idea of democracy, and that democracy never exists without nationalism' (Nodia in Diamond and Plattner (eds) 1994, 4). For Nodia, the two co-exist in a permanent tension, but they cannot be divorced. Nationalism can indeed foster democracy in certain contexts. Nodia's underlying reason for this claim is instructive. He maintains that at 'the core of democracy is the principle of popular sovereignty' (Nodia in Diamond and Plattner (eds) 1994, 5). Thus, democracy, via popular sovereignty, is integral to the concept and practice of nationalism. In addition, democracy is always situated within communities. It does not arise from an asocial condition. As Nodia comments, 'there is no record anywhere of free, unconnected, and calculating individuals coming together spontaneously to form a democratic social contract *ex nihilo*'. Thus, he continues, 'Whether we like it or not, nationalism is the historical force that has provided the political units for democratic government. "Nation" is another name for "We the People"' (Nodia in Diamond and Plattner (eds) 1994, 7). It is also significant here that Nodia does not see nationalism in any primordialist sense. He accepts what might be called the modernist thesis. Nationalism is a product of the French and Industrial revolutions. But even if it is a recent artifice – like democracy – this does not undermine its essential role in providing social cohesion.

There are a number of problems here with this supposed synonymity of democracy, nationalism and popular sovereignty, which can only be briefly touched upon. First, the history of popular sovereignty itself is long and tangled and by no means coincides with that of democracy or nationalism. Many European theorists in the last five centuries have articulated ideas on popular sovereignty, but only a small minority have been interested in democracy and it would be risible to call them nationalists. The serious and more widespread focus on democracy is largely a product of the twentieth century. Thus, before the twentieth century, the link between popular sovereignty, democracy and nationalism is, to say the least, historically extremely tenuous. Second, democracy itself is also a deeply contested idea. There are fierce, long-standing debates between notions of participatory, representative, pluralist, elite and postmodern difference conceptions of democracy, amongst many others. It is not at all clear whether all such warring conceptions of democracy are equally at home with nationalism. Third, the most politically successful notion of democracy – the representative idea – has not usually been conceived as a device for articulating popular sovereignty. Conversely, it has generally been seen as a device to limit and control the disruptive effect of the people and mass participation. For example, nineteenth century writers, such as Jeremy Bentham, James Mill and J. S. Mill (at points), all envisaged representative democracy in this more limited, instrumental and protective mode. In this sense, again, the connection with nationalism looks insubstantial.[26]

Despite the above arguments, if one still accepted the link between nationalism, democracy and popular sovereignty, it is arguable that they disperse powers and undercut the centralizing absolutist tendency of sovereignty. Nationalism is needed to provide an identity to the state, because personality theory is irrelevant. Two responses can be made to this. First, nationalism and democracy, in fact, provide a more 'mystical' substance to sovereignty and the state than that of absolutist argument, namely, that despite being a wholly dispersed multitude – for example, some fifty-eight million people in Britain – the nation *still* subsists as one unified corporate mystical body. The trappings of the absolute sovereign person are still ever-present here. In fact, the mysteries of state have become much deeper and more metaphysically obscure. Nodia's argument (above) supports this view. He suggests, for example, that 'national consciousness' is truly significant because it is, as he puts it, 'patterned on the blueprint of the individual human personality'. He elucidates this in two points. First, a nation is a community organized around the concept of self-determination and, unlike an ethnos, observes only those laws which it endorses itself. The national self only makes sense in terms of the concept of personality. Second, a national person needs partners for recognition. One person implies other persons who recognize one's personhood. For Nodia, therefore, a nation needs other nations. Both points exemplify what Nodia sees as the 'personality of the nation' (Nodia in Diamond and Plattner (eds) 1994, 11).

Second, it is important to grasp that nationalism is permeable and vacuous enough to alter with each differing account of sovereignty – absolutist or popular. Essentially, it arrogates the language of sovereignty, in the same way as it appropriates the languages of other ideologies to fill up its theoretical vacuum. Thus, popular sovereignty and democracy are both easily assimilated within nationalism. Despite the diversification and dispersal implied in popular sovereignty and democracy, the nation is able to assimilate this to the indivisibility and personality of the state. The notion of the indivisibility of sovereignty, linking together the whole of a people as a community of culture or ethnicity, provides an apparently deep historical root to sovereignty. This view is closely linked with early nineteenth century romantic and organicist discourse on nationalism. The co-existence of the state and nation, qua popular sovereignty, is presented in a pre-established harmony between culture, sentiment, tradition and force. If sovereignty is the metaphysical condition for the unity of the state, and this sovereignty is located in the people, and the people are identified with the historic 'natural' nation, then sovereignty also becomes 'naturalized'. Thus, as a recent study of sovereignty notes, 'If the classical concept of the state was based on a problematic ... identification of the person of the sovereign with the abstract space of power and interest, one could say with some simplification that the modern state is based on an equally problematic identification of state with nation, concealing its sovereignty by dispersing it at the ideological level' (Bartelson 1995, 210). The particularity of the state still exists, but in a more mysterious form.

Conclusion

In the context of the above analysis, the following comment from Paul Valery makes some deeper sense: 'The curious point in our historical and traditional way of defining nations is this: the present conception of grouping men into nations is ... anthropomorphic. A nation is characterized by rights of sovereignty and property. It owns, buys, sells, fights, tries to live and prosper at the expense of others; it is jealous, proud, rich or poor; it criticizes others; has friends and enemies ... In short, nations are persons, and by an immemorial habit of oversimplifying we attribute to them feelings, rights, and duties, virtues and faults, will and responsibility' (Valery 1963, 330). Essentially, my argument in this chapter has been that Valery is half right. It is largely sovereignty discourse, focused on individual and particular identity, which provides the driving energy for the nation. Without it, the nation would have little interest or significance. The nation idea parasitizes upon the language of individuality and identity, that is, notions of indivisibility, unified purpose, common interest and unified action. This language is embedded in state theory, via the concept of sovereignty and legal personality theory. It is thus still possible to speak of the individuality of the state *by* speaking of the nation, simply because it is the state and sovereignty language which fills the vacuity of the nation.[27] Nationalism, despite all its earnest rumblings over identity, has *no* language to express this identity, except via the more traditional discourse of sovereignty. Nationalism itself is a vacuous theory and without its use of sovereignty language it would be utterly bankrupt. Nationalism is particularist because both the state and sovereignty are particularist. The dilemma for nationalism now is stark. Doubts about collective entities such as states and sovereignties inevitably leach into doubts about nationalism. Thus, notions such as globalization, cosmopolitanism or multiculturalism are as much threats to nationalism as to statism, and nationalism has little or nothing to offer outside of sovereignty language. Terms such as cultural identity or regional self-determination, when deployed by nationalist writers, are just loose surrogates or stop-gaps, which try to avoid sovereignty language.

2   Nation State

It is important to be clear what is not being argued in this chapter. This at least clears the ground of some potential misunderstandings. First, this is not an argument against the state *per se*, in theory or practice. Second, there is no suggestion that nationalism does not exist, in some shape or form. Thus, this is neither an argument against the existence of nationalism, nor a surreptitious defence of cosmopolitanism or internationalism. Third, it does not deny that nationalism motivates, drives or influences behaviour and therefore has a strong political impact. Fourth, because there is a deep ambivalence amongst a number of contemporary writers over the question of the state and whether it is the best vehicle for the nation, this is not an argument against many of the preconceptions of contemporary nationalist writers. The focus of this chapter is rather on the compound term 'nation state', as it appears in contemporary political discussion.

The central argument of this chapter contends that the compound 'nation state' concept is largely redundant and needs to be disaggregated. As argued in the previous chapter, nationalism is a comparatively late addition to the European political vocabulary and trades upon the particularity and identity arguments implicit in sovereignty and state discourse. This chapter is however focused more intently on the relation between the state and nation. It is thus concerned with systematic doubts about the compound 'nation state', and argues, in effect, that it is a puzzle that it has persisted so long in political discourse. For some this may well be stating the obvious, for others this argument might just be mildly therapeutic.

The compound nation state

It was a well-established practice in nineteenth and twentieth century political speech to consider the state and nation as virtually coterminous or synonymous. This is, in fact, still the stock in trade vocabulary of politicians, international relations theorists, many political theorists and historians. From recent debates on the unified currency in Europe, the rights of ex-colonial states, *vis-a-vis* their former colonizers, or UN Security Council debates about humanitarian intervention, and so forth, the compound term 'nation state' is the dominant assumed background category for discussion. Thus, ironically, although interest in the theory of the state and 'nation state' waned in mainstream Anglo-American domestic academic political theory, particularly during the second half of the twentieth century, in international relations theory and the actual world of politics, it remained the basic hypostasized unit of analysis. The nation state terminology has thus been standard fare, particularly within the so-called realist, and later neo-realist, school of international relations, with writers like Hans Morgenthau or Martin Wight, and in a slightly different format, in Hedley Bull. Nationalism was not just an episode in state development, but was the linchpin or key factor of the state and international relations. The hyphen that sometimes appears in the term 'nation-state' is not therefore fortuitous. It indicates a definite compound entity of some sort.

In historical terms, also, up to the present day the 'nation state' has been the most popular form of political organization to aspire towards for developing or seceding groups. As argued in the previous chapter, the compound has a close conceptual resonance with concepts like sovereignty and self-determination. This popularity in fact accelerated exponentially in the twentieth century. In many ways, the concept of national self-determination is a comparatively recent idea, arising after the Versailles Treaty (1919). It then became enshrined in United Nations documents. Terms such as the League of Nations or United Nations, and the like, all largely presuppose the pervasive terminology of the self-determining nation state.[1] With the growing enthusiasm for this particular 'political form' over the mid-nineteenth and twentieth centuries, the older multi-national states were seen increasingly as anachronisms – 'prisons of peoples' to use the Mazzinian phrase – which had to be broken open for emancipation. This was the particular fate of the Hapsburg, Tsarist, Ottoman and British empires. The term 'peoples' remains unclear here; the usual shaky assumption is that it can be taken as virtually synonymous with nation. More recently, the same logic has been applied to the Soviet Union and even to Yugoslavia during the 1990s. Not only was the nation state envisaged, over the nineteenth century, as the precondition to genuine independence, self-determination and political freedom, but also – especially for some social science scholars – the ground for functional modernization and economic development. Some commentators have therefore seen a definite empirically identifiable pattern to this gradual evolution of the nation state.[2]

In summary, it has thus become a conceptual commonplace to link the state with the nation. This does not have to be a point of high-minded principle. Even on the most mundane level, the state is seen to provide a framework for nations – although whether nations provide the groundwork to states or vice versa is still an open and contested question. The conventional view here is that the state provides the forum or shell within which national identity can be articulated, represented and legitimated. This may be partly fortuitous, simply because of the context of a particularly strong European statist politico-legal culture, which not only developed on a practical political level, but was also given a powerful academic imprimatur by a large and growing band of lawyers, historians, philosophers and political theorists writing in the gradually expanding European universities of the late nineteenth and early twentieth centuries. Academic national history in universities and the 'nation state' itself have had an immensely close and symbiotic relation since the mid-nineteenth century. For some, this process has continued, with minor interruptions, to the present day.[3]

The terminology of the nation state has thus appeared consistently in academic political theory curricula. In German political thought Hegel, most notably, had signalled the importance of the compound terminology, and he was followed in this judgement by many jurists, historians and political thinkers across Europe (Hegel 1967, § 274, 178–9).[4] In Britain, the compound term 'nation state' was given its most well-known nineteenth century overt rendering by J. S. Mill. In the early twentieth century it became, more or less, a commonplace in political speech across Europe and elsewhere. Ernest Barker, for example, in a number of popular writings, like *National Character* (1927), summarized the idea quite concisely 'The history of the century since 1915 ... will teach us that in some form a nation must be a State, and a State a nation ... A democratic State which is multi-national will fall asunder into as many democracies as there are nationalities' (Barker 1927, 17). Despite some detractors, the compound term 'nation-state' still persists in political speech. In fact, as Anthony Smith has commented, 'The nation state [now] is the norm of modern political organization and it is as ubiquitous as it is recent. The nation state is the almost undisputed foundation of world order, the main object of individual loyalties' (Smith 1971, 2 and Kohn 1945, 17).[5] It even appears as normal fare amongst very recent political thinkers. Thus, Michael Walzer, for example, implicitly accepts it in thinking that a political community simply cannot exist except it 'favours some particular people who share a common life' (Walzer 1992, 524).[6] Or, as another theorist states, summarizing one aspect of the condition of contemporary political theory, at the onset of the twenty-first century, 'like it or not, most states are nation states and ... nationalism both as a generalized sentiment of attachment to one's national identity and as a form of organized political activity, is a salient feature of the contemporary world'.[7]

There is no suggestion here, by any means, that *all* modern commentators – even ironically nationalist commentators – accept this view. Far from it, as we will see. In fact, in many nationalist quarters there is some distinct unease, if not embarrassment, with this idea. Further, in developing the argument, it is important to be mindful of Margaret Canovan's comment that the first common move of a political theorist, particularly a liberal academic theorist, is to point out that nations and state do *not* coincide and that both can exist independently (Canovan 1996, 51–2). Usually, post-1945 liberal theorists have performed this ritualistic move as part of a more general demolition of nationalism, often, although not always, for the sake of some version of cosmopolitanism or international human rights. This is not my strategy. If there is a separation, in this chapter, between the claims of nations and states it is not for the sake of liberalism, cosmopolitanism or universal human rights.[8] Further, it is also important not to always expect too much rationality or sense from the compound. The idea of the nation itself is not noted for its conceptual or theoretical precision. In fact, as will be discussed, some theorists make a point, or a virtue, of emphasizing its vagueness. Yet, as with many political ideas, lack of precision or vagueness does not seem to have any debilitating affect upon political practice. If anything it can often enhance it.

This chapter now turns to a review of arguments which undermine the compound term nation state in contemporary political speech. The arguments examined are a mixture of empirical, historical, normative and conceptual claims, as well as overlapping composites of these. None of the arguments on their own would be decisive. However, if one looks at them together, then serious doubts should be considered about the utility of the compound term 'nation state'. However, in sowing seeds of doubt about the compound there is no wish to be seen to be undermining the conception of the state. As argued in chapter one, it is the state and sovereignty which provide the core theoretical substance to the nationalist focus on particular 'identity'. Before moving to these arguments the discussion focuses briefly on the attitudes to this compound in contemporary nationalist-orientated political theory.

What do our contemporaries think?

The modern literature on nationalism and political theory, although relatively scant up to around a decade ago, has more than made up for it. The present discussion will only look at some representative examples.

Up until the twentieth century, the link between the state and the nation was much clearer or at least less contested. This was certainly the case in theorists like J. S. Mill, J. G. Fichte, J. G. Herder, G. Mazzini and Ernest Renan. Thus, Herder noted, without any doubt or hesitation, that 'The most natural state is *one* nationality with one national character' (quoted in Ergang 1931, 243–4). Fichte also contended, in his *Addresses to the German Nation*, that it is language which always characterizes human beings. Language constitutes the real human essence. Fichte, however, draws a distinction between natural and compound languages. The German or Teutonic language is a natural *Urvolk* language, whereas French and English are compound neo-Latinate languages which both show the effect of admixtures. Fichte contends that all peoples who speak an original language naturally constitute a nation and ultimately such a nation must form a state. As Fichte notes, 'wherever a separate language is found, there a separate nation exists, which has the right to take independent charge of its affairs and to govern itself'. If a people has ceased to govern itself, then Fichte maintains that 'it is equally bound to give up its language'. Further, all genuine nation states to Fichte must speak an original language. The frontiers of such a nation state would therefore be internal to language speakers. As Fichte notes, 'the first, original, and ... natural boundaries of States are beyond doubt internal boundaries. Those who speak the same language are joined to each other by a multitude of invisible bonds by nature herself'. External boundaries of states are the outcome of internal boundaries. Geographical factors are for Fichte of little consequence compared to language. If such geo-graphical factors coincide with linguistic boundaries, as in the English, then it is fortuitous. Fichte adds here an ominous note, remarking that when the territory of a natural people has become too narrow or it wishes to exchange a barren for a fruitful region, it can 'enlarge it by conquest of the neighbouring soil in order to gain more room, and then it will drive out the former inhabitants' (Fichte 1979, 215–6, 224 and 226). This sense that state and nation are intimately linked still permeates much contemporary international relations theory. In the late twentieth century for more empirically inclined international relations scholars, such as Hans Morgenthau, Raymond Aron, Hedley Bull and Martin Wight, the interaction of 'nation states' has been the baseline or key premise for the whole edifice of the discipline. The conventional wisdom, of particularly the post-1945 generation of international relation theorists, is that the brute realities of power and nationalism, qua nation states, has to be accepted as a given datum.[9]

However, one of the interesting points to note about recent normative academic nationalist theorists is that, unlike their nineteenth century predecessors, there is surprisingly little unanimity on this 'compound' nation state issue. There are basically two forceful contrasting positions on the nation state compound in present literature. The first views nationalism as the stronger conceptual element and the state as a declining idea and practice. The second considers the compound as still being of some theoretical utility.

Thus, firstly, for Neil MacCormick, for example, the concepts of the nation and state need to be considered separately. On the one hand, he notes that 'states are political entities which have a legal definition'; he continues that wherever 'there exists a relatively independent and self-sufficient legal order having defined organs of government of a relatively centralized kind exercising jurisdiction over a … territory, there is a state'. The members of such a state are defined by law. MacCormick claims to be following Hans Kelsen here. It should be noted that Kelsen is the doyen of twentieth century legal positivism, namely, where the state is defined very strictly in terms of existing jural sovereignty and law. In this sense, there would be little, if no mileage in trying to derive any morality or cultural themes from a legal positivist state compound. Yet, for MacCormick, nations are clearly *not* legal entities (MacCormick 1982, 248).[10] Law and moral or cultural issues need to be kept distinct. Thus, whereas the state is taken to be a 'legalistic impersonal entity', nationalism is a form of warm 'popular consciousness', involving a common culture and incorporating a 'common way of doing and living'. Nation implies a form of personal kinship, based on common myths and traditions. MacCormick suggests that given the 'cold legal character' of the state, it is not surprising that many have wished to 'infuse it with the warm moral personality of "a nation"' (MacCormick 1982, 249). It is curious, but not wholly unexpected given the arguments of the previous chapter, that MacCormick should actually employ the term 'moral personality' here for the nation.

However, this 'common consciousness' includes, for MacCormick, 'the need for a form of common governance which recognizes and allows for the continued flourishing of the cultural and historical community' (MacCormick 1982, 261). Despite recognizing the need that national communities have felt for gaining their own 'state', MacCormick expresses profound scepticism about this expectation. He notes, for example, that the nineteenth and twentieth century 'nation state' has not added much to contentment or peace in Europe, or elsewhere, although whether this has been due to nationalism or statism, or the mixture of the two, is still an open question. MacCormick, however, does look with optimism to the retention of nationalism, but moving it beyond the state model. Thus, the nation state compound is envisaged as gradually being replaced by forms of diffused regional power in the context of federations, like those of the European Union. Multilevel plural governance thus provides the best vessel for national aspiration. In this sense, there is an appeal to a form of neo-medievalism, where Europe, once again, becomes cellular and disaggregated; although whether the European Union should be considered as the neo-Holy Roman Empire is anyone's guess. For MacCormick, in fact, 'the concept of a "sovereign state" is of much more recent vintage than that of a nation, and developments such as that of the European community suggest that it may have already had its day' (MacCormick 1982, 264). Historically, this appears an utterly skewed and odd judgement concerning the origins of the state and nation. Leaving this to the side, MacCormick further contends that those who consider that such regionally based nationalism is too weak are misled. Conversely, he suggests that regional federation can be a golden mean between the rejection of nationalism, on the one hand, and mindless xenophobia on the other. Thus, nationalism is something which MacCormick thinks can and should develop outside the dated cold and legalistic sovereign state.

The liberal nationalist writer, Yael Tamir, has comparable views to MacCormick. The nation is a particular type of cultural community. She, in fact, explicitly comments that a 'nation is *not* a state', although she admits that it is often 'assumed to be the case' (Tamir 1993, 58). She then identifies two meanings to the term state – although where precisely they come from remains obscure. One refers to 'a body of people that has organized politically'; the other implies 'the institutions of government' (Tamir 1993, 59). For Tamir, neither idea, nor indeed notions of territory, power or sovereignty, and the like, are essential characteristics of the nation. The coincidence of the terms nation and state is thus seen as a wholly *contingent* historical matter, bearing upon events and ideas surrounding the French and American revolutions of the late 1700s. Although she also adds that deliberate efforts by nationalists to foster the idea may have had some bearing on the issue. Most states now though are *not* nationally inclusive. Tamir indeed also speculates, like MacCormick, that the days of the homogeneous nation state are over and done with and that we now need to radically rethink. There has to be some notion of autonomy within states – although she does admit, in qualification, that a state adopting any kind of official language or public holidays quite definitely shows a cultural preference for one kind of national group or identity. But, like MacCormick again, the model of the federated European Union appears to save the day. This federated or regional idea can provide possibilities for self-rule, if not some self-determination. Her own thoughts on this utilize the consociational ideas of Lijphart. She thus remarks that 'accepting the idea that national self-determination might best be attained within a larger regional framework implies that political thought has entered a new age in which the principle of national self-determination no longer provides the sole justification for political organization. It also challenges the belief that a stable political framework requires cultural, linguistic, or religious uniformity' (Tamir 1993, 166). Thus, although nationalism is retained, for Tamir, as for MacCormick, the state is seen as a somewhat dated and arcane vessel which has had its day.

David Miller's case is less clear cut. He insists, like Tamir and MacCormick, in his book *On Nationality*, that the state and nation should not be confused. 'Nation' and 'state' are not synonyms – despite their common use in everyday speech. The nation is a community of people with an aspiration to be politically self-determining and the state is the set of political institutions they aspire to achieve (Miller 1995b, 18–19). Yet, he definitely does not see the state (or sovereignty) as a dated or arcane institution. In fact, the state is partly redeemed in Miller's argument. Thus, he argues that 'nation states have an underlying right to decide for themselves which rights of sovereignty they should continue to exercise' (Miller 1995b, 106). In an earlier article, he more explicitly insists that 'state boundaries should as far as possible coincide with national boundaries' (Miller in Brown (ed.) 1994, 143). It is also morally *desirable*, for Miller, that the nation be politically self-determining. National self-determination 'corresponds to the idea of nations as active communities'. Nations might well be less disruptive if tied to a state. For Miller, the state 'is likely to be better able to achieve its goals where its subjects form an encompassing community, and conversely national communities are better able to preserve their culture and fulfil their aspirations where they have control of the political machinery'. National self-determination usually 'requires a state with unlimited rights of sovereignty' (Miller in Brown (ed.) 1994, 145). This does not mean that either sovereignty or statehood should become a fetish for nationalists. In fact, there may be good reasons for transferring some legal powers to other bodies – as has actually happened in the European Union. But, nonetheless, there is a close symbiotic relation of states and nations.

In sum, there is little unanimity over the question of the state and nation in current writers who are sympathetic to nationalism. The more negative sentiments in Tamir and MacCormick argue that nationalism is a much more ancient phenomenon, which precedes the state and has now potentially outgrown it. Nationalism is thus prioritized over the state. Miller offers the most sympathetic rendering, but even he has many significant qualifications to make over the nature of the state. Despite this uncertainty in normative theory, the compound still persists as a commonplace in political speech. In fact, the most spirited defenders of the sovereign nation state idea in contemporary politics are often the newer postcolonial, developing and weaker states in the world. Iraq,

Sierra Leone, Yugoslavia, Croatia, and the like, are the states who most enthusiastically embrace the self-determining sovereign nation state compound. Further, much serious historical and international relations writing still works with the background theme of the nation state. In this sense, the compound continues to be a lemma or unquestioned datum of political analysis. The discussion turns now to some of the arguments which undermine the compound 'nation state'.

Nation to state or state to nation?

One of the ongoing themes in discussion of the compound concerns the issue of which if any is prior historically or normatively. Thus, do nations historically precede states? Neil MacCormick, for example, as mentioned, is convinced that the nation is characterized by longevity, whereas the state is a more recent phenomenon. For the conservative theorist, Roger Scruton, nations also provide a *natural* identity and sense of heimat which is completely distinct from that of the state and independent of and prior to any institutional forms. Loyalty and jurisdiction are rooted in this initial primordial membership. Even classical liberals are viewed, by Scruton, as nationalists, in relying on an unconscious background of prepolitical loyalties. The nation establishes 'a social unity suited to territorial jurisdiction' (Scruton 1990, 322). It is necessary here to query the desire of some nationalist writers to absolutely prioritize the nation as a natural or premodern entity, or, at least, something possessing antiquity, and thus to go on to suggest that pre-existent nations unproblematically create states in their own image. In fact, groups such as nations are simply what they make of themselves at any particular moment, regardless of any mythical past. Despite the labours of many scholars, in reality the mythic past provides no benedictions on the present, unless of course we allow it.

Further, apart from Anthony Smith's slightly more elusive arguments on the ethnic origins of nations, the historical evidence tends to point the other way, especially if one considers 'nations' rather than 'ethnie'.[11] The juridical state idea and practice historically precede the nation by many centuries and have subsisted adequately without it. If one included empires or, possibly, even politico-commercial organizations, like the Hanseatic League, as having aspects of 'stateness', then it is clear that all such juridico-political associations functioned without nationhood, nationality or nationalism. Similarly, dynastic, absolutist states preceded the existence of self-conscious nations by centuries. In fact, countless forms and types of social and political organization have existed without anything like nationality.

The other caveat to bear in mind here is that academic writing has itself been imbricated in the whole development of the concept of the nation. The academy often has a stake in its expansion. Nationalism was and is an extraordinarily adaptable tool for historians, poets, journalists and novelists. In interpreting the nation to itself these writers have a core social function in otherwise lonely and unappreciated professions. Thus, writings on the nation – no matter how scholarly – cannot be always treated as if they were abstracted commentaries on something *called* nationalism. Impartiality is implied, yet viewed from another angle, they are often part of and propagators of the mythic nation itself. The development of academic politics, law and history was, in fact, quite directly related to self-conscious policies of nation states in the nineteenth and twentieth centuries (see, for example, Berger, Donovan and Passmore (eds) 1999 and Soffer 1994). The nationalist myths, fantasies and aspirations – lovingly embodied in academic lexicography, academic historical writing, painting, poetry, literature and monuments during the nineteenth century – arose once again, phoenix-like from the flames, in the closing decade of the twentieth century. Old agendas were still very much the present realities of the 1990s, being re-fought with re-kindled hatreds. Those who service these agendas and hatreds are more often than not the scholarly literati. Thus, writings on nationalism, even the more abstracted and scholarly, are subtly interwoven into the very texture of nationalism. There is a sense here in which nationalism always contains its own self-fulfilling historical prophecy, wherever it occurs. In effect, it occasionally commandeers history and tradition to establish its own existence and ineffable continuity with the past. Academic history then becomes literally the history of the nation.

There are writers who obviously have deep reservations about this view. Some accounts associate nations with ancient ethnic groups or tribes. The nation is thus seen as a concept of great antiquity, virtually identifiable with a genetically based social instinct in human beings. Sociobiologically influenced writers are inclined to this form of interpretation, viewing nationalism as a biological rather than a normative category (see Kellas 1991). Nationalism is consequently understood as a distinctively premodern idea, expressive of either a form of ethnicity or a straightforward normative commitment to a common birthright.[12] Others see national differences becoming much sharper during the middle ages.[13] Anthony Black, for example, contends that 'the idea of the fatherland (*patria*) was ingrained in medieval culture, and one may assume it was not absent from popular consciousness'. He continues that 'many people, ... were aware of national identity and regarded it as a significant social fact about themselves: English, Franks or Frenchmen ... In the later Middle Ages there were trends towards a more articulate self-consciousness of nationhood' (Black 1993, 108–10). This sense of nationhood was based on factors like language, hatred of common foes and communal religious liturgy. For Black, therefore, many states, like

England, France, Poland, and Denmark, did emerge with an 'ethnic dimension' in the 1200s. He consequently sees an awareness of 'Scottishness' at the Declaration of Arbroath (1320) which referred to the Scythian origin of the 'nation of Scots' (Black 1993, 111). The historian Liah Greenfeld suggests that the sense of the nation arose much later, in the 1600s, as an elite device, but still long before modernization and industrialization processes. In Britain it was the Tudors who were decisive. She tracks similar developments across France, Russia, Germany and the United States (Greenfeld 1992). Hans Kohn coincides here with Greenfeld's view, also focusing on the late 1600s as the seedbed of nationalist ideas, although Kohn sees this as a more unconscious form of national awareness (Kohn 1945, 4). A similar view is also shared by the contemporary legal philosopher Neil MacCormick who sees evidence of national identity in the sixteenth century in England and more particularly Scotland. Thus, he comments that it is 'quite irrelevant that the term "nationalism" as a term of art in political theory comes into general usage only in the nineteenth century' (MacCormick 1982, 256 and 260). However, others do not agree. Lord Acton favoured the 1772 partition of Poland as the groundwork for European nationalism (Acton 1907). The Enlightenment of the eighteenth century is another favoured point of derivation for nationalism (Walicki 1989). Yet some scholars, like Elie Kedourie, were quite explicit in tracing nationalism to the revolutions in eighteenth century German philosophy. However, the most favoured point of origin is the period leading up to and immediately after the French Revolution.[14] Finally, some scholars have argued that nationalism is a product of the early nineteenth century. The historian Hobsbawm, for example, claims that the modern usage of nationalism is in fact comparatively recent. The modern idea probably only dates from the 1830s, although some aspects of its populist meaning were traceable to the American and French revolutions. This latter point more or less corresponds with the thrust of Gellner's and Benedict Anderson's work which also presents nationalism as a modern term corresponding with the growth and modernization of states in the nineteenth century (Hobsbawm 1992, 48–9; E. Gellner 1983; Anderson 1983). Hobsbawm however identifies three phases or periods: initially 1830–1880, which is dominated by liberal nationalism; then 1880–1914 which sees a sharp movement to the conservative right in nationalist thinking. Finally, the apogee of nationalism is identified with the period 1918–1950 (Hobsbawm 1992, 38ff).

The only point to note here in passing is that there is emphatically no settled view on the origin of nationalism. My own sympathies lie with those scholars who see nationalism as a distinctly modern movement emanating from the French Revolutionary era. This does not deny that there were earlier forms of group loyalty and allegiance. However they were not nationalist as we understand the term in the nineteenth and twentieth centuries. Undoubtedly, common membership, common legal structures and the traditions of stable absolutist states provided the ideal locations for 'proto-nationalisms'. Tudor England, for example, certainly possessed elements of proto-nationalism or elementary 'patriotism', and as Hobsbawm notes, 'It would be pedantic to refuse this label [patriotism] to Shakespeare's propagandist plays', or, as Bernard Bosanquet put it, in more vivid prose, 'when we read John of Gaunt's praises of England in Shakespeare's *Richard II*, we feel ourselves at once in contact with the mind of a social unity' (Hobsbawm 1992, 75; Bosanquet 1899, 12). But, it is worth reminding ourselves that the 'mind of a social unity' is not necessarily always national. In fact, for absolutisms, and other forms of political organization, it was more than likely religion or local custom which dominated perspectives. The full vocabulary of nationalism or nationality was not therefore really present even in the sixteenth or seventeenth centuries.

Yet, do nations and states in the nineteenth and twentieth centuries – the heyday of nationalist argument – coincide in such a way as to make a convincing case for the compound term 'nation state' in political vocabulary? Even here there are a number of obstacles to the coincidence of nations and states. States, *prima facie*, are, in one very pervasive view, impersonal cold juridical structures where membership is defined by law. This is a view that legal positivists espouse and is clearly acknowledged by many current nationalist writers. Conversely, nations are a different type of social entity, more personalized, culturally orientated, emotive and defined by other types of criteria (Smith 1991, 14–15.)

These points might be regarded as relatively innocuous. However, they become more problematic when linked with other issues, namely, the fact that there are clearly multiple nationalities, subnationalities and ethnic groups within the majority of world states.[15] Homogeneity is virtually non-existent. Heterogeneity is the norm. Multi-ethnicity and multi-nationalism have become the norm over the last half century with the decline of Western empires, increasingly global communication and market activity, international travel and large migrations of peoples, and so forth. This process has also been fostered, to some degree, by the growing interest in forms of decentralization, regionalism, secession arguments and federalism within states. Multiculturalism and multi-nationalism (on a more descriptive level) have become a more regular feature of states such as the USA, Canada, New Zealand and Australia, and are becoming an increasingly widespread, acknowledged phenomenon in many other states, including Britain, Italy, Germany and France, as well as Asian states like Indonesia or China; although, admittedly, states like Japan, amongst others, still appear deeply uneasy with the idea of multiculturalism.

The main suggestion here is that we have possibly – in the situation of the contemporary nation state – come to an historical impasse. We may, as even some nationalist writers intimate, be on the cusp of something politically quite novel. However, in this case, it may well not be the state which has had its day, but rather nationalism. Nationalism served a contingent historical role for the last two hundred years. That contingent period is now slowly passing and the evidence of that passing is around us, but nonetheless we are still *within* that contingent moment. Nationalism therefore still appears very relevant for many. Its appeal is very far from dead in political practice. What happens now though is open to debate.

In summary, forms of state have existed without nationality. The term nation state, even on the most simple descriptive level, appears quite odd conceptually. For a moment, in the nineteenth century, the nation-state compound had some sense and reference. Yet, whereas the old multi-national states and empires in the nineteenth century used to be generally derided by orthodox nationalists, it would appear to be the case now that the reverse is regarded as a more accurate social representation. Nation states are now the prisons of peoples. It is thus a fallacy to think of states – historically and sociologically – automatically coinciding with nations.[16] This is a view common to both critics and proponents of nationalism.

Normative argument

However, even if one acknowledged that states do not, as a matter of empirical fact, coincide with nations, nonetheless it might still be claimed that it is morally desirable that they ought to coincide. The point here is that, for the proponent, there is a possible moral, rather than an empirical *realpolitik*, case to be made for the nation-state compound. There are two issues to be considered here. The first concerns the question whether nationalists actually want to make a moral case for the compound. The second focuses on whether nationalism (let alone the nation state) can be said to be a source for morality.

The first point can be fairly quickly answered. Despite the fact that a number of nineteenth century and early twentieth century writers have wanted to make a moral case for the compound, this is not shared by all contemporary nationalist writers. The only exception to this might, unwittingly, be the argument for self-determination, which usually involves a transference from the individual human to the nation level, and given moral force *by* its link with nationality. This argument was briefly discussed in the previous chapter. Thus, for example, for Ghia Nodia or

Neil MacCormick, nationality is 'patterned on the blueprint of the individual human personality'. A nation is a community organized around the concept of self-determination and observes only those laws which it 'personally' endorses (Nodia in Diamond and Plattner (eds) 1994, 11). There are, though, two qualifications to be made here. First, this is a state-based language, concerning legal or moral personality and sovereignty, which furnishes nationalism with self-determination. Second, it follows, logically, that it is quite possible to have a theory of sovereign state self-determination without even mentioning the nation.

At root, self-determination asserts that a nation has the right to constitute itself as an independent state and determine its own government and laws. It is a concept which has figured particularly strongly in twentieth century discussions, although its conceptual lineage goes back into the early nineteenth century. However, there is a subtle, often unremarked, transposition in the argument on self-determination from a more conventional argument concerning the freedom of the individual. The supposition that a free individual is self-determining thus becomes transposed onto the proposition that the free nation is also apparently self-determining. Self-determination often implies the right of a state or community to its own independent and distinctive existence.[17] The nation becomes a synonym for the governed or the people. Apart from the difficulty of speaking about the 'self' of a nation – dealt with in the previous chapter – the crucial problem here is the fact that national self-determination does not necessarily fluidly correspond with individual self-determination. There is an unexplained 'carry-over', probably explained by the fact the nationalism relies on the background claims of sovereignty to establish notions of identity.

Nationality, in the above sense, is frequently seen to be the moral resource within the state; although this is a distinct argument from a moral case for the compound nation state. Viewing nationalism as a moral resource allows the agent to access all the virtues of nationality, without necessarily requiring a state. This seems to be the gist of what certain recent nationalist writers want to claim. Nationalism can thus provide moral and cultural resources within a regional or consociational federation. Thus, if anything is morally relevant, it is the nation and not the state, the state being impersonal and legalistic in character. This argument is reinforced by the fact that the majority of recent nationalist theorists see a clear distinction between nations and states and, indeed, some argue that states are no longer viable bearers of the morality of nationhood.

The second issue is the basic nationalist point, which is also recognisably communitarian, that moral goods cannot be determined by abstract reasoning. *Ethical particularism* is counterposed to *ethical universalism*.

As David Miller comments, 'ethical particularism ... allows existing commitments and loyalties a fundamental place in ethical reasoning' (Miller in Paul, Miller and Paul (eds) 1989, 68). We interpret an existing national tradition of ethical discourse. The national community becomes the locus of the good. We cannot totally step back to assess communities, morality or justice with a view from nowhere, although we can criticize them from within using internal standards of rationality.[18] Yet, a national culture does not, for Miller, have to be monolithic. It is rather a 'set of understandings about how a group of people is to conduct its life together'. Being French does not dictate the *kind* of French person one is or could be. Yet, for Miller, our obligations are always deeply coloured by the local ethos. Ethics can still be rational. In the best case scenario, national identity flows from this rational reflection. Nonetheless, it is still our prior obligations and loyalties which give substance to citizenship and justice concerns.[19] This particularism of ethics is also argued by Margalit and Raz. They suggest that group culture is crucial to individual well-being. Cultures are defined in terms of common language and shared history. Such cultural membership provides individuals with meaningful choices and the boundaries of the imaginable. Self-government for such cultural 'encompassing groups' is seen as immensely important (Margalit and Raz in Kymlicka (ed.) 1995a, 82–5). The encompassing groups they have in mind are national in character. The identity of the group should be respected and not subject to ridicule or discrimination and should be able to manifest itself in open public life in the community.

The above normative arguments come under three pressures. First, with the advent of globalism, the internationalization of culture, particularly the widespread recognition of international human rights and justice, it is now far from clear where the obligations of individuals do lie. Most liberal nationalists have been at pains to say there are no problems here – there is no ultimate incompatibility with international duties. Yet, for writers such as Miller, MacCormick or Margalit and Raz, national loyalties clearly come prior to any international duties. We do have special responsibilities to our fellow nationals. As MacCormick comments, in Herderian vein, 'could one learn to love mankind universally if one had not first learned to love people in the concrete in the narrower range' (MacCormick 1982, 253). For those who believe intensely in international justice and human rights, our obligations appear to be to human individuals, as individuals, qua human rights, irrespective of nationality, ethnicity, geography or culture. Thus, for Brian Barry, for example, justice does have certain formal universal characteristics and the validity of this proposition 'cannot be challenged by showing that a lot of people in some benighted society think otherwise' (Barry in Miller and Walzer (eds) 1995, 75). There is a deep conflict here between universalism and particular nationalism which cannot be simply elided.

A second pressure on normative argument for nationalism is the issue of internal moral resources. The question arises as to whether there are any unified normative resources available within nations. However, as opposed to there being a unified moral resource, for a theorist like Walzer, we are faced by a whole array of social institutions which are constitutive of our identities. This echoes Miller's point that being a Frenchman does not dictate the kind of Frenchman one is. Yet the point is even more complex than Miller's. Each self is potentially multi-faceted. We are constituted by an array of institutions, associations and groups. This means that the calls upon our loyalty and commitment, the factors that shape us and the demands we make upon others, come from a diversity of directions.[20] This is what Walzer calls the divided self (Walzer 1994a, 85–6). This point alone should make us uneasy with Margalit and Raz's somewhat claustrophobic conception of 'encompassing groups'. There are some institutional controls and limits on these spheres for Walzer. However, Iris Marion Young, for one, takes the divisiveness another step. She appears to accept the nationalist claim that groups are constitutive of individuals' moral identity. Groups are thus not fictions. They affect our sense of history, reasoning and feeling. But the 'affinity groups' she refers to are even more random, diverse, elusive and differentiated than Walzer's. Miller's account might be able to accommodate Walzer's liberal multiculturalism, but not Young's more radical thesis. Young's thesis is that, under the aegis of distributive justice and impartiality theories, many groups – because they are so different – are marginalized, silenced, subjected to violence or ignored. Thus, she 'seeks to show how ... a denial of difference contributes to social group oppression, and to argue for a politics that recognizes rather than represses difference' (Young 1990, 10). She suggests that we should respect the identity of all oppressed groups, who are at a disadvantage in the political process. Emancipation comes therefore through recognition of group difference and group rights. Nationalism, like communitarianism or impartiality theory, would be seen here as modes of oppression and domination.

This process of fragmentation has been explored even more vigorously in postmodern-inclined writers into a labyrinth of groups – almost diversity and difference out of its depth. For William Connolly, a postmodern position embraces strong difference and rejects *all* closure.[21] Where liberals try to shield society from strong identities, Connolly wants a future society to encompass them. Where nationalists offer a harmony of communal pre-understandings, Connolly wants real differences exposed to the full. Nationalists thus offer textual tropes that 'presuppose [harmonization's] availability'. For Connolly, the 'rhetoric of harmonization must be ambiguated and coarsened by those who have not had its faith breathed into their souls, particularly those moved by nontheistic reverence for the rich ambiguity of existence' (Connolly 1991, 90). The crisis of society is not one of fragmentation, but rather the attempt to fix identities. Connolly's vision of society is thus an 'agonistic democracy'.[22]

A third pressure concerns the issue whether normative resources can be found which do not require the nation *per se*. There is obviously a strong suggestion that this is the case with cosmopolitanism as well as with what might be called micro-particularism. However, normative resources can also be found even in the state. This argument is dependent on the Hegelian idea of the state being more complex and embodying institutions considered as constitutive ethical ideas. The state here would be a form of structured 'operative criticism'. An individual *per se* thus does not just exist in one group or institution. The individual is a process. Individuals stand in a 'mindful' constitutive relation to multiple institutions. Early development takes place in a family and local neighbourhood, from the family individuals move into the diverse spheres of civil society. They have to labour in the market and this need places particular imperatives and constraints upon them. They may have a family themselves and this adds a new dimension and a new inner layer of imperatives. The agent will often acquire some property and may also become an interested and concerned citizen, regularly examining public debates and even taking part in public bodies. These again place new perspectives and moral demands upon them. This whole developmental process which takes place within a more detailed and rich understanding of the state itself might be described as an ethical life in process. The individual becomes moralized through entering *mindfully* into established institutional spheres of the state. The critic may violently disagree with this view, but it is clearly still a viable reading of the relation of morality and the state, which does not even mention the nation.

To focus on nationality as *the* sole source of morality is thus profoundly contestable and narrow, not only from a cosmopolitan or statist standpoint, but also from the perspective of internal pluralism – a cryptic pluralism which is neatly implied in Rawls' 'reasonable pluralism' – a politics of metaphysical indifference, pushed wider open in Walzer's 'spheres' and 'complex equality', fragmented in Young's 'politics of difference' and irreconcilably and genealogically exposed in Connolly's or Foucaultian radical pluralism. Minimally, therefore, the contrast between cosmopolitan and nationalist morality seems overly simple. Further, contrary to the perception of nationalist writers, there are a range of alternative sources of morality other than nationalism. The state, for example, might be regarded as an ethical resource, without recourse to nationalism. The arguments for nationalism being a groundwork for morality are also vague and unsatisfactory. Finally, none of the nationalist arguments offer an effective normative case for the compound term 'nation state' itself. There are arguments, which derive from legal positivism, for keeping the legal (qua state) and moral (qua nation) spheres distinct, but there is nothing which offers a normative defence of the compound term.

Nations, power and pragmatism

However, another view on nationalism would suggest that we fundamentally misunderstand it if we think of it in moral terms. Nationality is a much messier, less salubrious idea and practice, which inhabits the world of politics and power, rather than the world of morality. It is thus a mistake to plunge our hands into the grubby waters of nationalism searching for its moral soul. It just does not have one. This argument is intrinsically appealing and, oddly, it can effectively redeem the nation state compound from another direction. The argument can have different, if overlapping, dimensions to it. There are what might be called the *tacit dimension* and the weaker *pragmatic governability dimension*.

The *tacit dimension* argument is ably and powerfully rendered in Margaret Canovan's work on nationalism. Nationalism here forms a tacit premise within political thinking. She offers a form of transcendental sociological argument, the nation becoming the transcendental unity of apperception for politics. All organizations (especially the state) require some kind of collective identity. The state is not enough on its own, it needs to be 'our' state. Thus there is a kind of 'ghostly presence' behind much political argument. It is even present in liberal cosmopolitan theories. To Canovan, for liberal justice and distribution to flourish, boundaries, powers and jurisdictions have to be presupposed. John Rawls' whole theory, for example, is thus seen to be shot through with such tacit assumptions. Nations are seen as powerfully present, in fact, conditionally necessary for states, yet, at the same time, often invisible. Nationality therefore 'makes possible the kind of community required by liberal democratic theories' (Canovan 1996, 68).

Canovan is absolutely correct, in my reading, in asserting that the large bulk of certainly recent political theory has been generally silent about boundaries, the character of our solidarities, the grounding of citizenship and justice and more particularly the sources of political power – let alone the state. Political theory largely, until recently, avoided such questions. Theorists might be said to have had such a high myopic success rate because they usually live in well-established nation states that have had early experiences of nation-building. The nation has become so embedded that it can exert an energetic 'us' feeling without effort. We thus leap, without exertion, into 'rights talk' or 'distributive justice', because we are oblivious to our deep starting point. Canovan thus claims that nations act subtly as batteries generating popular power and feeling when needed and lying dormant for long periods when not. The deeper rooted and more tacit the nation the more effortless its performance.

Canovan is insistent that this tacit notion is not the same as communitarian encumbered self argument (Canovan 1996, 53). Her nationalism moves at a murkier level of consciousness. She thus contends that we should not expect too much clarity. Conceptual clarity is not enough. Nations are indispensable, if hard to deal with conceptually. In fact, she suggests that nationalism may be a stage in the evolution of the nation itself; the presence of nationalism may even mean the absence of the nation *per se*, a point made consistently by many conservative theorists (Scruton 1990, 318). Nations may in fact be rarer than often thought. Further, Canovan admits that the terms nation and state are often used interchangeably (Canovan 1996, 51–2). This is a salutary reminder that nations are political. She thus chides writers like Bhikhu Parekh who contend that the state itself carries moral legitimacy in the context of commitments to the rule of law, respect for human dignity and common citizenship. Indeed, following Parekh, one might – if one were foolhardy enough – even suggest that patriotic commitment to the state is distinct from nationalism.[23] Canovan reads this as the state providing 'services' in a non-emotive way. For Canovan, however, consumer loyalty to the 'service station' state is not strong enough. Something far more visceral or earthy is needed (Canovan 1996, 61). The battery of nationalism has to be functioning.

My tack in responding to this argument is to take up Canovan's suggestion that conceptual clarity is not enough. The nation will not give itself up to conceptual clarity. It is possible in this context to begin to compare and contrast visceral emotions for a few moments. We humans are subject to many forms of visceral sentiments and loyalties. It sounds rather *ad hominem* to move this way, but how many readers of these pages – all of us subject to diverse deep-rooted feelings of duty – consider nationality, at this moment, as the most dominant or singular of such loyalties and impulses? Is national loyalty the key determinant of our deep sense of 'us' or 'we'? In other words, is it obvious to us that the nation is the transcendental condition for all other loyalties. It might, of course, be the case that even if we are not aware of it, this might be proof of its existence. Although, this could also be proof for many things – not least fairies at the bottom of my garden or personalized angels.

We are subject, on a daily basis, to pervasive identifications and deep-rooted loyalties with regard to religion, family, friendship, gender, ethnicity, colour, occupation or class, which can be just as, if not far more, invasive and conditional than nationalism. Islam, Christianity, sex, class, or skin colour have all claimed to transcend both nationality and, at points, states. Further, if Canovan admits that there is an intrinsic lack of conceptual clarity, how would one know that *what* one was dealing with was nationality? Might we not be in danger of mixing it up with other group sentiments? Defending a nation in war may, in fact, be a more real visceral defence of one's children or loved ones, a familiar and loved neighbourhood, village, town, landscape or religion. What do those who defend their state think about when defending it, probably more than likely their own survival, possibly their children, their vegetable plots or their dog, but surely not the nation. To think otherwise is not really to understand humanity. We might dress up the strong emotions and give them the honorific title of 'nation', but something more convoluted is going on behind it. Thus, unless we just trade hunches, by what clear *conceptual* criteria could one prioritize visceral loyalties? Why, for example, might I not fall back on the visceral loyalties to often dormant but diverse types of group feeling? There is no reason for citizens to have the same grounds for allegiance. Thus, for David Miller, on those rare but memorable occasions when 'we are suddenly confronted with the ties that bind us to our fellow nationals, ties which in everyday life remain hidden from view', we might not be encountering nationalism at all (Miller 1995b, 14). Further, there would be no way of knowing conceptually what we are encountering.

Therefore, even if nationalism now figures pervasively in much discussion, it is also important to recall that there can be, and indeed are, a host of other forms of loyalty, group identifications and modes of legitimacy. In fact, even beyond identification or loyalty there are a large bulk of reasons as to why people cohere on a day by day basis. Human beings are not rational actors. Apathy, mutual fear or anxiety over risk, a sense of personal security, levels of consumer satisfaction or economic well-being, being effectively socialized through an education system, religious feelings, a sophisticated power structure and surveillance system (CCTV acting like Foucault's vision of the Panopticon in encouraging self-discipline) and the permeation of various hegemonic ideologies concerning the value of order. All of these and many more factors, with nationality, contribute to elusive qualities of stability, social coherence and obedience within states. Why should nationalism provide the crucial tacit focus and how would one know it? There are, also, from another perspective, many possible political vessels for identification. Thus, regionalism, federalism, consociationalism and empire or imperialism have been routes for the representation of nationality, or, even, in fact, separate forms of identification distinct from nationalism. Nationalism is clearly but *one* contingent form of identification which has arisen in the last two centuries and it can be represented in associations other than the state.

The *pragmatic argument* suggests that a state is more governable if a nation coincides with it. There would then be shared ideals, resources and beliefs and possibly even more mutual concern between citizens, say, to facilitate redistribution of resources and welfare. Yet it is important to remember here that this is not a moral argument for nationalism or nation state identification. The above observation, however, could mean two things. First, it could be a simple observation that it is empirically the case that states which are nations are more governable with national sentiment, or, second, that nationalists (and state elites and bureaucracies) should deliberately foster the artifice of the nation in order to govern more easily. On the first point – acknowledging that we are not encountering a naturalistic argument here – it might well be the case that it is easier to govern if there is some harmony of sentiments and values. If you love or feel some greater affinity with your fellow citizens, it is easier to contemplate giving them your resources. However, it would be useful to see some empirical evidence that there are any such mutual moral sentiments or unforced affinities in any larger states. Common love or sentiment between citizens seems to have a very antique Rousseauist feel about it, and bears little relation to the reality of modern states. There may be complex and diverse emotional attachments, but the nation is just one of many and is, like the others, highly contingent. There is no sense that it is the key attachment and it is difficult to see how one could conceptually show this to be the case. Second, the remark about governability could imply that nations are artifices which states engineer, occasionally with clear intentions or policies. This corresponds broadly with the views of those, like Benedict Anderson or Ernest Gellner, who see the nation as an elaborately constructed functional 'device'. The history of common languages, particularly in unifying states – like the French under the Jacobins or the Welsh under English tutelage – shows us the unedifying spectacle of the conscious coercive imposition of language over the local patois. This was not an uncommon phenomenon with developing states into the twentieth century. As many scholars have noted, there is a very close connection between education, centralized curricula, the development of linguistic vernaculars and nationhood.

Thus, in summary, although partly accepting the *tacit* thesis, my qualification would be that what is tacit is by no means straightforward. There might be a pragmatic point to be made about the identification of the nation and state, although it remains slightly unclear as to the precise character of this identification.[24]

Conceptual argument

The final area focuses on the conceptual identification of nation and state. The common post-1945 argument on this issue suggests that we should not take the compound 'nation state' too seriously, since both are very different concepts.[25] One is comparatively clear, the other is in-coherent and fuzzy. As argued earlier, one could be disturbed by this incoherence and lack of clarity, or, conversely, find it normal, unprob-lematic and indeed fruitful.[26] Thus, whereas the concept of the state is more impersonal and juridical, nations are a distinct type of social entity, more culturally orientated, personal and nebulous. As noted earlier, this is also the position taken by many current writers on nationalism – although they still wish to valorize nationalism as profoundly important.

One issue to bear in mind here is the fact that the state concept is also subject to wide-ranging interpretations. Contemporary nationalist writers do not register this. MacCormick uses a limited, if standard, Kelsenian legal positivist definition. Miller falls back on Weber's hoary old sociological definition of the state as 'a body that successfully claims a monopoly of legitimate force in a particular territory' (Miller 1995b, 19). Tamir offers a more nuanced view, confirming that there are differing conceptions of the state. Minimally, on a juridical level, one can say that the state is a unique notion of public power, which is idiosyncratically distinct from other renditions of power. On an institutional level, this public power can mean the actual or fictive sovereign body or persons; the legal or constitutional structure of rules; the legal personality of the ruler(s), offices or institutions (see Vincent 1987, ch. 1). It can also denote the government, an element within a government, like the executive, judiciary or legislature, or a compound of these. It can further imply the collective or popular will of all the people (qua general will). It can also indicate something even more embracing, like the 'entire hierarchy of institutions by which life is determined, from the family to the trade, and from the trade to the Church and University'. In this sense, the state is conceived as the 'operative criticism of all institutions' (Bosanquet 1899, 150). The list could go on here. If one reviews the history of the state, there have been a wide range of theories and practices, each with its own interpretation, namely, absolutist, constitutionalist, ethical, pluralist, federalist and juridical theories. Each of these theories embodies long, complex and overlapping traditions of analysis. This does not mean that the state concept is vague, rather that the legal positivist and Weberian conceptions of the state are not very representative of that rich and complex tradition. It is not clear, though, whether any of the theories in this rich tradition link in *any* crucial way with nationalism. At its simp-lest, the nation is a concept which appears at a comparatively late period in the state tradition. It is a very powerful, if often unexplained and parasitical, addition to the state vocabulary.

One other side issue here on the state, which is worth mentioning, is that the state itself – even without the existence of the nation – can be viewed as slightly anachronistic. Many aspects of everyday life

– pollution, diseases, regulation of trade or environmental control –
are no longer simply state issues. None appear to be solely contained by
the state. Economies within states are characteristically subject to both
internal and external pressures. The rapid post-1945 growth of international trade and international trade treaties (like GATT); international
financial organizations (like the IMF or World Bank); international
legal, political and military organizations (like the UN, International
Court of Human Rights, and NATO); international travel and migration;
international communications like the internet and e-mail; the growth of
intergovernmental and non-governmental agencies, have all constrained
or changed the sphere of the twenty-first century state.[27] In Europe,
particularly, the growth of central European institutions, legal and trade
processes, the increasing emphasis on regionalism, common human rights
conventions and potentially a common currency, again limit the original
role of the sovereign state. Militarily, certain weapons, particularly nuclear,
entail a different mode of or attitude to warfare, which once again
changes the traditional modes of state conflict. To engage in conflict is to
risk complete mutual destruction. There is also now an awareness, most
significantly through environmental problems like ozone depletion, acid
rain, diminishing air quality or nuclear accidents like Chernobyl, that
such issues move well beyond the control of single states. In sum, changes
within international power and security, the growing influence of non-
governmental transnational organizations, erosions of sovereignty in areas
of state activity, have all changed the sphere of application of the state.

The state itself can thus look increasingly anachronistic in some of its
spheres of operation. States still have immensely important functions.
Particularly in times of crises, we still look to the authority and role of the
state to act as an agent in designing objectives and contriving plans to
realize them. But that role has been diminished and, more importantly,
most state functions could perfectly well be performed without a glimpse
of nationalism. Controlling domestic pollution, maintaining law and
order, regulating aspects of domestic economies, can be accomplished
by juridical states without nationalism. It is admittedly difficult to even
conceive, at the present moment, of a stateless world, although a nationless
world, or a world where nationalism is diminishing, looks more feasible.

Another facet of the state, which was briefly canvassed under the
normative issue, is the state qua other associations and groups. One
modern face of groups, which dominates contemporary literature, is the
multinational and polyethnic conception of the state.[28] This has led (as
noted earlier) some nationalists to dispense with the state in favour of
regionalism or consociationalism. Margaret Canovan, in commenting
critically upon Yael Tamir's abandonment of the state in favour of a more
idealized European Union of diverse cultures, remarks that 'the notion

that political theory and enlightened political practice might dispense with nation states and replace them with a combination of smaller communities and larger regional structures fails even more seriously than mainstream political theory to address the problem of the nation-state' (Canovan 1996, 117). The force of her remark here explains her later comment that perhaps only an external war could seriously unify the European Union. Canovan's comment represents an archetypal theoretical response to associations within the state. No matter whether the state is democratic, ruled by a Pope, or absolute sovereign, if sovereignty is regarded as one, indivisible and inalienable, it automatically expresses hostility to smaller unions. As J. N. Figgis put it: 'The great *Leviathan* of Hobbes, the *plenitudo potestatis* of the canonists, the *arcana imperii*, the sovereignty of John Austin, are all names of the same thing – the unlimited power of the lawgiver in the State' (Figgis 1914, 79). This was the state conception forged in religious civil strife, tempered by dynastic wars and settled partly at Westphalia in 1648. This was also the state system which acted as the womb of nineteenth and twentieth century nationalism.

However, it is worth noting two points here, firstly, that the hostility to groups and associations is a response of a particular state and sovereignty tradition, which nationalism, in its dominant mode, reinforced. It is not therefore primarily a nationalist response. The unity of the nation resonates with the centralized sovereign state, forged in the teeth of religious warfare. Internal difference always conjures up visions of modern St. Bartholomew Day massacres. Second, it is also worth noting that there are state traditions which have historically been more accommodating to groups. These traditions would either be confederal entities or internally complex states. Examples of the former can be found in Europe from the 1200s, in the Rhineland, Flemish leagues and Hanseatic League. The Swiss Confederation, set up in 1291, was particularly notable for surviving the religious civil wars of the sixteenth century. Confederations were essentially premised on contractual agreements and founded on distributed powers. This subsequently became a model for the United Provinces of the Netherlands and part of the background argument for the United States of America.

The internally complex state is a rarer phenomenon. Johannes Althusius suggested that we conceive of the state as an internally complex body of associations, each association being built out of other associations (Althusius 1995). Otto von Gierke's notion of corporate groups having a reality and legal right within a complex structure – a *communitas communitatum* conception of the state – also developed the same theme (Gierke 1990). In this vision, diverse interests are negotiated, neither delegated nor dictated from a higher authority. This complex model, it should be stressed, does not necessarily negate nationalism. However, it does configure it differently. Nations no longer have a place of moral privilege. The nation is one possible contingent loyalty. For some writers this theory means the end of the nation state, for others it is a fruitful path to follow in the face of heterogeneous human interests.

If we reversed the conceptual perspective to that of the nation, it is worth noting that the concept nation does not imply *any* particular type of state; in fact, it does not necessarily imply the state at all, if certain contemporary nationalist theorists are to be believed. Thus, if the nation aspires to self-determination, it can do so through vehicles like regional assemblies. The nation, in other words, is as likely to be at home with absolute dynastic monarchy, totalitarian one party rule, a liberal consti-tutional state or a regional assembly within a confederation. Further, the nation idea is flexible enough (or possibly vacuous enough) to be reflected within many differing ideologies. The nation appears, in fact, to derive its substance from host ideologies. Conceptions of the nation thus tend to follow the contours of the dominant host ideologies. The most dominant hosts have been liberal, traditionalist conservative and integral fascist conceptions. In sum, what we encounter in nationalism is not so much a clear view of the state and nation relation, as a site for contesting host political ideologies. Nationalism, in itself, has nothing significant to say.

Conclusion

The idea of the state encompasses a number of political languages. In fact, one might suggest there is no such thing as *the* state as such, there are rather *conceptions* of the state. The languages of the state do precede nationalism by many centuries. They were, however, often focused on themes of particular identity. The state was and is expressed in a form of personality, individuality and particularity, which provided a unity and coherence to its actions. The particularity of the sovereign state was originally set against the universal of the empire and church. Nationality is but one late facet of the sovereign state, often arising in situations of conflict, war or modernizing growth. Since the 1800s it has unquestion-ably also been immensely useful in standardizing language and cultures. Nationalism *per se* has consequently become slowly formalized, cus-tomary and often tacit in certain states. It has worked hard in concocting its own antiquity, an antiquity which continues to take in even its most intelligent votaries. However, war or conflict are as normal as peace to most states. One should be careful not to over-dramatize instability at the expense of peace, stability and diversity within states. What precisely generates belonging, a sense of place or identity, common concerns, or even loyalty, is unpredictable, even in war. Marxism, liberal democracy, human rights, race, a valued occupation, trade union, Christianity, the family, atheism, Buddhism, Islam, the idea of freedom, a belief in civilization, or weird and wonderful combinations of these, can all be visceral attachments. All have been seen as worth dying for time and again. Many have been renamed, recast and rechannelled as national aims. Yet, with the benefit of hindsight and reflection, one should not necessarily prioritize the nation. Human beings are at the interstice of many complex, often contradictory, and overlapping commitments, which, until recently, have often, but certainly not always, been contained by states. The fact that states contained these diverse commitments has often allowed the unifying national cloak to be draped over them. In the future this might become much less significant.

3   Citizenship

The central underlying questions in this chapter are – in what sense is citizenship linked fundamentally to a universalist or globalizing impulse? Further, what is the precise relation of citizenship language to particularizing pressures? My sketch of an answer involves two points. First, the slightly extended answer is that liberalism has been an ascendant force in nineteenth and particularly twentieth century politics in the industrialized, developed world. Further, citizenship discussion has tended to be dominated by this liberal discourse. A conception of liberalism has, as it were, marked out the terrain in which citizenship has been most frequently discussed. It is this more liberal, essentially 'right-based' approach to citizenship which leads it, almost by default, beyond the state arena. In other words, there is an implicit logic of citizenship which leads it into a universalist or cosmopolitan fold. It is the ambiguities of this conception that will be explored. My second point is more problematic and follows out from these ambiguities. It raises a number of sceptical arguments via two levels of enquiry: the first level of enquiry suggests that liberalism and citizenship have more complex histories than are often implied in the more dominant liberal account. The second line of enquiry focuses on the empirical practice of citizenship, as it has appeared in European traditions, embodying a paradoxical particularist and universalist legacy in tandem.

There are thus two theses concerning the relation between nationalism and citizenship which underpin this chapter. The first concerns the universalist implication of citizenship; the second concerns the particularizing criteria for citizenship within contemporary liberal democratic states. The central contention is that citizenship has a strong integral conceptual relation with liberalism. Thus, the manner in which citizenship is articulated links up closely with the character of liberal theory. Liberal theory, in one of its dominant formats, is intrinsically universalist by inclination. Yet, citizenship, in turn, also involves a close conceptual relation with the particularizing force of nationalism. Citizenship is thus at the interstice between two powerful social and political theories.

The discussion will first flesh out the cosmopolitan or universalist intuition, with the proviso that this is a sketch of something which will later be criticised. Second, it will review the concept of citizenship. Third, it will examine the character of liberalism. Finally it focuses on the nationalism and citizenship relation. Overall, the discussion draws attention to a complex of ideas surrounding the relation of citizenship and nationalism which form an unresolved subtext to much current legal, political and moral thought and practice.[1]

A universalist intuition

The present section unpacks what I have called the universalist intuition within liberal citizenship. The central premise to this argument is that citizenship embodies strong conceptions of agency and autonomy which are, in turn, central values for liberalism. Further, the compound term liberal citizenship is, as David Miller notes, the 'dominant view', although it has come under considerable stress in the last few decades (Miller 1995a, 450). Citizenship – although a concept with a broader ambit – can therefore be seen as a crucial component of the liberal perspective. Thus, citizenship figures as an important liberal motif. The citizen can, at points, literally and formally denote the individual person or agent with basic legal or moral rights to life, freedom, conscience and association. It is important to underscore this point.

First, the relation between liberalism and citizenship has deep philosophical roots in European thought, bound up with ideas of self-determination, autonomy and individualism. There is a strong ontological and conceptual linkage here. The *citizen* is conceived of as markedly different from the *subject* by dint of possessing agency, a capacity and right to make choices or withhold assent. The *subject* is, conventionally, seen as a creature of absolute or centralised authority, lacking the capacity for assent or dissent; however, the *citizen* is a creature of more constitutionally controlled or diversified authority which embeds the possibility of, and right to, choice. Citizenship thus denotes, intrinsically, the possibility of choice, an opportunity or space to act within some form of constitutional public setting, a setting which both implicitly and explicitly recognizes limitations on legal, political and moral authority. Citizenship thus has integral conceptual links with freedom and agency. This intrinsic connection between citizenship and human agency also combines with other fundamental ideas in liberal thought – freedom of conscience, natural, civil and political rights, basic equality, toleration of difference, free speech, and so forth. Citizenship enables liberals to deal with the issue of pluralism. Citizenship is a 'conditional public agency' allowing individuals to express their particular goods. However, at the same time, it embodies this agency in the formal terms of individual autonomy. Thus, there is a more than fortuitous connection between citizenship and liberal theory. Citizenship, specifically in the last two centuries, has been integrally part of a web of liberal values and beliefs. The question as to whether there are non-liberal conceptions of citizenship will be dealt with later in the discussion.

Secondly, the concept of citizenship does have a complex and diverse etymological history, which will be referred back to and examined later in the discussion. The critical focus, for the present, is upon the link with liberal thought. Since liberalism, above all social and political theories, embodies a belief in moral and political individualism and agency, and citizenship is intrinsically committed to individual agency and individualism, then it might be said to follow that liberalism is the most succinct modern bearer of citizenship claims. However, this argument is deeply problematic. If, for the moment, we can accept the compound term 'liberal citizenship' as virtually equivalent (for some) to the concept of the citizen, then there are further implications which follow from this logic of citizenship.

The logical implications which follow from citizenship can be summed up in the concepts of cosmopolitanism or universalism. Citizenship, in the manner in which it has been ontologically and conceptually linked with liberalism, gives rise to a universalist or cosmopolitan ethos. The argument, in its barest format, would go as follows: the core values of liberal citizenship – autonomy, agency, individualism, liberty, rights, equality, justice, and so forth – are tied to conceptions of reason and humanity which have no necessary connection with particular forms of life or political structures. Citizens have rights, qua agents, whatever their location. Citizens regulate their public conduct according to formal generic principles. There may be sufficient reason, with hindsight, for identifying such values within certain states or within particular structures of thought. However, the concepts and values themselves have no *intrinsic* or *necessary* particularistic connections. For example, the critic aiming to convince us of, say, the particularity of reason, would have to assume its universality to make the case. Reason thus appears to have a non-derivative universal value. Such concepts might therefore be described as intrinsically universalizing or cosmopolitan values. They contain an underlying logic which shows that when dealing with the justice, rights or freedoms of human beings, there are no rational grounds to stop at particular boundaries – state, community or otherwise.

In other words, to think within the ontology of the concept of liberal citizenship is to think oneself into the embrace of universalism. This ingrained logic would account for the stress often laid on human and natural rights, international justice, universal human equality, and the like, within many liberal democratic theories. Boundaries to human conduct become morally arbitrary in this context, since we are inevitably dealing with humanity as a single moral category. These considerations connect up with the concept of global citizenship.

There are direct parallels between the manner in which liberal citizenship drifts towards a universalist position and the way recent environmental political theory arguments on citizenship move in the same direction. However, the rights' element in environmentalism is not articulated as strongly as the duty component. Duty and care or compassion take priority over formal rights. Further, ecological duties are owed to peoples, not only beyond our borders, but also intergenerationally, beyond contingent times or places. Ecological duties are owed to strangers now and in the future. The reason for this would be that ecological problems are intrinsically universal and do not follow any established political contours. The logic of this argument has made some draw a direct connection between ecological and cosmopolitan citizenship.[2] Both encounter a similar range of problems and criticisms. Andrew Dobson, for example, sees this ecological citizen – or 'deep citizen' as he calls it – as giving rise to a new conception of citizenship. It bypasses the hard distinction between the public and private, although, at the same time, this is not just about private virtuous actions with public benefits. Public and private distinctions do not really work well within environmental theories. If anything, ecological citizenship, for Dobson, connects the local and the global and the public and private. It is about everyday living in general. In this sense, for Dobson, the ecological citizen is quite definitely 'non-national' and 'unencumbered' (Dobson in Pierson and Tormey (eds) 2000, 51). Ecology does not acknowledge nations and is therefore unconcerned about national membership. Ecological citizens are world citizens. Citizenship is thus thoroughly deterritorialized and denationalized. This corresponds quite directly with the underlying logic of liberal citizenship.

There are many problems here, not least the legal, moral, political, economic and social implications of global citizenship – both ecological or liberal. However, the central claim is that it is conceptually and ontologically *natural* for us – natural in the sense that it appears to be an unforced implication of the concepts we use – to read cosmopolitanism and universalism into citizenship. This is a position that both liberals and environmentalists almost unwittingly accept. In consequence, it is, therefore, a short step from being a good citizen of a liberal democratic state to being a good member of Amnesty International, a global human rights watch, a proponent of universal human rights or even Greenpeace. My own response to this issue is deeply ambivalent. The core intuition concerning cosmopolitanism and universalism is immensely appealing and compelling, but it also contains some fundamental problems. The deepest of these problems relates to the link between nationality and citizenship, which will be focused on later in the discussion.

Thus, the central claim in the above arguments is that liberalism embodies an underlying cosmopolitan impetus and that the ingrained logic of citizenship would appear to be directed towards a global perspective. The notion of the universal and cosmopolitan citizen long predates liberalism. One of the first Western philosophies to expound the cosmopolitan perspective was Stoicism. It involved a quite conscious rejection of the singularity and bounded citizenship of the Greek city-state. The citizen/barbarian distinction, common to such Hellenic thought, was anathema to Stoics. As Marcus Aurelius put it: 'my city and my country, so far as I am Antonius is Rome; but so far as I am a man, it is the *universe*' (quoted in Heater 1990, 12). This argument alone made it attractive to Christian thinkers such as St. Augustine. For Stoics, we dwell both in the community of our birth and the community of human argument, reason and aspiration. Our decisive moral values come from the latter. This is a moral not a legal community. This does not deny the separateness of peoples, but it argues that such 'separateness' is relatively unimportant in comparison with the wider moral community. Thus, world citizenship should be our ultimate moral focus.

Although there are strong intimations of a cosmopolitan perspective in the medieval *Respublica Christiana*, the cosmopolitan or universalist view, which developed under the aegis of Christianized natural law thinking, surfaces again most significantly, for the present century, in the work of Kant.[3] For a modern neo-Kantian, such as Thomas Pogge, most cosmopolitan arguments contain, firstly, a commitment to individualism, as against communities or tribes; second, a belief in universalism, namely, that all human individuals are valued equally; and, thirdly, a sense of generality, that is, cosmopolitan concerns are not limited to particular regimes. Persons are of concern to everyone, wherever they are. Our fellow countrymen are no more nor less important than anyone else in the world. Pogge also distinguishes types of cosmopolitanism. Legal cosmopolitanism is committed to a concrete juridical or governmental order under which people will have equal basic rights, as in international courts on human rights or international codes and covenants. Most commentators see the central problem here of jurisdiction, namely, will the courts be able to enforce their rulings? Moral cosmopolitanism, on the other hand, holds that all persons stand in certain moral relations to each other – mutual concern or respect is thus incumbent upon us. Every human being is an ultimate unit of moral concern.[4] Moral cosmopolitanism can, however, vary in its content with different moral positions

– utilitarian or Kantian. It can also either imply just leaving individuals alone and not harming them – which might equate with a more passive sense of civil citizenship – or, alternatively, taking a definite responsibility for others, even distant strangers, which might entail strong duties, as in the ecology argument.

In summary, the basic 'logic of the citizenship' argument would be this: citizenship, historically, has been used within nineteenth and twentieth century states to equalize, generalize and regularize treatment of humans as basic right-bearing agents – thus preventing exclusionary practices within states. It follows that if citizenship, within the state, is used *against* exclusionary practices, why should it not be extended (logically) beyond state boundaries? An 'exclusionary practice' remains an 'exclusionary practice' whether it appears in or outside a border. What is significant, qua citizenship values, about state boundaries? Citizenship is thus embroiled in the logic of a universalizing ethics which does not necessarily have to stop at the national boundary. Rights before the law, rights of participation and freedom, justice, the requirement for consent and duties to promote a social good (all implicit within citizenship), are *all* potentially universalizable. In fact, the logic of the concept appears to push them in this direction. For theorists such as Andrew Linklater, Brian Barry, Onora O'Neill, Charles Beitz and Jürgen Habermas (who also engage in this kind of generic reasoning), to 'universalize ideas about consent and dialogue which are intrinsic to citizenship in the domestic domain' enlarges 'the meaning of citizenship by conferring rights of participation on every member of the species'(Linklater in Keal (ed.) 1992, 32). Moral universalism thus arises out of domestic liberal citizenship, or as Habermas puts it, rights of national citizenship 'guarantee liberty because they contain a core composed of universal human rights' (Habermas 1992, 13).

Another comparatively recent example of the above argument is deployed by Martha Nussbaum. Using a Stoic analogy, she contends that we should think of ourselves as surrounded by concentric circles, the self, the family, the neighbourhood, the city, the country and humanity. We cannot ignore our locality, but we must work to make all humans part of our community – drawing all the circles towards the centre. For Nussbaum, we should therefore 'recognize humanity wherever it occurs, and give its fundamental ingredients, reason and moral capacity, our first allegiance as respect' (Nussbaum in Cohen (ed.) 1996, 7). Nussbaum puts the point well when she states that 'I believe ... that [the] emphasis on patriotic pride is both morally dangerous and, ultimately, subversive of some of the worthy goals patriotism sets out to serve ... These goals ... would be better served by an ideal that is in any case more adequate to our situation in the contemporary world, namely the very old idea of the cosmopolitan, the person whose allegiance is to the world-wide community' (Nussbaum in Cohen (ed.) 1996, 4). Even good nationalism, as incipient particularism, ultimately subverts the universal values it upholds.

Nussbaum contends therefore that we should automatically educate ourselves and our children in a cosmopolitan mode of thought. In so doing, we will learn more about ourselves. Education which focuses only within national boundaries encourages irrationality. To be ignorant of humanity is to be ignorant about ourselves. Second, we can only make headway solving international problems if we can acknowledge global issues. She also, unwittingly, makes the ecological point that the air that citizens breathe and the water we drink are not necessarily confined by national boundaries. Third, we should be troubled by the fact that our high living standards are not more widely available. We should therefore train children in a basic universalizing, as she puts it, 'Kantian awareness', otherwise we will train hypocrites. Nussbaum remarks, 'If we do believe that all human beings are created equal and endowed with certain inalienable rights, we are morally required to think about what that conception requires us to do' (Nussbaum in Cohen (ed.) 1996, 13). We should work to acquire knowledge that will enable us to consider these rights seriously. Fourth, nationalist writers often seek to encourage nationals to join hands across racial or economic divisions; why therefore, asks Nussbaum, stop at the boundary of the nation – 'what is it about the national boundary that magically converts people' (Nussbaum in Cohen (ed.) 1996, 14). Multicultural respect within a nation must also lead to wider world respect. The respect argument, in nationalist writers, must carry us in this direction. The latter two Nussbaum arguments clearly illustrate the logic of citizenship argument.

For Nussbaum and others, some of these cosmopolitan ideas have been translated into deeply practical concerns. The liberal rights of the citizen to freedom, conscience, procedural justice, speech, consent or dissent, can also be seen, synonymously, as universal 'human rights'. Although there are problems with ratification and application, human rights have also been codified and translated into positive legal rights. So far the main obstacle to the full realization of such rights has been persuading states to agree and work with the United Nations, international courts and international human rights conventions. The global citizen is therefore one who acknowledges universal human rights and believes, either on a personal level or on the institutional level of international courts and conventions, that we should accept the duties correlative on such rights.

There is a major problem here, namely, that state-based citizens have a rich panoply of well-established positive rights, whereas the global citizen's rights are, in comparison, thin. One way out of this dilemma for some liberal theorists has been to argue for an extension of international legal organizations, expanded international courts of human rights, and at the most extreme end, an elected parliament at the United Nations. In the latter scenario, states which recognized cosmopolitan citizenship would provide full diplomatic and economic support to the UN, promote arms control, uphold human rights, and provide generous foreign aid. These ideas are speculative, although not overly speculative. The fact that we have international commissions, like that on Global Governance with its report *Our Global Neighbourhood*, indicates that many take such ideas very seriously.

The discussion now turns to three overlapping and critical ambiguities, which are often glossed over in the above argument. These are, first, the ambiguity of citizenship; second, the ambiguity of liberalism qua citizenship; and, third, the ambiguous relation of nationalism and citizenship.

Citizenship

The first area of critical ambiguity is citizenship itself. This section of the chapter focuses on the complexity of citizenship. The gist of the argument is that citizenship is a far more heterogeneous concept than outlined in the previous 'universalist intuition' section. Although it would be true to say that the liberal view of the citizen has been a dominant view, it is also important to recognize that there are rival or distinct conceptions of the citizen. For example, in contemporary political theory, the most recent contender has been the republican conception. Firstly, rather than immediately settle upon the debate between liberal and republican theories, the present discussion focuses on certain broader categories which incorporate these ideas. These categories are civic and civil conceptions of the citizen, although another possible way of conceiving this distinction is between passive and active conceptions of the citizen. Second, the value of these broader categories is that they reveal that there is a longer and richer tradition behind these debates, and further that the theoretical categories of liberal or republican do not always neatly map onto the civic and civil abstractions.

The origin of the terms civil and civic or active and passive is open to debate. The civic/civil divide bears some conceptual parallels with the distinction, made by Benjamin Constant, between ancient and modern liberty (Constant 1988). The terminology active and passive can certainly be found directly discussed in, for example, Abbé Sieyes' writings. Sieyes' use is not quite the present usage, although there are parallels. For Sieyes, passive citizenship referred essentially to the domain of natural and civil rights of individuals. Such rights concern the protection of all persons equally in terms of their liberty and property. For Sieyes, despite the fact that all persons within a constitutional state possess passive rights, not all can take part in the 'formation of public power'. Passive citizenship is thus available to all. Active citizens, on the other hand, are those who 'contribute to the public establishment' and can be likened to 'true shareholders in the great social enterprise'. However, no class or group of 'active citizens' has more rights than another. At the time, Sieyes' active citizenship excluded children, foreigners and women, who were all regarded as passive citizens. It is worth noting here that active citizens are not discussed by Sieyes in the context of rights. Active citizenship, although it incorporated conceptions of political voting rights, also included a sense of a higher dutiful vocation. The taking part in the 'great public enterprises' is seen by Sieyes in terms of the performance of public duties. He thus remarks that 'It is ... a major error to envisage the exercise of public power as a *right*; it is a *duty*. The officers of the nation are distinguished from other citizens only in having more duties' (quoted in Forsyth 1987, 117–19).

In terms of the present discussion, certain aspects of Sieyes' use of the term 'passive citizen' can be picked up and developed. The passive or civil citizen is a product of the era of developing individualism and embryonic liberal thought. This is the idea which corresponds in large part to the 'universalist intuition' outlined in the previous section – although there are supplementations to this idea. The citizen is understood as separate and, at least, partially preformed, with distinct desires, interests and often basic natural rights. Humans uniformly possess these desires, interests, freedoms and rights, wherever they are found. Humanity is a singular universal category. The function of any public constitutional legal order is to protect and uphold these fundamental human interests and rights. Citizenship is thus conceived more negatively in terms of the legal protection of pre-existing rights to life, liberty and property, to use the older vocabulary. The private moralities of individuals are distinct from the formal but minimal public ethics of citizenship – although at the same time the notion of the citizen implies internal or private agency and autonomy. Civil citizens are publicly free, within certain constitutional agreed constraints, and also privately autonomous, within defined parameters of harm and the like. For all classical liberal theorists, throughout the nineteenth and twentieth centuries, although individuals may have lost some of the benefits of close communal life, nonetheless, they have gained from the privacy, modern liberty and new-found prosperity of commercial liberal society.

In summary, civil citizenship, in my use, is conventionally associated with the classical liberalism, implying negative rights – understood largely as side-constraints – to protection of one's person, property and liberty. The classical liberal view of citizenship thus favours in consequence limited political rule, a framework of laws and minimal welfare. Markets, within this perspective, are the preferred economic technique for allocation of resources. Essentially, this is a more procedural, minimal constitutional, and rule of law view of politics. Politics does not pursue any particular social or moral goals. The consequence of this for citizenship is that individuals are secured maximum negative liberty. They are left alone and free from coercion. The good citizen upholds the rule of law and equal liberty for all. This is the conventional liberal *Rechtsstaat*. This is also the conception of liberal citizenship which contains at root an inner logic of universality, a logic which drives the arguments for universal natural and human rights discussion.

However, this civil view is not necessarily completely passive. Later nineteenth and twentieth century versions of this understanding of citizenship extend into political representation. Political rights to vote or stand for office invoke ideas of active informed participation. The argument about political rights to vote depends on how significant one regards them. Such political rights can, for example, still be viewed as passive. As one recent writer has noted, 'the occasional visit to the polling booth has seemed to many a pathetically inadequate definition of citizenship' (Heater 1990, 96). Some writers, such as Schumpeter, amongst many others, have made a virtue of the passive or apathetic voter. However, the intuition to grasp here is that political democratic citizenship, as it has been conventionally understood, can still be viewed as constrained, passive and perfectly in accord with classical liberal theory. In sum, citizenship in classical liberal thought is generally confined to a relatively narrow moral and legal field. It is defined in terms of the constrained political rights and legal or civil rights of persons. Classical liberal thought on citizenship generally excludes rights and entitlements to economic and social resources. The citizen of classical liberal individualism could be described as a more 'minimal citizen', essentially being the other side of the more minimal procedural concept of the state. However, it is this very minimalism or generality, for some, which allows its potential universality to work. Generic liberal citizenship rights move without a murmur into universal human rights.

There are two ambiguities here: firstly, the liberal citizen perspective has been subject to significant 'rights' developments, in twentieth century liberal democratic states, which have changed both the theory and practice of citizenship. More particularly it has shifted uneasily between civil and civic ideas. Second, the liberal perspective is clearly not the only view of the citizen.

First, this conception of definite individualistic rights was more characteristic of civil citizenship. Rights expressed, ontologically, the separate or independent identity of individuals. They were claims asserted against

other individuals, groups or states. The more general of such rights
– natural and human rights – were fundamental claims to life, liberty,
happiness, property, speech, conscience, opinion, association, and so
forth. Such rights correlated loosely with duties of forbearance or non-
interference, usually with the proviso that such rights did not overtly
injure or harm others. These rights did not, characteristically, demand
positive public action by any individual – except, for example, in the duty
to discharge one's debts or fulfil contracts. Such rights were usually more
negatively protective rights, implying (on one reading) passive, relatively
costless duties. This latter conception of rights is, to some extent, encapsulated in two of the categories of citizenship – civil and political –
discussed by T. H. Marshall in his *locus classicus* account of citizenship,
Citizenship and Social Class (1950). For Marshall, *civil* citizenship, which
he saw developing from the eighteenth century, implied a comprehensive
equality of rights to civil freedoms, which might broadly be called generic
constitutional liberal freedoms. *Political* citizenship, which developed for
Marshall gradually over the nineteenth century, concerned the extension
of suffrage rights, namely the right to participate in the political process
which determines the condition of one's life. Neither of these categories,
as stressed earlier, necessarily causes any problems for classical liberal
thought on citizenship.

The problematic category, for classical liberalism, in the Marshall
scheme, is the third concept of *social* citizenship. On the one hand, it was
still individualistic and rights-orientated, but it also embodied conceptions of collective goals and claims to social resources. Social citizenship,
as it developed in the twentieth century, was more of a hybrid between
the civic and civil aspirations. It was also more characteristic of a different
conception of liberalism. The social citizenship perspective was essentially that individual citizens are morally justified in claiming a particular
economic status and a right to resources, via the welfare state and social
justice. In the mid-twentieth century, this idea crystallized around a more
administrative static model of social rights. 'Duty', for most citizens,
became the basic willingness to pay marginally higher levels of progressive taxation, which, over time, became for many a bureaucratized
burden. In consequence, clientalized recipients of welfare claimed passive
entitlements without any sense of civic responsibility. In summary, the
strong emphasis on the social rights of citizenship, the indirect undermining of solidaristic duty, the bureaucratization of social rights and the
gradual decline of communal consensus in mid-twentieth century
industrialized societies essentially eviscerated any sense of public duty.
Marshall recognized that this created immense problems and strains for
a liberal capitalist society – problems which he never claimed to resolve.
This opened social citizenship up to 'new right' criticism during the

1980s. The assault on the welfare state incorporated an attempt to prise apart civil from civic duty-based citizenship. Essentially the 'new right' theories were trying to return citizenship to a more predictable world of passive civil rights.

In summary, classical liberal citizenship implied basic negative civil or political rights. The correlative duty of such civil rights was forbearance from harming others. In effect, this conception unwittingly devalued any but the most minimal duties. The idea of social citizenship was initially theorized in terms of civic duties, as well as a more expansive vision of rights. This civic duty component was crucial to the initial justification of the welfare state. Yet, the stress on 'social rights' also maintained a self-conscious continuity with classical liberalism. The emphasis on rights slowly weakened the idea of public-spirited duties as correlative to such rights. By deploying rights language, exponents of social citizenship, unintentionally, set the stage for the gradual decline during the twentieth century of solidaristic notions of public-spirited duty. From its inception, the social citizenship idea embodied a complex tension *within* liberalism, which has carried through to the present day. This tension focused on the conflict between civism and civility, between an essentially 'rights-orientated' passive recipience vision of welfare and civic activist vision of duties to the common good.

The latter conclusion leads to the second issue: namely, that the liberal view is only one dimension of the citizenship tradition. It is a well-established criticism of civil liberal citizenship that it ignores the socially and historically embedded or encumbered character of individuals and abandons any clear sense of perfectionism, community and, more pertinently, nationality. This is the standard criticism made of deontological and consequentialist liberal individualism by communitarians. This civic sense of the citizen implies a more rigorous conception of political involvement, which was most succinctly focused on – in recent history – at certain key moments during the French Revolution; however it also harks back to an older tradition. Such an idea can be found, in differing formats, in the doctrines of Aristotelianism, some civic republicanism and the later Rousseauist and Hegelian traditions. It can also be found implicitly and explicitly in some recent expressions of communitarian thought.

The civic category is the oldest conception of the citizen. The citizen is seen to be morally identified with the community. The good of the individual citizen is tied to the good of the state. For example, citizenship implied, for Aristotle, membership of a city-state, the possession of certain claims and duties based on that membership; more importantly, the duty to participate in the adjudication and ruling processes of the polis, and, finally, an inner capacity for rational virtue, entailing the internalization of communal norms. The themes of self-discipline, public spirit, a conception of the common good, unease with private gain and self-interest, a belief in formal simplicity and piety of life, were also reasserted in the later civic republican tradition. Overall, the civic citizen is regarded as one who – mythically or not – gladly and intelligently participates in the promotion of the public good. The idea was facilitated in the smaller scale of the city-state. Yet, this citizenry, despite being mobilized to a common task, was, nonetheless, parasitical upon a large body of non-citizen slaves and foreign workers who performed all the domestic and menial tasks.

The older tradition of civic citizenship did not have a rich vocabulary of rights at its disposal – although it was partially developed in the nineteenth century. Aristotelian-influenced proponents of civic citizenship tended to speak more in terms of the duties of the citizen or what was due to the citizen. The assertion of the importance of citizens performing their civic duty was not therefore necessarily premised on any correlative right, rather what was due to and from the public good. Later civic exponents, such as T. H. Green, transformed this form of argument into the vocabulary of rights, although, characteristically, it was usually the vocabulary of socio-legal rights, not natural or human rights. Such socio-legal rights were also conceptually tied – in the case of Idealist thinkers – to a conception of the common good. The civic citizenship tradition further embodied a strong correlativity thesis. Rights were premised on the common good. Such rights implied that the citizen had correlative duties to the common good. Citizenship implied the consciousness of the ends of human life as embodied in the institutional forms of the public life. It was an ethical disposition, where the individual developed to a level of self-consciousness and ethical awareness inclusive enough to be identified with the public sphere of the whole community. For some, this spectre of civic citizenship developed again with the rise of nationalism in the nineteenth century. Its ethos was though 'more creative and protective, stressing liberation rather than defence' (Kelly in Beiner (ed.) 1999, 91).

One major criticism of the civic view is that the citizen will be asked to participate continuously in every aspect of political life. The public realm would totally absorb the private realm of the individual. Liberals, from Benjamin Constant to Isaiah Berlin or John Rawls, have been profoundly worried by such arguments as potentially undermining the value of individual liberty and privacy. Ralph Dahrendorf has referred to this civic conception as the 'total citizen' (Dahrendorf 1974). In extremis, the total citizen and the total state would be seen as two sides of the same coin. This civic caricature provides some credence to the claim, made by recent republican theorists, that the republican conception of the citizen is a *via media* between the civil liberal and more Hegelian or Aristotelian civic conceptions.

The problems in this area can only be briefly touched upon. However, many critics of republicanism have argued, with considerable justice, that republicanism also has strong civic components. The question is the balance of the civic and civil within republicanism. For critics, the civic clearly overwhelms the civil. Thus, if one looks at the history of republican theory, the bulk of its original advocates clearly envisaged citizens as being contained within the disciplined confines of a virtuous republic, still modelled mimetically on the claustrophobic vision of the ancient city-states. Despite the massive growth of territorial states in the nineteenth and twentieth centuries, the model of the cohesive, inertial, homogenized, face to face, loved republic still haunts the modern republican imagination. Thus, even if we focus on recent republican theories, there is still a lurking assumption of some form of common or consensual culture, if only focused on liberty as non-domination. This critical point forms the basis to Habermas' main objection to republicanism (Habermas in Gutman (ed.) 1994). He contends that republicanism is too intently focused on identity and membership of an ethical community. Republicans are thus directly comparable to communitarians. For Habermas, this homogenizing ethical vision overburdens the modern democratic process by forcing politics into burdensome and suspect visions of collective identity.

The complexity of this whole debate can be partly revealed in Iris Marion Young's critique of republican ideas. She sees republicans as, again, deeply committed to stultifying notions of unifying identity and impartiality. In the same manner as Habermas, Young sees this as an enforced homogeneity which takes no account of real difference. However, one of her prime exemplars for this republican uniformity is Habermas! (Young 1990). One way forward here, to account for these anomalies, would be to draw a distinction between weaker and stronger forms of republicanism. In effect, the stronger emphasizes the civic over the civil, whereas the latter seeks the converse. The older civic variant entails more cultural and moral uniformity. It emphasizes a virtuous active citizen and a unifying public good, which takes priority over private goods. The weaker conception, which prevails in most recent expositions, entails a more restricted pragmatic conception of impartiality. It does not demand that individuals share values, but only that they are prepared to debate their views rationally in a public setting. Each person's good is implicated in this public debate. Law is consequently viewed as the outcome of a reasonable process. This does not imply that the majority of individuals would have to set aside their individual goods. This is the civil liberal component. However, individuals are required to be willing to engage in public debate or dialogue. They must connect their reasoning to publicly accessible understandings of reason. This is the weakened civic component. Weak republicanism does not adjudicate between the demands of groups or individuals. It only requires that demands be expressed or articulated in certain ways.

David Miller, in a sympathetic rendering of this weaker republicanism, suggests that there is little limitation to the kind of argument which could be made. The republican grounds all rights in open public discussion where there are no prepolitical justifications. Republican debate is more pragmatic and does not enjoin agreement with established principles, other than those implicated within rational communication or dialogue. In this reading, republicanism, for Miller, has clear analytical resources to deal with the ordinary problems of pluralism (Miller 1995a, 449). However, he does admit that it would not be able to cope with radical difference. One additional paradoxical element here is that it is fairly clear that recent republicans, such as Philip Pettit or Maurizio Viroli, have no truck whatsoever with nationalism, qua republicanism. Nationalism is anathema. A culture of patriotic liberty should suffice. Ironically, Miller does suggest that republicanism also requires supplementation with what he calls 'sensible nationality' (Miller 1995a, 450). Nationality provides a unifying cement which enables republicanism to deal with the more intractable problems of pluralism – implying that republicanism *per se* is not quite enough.

Liberalism

The upshot of the previous section is that despite the dominant cultural position of civil liberal citizenship – which partly accounts for the manner in which the 'universalist intuition' has been widely assumed – there are clearly, firstly, deep ambiguities in the manner in which the rights discourse of citizenship has evolved during the twentieth century. Social citizenship rights, specifically, contain strong elements of civism and particularity.[5] Second, the citizenship tradition itself is clearly more elaborate and varied than can be summed in the civil conception. Further, liberal and republican conceptions of the citizen cannot easily be mapped onto the civic and civil traditions. There are subtle and complex overlappings.

The discussion now turns to a second critical ambiguity, focused on the concept of liberalism. Does liberalism present a consistent enough face to allow the universalist intuition to develop? There have been many typologies of liberalism. The following discussion draws a distinction between three types of liberalism: classical liberalism, social liberalism and cultural liberalism. The classical view, which is a predominantly procedural view in its modern guise, insists that individual rights must

always come first and must take precedence over collective goals.[6]
Michael Walzer characterizes this procedural liberalism as 'committed in
the strongest possible way to individual rights and, almost as a deduction
from this, to a rigorously neutral state, that is, a state without cultural or
religious projects or, indeed, any sorts of collective goals beyond personal freedom and … physical security' (Walzer in Gutman (ed.) 1994,
99; also Habermas in same volume, 123ff). This is a view that one
finds, according to Charles Taylor, in writers such as John Rawls, Ronald
Dworkin and Bruce Ackerman.[7] This conception of liberal society has no
substantive view about the ends of human life. Society is rather united
behind an idea of equal respect for individuals. For Charles Taylor, the
roots to this procedural view are culturally very deep. He sees Kant as
probably the single most important figure articulating this perspective.
Human dignity focuses on autonomy and the ability of the individual to
determine their own notion of the good life. Thus, procedural liberalism
enshrines a politics of equal respect which is hostile or indifferent to
difference, because it insists on the uniform application of rights and is
thus suspicious of any collective goals. Taylor has his own thoughts on the
problems that this notion of liberalism has caused in the Canadian
situation, qua Quebec.

Social liberalism appeared in Britain in the 1880s and 1890s; variants
also developed in America with John Dewey, in Italy in writers such as
Guido de Ruggiero, and in Germany in the writings of Albert Lange and
Karl Vorländer. Social liberal thought was committed to collective welfare
goals pursued through the state. It was thus more statist by inclination,
but not overtly nationalist. Essentially, social liberals were reacting to
certain themes present within classical liberalism, notions like atomized
individualism, the negative conception of liberty, the radically free market
economy and minimal constitutional state theory. They wished to replace
these with a socialized and developmental understanding of the individual; a 'positively inclined' conception of liberty, linked to notions like
self-realization and self-development; a conception of a mixed economy;
and a more responsive, collectivized and ethical conception of the state.
State intervention was premised upon the common good and the realization of human personalities. One of the characteristic forms of social
liberal thinking is T. H. Marshall's concept of social citizenship. Marshall
himself was a classic example of a social liberal. The doctrine implied a
delicate balance between self-government and corporate government
action.[8] The social liberals were, in effect, developing the embryonic form
of the welfare state. Their arguments were rooted in evolutionary theory,
social utilitarianism and philosophical idealism.

Cultural liberalism developed in reaction to procedural liberalism.
How self-conscious it is as a political movement is open to question.

Cultural liberals promote the conception of collective cultural goods, as in the French-language policy in Quebec. This view of liberalism has been developed by Will Kymlicka, amongst others. Classical procedural liberalism emphasizes individual rights against collective goals; communities and collective cultural goals (or rights) have no real moral existence. For Kymlicka, however, group and individual rights are not necessarily opposed. He thus tries to defend the conception of group rights within the framework of cultural liberalism. The crux of his argument is to suggest that when we exercise our liberty it is 'determined by our cultural heritage' (Kymlicka 1991, 165). Agency *requires* culture. Culture provides the content of choice. It also provides the norms and historical heritage. Thus, 'the primary good being recognized is the cultural community as a context of choice' (Kymlicka 1991, 172). Contrary to his perception of communitarian theory and stronger accounts of civism, Kymlicka thinks that we can abstract ourselves from communal ways of life and criticize them. We can be partly unencumbered. We neither just discover cultural views, nor are we irrevocably trapped by them. Cultural liberalism, therefore, distinguishes fundamental liberties from privileges and immunities. Provided the exponents of collective goals and cultural goods respect the fundamental rights of minorities and individuals, they can still be considered liberal for Kymlicka. This liberalism is seen as more sensitive to 'cultural survivals', and, for Charles Taylor, is the more relevant model for contemporary, porous and culturally diverse societies. Liberalism has more to do than negatively letting difference exist. Cultural liberalism therefore positively recognizes the 'worth' of different cultures.

Some very general conclusions can be drawn from this cursory typology. First, cultural liberalism, *per se*, tells us little about the nature of the state or welfare. Thus, it might or might not share beliefs with social liberals about, say, the market. It only affirms that culture is immensely important for choice and that groups, as well as individuals, have rights. There is, therefore, nothing inherently to stop cultural liberalism from being assimilated with either an older variant of classical liberalism, or, alternatively, social liberalism. Cultural liberalism might legitimately share even a classical liberal antipathy to distributive justice and the welfare state – especially if the existent cultures embody that antipathy. Thus, as long as different cultures are respected, then cultural liberalism is content. The only sticking point would be whether procedural liberalism could accept moderate formulations of group rights. Cultural liberalism therefore seems to have no specific economic or political content. It is not necessarily 'theoretically' committed, for example, to social justice.

Secondly, cultural liberalism arrests, but does not undermine, the argument for civil citizenship leading to cosmopolitanism and universalism.

However, because cultural liberalism tends to be more sympathetic to liberal nationalism, its universalizing appeal is partly blunted. Thirdly, because social liberalism is statist and centralist in intent, it is ideologically antipathetic to procedural liberalism. It would also have little sympathy with cultural goods and group rights taking priority. Further, because it views citizenship in the context of the state, it would also inhibit the force of any cosmopolitan argument. Fourthly, classical liberalism is intrinsically critical of the statism of social liberalism. It also feels deep unease with the cultural goods and group rights being pursued at the expense of individual rights and procedural justice. Classical procedural liberalism is most susceptible to the 'universalist intuition' argument. It is, literally, much easier to universalize the generic negative individual rights of classical liberalism, such as life, liberty, property. Yet, at the same time, most recent postcolonial writers see procedural liberalism as an expression of a particular oppressive colonizing community. In this latter scenario, minimal generic rights are no longer considered through the lens of cosmopolitanism, rather through the medium of imperialism and colonialism. This critical argument has also, paradoxically, been applied to the treatment of internal minorities, even within the USA, by Iris Marion Young. For example, rights-talk and notions of procedural neutrality are conceived as modes of group and cultural domination.[9]

The upshot of this section suggests that, given the profoundly contestable character of liberalism, the initial universalist intuition concerning cosmopolitan citizenship looks increasingly insecure. Indeed, some senses of liberalism might be profoundly at odds with universalism.

The empirical citizen

One implication of the conceptual analysis of citizenship, qua liberalism, is that the 'universalist intuition' argument looks less clear. Further, there are elements of both the concepts of citizenship and liberalism which might be described as deeply particularistic. So far, this particularist argument has not been made explicit; however, if we turn to the empirical practices of citizenship, then it becomes more obvious. However, what becomes obvious is not so much any overt particularism, as a set of confused aspirations which embody a tension between universalism and particularism.

The more empirical approach to the citizenship issue raises a different range of problems. First, citizenship, despite all that has been said earlier, is an empirical technique of exclusion. This is a particularly potent issue with regard to immigration. States always involve a bounded citizenry. Citizenship is largely about closure and control. Citizenship creates the concept of the foreigner and alien. Second, the character of citizenship itself mutates between state traditions, even between liberal democratic states. These empirical dimensions cut across the civic/civil distinction outlined earlier.

Turning to the empirical character: the two best known ways of conceiving the citizen have been the *jus soli* and *jus sanguinis* conceptions. *Jus sanguinis* associates citizenship with direct descent and blood relations or blood lines. It is not concerned with where one is born. If one can trace direct blood or birthright descent, then citizenship is automatic. Germany is the clearest example of this tradition. In *jus soli* citizenship follows prolonged residence or birth within a territory. France is the best example of this tradition. There are usually combinations of these traditions in most countries. Thus, in Britain, since 1981, where one parent must be lawfully resident and settled, then birth in the territory provides citizenship. The British case on citizenship is also complicated by the fact that the British are more formally defined as being subjects of the Crown, rather than citizens.

Two phenomena affected the German *jus sanguinis* case – the Prussian state and romanticism. The Prussian state view of the citizen was a corollary of the absolutist state, in intrinsic conflict with the older medieval *Standestaat*. Territorial residence took precedence in the Prussian conception. The romantic movement provided more of a background 'pattern of thought'. The aesthetic socio-historical idiom of romanticism was ideally suited for the misty formulations of ethnocultural ideas, namely, conceptions of uniqueness, inwardness, feeling over reason and organic growth over conscious artifice. These latter ideas provided a frame for *jus sanguinis*, which developed gradually between 1871 and 1913. Before 1913, German citizenship was partly contradictory. The older Prussian absolutist model of the citizen, namely, a member of a territorial community, jostled with the ethnocultural 'community of descent' idea. The community of descent idea won out, largely in 1913 citizenship legislation which established the concept of *Auslandsdeutsche*. This legislation aimed at the preservation of the pure German *Volkstum*. Citizenship was severed from questions of residence. Blood and descent became crucial.

The difference between the Wilhelmine and 1930s national socialist ideas of citizenship was that in the latter there was a definite ideology of ethnocultural dominance, coupled with a desire to *deprive* groups of citizenship. In the Wilhelmine case, the ideology was not so well developed and the desire was to *prevent* immigrants acquiring citizenship. As Rogers Brubaker comments, 'Remarkably, German citizenship today remains governed by a law of the Wilhelmine period'. He continues, 'As a result of this continuity across two world wars, three regime changes, and the division and reunification of the country, the marked restrictiveness of citizenship law towards non-German immigrants was carried over from the Wilhelmine Germany into the Federal Republic and, in 1990, into the new German nation-state'. He continues, 'the 1913 system of *jus sanguinis*, with no trace of *jus soli*, continues to determine the citizenship status of immigrants and their descendants today' (Brubaker 1994, 165). The end result of this in Germany is the well-known issue of the *Gastarbeiter* (guest workers). General estimates puts their number at approximately 7.3 million foreign workers, living in Germany, more than half of whom have been resident for over ten years. Many came initially to work in German post-war reconstruction and development. None of these can acquire citizenship since they do not have the 'blood line' descent.

Since the late 1990s election of the Social Democratic Party (SDP)-led government in Germany, there have been determined efforts by the administration of Gerhard Schröder, with the support of the German Greens, to reform the 1913 citizenship laws. Habermas' and others' interest in the concept of *Verfassungspatriotismus* (constitutional patriotism) forms a background theme here. An optimistic reforming parliamentary Bill was put forward to change the old 1913 law. It aimed to undermine the 'blood and descent theory' and to cut the length of residency required before citizenship was granted.[10] The proposed law also formulated a conception of 'dual nationality'. However, the Bill ran into obdurate and determined opposition from the powerful Christian Democratic Union and Bavarian-based Christian Social Union parties. The widespread fear was expressed that Germany would be flooded with foreign workers. The issue then became a focus for certain state elections, such as Hesse, causing SDP losses in the second chamber of the German parliament – the *Bundesrat*. Consequently, the whole process of citizenship law reform faltered and was watered down. Children of foreigners would be allowed to hold dual citizenship, if one parent had worked in Germany for over eight years. The children of foreigners must then decide at eighteen (within five years) which citizenship they wished to hold. Although these changes alone signal a historic shift, the blood and descent theory obviously still holds very strongly in the German tradition. It is important, however, to remind ourselves that we are still looking here at a mainstream liberal democratic state in Germany, probably the most self-consciously liberal and democratic in Europe. But the concept of citizenship is still exclusive and measured by blood descent.

The French case is even more interesting, for my purpose, namely, the question concerning the universalizing intuition within citizenship. In France, *jus soli* is the more predominant perspective. The drive for citizenship was always a political state-centred, integrationist and assimilationist idea. France did not, and still does not, really consider itself as a pluralist society, even at the millennium with an increasing multicultural dimension and fierce public debate about the Islamic headscarf in schools (Moruzzi 1994). The French citizenship argument was integral to a revolutionary, democratic, secularist and republican tradition. The events of 1789 were conceived of as a decisive break with the past. Republican citizenship law emancipated all individuals from their particular groups or associations under the banner of natural rights to liberty and equality. In its purest universalist reading, the only foreigner in France would be the bad citizen. Self-determination – in individuals or nations – was conceived in terms of the universal demand for liberty. The doctrine of the 'citizen' and the 'citizen-nation' moved hand in hand. Republican ideology usually emphasized military service or education as key factors here. Schools and the army were engines of assimilation. Second and third generation immigrants in France became citizens and were expected to serve the nation militarily. National purpose and assimilation were reinforced in the Third Republic by the apparent civilizing mission of the French nation for the world. The French state conceived of imperial unity in legalistic and *étatiste* terms. The state was seen to be an organ for solving problems, via a trained self-confident, public-spirited bureaucracy. The colony was an investment of the French state itself. If there were commercial interests, they came via the state. The colony was only separated from France by a geographical accident. Law was thus conceived as an emanation of the state itself. In no case were even the most advanced colonies of France, such as Algeria, allowed to move independently. Universalist civilization came though the French state, culture, language and fundamentally citizenship. French citizenship was therefore always a peculiar blend of chauvinism and universalism. Before the 1870s it was very much a liberal and radical push, after the 1870s it partly migrated to the right, reaching an ascendancy in the Dreyfus affair. However, the French left still carried on promulgating universalism and the civilizing mission of citizenship, even through the processes of imperialism and colonialism.

As mentioned, ethnocultural criteria did appear in France in the mid-1800s.[11] As ethnocultural criteria developed, the French idea of the citizen lost some of its universalizing aspect. In Arthur de Gobineau's work citizenship and nationalism began to take on racial dimensions – a theme partly reflected in the work of Taine, Renan and Thierry, particularly after the Franco-Prussian War. Still, the French republican tradition, to the present day, has been fundamentally exercised by the issue of citizenship. Whereas the Dreyfusard ethnocultural line of thought is still represented in groups such as the *Front National*, republican thought is still motivated by an underlying, if at times semi-dormant, strongly held abstract cosmopolitanism and universalism.

Nationality and citizenship

Citizenship is clearly a very immediate issue for a number of pressing empirical reasons, such as deep fear of mass immigration and asylum-seeking, anxiety over multicultural tensions and serious unease with the effects of globalization. Another subtext within this empirical discussion, which should be underscored, is that citizenship law is synonymous with nationality law. The two terms 'citizenship' and 'nationality' are virtually interchangeable. This is not a synonymity which would be acknowledged by theoretical republicans or procedural liberals, except as a convenient policy shorthand. Although, one suspects that on the ground, this synonymity is what most people believe about citizenship, namely a citizen is a member of a nation. However, could one conclude from this that those who promulgate the 'universalist intuition' are just empirically wrong?

It might thus be concluded, therefore, both from the earlier *conceptual* analysis of citizenship and liberalism, and the *empirical* use of citizenship in present-day states, that the 'universalist intuition' is completely erroneous. However, despite appearances, this is not necessarily the case. It was argued earlier that there is some conceptual case to be made for the intuition. However, even the empirical issues reveal ambiguities. The French debate is particularly instructive here. French republican citizenship – which is distinct from both the weaker and stronger civic republican variants outlined earlier – traditionally involved a core of universal human or natural rights. The declaration of 1789 speaks openly and stridently of the rights of 'man' *and* the 'citizen' – almost as if they are coterminous. The rights involved are described as 'imprescriptible' and 'inalienable'. Governments are contractually instituted to uphold them. Thus, 'the end of all political associations, is the preservation of the natural and imprescriptible rights of man'. The French National Assembly, in this context, 'recognizes' such 'sacred' rights. It does not create them. *All* men are born free and equal, with respect to these rights, thus 'civil distinctions ... can be founded only on public utility'. Yet, at the same time as the above assertions, the nation is also conceived as sovereign! Thus, no individual or group is 'entitled to any authority which is not expressly derived from it'. What is the relation here between the nation and the universal cosmopolitan rights of man? The profoundly direct, if equivocal, answer is that the nation is the will of the whole community of citizens and it embodies the imprescriptible rights of humanity *within* its own prescriptions. Law and government, as an expression of the national will, are only there to give 'security to the rights of man and of citizens'. Thus, 'the acts of the legislative and executive powers of government, [can be] ... every moment compared with the ends of political institutions'.[12]

The above issues form the substance to my analysis of this question and the key theme. Particularistic nationalism and cosmopolitanism co-exist, simultaneously, in citizenship. In fact, it is possible to assert simultaneously an extreme chauvinism and an extreme cosmopolitanism. In the case of *jus sanguinis*, the particularism and inclusiveness come to the fore quite unproblematically. Ethnocultural citizenship links easily with racism, nationalism or cultural liberalism. The citizenship and nationalism connection is thus more obvious here. However, *jus soli*, particularly in the French republican tradition, reveals more clearly the intrinsic and deep-rooted ambiguity of citizenship, namely, its continual alternation between cosmopolitanism and particularism.

Liberalism, generically, often represents itself as a form of historical emancipation from older political traditions – the conventional portrayal of status to contract, or the release from the medieval *Standestaat*. Liberal citizenship sees itself removing feudal shackles. It casts off the 'subject-hood' status of individuals under absolute monarchy or feudalism. Liberal rights theory thus rejects conceptions of status, based on birth or position. There is therefore an insistent 'progressive Whig' logic or dialectic to ideas of equality and freedom. Such ideas, it is suggested, cannot be checked by any hierarchical regime. Liberal citizenship iden-tified equal rights with individuals *as* individuals. Citizenship *is*, therefore, a central motif within liberalism and liberalism has always believed in equality of individual rights, regardless of race, gender, class or birth. In the French republican tradition particularly, and in the classical liberal tradition, there has consequently been a move to some form of cosmo-politanism. Yet, co-existing with this universalizing dialectic is the nation – usually read through the state. As one commentator has put it: 'Almost all [states] claim to derive state power from and exercise it for (and not simply over) a nation ... A state is a nation-state in this minimal sense insofar as it claims (and is understood) to be a nation's state: the state "of" and "for" a particular, distinctive, bounded nation ... *How* the state-bearing and state-justifying nation is culturally or legally bounded is irrelevant; *that* it is bounded is what matters' (Brubaker 1994, 28).[13] One has only to think of the commonplace usage of 'citizenship law', as directly synonymous with 'nationality law', to see the truth of this point.

The above argument does create an oddity in the liberal position. In the context of the nation, the citizen has rights which are premised on the natural arbitrariness of birth, even in the *jus soli* setting. In one sense, closure is pragmatically necessary, for the purpose of military service, taxation and public administration. Yet, the nation, birth and citizen relation is stronger than simple pragmatism. Given the history that liberalism relates, and given its lurking cosmopolitanism, something odd is taking place. As one recent scholar comments, citizenship 'represents a striking exception to the secular trend away from ascribed statuses. And it is difficult to reconcile with a central claim – perhaps the central claim of liberal political theory: the idea that political membership ought to be founded on individual consent' (Brubaker 1994, 31–2). The ascription of rights based on birth or blood descent is at odds with the panoply of liberal rights and liberal agency, in general, and yet they *all* co-exist within liberal citizenship.

Liberal citizenship is consequently at the interstice between a number of contradictory forces. Even procedural liberalism subsists with a potential for radical exclusion.[14] It incorporates both an embracing cosmopolitanism and an exclusive nationalism. There are though a number of forms of national exclusion and some are more problematic than others. But still, any of the exclusions entailed by citizenship do not rest easily with the universalist intuition. The nationalist-based 'birth connection' of citizenship also does not join with the liberal narrative. Therefore, the two theses discussed in this chapter – the cosmopolitan implication of liberal citizenship and the potentially illiberal nationalist and particularist criteria for any and all citizenship – encapsulate a dilemma.[15] Thus, the fate of nationalism and citizenship appears to be inevitably interwoven in a complex and tense relation, which gives rise to continuous reverberations in contemporary public policy. Universality and particularity vie with each other within the confines of citizenship.

4   Liberalism

The key theme of the previous chapter was that liberalism embodies an ambiguous and complex relation with both citizenship and nationalism. One conclusion is that 'liberal citizenship' is caught between contradictory forces. However, there is one possible solution to this tension, which was not canvassed in the previous discussion, and that is to seek some form of much deeper philosophical rapprochement between liberalism and nationalism. If liberalism – and its panoply of universalist values – can be reconciled successfully with some form of particular nationalism, then, it would largely overcome the conflict discussed in the previous chapter. This is an alluring possibility for many political theorists. It has consequently given rise to a strong set of arguments for a new theoretical hybrid – liberal nationalism. As one very recent liberal nationalist notes: 'Underlying nationalism is a range of perceptive understandings of the human situation, of what makes human life meaningful and creative ... Liberals are challenged to accommodate those worthy elements'.[1] This chapter will focus on the arguments for this hybrid which tries to bring together the universal and particular.

It is still ironic that until comparatively recently one of the worst insults one could deliver to most liberals or socialists was to associate them with nationalist beliefs. Internationalism and universalism were the norm. In the second half of the twentieth century, up to 1990, there was a heightened sensitivity to this question in the context of national socialism and fascism. Nonetheless, in the last decade, there has been a resurgence of interest in the idea of nationalism within liberal thought in particular. This chapter places this interest in liberal nationalism into a longer time frame, reviews the arguments of some of the recent enthused renderings of liberal nationalism, and then unpicks them in critical vein. In conclusion, a distinction is drawn between the pragmatic and ethical significance of nationalism for liberalism. Pragmatically, nationalism is unavoidable in contemporary world politics. If it is to exist, then it is infinitely preferable to have a relatively innocuous form which accords with liberal intuitions. However, we should hesitate to search for ethical justifications. Thus, my critique of the ethical arguments for liberal nationalism should neither be taken as a dismissal of nationalism *per se* nor as a defence of liberalism against nationalism. My argument rather tries to decouple ethics from nationalism.

Nationalism and liberalism in context

The first contextual problem concerns nationalism itself. One of the areas which was not examined in the previous chapter concerns forms or types of nationalism. It is important to consider this issue since it forms a crucial presupposition to the whole of the liberal nationalist case. There are a large number of typologies within the literature on nationalism. In considering such typologies, a great deal depends upon the particular theoretical approach adopted. Thus one could construct a typology premised upon diverse nationalist *strategies*. In this context one might distinguish unificatory from secessionist nationalisms. Alternatively, one could focus on *historical* phases in the growth of nationalism.[2] Other forms of typology concentrate on the distinctive *ideas* of nationalists. Typologies of ideas range from twofold to fivefold classifications of nationalism.[3] The typologies of the ideas of nationalism are in many ways much less settled than most other ideologies. Thus, selecting a particular typology is a hazardous affair.[4]

Much contemporary liberal interest in nationalism is premised upon a twofold classification. John Plamenatz's work is particularly apposite here as one of the unwitting prime movers of liberal nationalism, although in my reading, he merely reflects Hans Kohn's earlier formulation. For Kohn, nationalism was divided into two opposed types: Western and Eastern (see Kohn 1945).[5] This distinction keeps reappearing – in slightly different dress – in contemporary debate (for example, Michael Ignatieff 1993). The former, premised on Enlightenment values of reason and universalist humanism, aimed at a more open, plural, outward-looking society. It tended towards democracy, liberalism and constitutional rule. Its aim was to liberate the individual. The latter was more overtly authoritarian, closed, inward-looking, particularist, pathological, bellicose and xenophobic. The only important factor was that the nation should be free from others' hegemony. Plamenatz echoed this distinction directly. He distinguished, qua Kohn, between an acceptable 'moderate' Western civic nationalism – essentially the candidate for liberal nationalism – and a more bellicose Eastern European cultural nationalism (Plamenatz in Kamenka (ed.) 1976, 23ff). For Plamenatz, many critics often saw the whole of nationalism as tainted with illiberalism, particularly liberal commentators. He commented: 'No doubt, nationalists have quite often not been liberals, but that, I suggest, is largely because they have so often been active in conditions unpropitious to freedom, as the liberal understands it. I see no logical repugnance between nationalism and liberalism'. By and large, the brutality or unpleasantness is dependent on historical context (Plamenatz in Kamenka (ed.) 1976, 27). He continued that in Western European societies, nationalism was more usually liberal, particularly in the nineteenth century. However, Plamenatz was clear that this liberal form should be kept distinct from Eastern nationalism. Eastern nationalism was both imitative and hostile to Western liberal nationalism and was invariably illiberal and authoritarian in character. It is this later species which has given 'nationalism' a bad press in the twentieth century.

There is some truth to the view that there was a surge of interest in liberal nationalism in the early to mid-nineteenth century. Giuseppe Mazzini (1805–72) was one of the more important early figures here. His position was undoubtedly liberal – almost cosmopolitan in an ironic way. His liberal *Risorgimento* nationalism was linked to the promotion of most of the core classical liberal values. In fact, writers who adhered to some form of liberal nationalism from the nineteenth century to the present have not seen it as necessarily incompatible with either cosmopolitanism, universalism or pacifism. In many ways, President Wilson's Fourteen Points, promulgated after World War One, represent, if only symbolically, the high point of a certain kind of liberal nationalism, insofar as the points stressed 'the absolute sovereignty of the national state, but sought to limit the implications of this principle by stressing individual liberties – political, economic, and religious – within each national state' (Hayes 1949, 135). Formally, for the Fourteen Points, each nationality should have its own state, but it must instrumentally underpin constitutional government and democracy, and enshrine the rights and freedoms of the individual.

The general excitement in nineteenth century Europe over the Greek struggles against the Ottoman Empire and the Polish struggle against the Tsarist Empire in the 1830s attracted the attention of Mazzinian-inspired liberal nationalists. Thus, this original form of liberal nationalism was at its most potent in the century from the Congress of Vienna (1814–15) to the Treaty of Versailles and Wilson's Fourteen Points. The underlying theme was the liberation of peoples, through political independence and sovereignty, with the proviso that such independence would inevitably lead to or promote constitutional liberal democratic rule. By the time of the Fourteen Points, such independence was expressed in terms of the concept of 'self-determination'. One of the major problems with this form of nationalism (which will be returned to) was that, once having promulgated the idea of the sovereign independent or self-determining nation, it was difficult to know where to call a halt. As President Wilson was to bemoan, how could one prevent every moderately sized community perceiving itself as a nation, and thus a state? In addition, how was one to resolve conflicts between liberal nation states and, even more problematically, secessionist movements *within* liberal nation states.[6] Liberal nationalism did not appear to have the perspicuous resources to meet such challenges.

Overall, the case for liberal nationalism therefore presupposes a fundamental distinction between two types of nationalism. The distinction, which usually always occurs in late twentieth century liberal nationalist literature, is between a liberal as against an ethnic form. Liberal nationalism, *per se*, cannot afford to be tarred with the same brush as nationalism in general.

The other issue to consider focuses on what form or type of liberalism is involved in the compound 'liberal nationalism'. The question is raised by the fact that three forms of liberalism were discussed in the previous chapter. At first glance, cultural and social liberalism look more appropriate vessels for nationalist sympathies. Both have, by definition, intrinsically more appreciative views on communal aims or collective goods. Liberal nationalists have found it much easier to reconcile a sensible moderate national sentiment with some form of more responsive social or cultural liberalism. This claim would be supported by the additional fact that classical or procedural liberal arguments, in the post-1945 era, usually took the lead in asserting the incompatibility between liberalism and nationalism. Classical liberal writers, such as Friedrich Hayek and Karl Popper, clearly associated the collective goals of nationalism with tribalism. The strong-minded methodological individualism of classical liberal writers added moral gravitas to this position. The obvious weakness in this latter argument is that one of the candidates standardly rolled out by contemporary liberal nationalists to support their position is J. S. Mill. However, Mill's position in the history of liberalism is contested. Like Alexis de Tocqueville, Mill was unquestionably sympathetic, in some areas, to a classical or procedural liberal position. Despite this point, both Mill and Tocqueville also saw considerable importance in nationalism.

However the above argument is still incomplete. As Fred Rosen has maintained, early British classical liberalism did actually have a 'deep repugnance' to nationalism. Raising the spectre of Mill or Tocqueville (as above) does not undermine this argument. Rosen contends that 'because Mill did not dwell on the hostility between liberalism and nationalism, it is assumed that he did not accept this hostility'. For Rosen, the assumption is wrong. Mill's *Representative Government*, quite simply, does not deal with the problems of nationalism – particularly brutish issues surrounding the nineteenth century Greek nationalist struggle for independence from the Turks. Mill assumes, in the above work, that national government will be good government. He does not deal with illiberal nationalism. Rosen thus argues that the use of Mill by recent liberal nationalists 'suggests a greater compatibility between liberalism and nationalism, than Mill himself would probably have conceded' (Rosen 1997, 186). At first glance, this would appear to give credence to the Hayek and Popper view that classical liberalism is incompatible with nationalism. However, again this would be a false conclusion to draw. It is still important to realize that Mill was sympathetic to nationality, even if it is to only one shape or form of nationality, namely, something that upholds good liberal government. This view turns the argument around again and appears to support the contemporary liberal nationalist view, in drawing an implicit distinction between liberal as against more brutish forms of nationalism.

However, there are two weaknesses in the above contemporary liberal nationalist view. First, Mill's substantive liberalism – in terms of what is appropriate, for example, for the sphere of government regulation – is still classically liberal in character, whereas, the liberalism of Tamir, MacCormick, Raz, Kymlicka, and other recent exponents, appears self-consciously social liberal in texture. Thus, when examining liberalism, we are addressing different species of the genus liberalism. We are discussing liberalisms not liberalism. Mill's liberalism is not necessarily the same as, say, Tamir's. Second, and more significantly, do Mill and the recent exponents of liberal nationalism, both see the same *type* of relationship between moderate nationalism and liberalism? It may well be that in drawing a distinction between types of liberalism, in order to show different outlooks on nationalism, we are approaching the issue in the wrong way, or with inappropriate tools for analysis. Consequently, a more helpful distinction here would be to focus on the ways in which the relation between liberalism (of whatever type) and nationalism is configured. Thus, a distinction can be drawn between *intrinsic* and *instrumental* relations.

The basic point of the above distinction is that many liberals, over the last two centuries, including social liberals such as Hobhouse, and more classically minded liberals, such as Mill, have viewed nationalism from a more instrumental perspective. Nationalism is not viewed as intrinsically good, but rather, prudentially, it can enable (or hinder in some cases) more effective liberal government. Unreasonable nationalist sentiments, jingoism, and the like, should be resisted. Only nationalism which instrumentally enables good government is acceptable. Good constitutional government, public reasonableness and liberty take moral priority. In the words of Erica Benner, this instrumental view, 'is a pragmatic recognition of currently salient facts, not a statement of nationalist principle'. She continues that 'For Mill, Hobhouse and Sidgwick, the "principle of nationality" is derived from brute historical facts, not from any intrinsic connection to generous fraternal impulses'.[7] However, it is important to underscore the point that nationalism is not an intrinsic good. This is the nub of the difference between earlier liberalisms, which expressed sympathy with nationalism, and the liberal nationalism of the 1990s. The latter is committed to the intrinsic good argument. Nationalism or nationality embody the intrinsic goods of liberalism. Their relation is integral and mutually reinforcing, consequently nationalism becomes liberal in itself. This does not refer to all nationalism, but only this particular liberal expression. Thus, as Benner concludes (correctly in my view), an argument like that of David Miller's 'turns an essentially pragmatic and conditional set of policy arguments into a defence of "intrinsic", non-negotiable national values' (Benner 1997, 202).

One additional social and historical point which is missed in more recent expositions of liberal nationalism, which is worth noting, in passing, is the context of the distinction drawn by Kohn and Plamenatz *et al*, as well as Popper's antagonism.[8] Much of the debate over nationalism in the period from 1930 to the 1950s must be understood in the context of what might be termed the 'Weimar debates'. Most of the liberal-minded writers, such as Hans Kohn or Karl Deutsch, and many others, who generated the academic debate over nationalism, were European *émigrés* to America in the 1930s. They had either experienced first-hand, or second-hand through teachers, or through reflections on the World War Two experience, the rise of national socialism in Germany. There was a deep sensitivity about the role of nationalism. However, one could hardly say that nationalism, in itself, was a pressing problem in America in the 1920 to 1950s period, comparative to, say, Germany. Thus, a large contingent of German-speaking writers took their anguished debates with them into the USA. Some retained a profound antipathy to anything nationalist. Thus, the Austrian *Anschluss* contingent – Karl Popper and Friedrich Hayek – identified all nationalism with virulent authoritarianism. Others, such as Kohn or Deutsch, wanted to save an aspect of reasonable cohesive nationalism for a Weimar-type constitutional liberalism. It is slightly harder to locate the source for the urgency of the contemporary debates about liberal nationalism, other than, say, legal and political developments in the European Union.

In summary, liberal nationalism rests on an implicit distinction between liberal and other variants. Further, it is not the type of liberalism which is at issue, in considering liberal nationalism, all types of liberalism can potentially function with nationalism. It is more a question of the nature of the relationship between liberalism and nationalism. The difference between writers such as J. S. Mill and recent exponents of liberal nationalism is that the former viewed nationalism in an instrumental manner, whereas the latter have tended to see nationalism as an intrinsic value. The focus of the rest of this chapter will be on the more recent intrinsic argument.

Liberal nationalist arguments

The post-war Austrian liberal contingent had a powerful effect on social and political thought in the English-speaking world. Ironically, this liberal contingent shared with the internationalism of Marxism a common opposition to nationalism. For those educated in politics during the period 1950–80, it still appears slightly odd to find liberal political philosophers waxing lyrical over nations. The only exceptions to the rule are the socially acceptable liberationist and secessionist anti-colonial nationalisms which have a form of quasi-socialist imprimatur. Yet, even if one pays little attention to the Austrian contingent, there is still the shade of Lord Acton to warn us off nationalism from another, more Whiggish, dimension of the liberal perspective. As mentioned, twentieth century classical liberals, such as Hayek, have usually been profoundly uneasy with collectivities in general. Collectivities such as states, which can be juridically rationalized, are bad enough, but collectivities such as nations, which often appear to play upon irrationalism, are beyond the pale. The most that classical liberal writers have usually been prepared to admit is that collectivities, such as nations, are fictional aggregates of individuals or atoms (rather as David Hume suggested) which, occasionally, could be said to have some form of fictional legal or moral identity, if we strain hard (Hume 1994). Admittedly, twentieth century social liberalism has been more accepting of collectivities and public goods, but still the crucial importance of individualism holds strong in all forms of liberal thinking. Thus, minimally, nationalism does present a dilemma.

It is consequently diverting to find Neil MacCormick, the well-respected contemporary legal philosopher, whose credentials have always been impeccably liberal and individualistic, writing essays in praise of nationalism. In MacCormick's case it is premised upon a deep attachment to Scotland and a consequent irritation with English hegemony and a commitment to the SNP (Scottish National Party). Still, MacCormick himself, at times, gives the impression of being partly surprised by his own nationalism. He freely admits that nationalism has a brutal history, but he is certain that it has a 'reasonable' side. Yael Tamir has also utilized a very similar set of arguments to MacCormick's, writing one of the most well-known studies of liberal nationalism in the last decade (Tamir 1993).[9] David Miller has also attempted to capture nationalism for 'market socialism'. However, market socialism, in the manner that Miller describes it, might just as well be described as a form of social liberalism. This is the more statist version of liberalism discussed earlier. For Miller, the nation can be defended as a self-sufficient and worthy object of allegiance and 'one that is subject to rational control' (Miller 1988b, 658). Miller's arguments are directed to a moderate particularism (and moderate communitarianism), as opposed to a 'narrow-minded' nationalism (Miller 1988b, 648). This is a direct transposition of Kohn's and Plamenatz's distinction. Nations, for Miller, share common traits. The nation is 'constituted by mutual belief, extended in history, active in character, connected with a particular territory, and though ... marked off from other communities by its members' distinct traits – served to distinguish nationality from other collective sources of personal identity' (Miller in Brown (ed.) 1994, 141).

There appear to be three major elements to the liberal nationalist case which are stressed with varying intensity. First, there is the communitarian argument that we are socially contextual or embedded beings. We are constituted through the community and its values. We cannot be prior to society in any way. MacCormick consequently advocates a social, embedded or contextual individualism, as against an atomistic individualism. One can be a normative individualist whilst rejecting methodological individualism. In fact, he suggests that the more atomistic liberal concept which allows individuals to form their own sense of the good life is deeply implausible (MacCormick 1991, 13).[10] Thus, he states: 'The truth about human beings is that they can only become individuals – acquire a sense of their own individuality – as a result of their social experiences within human communities' (MacCormick 1982, 247). Families, local communities, nations, education, jobs etc. have a formative effect on the individual. MacCormick feels that he is offering a supplementation and corrective to the 'apparent individualism' of some of his other work. However, he adds that 'individuality goes beyond all that – but not in any way that renders all that superfluous or meaningless; human individuality presupposes social existence' (MacCormick 1982, 251). For MacCormick, though, despite the social constitution argument, 'I continue to affirm that the good society is one in which individuals – each individual – are taken seriously' (MacCormick 1982, 247, see also MacCormick 1990, 14–15).

Membership of groups, including nations, lets individuals transcend the constraints of time and place; it also provides a conceptual framework which permits them to 'comprehend [their] own existence as belonging within a continuity in time and a community in space' (MacCormick 1982, 251). Human beings take pride in tradition, it allows them to transcend their 'earthly existence' (MacCormick 1982, 252). For MacCormick, churches, trade unions, political parties, schools, universities and even supra-national groups 'can have a like significance to human beings in just the same way as can nations' (MacCormick 1982, 252). MacCormick confesses that he is very much against the notion of ranking such loyalties. It is but a step from ranking nationalism against other loyalties to ranking nations themselves, which he finds intolerable.

Miller also accepts the communitarian contextual individual claim in terms of his moderate particularism. For Miller, national communities exist through belief, not race or language. Like Tamir, and Benedict Anderson for that matter, Miller also partly accepts the artificial dimension of nationalist thought (Benedict Anderson 1983). Yet there have to be some shared substantive beliefs or 'attitudes, ritual observances and so forth' for nationalism to exist (Miller 1989a, 244). It is not, however, a belief system which can be totally conjured out of thin air. There is a pre-political element to it which forms a precondition to politics. It is an active identity which embodies historical continuity.[11] Yet Miller also suggests that this national identity can be fostered through education. This is a point which is not stressed by MacCormick or Tamir – although oddly it does bear a close affinity with Johann Gottlieb Fichte's views (Fichte 1979, see 2nd Address). Political education must 'try to shape cultural identities in the direction of common citizenship. It must try to present an interpretation of, let us say, Indian culture in Britain that makes it possible for members of the Indian community to feel at home in, and loyal to, the British state' (Miller in Mendus (ed.) 1988a, 253). In this sense Miller expresses unease with multicultural education, which rests on a spurious neutrality.[12] Nationhood is the crucially valid source of human identity.

In addition, like MacCormick and Tamir, Miller thinks that the distinction between the universalism and particularism of nationalism can be overdone. Local loyalties can be linked with universalist claims. Particularism can be reconciled with universalism. The nation is a valid form of ethical community. For Miller, a 'strengthening of commitment to a smaller group is likely to increase our commitment to wider constituencies', the point being, for Miller, that 'if we start out with selves already laden with particularist commitments ... we may be able to rationalize those commitments from a universalist perspective' (all quotations from Miller 1988b, 661–2). Put in another way, the bad nationalist is one who *fails the universalizability test*. As MacCormick puts it, 'A part of the *odium philosophicum* attaching to nationalism ... lies precisely in its failure to universalize and treat essentially like claims in like manner. But this in itself can no more discredit the legitimate claims of reasonable nationalism than the rampant selfishness and non-universalism of some individualistic persons discredits of itself universalistic doctrines of political individualism' (MacCormick 1990, 18). In general terms, for Miller, a state is more governable if it is a national community. A state – especially a welfare state with programmes of distributive justice – needs trust and voluntary cooperation to achieve its goals. It is thus, apparently, 'self-evident that ties of community are an important source of ... trust between individuals who are not personally known to one another' (Miller in Brown (ed.) 1994, 142). A crucial concept which figures in Miller's position and links with his arguments on both moderate particularism and distributive justice under market socialism is 'need'. For Miller, the 'universalist case for nationality ... is that it creates communities with the widest feasible membership, and therefore with the greatest scope for redistribution in favour of the needy' (Miller 1988b, 662). Miller is deeply concerned with the necessary pre-conditions for redistribution. Social justice and redistributive policies will be considerably facilitated if people see themselves as conationals.[13]

The second component of the liberal nationalist argument – respect for nations – is more strongly emphasized by MacCormick. It is supposedly, for MacCormick, Kantian – although what Kant actually had to say about nations certainly does not square with MacCormick's views. In fact Kant's material on nations is just deeply cranky.[14] For MacCormick, nations make up a part of our identity. Identity is deserving of respect. The principle of respect obliges us to respect that 'which in others constitutes any part of their sense of their own identity'. Thus MacCormick concludes, 'I assert it as a principle that there ought to be respect for national differences, and that there ought to be an adoption of forms of government appropriate to such differences' (MacCormick 1982, 261–2).[15] Autonomy does not necessarily conflict with national context – 'Autonomy is ... a fundamental good, and thus it is a great social value to uphold societies which facilitate it' (MacCormick in Twining (ed.) 1991, 14). A free society and free nation can be linked. If autonomous individuals require a context of freedom-enabling, 'then the collective autonomy of society itself seems a part of the necessary context' (MacCormick in Twining (ed.) 1991, 15). In other words, self-determination by the nations is linked to the self-determining individuals within them.[16]

The third component of liberal nationalist argument, which follows closely upon the previous points, entails specific recommendations for political arrangements. Nationalism can underpin liberal individuality and democracy, although MacCormick and Tamir add that nations are not necessarily coincidental with states. National communities should have the 'political conditions hospitable to their continuance and free development ... the whole idea of the desirability of creating the conditions for autonomous self-determination both of individuals – contextual individuals – and of the groups and collectivities constitutive of them leads back to the claim of self-determination as quite properly

a claim on behalf of each nation on similar terms to any and every other'
(MacCormick in Twining (ed.) 1991, 17).[17] MacCormick suggests that
'any tendency toward a greater democratization of government, a greater
re-inclusion of the nation in the state, would surely be welcome, and that
on simply democratic grounds' (MacCormick in Twining (ed.) 1991,
11).[18] However, he does express distaste for the concept of sovereignty –
an issue discussed in the first chapter of this book. Sovereignty and statehood are part of what MacCormick calls the 'inept model' of nationalism
derived from 1789. Yet, he still thinks that 'The mode of consciousness
which constitutes a national identity includes a consciousness of the
need for a form of common governance which recognizes and allows for
the continued flourishing of the cultural and historical community in
question' (MacCormick 1982, 262 and MacCormick 1990, 18–19).
MacCormick sees more hopeful signs in the European Community,
subsidiarity and the development of regionalism rather than in statehood
or sovereignty.[19] Scotland would become an independent regional government within the European framework.

For Miller, though, state boundaries should as far as possible coincide
with national boundaries (Miller in Brown (ed.) 1994, 143). National
self-determination is valuable because it corresponds to the idea of
nations as active communities (although he acknowledges that they act
through representatives). Self-determination follows from the identity
argument. If people share substantive beliefs which are reflected in their
acting representatives then the nation can be said to act and determine
itself. Miller also suggests that nationalism and democracy might be
linked (Miller in Brown (ed.) 1994, 144). The particular notion that he
has of democracy is deliberative. Citizens actively participate, shaping
society through public discussion. For Miller, the state is 'likely to be
better able to achieve its goals where its subjects form an encompassing
community and conversely national communities are better able to
preserve their culture and fulfil their aspirations where they have control
of the political machinery' (Miller in Brown (ed.) 1994, 145). Where
nation and state do not coincide, Miller distinguishes ethnicity and
nationalism. One can thus have a nation with multiple ethnic groups
within it. For Miller we are thus saved from the problem of giving every
ethnic group a state (Miller in Brown (ed.) 1994, 156).[20]

Another element of Miller's case is concerned with the questions: does
nationalism require state sovereignty, and are there any obligations
holding between nation states? Miller takes it for granted that 'each
nation in asserting its claim for self-determination must respect the equal
claims of others who may be affected by its actions' (Miller in Brown
(ed.) 1994, 145). This is essentially the universalist element in particularism. He suggests that complete sovereignty does not follow from

nation statehood, trade-offs are possible. Sovereignty should therefore not become a fetish for nationalists. Yet, nation states still, for Miller, retain a right to decide what to secede. There may be good reasons for transferring powers to a confederal body, but the most crucial elements are still rescindable. Miller is thus not interested in applying (like Charles Beitz) the Rawlsian difference principle internationally. Yet international justice can, and frequently does, limit national sovereignty (Miller in Brown (ed.) 1994, 150–2). Miller is perfectly content with this. There can be justice across boundaries if nations choose to act reasonably.

Liberal nationalism: a critique

The main arguments above can be systematically stated as follows. Individual identity is socially 'embedded' and the material in which it is embedded is national culture. Individual identity is deserving of respect. Since national culture is constitutive of individual identity, national culture is therefore deserving of respect. Constituents of individual identity which are valued, like freedom, if promoted by the national culture add substance to the case of respect for national identity. Institutional or political arrangements which embody and foster national culture and maximize the conditions of individual self-development are also deserving of respect. If free self-determination by the individual is valuable, then free self-determination by a nation (state) is valuable, as long as the nation state is promoting individual self-determination (this latter point is not always made explicitly clear enough, but I think that it is what liberal nationalists want to say). If the individual has a *right* to self-determination and the constituents of the embedded individual are made up from elements from national culture, then the nation state also has a right of self-determination in the international sphere. There are certain additional claims – nationalism nurtures cooperation and mutual obligations, which, for Miller, for example, form the groundwork for distributive justice. Miller also suggests that the substantive beliefs which are crucial to nationalism can be cultivated through education policies.

Embedded individualism

Taking the 'embedded argument' seriously, there are a number of critical points which need to be addressed: firstly, individuals have multiple and often conflicting group allegiances, including nationalism. What is the relation between these allegiances? Individuals are also more deeply embedded in some groups rather than others. The position of the nation in this context remains ambiguous. Secondly, group life entails responsibilities, how are these to be ranked with nationalism? Thirdly, nations might claim some priority to other groups either through their size or through their relation to the state. However both these latter points remain suspect. There is in fact a general unwillingness of nationalists to consider the sheer diversity, significance and range of group life. Fourthly, nationalism might seek solace in the argument that liberal beliefs are so deeply embedded already in certain polities that to be a liberal is implicitly already to be a nationalist. Again this argument has unforeseen consequences which liberal nationalists might not be able to accept. Fifthly, does the fact of being embedded imply that the agent 'ought' to be embedded, or, alternatively, does the fact of being embedded give rise to normative rules? This is connected to another issue, namely, if the agent is embedded what is the role of nationalist theory?

Thus, firstly, most liberal nationalist theorists recognize, within the embedded claim, that families, local communities, education, workplace, religious groups or clubs etc. also have profound formative effects on the individual.[21] A number of issues remain profoundly obscure here. If such groups and associations are formative on individuals, it remains unclear how far and in what manner nations relate to these other groups, especially in the constitution of the self. Such primary groups (families, villages, clans, neighbourhoods etc.) may overlap several nations or conflict in diverse ways with the nation. In fact, individuals are quite commonly at the interstice between multiple allegiances, many of which can be deeply opposed. Some allegiances, say, religious or political (Catholicism, Islam, Marxism, or cosmopolitan liberalism), may in fact entail denying the significance of national commitment. In addition, individuals are also usually more deeply embedded in families, workplace, churches, unions or clubs than nations. Nations are not ephemeral, but they certainly have little everyday significance for most individuals – at least for most of the time – whereas groups such as families, religious affiliations, occupations, and the multiple associations of everyday life press upon us all with depressing (or joyful) regularity. Thus, the idea that the nation forms anything more than a small aspect of embedded identity appears as simple commonsense, even ironically from a liberal nationalist position.[22]

Secondly, and more significantly, such diverse types of group entail a complex range of duties. There are shared ways of life in each of these diverse primary associations which often create moral responsibilities. Can we rank such responsibilities? MacCormick, for one, resists ranking (MacCormick 1982, 254–5). It is admittedly difficult to see, without much more elaborate argument, how such rankings could take place.[23] If one cannot easily rank priorities then nations become no more nor less significant than other group loyalties – in fact other loyalties are often more immediate and pressing. An additional small, but significant point, is that we do tend to recognize that some groups or associations can be immensely destructive and negative in their demands. We could cite the Mafia here, but family life, political parties or neighbourhood groups, at times, can be more than adequate examples. We also usually recognize that individuals can be subject to multiple, often conflicting allegiances, within and between groups. For some unaccountable reason, we do not so readily recognize nations within this setting. Nations can be potentially invasive and threatening even in their civic format.

However, thirdly, one ground for ranking national groups against others might be premised on size. It might be argued that nations are larger than other groups – certainly historically the largeness of nations over tribes or clans gave some credence, initially, to their priority. The altruism of the clan was extended to the nation. But this larger aspect of nations encounters problems if even larger units are identified – co-religionists (Islam or Catholicism), social democrats or utilitarians across the world, international legal, military, trade or political organizations, international corporations, or even those who believe in Europe. If size is the determinant, then nationalism immediately loses its privilege. If feeling and everyday pressing relevance are at issue, then it also loses out to smaller associations. If one placed these observations of groups into the Burkean language of the little platoon (favoured by some conservative writers), one wonders what the average citizen would make of it all. If one explained that the little platoon meant a congeries of platoons including the local sports club, neighbours, family, church, colleagues at work, and so forth, she might be more receptive. However she might be slightly more baffled, except when inebriated or watching the World Cup, that she belongs to a really big platoon with some twenty, fifty or eighty million members. It takes some form of inebriation and loss of common-sense to appreciate such an idea.

Yet again, it might be contended that nations gain importance and priority through their association with the state.[24] As argued in chapter two such a compound association is suspect, except as a figure of speech. Homogeneous 'nation' states are a rarity in the world. Most states contain many subnationals.[25] The link between the nation and the state is thus merely a transient phenomenon of the nineteenth and early twentieth centuries. As was quite clearly seen, even by President Woodrow Wilson in his later, clearer moments, if all national or ethnic groupings were granted statehood then international mayhem would break out. The fact about nations is their ahistorical arbitrariness. In addition, the most worrying phenomenon *is* the state which claims exclusively one par-ticular national identity. It is this demand for exclusivity which raises most problems. Contrary to the older nineteenth century nationalist view, it is exclusive nation states which are now the prisons of peoples.

Multi-national states or political organizations seem to be the only way forward.

The important general point which is missed by nationalists is that they are still under the pall of an older statist dualism, which has predominated in state discussion since the early modern period of European thought. Paradoxically, this dualism also affects their critics – the more cosmopolitan-minded liberal Kantians and utilitarians – whose solution to the 'nation/individual' dichotomy is to emphasize the global significance of individualism. In the latter it turns out by logic (if not in reality) that we have no special duties to our conationals, but rather general duties to the whole of humanity.[26] This is simply the obverse of the nationalist emphasis on the particularities of the nation state. For both cosmopolitans and nationalists there are 'nations or states' and there are 'individuals' and then, as Hobbes put it, there are worms in the entrails of the body politic – namely, cellular groups which are either regarded with antagonism (because they interfere with the life of individuals or nations) or are simply ignored. Communities are always generally regarded as 'large' things, which virtually coincide with states. However, contrary to this reading, states have always been multilevel entities. Nationalists and liberals both neglect the *corps intermédiaires*. States are made up of diverse constituent communities, associations and corporate groups – some groups transcend and cross many states.[27] In sum, nationalism has no particular position of privilege within our complex array of allegiances.

One reply to the above claim is that one can still retain some of the cultural priority of nations without appealing to size or statehood. Nations, in this reading, would retain a special form of respect as embodying the cultural aspirations of a significantly large group, without affecting allegiance to other groups or institutions. One could thus be both a Welsh nationalist and a good European. This is a point which will be looked at more closely in the next section. The gist of my response again is to ask why liberals or anyone else *should* see any virtue or importance in nations above other types of group loyalty? Why should there be a virtue in giving political expression to nations above other groups? It is not clear where the systematic account of the priority lies.

Yet, fourthly, perhaps liberal nationalists should not be so concerned here. If liberal values are embedded in the political and moral fabric of communities, then national members can form themselves through such liberal beliefs, without even raising the question of nationalism. In this view, which implicitly asserts the universality of liberal ideas, liberals appear to be tacitly proposing the content or substance of what individuals should want or desire. They also maintain that we should realize such content through the institutional processes of an 'embedded' liberal polity. There is some commonsense truth to the argument, at this point, that liberals, even where they express a strong antipathy to nationalism, nonetheless assume the background of a national unity on primary goods such as justice, liberty and individual rights. Therefore, they simply do not have to address the question of nationalism, *because* liberal values are so embedded within the community. Insofar as liberals seek a collective or general education system, economy, welfare system, army, police, bureaucracy or government, they could be seen by some to be nationalists of a type. Adam Smith, after all, wrote about the wealth of *nations*, not the wealth of the cosmopolis. Thus, as Tamir remarks, 'liberals were thereby able to circumvent such thorny issues as membership and immigration, as well as the more general question of how groups are structured ... Except for some cosmopolitans and radical anarchists, nowadays most liberals are liberal nationalists' (Tamir 1993, 139). This is an argument one can find stressed by economic nationalists, such as Friedrich List, in the nineteenth century.[28]

However this above argument is elusive and problematic even for liberals.[29] If the nature of human beings is reduced to distinct national histories, and particularly to distinct narratives, then they become simply an *aspect* of the distinct languages and cultures. Human nature is articulated in a fragmented form through a series of separate narratives, narratives which figure in the distinct nations. Human nature is thus 'constituted' within different narratives. We could, therefore, have no access whatsoever to any objective factors or psychology of human beings outside of the constitutive national discourses. Liberal nationalism, in this reading, would therefore have no purchase beyond a particular localized liberal narrative. The embedded sense of liberal beliefs is thus taken with full seriousness and liberalism becomes swamped by a strong communitarian thesis. However, I do not think that liberal nationalists would be totally happy with this outcome since it would leave them with no objective, or minimally transnational grounds whatsoever to assert any preferred way of life.[30]

Fifthly, does the fact of being embedded imply that the agent ought to be embedded, or, alternatively, does the fact give rise to a normative imperative? The fact itself of 'being embedded' is multi-faceted, as pointed out. However, regardless of the type of social structure, what would be the precise logical connection between being embedded in a particular social structure and deriving all one's values from that structure? The argument itself is problematic for a start, since each dimension of a multiple group life could provide norms; thus, where and how national culture appears in this scenario remains completely obscure. Leaving this point to the side, it is still not clear how one moves from being in a community, to deriving norms from that community.

There are two possible ways to read this latter issue. Firstly, it could imply that, factually, we only have the national group to derive norms from. This is empirically completely false; however, it still does not explain the logical move from a sociological fact to a moral 'ought'. Thus the sociological reportage alone is inadequate. Second, it could imply that we 'ought' to derive our norms from the community. Yet, it is not clear here where this 'ought' comes from. Is it an 'ought' that derives either from a group or community, or from transnational or universal norms? If it is an imperative that derives from a group, then it has no reach beyond that group and is consequently false as a universal proposition. If it derives from outside any groups, then the argument confutes itself. Further, if all groups or nations contain a structure of norms which constitute our normative life, how could one differentiate between them, everything becomes possible and moral. There would, by definition, be no objective criterion to differentiate between moral beliefs. If there were such a criterion, it would again be contradicting its own major premise.

The above is connected to another issue (already partly touched upon), namely, if the agent is embedded, what is the role of nationalist theory? To be embedded is, by definition, not to be intentionally constituted.[31] If therefore nationalist theory does act constitutively, then there is no embedded national culture. The populace would always be reliant upon ideologists to create and feed them their nationalist ideas. Nationalism itself would always be an artifice superimposed on idiosyncratic political affairs, even when claiming to be natural. Nationalism, in this reading, is an abstract theory. Within its abstractions is a false, if effective, claim about the importance of natural embedded particulars. In this sense, nationalist theory, throughout the twentieth century, has been an elaborate, if profoundly successful, charade. Alternatively, nationalist beliefs could be said to be already deeply embedded in the community, in which case an appeal to a theory called nationalism would be utterly superfluous. Nationalist theory would have no function. The problem with this embedded view is precisely the problem of particularity. How can an untheorizable embedded particular become a universal theory?

Respecting nations

If we move now to the respect argument: for liberal nationalists nations make up a part of human identity and identity is deserving of respect. We are therefore obliged to respect that 'which in others constitutes any part of their sense of their own identity'. Thus MacCormick concludes, 'I assert it as a principle that there ought to be respect for national differences, and that there ought to be an adoption of forms of government appropriate to such differences' (MacCormick 1982, 261–2).[32] The central idea is that national culture is constitutive of individual identity, therefore national culture is deserving of respect. There are three objections which are considered here: first, the notion of constitutive identity tied straightforwardly to respect appears downright odd; second, it is not clear why respect for a nation implies any separate political organization. Third, the idea that self-determination is a ground for respect fails to translate from the individual to the national level. This links to the issue of democracy and nationalism.

Firstly, it would appear to follow from the liberal nationalist argument that anything which constitutes part of our identity is deserving of respect. It is unclear how one could find a criterion to distinguish between content. If there is no criterion, it follows that it would license respect for the most abominable practices and this cannot have been meant by liberal nationalists. On the level of nation states this 'open-ended' content claim might of course be tolerated by a strict legal positivist. Yet, is this really acceptable or reasonable? Because something constitutes 'part' of basic human identity surely does not entail automatic respect of that part. Human identity alone is a very convoluted and messy thing which remains subject to immense philosophical and psychological contestation. Persons may have neuroses, recurring odd fantasies, unpleasant or harmless habits etc., which may have been communally derived (even from a national culture or historical tradition – such as duelling, cannibalism, genital mutilation, racial contempt or infanticide), but surely we would not automatically render them respect simply because they constitute part of an autonomous person. Also, what if someone conceived of their identity primarily in religious terms? Respect would be due to their religious beliefs as a constituent of their identity. Respecting the constituents of that person's identity would in no way link with or carry over into respect for a nation. In fact, respect for their religious beliefs might entail antagonism to nationalism and even transcendence of the nation state. Thus, although it might be partly granted that autonomy requires a cultural context as a precondition to choice, and that acts performed in cultural contexts are both individual acts and cultural manifestations, nonetheless this would not necessarily lead us to respect on principle either the substantive act or the cultural manifestation.

Secondly, does respect for nations imply separate political organization? There is another absurdity lurking in the wings here. The groups mentioned in the first arguments (families *et al*) all have separate existences and are often central to a person's identity, but it would be odd, even on the basis of established respect, to accord them separate political recognition. If, as argued above, national allegiance cannot be established as having *any* moral or political priority, then there is no reason not to grant each family or neighbourhood association statehood or petit-sovereignty. Surely, it is also doubtful that one would want to accord groups immediate respect without careful empirical assessment. Groups (including families, religious communities or nations) may perform monstrous acts which might in fact require guardianship of persons within them, even by international bodies or other neighbouring states. Nations are surely no different in this regard from any other groups.

Thus respect for a person is not something we would want to carry over automatically to groups without careful consideration. Group identity is certainly a feasible notion, but it needs to be carefully and juridically circumscribed and argued. There is clearly a strong and im-mensely articulate tradition of argument on the state and law. However, in comparison, the vagaries of national groups do not exactly evince clarity, any more than granting moral identity to a sports crowd would be viewed as immediately reasonable. For writers such as Miller or Tamir particularly it is also important to have a substantive national public culture. The problem here is what is the national identity and culture of Britain, Canada, Australia, Germany, America or Israel? Is there a central public culture or distinctive set of values acknowledged by all the citizens? Taking Britain alone, there are so many cross-cutting differences of class, age, ethnicity, belief systems and gender that such a judgement seems simply frivolous.

One counter argument to the above might be that: first, respect could still be forthcoming for all groups, including nations, but such respect would be defeasible or trumped by some higher-order liberal consti-tutional or moral principle. Thus, respect can still be integrated with the above criticisms – small groups and nations could be given political and even legal recognition, once we have abandoned the sovereignty vocabulary. Second, taking a leaf out of the European Community book, one could anticipate that 'subsidiarity' might give leeway for complex allowances to group life, regional and local loyalties within a much larger federal framework. In this context, one could anticipate very small to much larger regional groups having some participatory role and having respect accorded to them. The competence of larger bodies could thus be reconciled with the competences of local or regional bodies.

My response to this is to suggest that the above reply, although establishing the point that recognition could be given to the multiple groups, still does not solve the problem of how such group loyalties can be ranked. There is certainly a suggestion in MacCormick's argument that some form of significant 'regional' political organization should be accorded to nations such as Scotland. Yet my original question still holds – what is so special or what is the special virtue of a national loyalty above other group loyalties? Unless this priority can be clearly shown then it follows that all of the above groups should be granted some form of significant political organization, which, as suggested, is an odd idea.[33]

This latter point is clearly connected to the subsidiarity issue which might be seen to resolve the complex question of recognition and political organization. We do not of course have to debate subsidiarity in the abstract, since it is enshrined in the European Maastricht treaty. The principle of subsidiarity, as it has arisen in European Union debates, indicates that there is a presumption in favour of local decision-making and the involvement of a higher authority only when lower authorities are unable to fulfil a given task.[34] *Prima facie* the competence belongs to the member states, since the Community only has those powers attributed to it by member states. As yet, though, there is very little consensus on the interpretation of subsidiarity: views range from it being a cover for further centralization, to a genuine encouragement to local autonomy (including regional autonomy).[35] Overall, though, 'people have changed its meaning to suit new needs and circumstances. Hence lawyers still see it as an essentially political concept, if not a state of mind. As such it is not susceptible of easy definition let alone effective legal enforcement' (Church and Phinnemore 1994, 70).

One strong interpretation, however, is that subsidiarity was designed to slow centralization to Brussels. The competences of the Community would tend, as much as possible, to devolve to the member states or possibly regions. However, the opaqueness of subsidiarity, its lack of any clear statements as to who does what, and its abstract formulation (partially to avoid mentioning federalism) do not evince much confidence (Church and Phinnemore 1994, 72–3 and Dehousse 1995, 126). Not only can it be interpreted to mean restoring powers to national governments (which is the British view), but also to subnational units, which is where some regional nationalists in Europe would see leverage. However, the subnational reading is but one of many.[36] Thus, subsidiarity in practice does not seem to provide any clear insights into the subnational question or political recognition. Conversely, it introduces further obfuscations of a basically federalist impulse, which, again, does not really address the subnational or multiple group questions.

Nations, democracy and justice

Moving to the third objection. If we focus on formal self-determination and willing – as the grounds for respect – then further ambiguities remain. Many of the liberal nationalist arguments focus on ideas of self-determination in both individuals and nations. In fact they often envisage a close relation between individual and national self-determination. Nations are or ought to be self-determining, and this, like the individual's capacity for autonomous self-determination, should be respected. What we have here though is a deeply ambiguous transposition of the argument of self-determination from the individual to the collective level. The free individual is self-determining, thus the free nation ought also apparently to be self-determining. The nation becomes the self-determining higher-order individual or self. Despite its cryptic history in the twentieth century, self-determination is admittedly often identified as a strong liberal, as well as nationalist, motif. The self-determining individual and the self-determining nation are thus parallel in some liberal minds.[37] The nation usually becomes a synonym for the governed, via ideas of democracy and popular sovereignty. Apart from the ontological difficulty of speaking about the 'self' of a nation (discussed in chapter one), the crucial problem here is the fact that national self-determination does not necessarily correspond with individual self-determination.[38] There is no automatic 'carry-over'. All self-determining nations would somehow be liberal nations, which is nonsensical. Yet, self-determination can imply the right of a state to its own independent and distinctive existence. The right of the German *Volk* under the national socialists, or any other such autocratic regime, also becomes legitimized by self-determination.

The salve for the above argument is internal self-determination and participation. It is here that we encounter the link between democracy and nationalism. Respect for nations translates into respect for liberal democratic nations. It is thus argued that representative democracy should be embodied in the substantive institutions of the nation. Self-determination at the individual level would therefore mean that the government would be determined by the voters. In this latter context, individuals participate or identify themselves with national policies.[39] Ironically, to insist that the substantive content of all nationalisms ought to be democratic contradicts an important dimension of the nationalist respect argument, which insists on tolerance and respect for particular difference.[40] The democracy argument appears to dictate the actual content of regulative beliefs within diverse nations. In addition, there are clearly many civic-inclined nations, embodying multi-ethnicity, acceptance of equal civil rights – many South American states and South East Asian nations such as Singapore – which are not particularly democratic (or at least claim to have a different understanding of democracy). Further, it is also worth drawing attention to the fact the liberalism has not historically always been attracted to democracy. The alliance between liberalism and democracy is contingent, liberalism usually seeing democracy as one amongst many instrumental constitutional devices for limiting governments. For many liberals, democracy itself should always be hedged around by what Madison called 'auxiliary precautions' to control the effect of the 'ignorant masses'. The capacity of countries such as Weimar Germany to vote in a national socialist regime bent on destroying party democracy made liberals, such as Hayek for example, deeply suspicious of the reach of democracy.

Further, to participate rationally in politics is not necessarily to identify with a nation. In addition, a people is *not* necessarily a nation. Popular sovereignty is not necessarily national sovereignty. History and tradition, within most states, are not things always shared in common. We have ordinarily many different allegiances and loyalties. The majority of states have no national, ethnic or cultural unity. It is possible however to have widely accepted structures of authority without raising the spectre of nationalism. Indeed it is questionable how helpful nationalism is in any democratic scenario.

There is one final point which needs to be mentioned on the issues of democracy, social justice and nations. The issue of democracy and nationalism was discussed in chapter one, under the rubric of popular sovereignty, thus I will not dwell upon it. However, one further point should be noted. It might be argued, in response to the above analysis: how can a state (or community) hold together, promote justice, welfare and democracy without nationalism? Nationalism nurtures cooperation and mutual obligations, which for David Miller, for example, forms the ground for distributive justice and deliberative democracy. Without nationalism, it is difficult to see how social justice, minimal social solidarity or democracy could be maintained. There must, in other words, be some kind of social cement; the centrifugal forces of liberal society would otherwise be too strong.

There are two answers to this question. The first is prefigured in what has already been argued, namely, that nationalism is but one of many different types or species of solidarity and is by no means the most pervasive or significant. Second, apart from the fact that there is no solid agreement on what a nation is, it is also worth bearing in mind some very obvious, if often overlooked, points. When contemporary liberal nationalists suggest that nationalism underpins justice, particularly distributive justice and welfare, by generating trust and voluntary cooperation, it is important to note that nationalism in the twentieth century has not necessarily generated any concern for neighbours, the poor or the oppressed, even in extreme war situations. Generally warfare will generate strong national sentiment, but low levels of interest in democratic processes. Britain under Margaret Thatcher, Chile under Pinochet, Argentina under the military Junta, America under the Ronald Reagan administration, Germany under Hitler in the mid-1930s, Spain under Franco, and many other such examples, although *all* expressing very strong levels of nationalist or patriotic sentiment, are not exactly noted historically for their interest in social justice, strengthening democracy, freedom, or the plight of the poor and oppressed. American patriotic sentiment, in general, cannot be doubted, but it could hardly be said to coincide with widespread North American interest in social justice or welfare. These facts are so obvious it is strange, in the extreme, that anyone should think otherwise. In parallel, it is possible to have regimes with very low levels of assertive national identity, but with strong programmes of welfare and social justice – as in Canada. Similarly, Canada has distinctively high levels of democratic participation and comparatively low levels of national identity. Ironically countries such as Germany, in the 1930s, had very high levels of nationalism and little interest in democracy. Conversely, in the 1990s, Germany has comparatively high levels of democratic participation and painfully sensitive juridical awareness, but an understandable paranoia about nationalism. The list of the 'obvious' could go on here.

Overall, it is very difficult to see how pure individual self-determination could be easily reconciled with national self-determination even in the liberal democratic format. Would anyone seriously contend that representative democracy really carried individual self-determination into the realm of national self-determination?[41] The two appear to be potentially at odds, depending upon exactly how one interprets the relation of the individual with the nation. Formally, nationalism as self-determination is as compatible with fascism as with liberalism. The idea that nationalism is a crucial social cement and necessary for justice, freedom, democracy and participation is just factually mistaken. There is no necessary connection between democracy, social justice and nationalism.

Conclusion

Nationalism is undoubtedly not going to disappear from the scene of world politics. It will be with us for the foreseeable future, well into this century, influencing the character of political activity. If this is the case, then liberal nationalism is, without a shadow of doubt, the most acceptable form of nationalism. But there is a distinction to be made here between, on the one hand, the pragmatic acceptance of nationalism and, on the other hand, a principled ethical reception of nationalism which tries to seek a rapprochement between liberalism and nationalism. It is a very different matter to accept nationalism, with some reluctance, pragmatically, as a pervasive form of group allegiance, and, alternatively, to try to bestow some intrinsic ethical and liberal significance upon it. Humans are constituted by many and diverse forms of group and association. Brutal families, religious fanaticism, criminal associations and large business corporations also have a constituting role. However, although realizing that it is very difficult, most of the time, to do anything but control the peripheries of such constitutive entities, we certainly would not accord them any ethical importance *per se*, simply because they are social entities which have a constitutive role. Such social entities will not disappear and will not be eliminated. We have to live with them, but we do not necessarily have to like them or approve of them. Such is my response to nationalism. Pragmatically, it is, at the present moment, an inevitable form of allegiance. If it is to exist, then it is infinitely preferable to have a relatively innocuous form which accords with liberal intuitions. However we should hesitate to search for ethical justifications for it. Nationalism, in the final analysis, is an empty husk of a word which will always resist being assimilated into liberalism alone. It will always tend to invite its brothers and sisters and thus easily collapses into the lowest common denominator – shallow expressions of blood, soil and xenophobia. Nationalism is a contemporary inevitability which should be minimized. It is not a virtue to be promoted.[42]

In conclusion, the central arguments of recent liberal nationalism are both confusing and unpersuasive. The complex character of the social constitution of the individual is assumed as unproblematic. Their arguments for transferring respect from individuals to nations also appear woefully inadequate and unsatisfactory. In addition, self-determination is a profoundly difficult and elusive notion, particularly if carried over into nations and states. It is certainly not impossible to deploy the term and it may of course be used in a trivial sense by international relations theories, indicating that states appear to act in a unitary manner – however, liberal nationalists want the idea to work harder for them. This 'harder' application is unconvincing, if not irresponsible. Further, self-determination, by individuals or states, does not lead to or guarantee any particular institutional arrangements. Autocracy or liberalism are equally possible outcomes. In sum, liberal nationalism still needs to explain itself. Its rapprochement between nationalism and liberalism does not work.

5   Patriotism

One of the main aims of liberal nationalism, discussed in the previous chapter, is to seek a philosophical rapprochement between two apparently disparate doctrines, liberalism and nationalism; in effect, trying to unify the particular and universal. This might be described as the philosopher's stone of contemporary political theory. The interest in liberal nationalism is understandable. On the one hand, there is a realization that to favour universalism, qua humanity, is not practical for most human beings. Despite this fact, political theory, as a discipline, has often tended historically to favour the universalist path. On the other hand, there is a sense that nationalism, when it has been politically dominant, also shows little concern for neighbours or strangers and tends to exhibit irrationalism and xenophobia. The experience in the Balkans has not exactly illustrated the endearing aspects of national sentiment. If both nationalism and liberalism are unacceptable, why not move the universal closer to the particular – thus liberal nationalism?

The latter theme also explains the impetus behind patriotism. On the one hand, many contemporary theorists find nationalism utterly unacceptable, in whatever shape it appears. Nationalism, for these theorists, remains unequivocally caught in the particular – and usually a bloody and messy form of the particular. Yet, these same theorists still see the need to embody the universal in some form of the particular. Consequently, empty universality is also seen as inappropriate. A new form of particularity is needed within which to nest the universal. This has led to a renewed search for older vocabularies to dress in modern clothes. Two such vocabularies have arisen in the last decade to fulfil this urgent function – patriotism and republicanism. Patriotism has not been limited to republicanism (as I will argue); however it was and is, undoubtedly, a strong virtue appealed to by republicans and, in recent theories, it is one of the key devices through which republicans have tried to link the universal and particular, whilst circumventing the detested nationalism. The 'philosopher's stone' is therefore being sought, once again, in both patriotism and republican patriotism. Patriotism fills the particularist void left by nationalism. Republican patriotism rejects both the universal of liberalism and the particularity of nationalism. Patriotism is therefore seen as a particular loyalty compatible with universal reasonable values. It allows citizens in particular territorial states to adopt values compatible with both their own particular situation and potentially with even world citizenship.

Yet, in re-embracing such older vocabularies, unresolved problems are reopened in the arguments surrounding patriotism and republicanism. This chapter focuses critically upon patriotism, and specifically on republican arguments used to achieve the separation of nationalism and patriotism. In the course of the discussion, the argument concerning the relation between these terms is broadened. It concludes with a claim that they can be separated in certain contexts, although the gist of that claim is negatively articulated. Patriotism has no intrinsic value in itself. It largely depends upon the state within which it is articulated. In fact, if anything, patriotism is closely connected with 'reason of state' doctrine.

Republican patriots

Patriotism does have an important intellectual resonance with republicanism, although the etymology is complex. The roots of the word patriot lie in *patria*. *Patrie* and *patria* refers to father (as in pater, père, Vater, padre), and, in addition, to the land, property and dignity associated with the father. The attribution of father also has direct links with the authority (*auctoritas*) – originally meaning the capacity to influence. The term 'patriarch' derives from this dimension.[1] *Patria* also has the same etymological root as *pays* or *Vaterland*.[2] *Patria* thus referred to both the land *and* the authority – thus capacity to influence – of a father. This again has conceptual ties to notions of family or clan, as in the term *paterfamilias*, namely, referring to one who is not only the master of a house, in respect to ownership, but also the proprietor of an estate and head of a family.

The blunter dimension of this linkage between authority, land, family, property and influence can be observed in the Roman *patrician* class, who possessed considerable wealth, in land resources particularly. Patricians were the dominant class in, what loosely might be called, the older Roman state. They also claimed to be the most ancient families of Rome. Their property enabled wide-ranging political influence. This is connected to the original use of the terms patron and patronage. Early Roman political factions worked through the context of powerful families. Loyalty to kin in politics was supremely important for survival and political success. *Pietas* was, thus, originally loyalty to the family hearth. However, Roman republican writers, such as Cicero, also saw a wider *patria* in the *res publica*. The later Roman legal *Digest* and *Institutes* thus commonly referred to two *patriae* affecting the citizen: the local (*patria sua*) and the more abstract public Rome (*communis patria*). Under the later Roman Empire this second *patria* became increasingly more abstract and legalistic. It was also linked closely with the juristic theme of Roman citizenship. The citizen – a *legalis homo* – is one who is free by law and consequently expects the law's protection, but also owes loyalty to the *communis patria*.

The qualities of 'local familial emotive identification' and 'abstract legal loyalty and entitlement' have remained part of the curious conceptual baggage of patriotism to the present day. Emotive identification implies a more visceral loyalty. For some twentieth century commentators this visceral idea has been the preserve of nationalism. Yet, this is clearly mistaken. This is why some commentators still insist, unwittingly, that patriotism is more of an *emotion* than an intelligible political or legal idea![3] It is difficult to love consistently a legal abstraction, such as *res publica*, or, alternatively, a legal constitution. Love of home or family (the *familia* and thus what is both familiar and particular) consequently remains intrinsically part of the concept of *patria*, partly to compensate for the remoteness of the legal abstraction (*res publica*). Patriotism, in its etymological roots, therefore embodies an unresolved duality.

Yet, the legal abstraction (the public thing) was only worthy of patriotic loyalty – particularly for Roman republican writers – if it embodied a commitment to particular values such as liberty (under law). The conjuncture of devotion to *patria* (love of country), moral and religious piety and commitment to abstract legalistic values, such as liberty, was given its most forceful rendition in the civic republican tradition. The term republic is an anglicized form of *res publica* (public thing), as opposed to *res privata* (private thing). The *res publica* of Roman thought was a remote but attractive abstraction. It retained this attraction even for Roman emperors who tried to continue the republican terminology for several hundred years after it was no longer politically meaningful. *Res publica* refers, more generally, to the common weal, common wealth or *civitas*. In this generic sense, the term republic (the public thing) is not a particularly helpful term, since it could refer literally to *any* form of political regime.

The more specific normative concept of republicanism, which derived from a somewhat rosy reading of Republican Rome, implied that the people (*populus*), or more specifically the citizens, had a decisive role in the organization of the public realm, although we should not mistake this for democracy. The republican citizen, in this scenario, exhibits virtue and rational self-control in the public realm. In late medieval, Renaissance, sixteenth and seventeenth century versions of republicanism, this also clearly implied a belief in Christian truths and virtues. It was only eighteenth century republicanism which became linked with secular themes. Further, the citizen was viewed as an independent agent in the public arena, but, such independence implied basic property ownership. Property ownership implied that one had a 'stake' in political order and a consequent sense of social responsibility. The language of republicanism is also one of the right to resilient individual liberty, but intimately tied to the correlative duty of active service for the community. Each citizen has to be formally willing to renounce private concerns for the common good, order and flourishing of the community. There was, in addition, a continual fear in such earlier republican thought of potential degeneracy, institutional decay and corruption. This often led to a pervasive conservative and pessimistic demeanour, which favoured political stasis.

Whether or not republicanism submerged in the medieval period and re-emerged in Renaissance city-states is a subject of scholarly debate. The conventional view amongst recent neo-republican writers is that the theory passed via the Italian Renaissance city-states, with Machiavelli as a founding father, to the seventeenth century English civil war period, emerging also in the Dutch Provinces in their struggle against Spanish monarchy.[4] It was seen to be revived by writers such as Henry Neville and Algernon Sidney in the 1680s, given an opportunistic rendering in Lord Bolingbroke in the 1720s and restored again by Richard Price and others to defend the American colonists in the 1770s (Skinner 1998, 10–13). The fruits of classical republicanism can be found in doctrines such as the mixed or balanced constitution and American Constitution separation of powers of the next century. The French Revolution is, however, standardly seen to transform republicanism into a debate about forms of democracy.

Most scholars of republican thought thus conventionally see it dropping out of use in the nineteenth and twentieth centuries in the face of the rise of liberalism, conservatism and socialism. However, from the 1960s, some commentators, critical of the idea that American politics was founded in Lockean individualism, identified the real roots of American politics in a civic republican tradition. The culmination of this process was J. G. A. Pocock's magisterial work *The Machiavellian Moment* (1975). Pocock interpreted many important strands of Anglo-American political culture of the early modern period as part of a civic humanist or civic republican tradition, derived from Renaissance Italy. Similar views were developed in the work of Hans Baron, Adrian Oldfield and Quentin Skinner (Oldfield 1990, Baron 1966, Brugger 1999 and Skinner 1998). However, Skinner, and more recent writers, such as Philip Pettit, have moved away from the historical commentary into direct normative claims concerning the contemporary relevance of republicanism (Pettit 1997).

Skinner is more opaque here. But he certainly uses republicanism to question the current 'liberal hegemony', namely, 'by attempting to re-enter the intellectual world we have lost'.[5] In other words, republicanism provides a resource for contemporary political theory and practice to counter the hegemony of liberal theory. This is largely where the contemporary interest in patriotism arises. With republicanism, however, comes a very specific reading of patriotism. It would thus now be a truism to say that much of the very recent political theory-based argument about patriotism, as set against nationalism, has arisen from within the republican position. One of the central claims of the republican perspective, in recent years, is that there is a clear and important separation to be made between patriotism and nationalism. Patriotism is the great lost, liberty-based language of the ancients, nationalism is a modern aberration. Patriotism saves populations from nationalism.

The only caveat to enter here is one discussed briefly in chapter three on the question of republican citizenship, namely, that there is a distinction to be drawn between the older and the more recent manifestations of republicanism. I formulated this distinction in terms of weaker and stronger variants of republicanism. The stronger format emphasized the civic over the civil, whereas the weaker seeks the converse. The stronger civic variant thus entailed more cultural and moral uniformity. It placed a powerful emphasis on virtuous active citizens and an integrating and unifying public good, which took priority over private goods. The weaker conception, which prevails in most recent expositions, entails a much more restricted pragmatic conception of impartiality. It does not demand that individuals share values, but only that they are prepared to debate their views rationally in a public setting.

The above argument might lead to a distinction between weaker and stronger forms of republican patriotism. There is some truth to this point. However, even giving ground to this point, there is still a pervasive assumption in recent exponents of a consensual integrating republican culture, if only focused on liberty as non-domination. There is also a clear and unequivocal repudiation of nationalism. Most recent republicans would therefore accept the following generic points. First, patriotism means the intentional political identity of citizens within a free rational polity, whereas nationalism implies unwitting ethnic or cultural identity. Second, patriotism is often regarded as much older, more settled and civilized than nationalism. Nationalism is a crude recent addition to political argument.[6] Third, patriotism is often seen to have closer links with the vocabulary of constitutional republican states. Nationalism is more focused on the issue of power within any state. Fourth, patriotic language, in France and North America, during the revolutions, converged on universalist themes, such as liberty (Hobsbawm 1992, 87).

Nationalism is only peripherally or indirectly concerned with liberty. Fifth, patriotic loyalty expresses rational willing and consent, whereas nationalism relies upon prepolitical naturalistic issues such as birth and blood. Sixth, nationalism tends towards tighter conceptions of exclusivity and is often aggressive and bellicose, whereas patriotism is seen as more inclusive and defensive.

The elusive republic

The problem with the above claims – which are admittedly shared by many both within and outside the republican frame – is that they provide an ersatz picture of the patriotism and nationalism relation. This issue is complicated by the fact that we have to examine two lines of argument – republican and patriotic – which some see as intimately linked. The discussion now turns to a series of enquiries into the structure of patriotic and republican arguments.

Primarily, as mentioned, the conception of republicanism remains elusive. However, it may well be that the issue is even more complex than a distinction between weaker and stronger variants. There are as many differences between the republicans of the seventeenth and late twentieth century as there are between Roman republicans and seventeenth century variants. The modern variants no longer have a primary focus on independent property ownership in the citizen body. Further, the seventeenth century strong republican emphases on almost suffocating civic virtue, strict conditions for military service, good arms, an underlying deeply conservative, inertial and pessimistic demeanour, belief in universal Christian truths and obsessive fear of institutional decay, instability and degeneration, do not sit comfortably with modern, dare one say, more liberal republicans' preoccupations.

Thus, initially, it is difficult to speak of *the* republican perspective. There are four generic contenders for the republican heartland: first, classical republicans (Aristotle, Cicero, Livy, and Machiavelli – unless one separates out the Hellenic Greek, Roman and Renaissance versions); second, the complex seventeenth and eighteenth century variants (Henry Neville, Algernon Sidney, Richard Price); third, neo-classical republicans in the twentieth century (Hannah Arendt and most recently Viroli, Skinner and Pettit), and, finally, communitarian republicanism (Charles Taylor, Robert Bellah and Michael Sandel *et al*). In this more complex scenario, Maurizio Viroli's attempts to dismiss, for example, recent communitarianism from republican ranks looks more partisan than scholarly. Another more subtle definitional point here is Skinner's claim that true republicans ('neo-Romanists' as he now calls them) have a distinctive and unifying characteristic, namely, that they are all anti-monarchist. Those who resisted monarchy are therefore 'republican in the strict sense' (Skinner 1998, 22, ns 65 and 67, also 54–5 and 55, n. 176).[7] This anti-monarchical aspect is taken as more significant than their distinctive view of liberty or their commitment to the politics of virtue. The problems here are that, first, although all anti-monarchists would be by definition republican, not all such republicans would be classically or neo-classically republican. For example, anarchists, Marxists, most socialists and many liberal theorists, *et al*, would be republican, in the minimal sense of being anti-monarchical. But, none would be republican in the substantive sense advocated by Viroli (or one suspects Skinner). Second, other contemporary neo-classical republicans, such as Pettit, seem more directly focused on the distinctive concept of 'resilient negative liberty' (or liberty as anti-power) as the decisive component of republican argument. Thus, the monarchy theme is far less evident. Further, monarchy itself is a contested concept. Constitutional monarchy, although different to absolutist monarchy, is not necessarily so different a category to republican theory as Skinner might suggest.[8] Thus, in speaking of 'the' republican perspective it still remains far from clear as to what precisely is being addressed. Republicanism remains inchoate.

Designer patriotisms

This whole issue becomes that much more complicated when one re-focuses the argument upon the broader canvas of contemporary expressions of patriotism in political theory.[9] Despite the fact that patriotism has appeared continuously in ordinary political discussion (and poetry) over the nineteenth and early twentieth centuries, there has been, as discussed above, a sense of a *rediscovery* of its language in recent years within political theory. In my reading, however, there are five different renderings of patriotic argument, some of which (but not all) arise from the broad church of republican theory. These strands can be categorized as strong communitarian patriotism, neo-classical republican patriotism, moderate communitarian patriotism, moderate liberal patriotism and constitutional patriotism. This list is not exhaustive but encompasses many dimensions of current discussion.

Alisdair MacIntyre's version of the strong patriotism argument links seamlessly – if possibly unwittingly – with nationalism. Thus, another term for it might be *nationalist patriotism*. This argument would accord with the general fact (not denied by anyone) that nationalist argument did tend to absorb much patriotic discussion in the nineteenth and twentieth centuries. We might call this the 'positive assimilation model'. In his 1984 essay, 'Is Patriotism a Virtue?', Alisdair MacIntyre clearly accepts the synonymity of patriotism and nationalism as unproblematic.

He remarks, in the course of a critique of liberalism, that a 'national community' which 'disowned its true history ... would be one towards which patriotism would be ... an irrational attitude'. There is still some confusion within this communitarian orientation, as to the precise nature of the concept of community. Proponents appear to be unconcerned by the conception of community, qua nation or patriotism, others are clearly worried.[10] MacIntyre falls, a little uneasily, into the former category, certainly in the above essay, although he might, of course, simply be unaware of any difficulty concerning these concepts.

Patriotism is one of a class of what MacIntyre describes as 'loyalty-exhibiting virtues', with marital fidelity, love of family, friendship, and so forth. Such virtues exhibit what he calls 'action-generating regard for particular persons, institutions or groups', and they are usually founded in highly particular relationships. Yet, for those who see morality as universal and impersonal, patriotism cannot be a moral virtue because of its particularity. Liberal universalist morality would appear to require the agent to abstract herself from all particularity. This view of morality, implicit in Kantianism, utilitarianism and contemporary contractarianism, denies that the patriotism/nationalism synonym can be moral. For MacIntyre, however, 'where' and 'from whom' I learn morality is of crucial significance. Morality is learned within a way of life, from other agents, within a particular community. It presupposes a set of particular institutional arrangements. Goods are never encountered except as particular goods of communities. The morality of patriotism/nationalism is thus seen as perfectly natural to us as particular communal beings and is thus compatible with all expressions of patriotism.

Before moving on from this argument, it is worth noting that the synonymity of patriotism and nationalism can be viewed both positively and negatively. MacIntyre articulates the positive view, which involves the direct normative assimilation of the two languages to communitarianism. The negative view would take the synonymity as exemplifying – what many would take to be – all the worst excesses of nationalism. Both terms are thus viewed with contempt. We might call this latter argument the 'mutually disagreeable model'.

There are a number of background points to the 'mutually disagreeable model'. First, patriotism is seen as a verbal 'sleight of hand' to avoid the pejorative and unpleasant connotations of nationalism. The separate use of patriotism thus has a face-saving character. Second, it might well be the case that patriotism did have an older and more distinctive meaning, but, since the nineteenth century, that older sense has been lost in all but theory. As one writer has commented, 'from the nineteenth century onwards, the meaning of patriotism shifted to allegiance to the nation and the nation-state, and came to be synonymous with nationalism' (Alter 1989, 6). Another writer speaks of patriotism losing all its 'sting' in the nineteenth century, moving from being a 'critical springboard' towards a myopic 'my country right or wrong' attitude. Patriotism, in these readings, has become the *same* vessel as nationalism. They are two sides of the same unpleasant currency. Any trace of old republican virtue in this reading has been swamped. Thus, patriotism should share all the opprobrium heaped upon nationalism (see Dietz in Ball, Farr and Hanson (eds) 1989, 189).[11]

The 'mutually disagreeable model' is well formulated by Leo Tolstoy at the beginning of the twentieth century, although he does express a more generic perspective characteristic of the whole century. Tolstoy found both ideas utterly abhorrent, commenting that 'it is taken for granted that the feeling of patriotism is, in the first place, a feeling innate in every man; and secondly that it is ... a lofty moral feeling. But neither the one assumption nor the other is correct. I have lived half a century among the Russian people, and during all that time I have never seen or heard a manifestation or expression of patriotism amongst the great mass of real Russian peasants'. Patriotism is seen by Tolstoy as a form of 'collective hypnotism', grafted onto a people by state institutions for their own nefarious purposes. Despite great efforts by states to foster patriotism, indifference rules amongst the great mass of the people. Tolstoy notes 'what is called patriotism is merely ... on the one side a certain frame of mind constantly produced and supported among the people by the schools, the Church, and the venal press, for the purposes of government; and on the other side a temporary excitement aroused in the classes of the lowest mental and moral level by special means adopted by the ruling classes'. Tolstoy admits that patriotism is a useful doctrine for the state, but it is still, nonetheless, a 'very stupid and immoral one'.

Tolstoy admits that in ancient Hellenic states, patriotism coincided with religion and morality and was bound up with defence. In modern states these themes are no longer linked or relevant. Patriotism, in our day, is 'a cruel tradition surviving from an outlived past'. Its essence is the power of ruling classes to befuddle and manipulate the people. In the final analysis, to espouse patriotism means the renunciation of human dignity, commonsense and conscience. States cannot exist without it, but it remains utterly immoral (Tolstoy 1974, 498–517). This deep moral suspicion of patriotism – without the Tolstoyean preconception on Christian anarchy – is also shared by other contemporary writers, such as Martha Nussbaum (on a more Kantian and cosmopolitan basis), who is also clearly not prepared to countenance the separation of patriotism and nationalism.[12]

A second strand of argument sees both the negative and positive accounts of fusion between nationalism and patriotism as a deep betrayal of 'true patriotism'. True patriotism must be kept completely distinct from nationalism. This is a *neo-classical republican patriotism*. One of the most articulate recent defenders of this thesis is Maurizio Viroli. He insists that these concepts 'must be distinguished'. For Viroli, the language of patriotism 'has been used over the centuries to strengthen or invoke love of the political institutions and the way of life that sustains the common liberty of a people, that is love of the republic, [whereas] the language of nationalism was forged in late eighteenth century Europe to defend or reinforce the cultural, linguistic and ethnic oneness and homogeneity of a people' (Viroli 1995, 1). The enemies of patriotism are tyranny, despotism, oppression and, inevitably, corruption. The enemies of nationalism are cultural contamination, heterogeneity and racial impurity. Whereas, patriotism emphasizes a free way of life within a republic, nationalists focus on the cultural and spiritual unity of the people; therefore, the republic is unimportant.

Viroli admits, however, that both terms have protean and shifting meanings. But he still insists that 'the language of modern nationalism came about as a transformation or adaptation of the language of patriotism, by which words like "country" and expressions like "love of country" were given new meanings, while a number of themes like cultural or ethnic unity and purity that republican patriots did not address at all or treated as minor compared to the main question of common liberty, assumed a central role'. Consequently, he argues that 'to understand nationalism, we must then begin with patriotism and think in terms of two languages, not a single language unfolding and changing over centuries' (Viroli 1995, 8). Cultural or religious homogeneity is considered by Viroli as a vice. National homogeneity asphyxiates a community and encourages boring, intolerant bigotry (Viroli 1995, 13). It is therefore deeply pernicious to confuse patriotism and nationalism, since for Viroli republican patriotism *is* the theoretical and practical antidote to nationalism. However, he still admits that republican patriotism has been historically largely pushed, for various complex reasons, to the periphery of political thought during the nineteenth and twentieth centuries (Viroli 1995, 161).

For Viroli, the distinctive character of patriotism is that it is focused on political liberty, civic virtue and love of country. Love of country is, though, not love of a language or ethnicity, but rather of common political liberty. This is not a love of particular liberty, but generic nonexclusive liberty. Love of liberty can extend 'beyond national boundaries and translates into solidarity' (Viroli 1995, 12). 'Particularity' is here saved for 'universality' – an argument also found in liberal nationalism, liberal communitarianism and all forms of rooted cosmopolitanism. Patriotic language is particularistic, for Viroli, 'in the sense that it makes the republic particular; it does not fly the field of particular loyalties on which nationalism flourishes, but works on it to make citizenship grow' (Viroli 1995, 14–15).[13] The ideal, for Viroli, is therefore the republic. Republican patriotism counters both nationalistic and communitarian arguments. A republic is not, however, just political. It also has some common traditional memories. It also needs some sense of solidarity and commitment. For Viroli, the left – in ideological terms – have unfortunately allowed the right overwhelming access to the language of patriotism. In the nineteenth century, left radicalism was dominated by the language of internationalism and universalism. Republican language can, however, be adapted to socialist projects. It is, thus, a viable alternative to both current liberal foundationalism and ethnic nationalist claims, linking particular loves with universal themes.

A third strand of argument is *moderate communitarian patriotism*. Theorists, such as Charles Taylor, Michael Sandel and Robert Bellah, amongst others, have directly linked patriotism and republicanism (and thus civic humanism) with communitarian motifs. Communitarians, *vis-a-vis* MacIntyre, are clearly not of one mind on the issue of the synonymity of terms. Some admit that patriotism is not one single entity. In this sense, minimally, one should distinguish moderate patriotism from strong patriotism. This also has some parallels with the distinction between stronger and weaker senses of community, within communitarian theory, and ethnic as against liberal senses of nationalism. Thus, unlike MacIntyre's acceptance of the synonymity (outlined above), Charles Taylor seeks a definite separation. He sees 'patriotism' as 'a strong sense of identification with the polity and a willingness to give of oneself for its sake'. Being a citizen thus takes priority to other forms of identity. One ground for this identity, Taylor admits, is nationalism, so much so that, he admits, it is often now difficult to distinguish them. However, Taylor argues that it is nonetheless very important to try to distinguish them, remarking that, 'if we think of patriotism as strong citizen identification, then nationalism is one basis for patriotism but not the only one'. Religious, cultural or ethnic identities are *not* the same as patriotism, although, they also fuel nationalism. What is distinctive about nationalism, for Taylor, is that it is tied up with a claim for 'prepolitical' identity – a point also made by Habermas. Patriotism, however, has no such 'prepolitical' reference. It implies intentional love of country and its laws. *Patria* is thus always 'politically defined', as in the American and French revolutions – neither of which was, for Taylor, nationalist in intent. Later, however, he admits 'so much did nationalism become the rule, as a basis for patriotism, that the original prenationalist societies themselves began to understand their own patriotism in something like nationalist terms'. Thus, now, for Taylor, 'nationalism has become the most readily available motor of patriotism' (Taylor in McKim and McMahan (eds) 1997, 40–1).

For neo-classical republicans, such as Viroli, Taylor's moderate communitarian theme utilizes a notion of liberty, which, Viroli contends, is completely alien to the republican tradition. Thus, Taylor's more positive rendering of liberty, as participatory self-rule, is *not* seen as part of the republican perspective.[14] For Viroli, communitarians also lay too much stress on the 'particularity' of morality, as a local narrative and native solidarity. However, the situation is more complex here than might appear in Viroli *et al*, partly because republicanism is itself a contested and unresolved category. Given that Viroli's own republicanism is so different from Roman, seventeenth and eighteenth century versions, it is not clear why we should simply accept his own stipulations concerning doctrine. Taylor certainly views himself as a form of republican. He also separates out patriotism and nationalism in a form akin to Viroli. He also does not articulate anything like MacIntyre's strong thesis. Thus, the argument here becomes slightly more cryptic.

A fourth strand of argument is *moderate liberal patriotism*. This can be found in recent writers who shade across into liberal nationalism. Stephen Nathason, for example, directly contrasts his moderate liberal-minded patriotism with 'extreme patriotism', qua MacIntyre. Moderate liberal patriotism sees certain liberal universalist moral constraints acting upon patriotic goals. Too much patriotism or too much liberal universalism are not seen to be good things. One needs a *via media*. Thus, as he argues, 'liberal universalism does provide a plausible basis, rooted in both history and theory, for limiting the ways in which people pursue their conceptions of the good life' (Nathason 1989 and 1993). Nathason's position is at least a salutary reminder to earnest neo-republicans that liberal language is not necessarily anti-patriotic. Thus, patriotism cannot be confined within republicanism, in some kind of perennial historical struggle with liberalism.

A fifth strand of argument is *constitutional patriotism* – Jürgen Habermas' *Verfassungspatriotismus* – which is basically a Kantian-orientated loyalty to the universalistic political principles of liberty and democracy embodied in a legal constitution (see Habermas 1992, also Ingram 1996). Constitutional patriotism is thus an allegiance to a particular constitutional tradition embodying certain political values. The background to this is Habermas' own deep sensitivity to the events of World War Two in Germany, particularly qua nationalism. In Habermas' case, it is patriotic loyalty to universalistic political principles of liberty and democracy embodied in the German constitution. As Attracta Ingram comments, citizens, in this scenario, 'are thought of as bound to each other by subscription to these shared values rather than by the more traditional pre-political ties that nation-states have drawn on as sources of unity ... So it has to be an identity in which membership is constituted by recognition of a common system of authority erected and maintained by a constitution. Unity and legitimacy come from the constitution and the formal tie that holds people together is their continuing voluntary recognition of the constitution, their constitutional patriotism' (Ingram 1996, 2). Constitutional unity does require a certain kind of citizen solidarity. But its source need not be nationalism, which is viewed as a prepolitical claim. This kind of general theme can be found, for some, in the polity of the USA and, possibly, the burgeoning European Union. Shared values in democracy and liberty could, in fact, be viewed as a stage towards world citizenship. This is a partial reconstitution of the more abstract juridical conception of Roman thought.[15]

Thus, the first point to note is that there are a number of differing strands of contemporary patriotic argument, many of which do not necessarily coincide with republicanism. Further, not all strands of patriotic argument necessarily repudiate a synonymity with nationalism, either from a positive or negative perspective.

Republican assumptions

If we home in on recent republican writings a little more closely, there are certain background assumptions which require further explication. Primarily, there is the mundane assumption of a community made up of rational, independent-minded citizens. Further, there is a supposition of some form of minimal public culture – usually focused on a particular and quite idiosyncratic reading of liberty, distinct from notions of negative and positive liberty. Republican laws, in this reading, should make men good. Law socializes and controls natural selfishness. Liberty is most likely to be preserved under republican institutions and laws which facilitate individual self-rule. Strengthening individual liberty therefore means strengthening institutions. Consequently, republicans emphasize the need for laws to ensure that people act with virtue and within the same generic framework of values. The rational virtues espoused by the republic are secular in character. Modern republicans are also keen to foster homogenization through civic education and institutional design.

Firstly, there is the assumption here of a uniform rationality amongst citizens. Although this is also crucial to a number of contemporary political theories, it bears little relation to the realities of life for most human beings, except at the most minimal level. Humans are simply not like this, except in theory. Second, as regards liberty, republicans stand in a negative relation with multiculturalism, specifically multicultural education. In being focused on social virtue and the legal coercion of individual behaviour, republicanism implies a greater homogenization and much more constrained sense of pluralism than found in liberalism. Of course, the older stronger versions of republicanism would find multiculturalism and pluralism quite simply intolerable. The demand made by the recent weaker variant is that there should be public dialogue and that equal resilient liberty should be respected. Yet, although accepting a weak pluralism, there is still, in this latter variant, a pervasive view that a better society is a more homogenized society (which corresponds to the ancient polis model in theory). Thus, deliberately fostering republican patriotism through education does not rest easily with the obvious difference contained in most large modern states. Cultural diversity is an accepted fact of life for most people, even, oddly, for the ancient Hellenistic Greeks and the Romans (in practice). The mundane messy reality of diversity does not seem to have been registered by modern republicans.

Further, republican patriotism, embodying the implication of moral exclusivism, can all too easily slip into moral chauvinism. Despite the more secularized vision of patriotic republicanism presented by late twentieth century exponents, others have drawn attention to its deep Christian roots. This explains partly some of the moral uniformity presupposed within the republican perspective. For Anthony Black, for example, the Christian perspective on republicanism – which dates to the medieval period – did not simply disappear with the Reformation, the scientific revolutions, and other such harbingers of modernity. It rather penetrated deep into the psyche of all republican thought. Although there are marked differences between modern republicanism and earlier forms, it is still clear to Black that Christianity (being a deeply malleable political doctrine) helped shape the substance of republican thought. Modern republicans would no doubt reply that 'resilient' secular republican liberty provides an ideal ground for respecting difference in modern civil societies, including religious difference. Liberty is concerned with the absence of the danger of interference. Yet, it is still not clear that a common culture, even of resilient liberty, actually avoids or diminishes illiberalism or intolerance; in fact, it may well exacerbate it. The recent case in republican France of the Islamic headscarves issue illustrates some of the problems here (see Moruzzi 1994). The upshot of this reading of liberty is that it may be more intrusive than negative liberty, in a more traditional liberal understanding. Further, the love of the republic's freedoms, laws and constitution does not necessarily solve problems of difference and cultural tension.

Habermas is distinctly uneasy with republicanism, specifically over this multicultural issue. For Habermas, republicanism focuses too strongly on membership of an ethical community. He notes that the republican perspective is essentially the same as Charles Taylor's communitarianism, in emphasizing that the 'citizen must identify himself "patriotically" with his particular form of life'. Taylor's view implies a 'collective consciousness' within an ethical community. In arguing this, for Habermas, Taylor suggests a conceptual, not just a contingent historical relation between republicanism and nationalism. For Habermas, the 'classic republican idea of the self-conscious political integration of a community of free and equal persons is evidently too ... simple a notion to remain applicable to modern conditions'. Republicans, for Habermas, are thus like communitarians and nationalists in regarding the citizen as 'fully integrated' within a communal identity. Habermas' solution is 'constitutional patriotism'. He sees the USA as an example of a state in which the political culture 'sharpens an awareness of multiplicity' (Habermas 1992, 6, 7, and 11). Habermas explicitly uses the Rawlsian term 'overlapping consensus' to explicate this idea.

For Viroli, however, Habermas' unease with republicanism is due to a basic misunderstanding, the source of which is Habermas' reliance upon Charles Taylor's work. For Viroli, Taylor is not a republican, whereas Habermas unknowingly is. Viroli assumes, of course, that in republicanism we are speaking of one singular clearly identifiable entity, which is in fact false. For Viroli, Taylor's understanding of civic freedom is not negative freedom, but participatory self-rule. He continues that, 'if one reads the canonic texts of classical and modern republicanism ... [that is Livy, Machiavelli and Rousseau] it is easy to see that, in fact, republican theorists place the highest value on liberty understood as "negative" liberty under the shield of just law'. Citizenship is not therefore about self-rule in an ethical community, but rather the Roman juristic 'enjoyment and exercise of civil and political rights as a member of a *respublica*' (Viroli 1995, 171, n. 23). Love of country is love of a free republic which is a love of political liberty. Viroli also suggests that Habermas' constitutional patriotism needs a stronger connection to culture and history, but not so much so that the political liberty is overwhelmed.[16] The particular must manifest the universal. For Viroli, whereas Habermas stresses political and legal factors, others, such as MacIntyre and Taylor, stress the need for particular communal moral values. Patriotism is a virtue in conflict with universalism. MacIntyre's argument stresses that we need our national community narrative as part of a personal narrative conception of the self. For Viroli, MacIntyre's patriotism is thus 'really nationalism' – hardly a startling supposition – and the crucial issue is that political liberty disappears in this nationalist setting.

Viroli's argument walks a fine line here. He notes that 'the republican prescription for civic virtue seems to have worked in nineteenth century America: if the *patria* treats the citizen justly, if it allows them to participate in public life, they are likely to consider her as their own common good and love her with passion and reason' (Viroli 1995, 177 and 182). Republican patriotism is concerned with the rule of law. It is not premised upon any notion of social, religious or ethnic homogeneity.[17] Citizenship does not need homogeneity. For Viroli, it was thus 'republican outrage' in the USA which fuelled the campaign against President Nixon [sic]! In essence, however, republican patriotism, as presented by Viroli, is not really very different at all (except by sleight of hand) to liberal nationalism, liberal communitarianism, moderate liberal patriotism and rooted cosmopolitanism. They are all trying to contain particularity within universality.

One final point to note, with regard to the mimesis of ancient republics in writers such as Viroli, is that no one actually believes that modern communities are like this in practice. Republicans usually describe the world through the model, and, in a peculiar reversal of priorities, argue that the world often fails to live up to the quality of the original. Republican theorists thus recast their mimetic model and try to read it into the present conditions. The model itself does have a perennial appeal. Yet, the underlying republican vision of hermetically sealed good polities, reflecting the self-government of upstanding rational citizens and possessing the capacities for effective clear-headed policy-making and institutional design, is also strangely inappropriate and unrelated to the global complexity, frequent irrationality, wide-scale immigration, cultural mixing and often deep incoherence of modern polities.

Patriotic objects

It is important to underscore the point that republican thought does not have a monopoly on contemporary patriotic language, despite the fact that its Roman origins had a powerful later impact on the discourse surrounding patriotism. Patriotism is formally compatible with *any* political creed or object of attachment. Family, locality, capital city, tradition, land, absolute monarch, totalitarian state or republic can all theoretically be the *patria*. In the next three sections a different account of patriotism is offered.

In the medieval period, *patria* was identified with a number of generic objects. First, it could be – as in Roman and Greek thought – a familiar locality, hamlet, village, township or city. The patriot was one who submitted to the city or village and was prepared to defend it. Second, in terms of the feudal structure, defending homelands could also entail defending the lands of a local lord or prince. In this sense, feudal and vassal relations became integral to much patriotic argument. Third, in Augustinian Christian thought another dimension appeared. The significant *patria* was the city of God – the eternal fatherland – which could, admittedly, be confused with the empire as *Respublica Christiana*. This transcended all cities or states. Papal authority and government became additional confusing components to this area of argument. The idea of the *patria*, as the city of God, which transcends all states, re-appears later as an anti-patriotic theme in, for example, Tolstoy in the early twentieth century; this was partly due to the manner in which patriotism was corralled into nationalist vocabulary.

During the later medieval period, Roman imperial thought was increasingly utilized by secularizing *patria* (states) in Europe. Citizens were thus still subject to two *patriae*: the locality and the abstract juristic Rome, *communis patria*. However, 'abstract Rome' became a movable feast. Rome could, in effect, be Paris or London. As one scholar has argued, 'the loyalty to the new limited territorial *patria*, the common fatherland of all subjects of the Crown, replaced the supra-national bonds of a fictitious universal empire' (Kantorowicz 1957, 247). Monarchs became, in effect, supreme law-makers (sovereigns) and emperors in their own domestic realms. Patriotism kept pace with this logic. However, the belief in *patria* retained deep roots in both theology and juris-prudence.[18] Religious sentiment lay within the political goals of the new national monarchies. The biblical ideas of Davidic kings, priest kings and the stipulations of St. Paul's Romans XIII and St. Peter's Epistles gave a strong impetus to the idea of God's role in governing processes. Monarchs became, in some readings, saintly and divine healers – the 'royal touch' has its source here. The family origins of monarchs were also traced to remote divine antiquity – Adamite or Trojan.

From the twelfth century, the notion of *patria* often arose in the con-text of defence of a territory. Defence of *patria* was a legitimate ground for 'just war'. Religious language, again, was immensely important here. God also appeared, in the eyes of rulers, to embrace certain kingdoms with a special affection, such as Italy or France. Thus, defence of king-doms took on a value-added religious lustre. One of the important pious linkages here was provided by the crusades. The crusader, defending God's *patria* against the infidel, was thus looked at through the lens of religious martyrdom. However, if the 'crusades idea' is extracted from the equation, then one is left simply with defence of the fatherland (*patria*) as a religious duty. As the historical logic of Europe slipped over into territorial monarchies, the logic of the crusader's patriotism pervaded the soldiers who fought for liege lords or secular monarchies. Death for the kingdom (*patria*) became death for the heavenly kingdom.[19] Absolution and salvation were linked to service of the Lord and *patria*. *Pro patria mori* was the work of Christian *caritas*. Christian love thus became unmis-takably political. By the thirteenth century, martyrdom was descending upon all the soldiers of European states. At the extreme, even parricide or matricide became forgivable for the sake of the *patria*'s defence.[20] This deep identification with *patria* intensified with the study of writers such as Cicero, and later, with the thirteenth century rediscovery of Aristotle. Thomas Aquinas also touched upon the issue of the religious duty of the citizen to render themselves vulnerable to death for *patria*. In summary, death for *patria* and death for the Christian faith were virtually coeval. The religious memorials, thanksgivings and formal recognition we still give to war dead are a testimony to how deeply this idea has permeated state theory. This is an immensely important theme, central in the understanding of patriotism to the present day.[21]

It should be remembered that patriotism has been subject to many changing meanings over the course of its history. The republican episode was a brief moment in a longer and more detailed history. The strong conceptual components of patriotism have been the linkage of love of locale with the attachment to the legal abstraction of the state. Patriotism was not a forgotten term during the nineteenth and twentieth centuries. It was used extensively, although it just did not appear in a republican format.

Imitatio Christi and *Imitatio Patria*

When patriots feel uncomfortable with either the lustful emotive excesses of nationalism, or, alternatively, the colder abstractions of legal citizenship or constitutions, they usually speak of love. Thus, for Viroli, 'modern citizens ... can love their republic, *if the republic loves them*' [my italics]. The republic 'protects their liberty, encourages political participation, and helps them to cope with the inevitable hardships of the human condition'. This love, we apparently all experience, is a rational, charitable and generous love, whereas with nationalism it is an 'exclusive attachment' (Viroli 1995, 184 and 2).

First, what is meant here by love – as in 'love of country'? Love implies more than just affection, liking, fondness or tenderness – although it *is* still linked with these. Love is an attachment, but not all attachments are love-based. Further, love is not just feeling or emotion. It has a cognitive component. Some would also associate love with sexuality – depending on what is meant by sexuality. However, most commentators agree that love is a much larger issue than sexuality. The root problem is that the English word *love* covers many things. There are though certain more formal themes which run through all discussions of the concept. Thus, from Greek thought, there is 'eros' (a yearning for satisfaction at any level, not just sexual or physical love), 'philia' (friendship of equals) and 'agape' (a selfless or self-sacrificing love). In Latin there are three rather more blurred terms for love: *caritas*, *dilectio* and *amor*.

Anders Nygren famously saw *three* major religious perspectives having differing conceptions of love – Hellenism, Judaism and Christianity – as manifesting eros, nomos and agape (Nygren 1982). Eros, at its height, is found in ancient Greek thought and early non-Christian religions. Probably, it is most perfectly expressed in Plato's dialogue the *Symposium* (Plato 1971).[22] Eros implies an acquisitive longing for a higher, transcendental level of being – stretching from sensual longings up to the intelligible world of Platonic ideas. Ultimately, in the above Platonic dialogue, the self moves from sensual beauty to the soul's contemplation of the idea of the 'absolutely beautiful'. This is not a 'giving' notion of love. Eros remains largely egocentric, in terms of an orientation or desire. It is a longing for union with an object which will fulfil the promise of self-completion. Love is thus the quest for completeness. It presupposes incompleteness and desire. It implies a lover, an ego, who remains self-centred and seeks fulfilment in the other. The Greek conception of God is not therefore based on love, since love implies insufficiency and imperfection. Love as Philia also existed in Greek thought. Yet, Philia had no initial philosophical implications. It denoted affection, including friendship and family feeling. It was not concerned with the inner nature or drives of human beings. For Nygren, Judaism looked at love in terms of obedience. The agent attains loving fellowship with God through obedience to the law (nomos).

Agape – a word little used in ancient Greek thought – is largely God's self-sacrificing love of humanity, revealed in Jesus Christ. It is outside the range of natural possibilities; rather, it is revealed to us. It is theocentric and selfless. It can flow through us, but it is not 'ours'. We only love, according to I John. 4, 19, 'because he first loved us'. Agape therefore came, largely, to express Jesus' teaching.[23] Love of neighbour is being responsible for her, because she is made in the image of God. Such love is unselfish, sacrificial, freely given, irrespective of value or merit. Agape *creates* value in its object. It does not depend on affection, friendship, attractiveness, fondness or even attachment. Agape does not seek a response. In one sense, it also has ties with justice. It entails putting oneself in another's shoes or treating like cases alike. Western thought has tended to mix these various traditions on love.

Second, to whom or what is love applicable? There is a strong sense, in ordinary discourse, that to speak of love usually implies the existence of a particular person or persons. When we love, there is a sense that we focus on a particular person or, at least, a particular sentient creature. To love, and be loved, implies that 'the loved', minimally, has sentient interests, or some elements of personality. Therefore, can we love the non-sentient? We often say we love a car, the sea, boats, home, beer or a landscape.[24] Yet, is this anything more than a figure of speech? Can one literally love non-sentient or inanimate objects? We can have strong concerns about inanimate objects, but it is difficult to see why this is described as love. The convinced animist or pantheist might find this possible, but otherwise it seems risible. Loving a country, state or liberty, in this context, does sound distinctly strange. Does 'loving a country' mean we have a strong cognitive and emotive attachment to fifty million people, or the collective persona of fifty million? Can we love non-sentient customs, language or culture? Viroli himself suggests, at one point, that we can only really love particulars. Only saints rise above the particular. Yet, what has this particular love got to do with basic political loyalty? An inexplicable jump is made in the discussion from 'love of particular' (friend, family member or spouse) *to* 'love of country'.

Yet, even stranger, can a country or republic love me – as Viroli suggests?[25] Does a republic possess a personality capable of loving and can it really perform such intimate feats? Would one want it to perform them? This is all utterly baffling. I can offer no insight here, except to register – if we think about it for one moment – the extreme oddity of the phrase 'love of country', in terms of what most of us, in our ordinary existence, usually mean by love, qua particular children, parents or friends. It is unsettling that such otherwise intelligent and perceptive people should go on using the phrase, unless, as suggested, it is either a vacuous figure of speech or rhetorical flourish with no precise meaning at all.

Third, if there are different senses of love, as outlined above, how do they affect the objects or subjects of love? One key to the problem with patriotism – as love of country – may well lie in the difference between Greek eros and Christian agape. Greek eros, as argued, retains the person. It is a love which identifies with a form of satisfaction of the self in a higher and intelligible idea. The self is retained in a desire for greater completeness. However, in agape, in its highest form, there is a complete giving up of the self – a 'dying to the self' in St. Paul. The central theme is that God so loved the world that he 'gave up' his only son. Self-sacrifice and martyrdom are written into the Christian psyche via love. This love is theocentric and selfless. Its source is divine grace. We do not deserve anything as such. We are not worthy to be loved or to love. The giving up of the self to love one's enemy is the most perfect love (agape). It is exemplified most perfectly in the life of Christ (*Imitatio Christi*). This perfect love remains essentially mystical, emanating, as it does, from the divine not from humanity.

If we transpose the above claims onto patriotism, as love of country, then, in the Greek or Roman worlds, *patria*, understood through eros, meant that the self was retained, but that the polis or republic, in its most perfected form, embodied a telos, which provided a higher form of rational satisfaction or well-being for the self. In fact, the love of the polis or republic was love of the purpose and idea of the polis. This was equated with reason, balance and the true satisfaction of the person. This also allowed a distinction between the good and bad commonwealth or republic. However, if one viewed 'love of country' in the context of Christian agape, then something quite different occurs. There is, of course, not one Christian response here. In writers such as St. Augustine, there is a clear appreciation of the point that the earthly *patria* is an inappropriate vessel for love. In this case, the Christian abandons the earthly states and stresses that God's kingdom, a love that surpasses all *patria*, is primary. This is, partly, Tolstoy's Christian anarchist path.

The other path is to accept (contrary to Augustine) that Christian virtue is compatible with life in the *patria*.[26] However, this can imply transposing the self-sacrificing agape onto the *patria*. This produces a totally different patriotism to the Hellenistic or Roman. *Patria* did in fact become deeply and subtly linked to Christianity in the medieval period. Agape, *per se*, does not expect happiness. It anticipates pain and possible martyrdom as part of this love. It does not expect personal satisfaction, qua eros. This is the odd attraction, for many, in Christ's death. He was rejected; a man of sorrow acquainted with grief. When this self-sacrificing love is transposed to *patria* (the earthly *patria* taking on the accoutrements of the heavenly), then the love of country can also demand self-sacrifice. In the Church of England hymnal there is still an exaltation to this love sung every 'Remembrance Sunday'. In the words of the hymn, 'The Two Fatherlands', this is 'the love that asks no questions, the love which stands the test, That lays upon the altar the dearest and the best … The love that makes undaunted the final sacrifice'. Love of country means that the *patria* can expect this final personal sacrifice from us. The logic of this process was aided and abetted by the deeply seductive divinizing of *patria*, via the popes and then national monarchies, from the twelfth and thirteenth century onwards. When the first national monarchies (such as Henry VIII's or Elizabeth I's in England) claimed imperial independent sovereign status for themselves, it was as direct successors to the divine imperial power of Roman emperors and popes. Divine authorization flowed through all of these.

Whether one examines the divine imperial monarchies, absolutist states or quasi-spiritualized national states from the seventeenth to the twentieth centuries, the basic elements of this sanctification of the *patria* are present. Christ's agape is the inner purpose, drive and energy of Christianity in Europe and elsewhere. This *is* intrinsically part of the rich continuing attraction of Christianity. It appeals to a deep-rooted idea within us and provides a spiritual rendering of its significance: to die for one's children, family, friends, or community, prioritizing their survival and well-being over our own, is the highest of all sacrifices, which cannot but move us – no matter how grudgingly. Communal or family self-sacrifice – the defence imperative – links up with the cosmic principle of Christianity, the God who sacrifices himself for us. The whole phraseology of patriotism thus becomes spiritualized. We have now lost pretty much all of the original 'eros' conception of love – although it is this which underpins the Hellenistic and one suspects early Roman Republican love of *patria*. We would be hard put now to make much sense of the idea that to love implies incompleteness, imperfection and lack of satisfaction. We are the offspring of a different tradition. If the *patria* 'loves us' (as Viroli suggests), and if we emulate that love (*imitatio patria*), we must be prepared to give our selves (via agape) unquestioningly to *patria*. We must be prepared, in love, to sacrifice our bodies and selves on the altar of *patria*. The citizen soldier's death for *patria* becomes therefore a beatification.

Patriotism and reason of state

For Viroli, Mazzini anticipated a corruption of language with regard to patriotism. He notes that 'in the Europe of Monarchies, the "principle of nationality" was corrupted into a "mean nationalism"; a politics of sheer force and interest replaced a politics of free and spontaneous development'. For Viroli, this was the victory of *raison d'état* against the politics of the republic and patriotism (Viroli 1995, 156). Contrary to Viroli's assessment, there is a profoundly subtle link between patriotism, the above religious themes and reason of state argument. In Christian thought, whether in republican, absolutist or liberal democratic state theory, in the nineteenth and twentieth centuries patriotism implied a self-sacrificing love. It was impossible for any of these theories to recover the Greek sense of love. Christianized virtue and love inevitably predominated. The survival of the *patria* was given a priority, partly because the *patria* was an encompassing political entity (a sovereign state), but, more importantly because it had a spiritual imprimatur.[27] Survival of the spiritual *patria*, as a priority, gives clear and unambiguous *reason of state*. Patriotism is thus, at root, an obedience to an hypostasized spiritual reason. The defence and survival of *patria* are a religious duty.

It is too easy to caricature 'reason of state'. There are three general ways in which it can be understood. The first and most unrefined way is what Friedrich Meinecke calls a 'materialistic ability for calculation'. A crude form of instrumentalism inhabits this conception (Meinecke 1957, 194). This is the reason of state which is considered in terms of pure expediency and power. Political survival means that any regime will wish to survive and any type of action is permissible for survival. This is the most caricatured understanding of Machiavellianism, as equivalent to political opportunism and cynicism. It presumes there is no morality between states, only power, cunning and political endurance. The second view maintains that the ultimate value of reason of state argument is the well-being and health of the whole state – including therefore the well-being of the whole people. It is not expediency, but a form of political realism in a brutal world. Certain acts have to be performed for the good of the state and well-being of the whole people. Many exponents of reason of state were not, for Meinecke, just crude amoral manipulators, but rather public servants who performed actions for (what they perceived to be) reasons which were most conducive to the survival and well-being of the state.

The third conception of reason of state relates to the origins of the term, which incorporate the religious dimension of *patria*. The sovereign authority of *patria* was the source of justice and law. The *patria*, with its authoritative sovereign, is an imperfect image of God's *patria*. The ends of the *patria* are intrinsically religiously legitimated. The sovereign, especially, is seen as the personification of the state and the linchpin for order and well-being. Whatever are the *interests* of the sovereign (whatever shape or form that executive takes) are in the *interests* of the state and are thus compatible with Christian values. In this sense, there is no division between political realism and morality. This is precisely the argument for patriotism. The *patria* embodies public authority. The good of the *patria* (and sovereign) and the good of religion amount to the same thing.[28] Spiritualized reason of state provides *patria* (and patriotism) with a transcendent gloss, which, although flaky at the edges, has never quite worn off during the nineteenth and twentieth centuries. The continuity of the state is still surrounded with a mystique. The more overt patina of religiosity may have worn off the surface of the state, thus more purportedly secularizing forces have filled the gaps – nationalism and revivified secular patriotism are the most obvious examples. Yet, the banal symbolism and emotive rhetoric of both nationalism and patriotism still retain the underlying force of the spiritual or mystical dimension of the state.

The major difference between nationalism and patriotism is that patriotism (or at least the devotion to *patria*) does have a much longer etymological and practical history.[29] Further, patriotism has a much stronger intellectual connection to the state, and reason of state, than nationalism. This connection to the state (which some interpret as a positive good qua constitutional or republican patriotism as distinct from asphyxiating nationalism) is, in fact, part of the distinctive mark of patriotism. Patriotism, as love of country, captures a tragic duality within the state. The state is both a legal abstraction embodying, in the same moment, a multiplicity of quite brutal powers – whether in the republic, sovereign person or representative constitutional democracy – and moral and religious themes which inspire love and self-sacrifice. The work of state is, officially or unofficially, apparently, *opus divinum*. The state, as well as being a remote abstraction, is still an object of awe, and thus actions of state, even if overtly evil, are nonetheless worthy of devotion, love and obedience. Reason of state and patriotism together encapsulate this tragic duality.

Conclusion

What is the relationship between nationalism and patriotism? It is tempting to adopt the sceptical view of Michael Billig, namely, that '"Our" nationalism is not presented as nationalism, which is dangerously irrational, surplus and alien. A new identity, a different label, is found for it. "Our" nationalism appears as "patriotism" – a beneficial, necessary and, often, American force' (Billig 1995, 55). For many contemporary statements of patriotism this is the usual spurious logic. However, there are negative and positive arguments for both separating and fusing nationalism and patriotism. The *positive* statement for their fusion is contained in a stronger statement of communal identity. Both concepts are seen as powerful statements of the ontological priority of the moral community. The positive view thus involves the direct normative assimilation of the two languages to communitarian themes – the 'positive assimilation model'. The *negative* reading of the fusion – the 'mutually disagreeable model' – views both terms with equal contempt as 'blots' on political discourse. The positive reading of the separation can be found in a number of recent writers, but it has been most forcibly rendered by neo-classical republican writers. This is a flawed model relying upon a series of highly suspect assumptions. The negative reading of their separation has not really been articulated. The present argument opts, nonetheless, for separating patriotism and nationalism on negative grounds. The concepts are different, but they are both equally to be mistrusted, for different reasons.

Before moving to summarize my argument, there is one important parallel between patriotism and nationalism which is worth noting. Both concepts rehearse the universality and particularity of the modern state.[30] Both the United States and France have produced their own versions of this point. In France and America, patriotism (and nationalism by default) contain strong claims for the universality of their own particularity. The particularisms of patriotism and nationalism are thus conflated with the universal. In trying to overcome micro-localism, both concepts can often, unwittingly or wittingly, provide part of the logic for internationalism. At it most stark, liberal democracy or republican democracy, as practised in France or North America, ought to be the model for *all* other societies to follow. This is an ideal thesis for neo-colonialism and empire, as well as more benign conceptions of human rights, but it also raises many paradoxes which will continue plaguing us in the new century.

What is significant about patriotism? Patriotism, as a concept and practice, does have an identifying tag which makes it different to nationalism. But this tag does not make it a more acceptable idea. In this chapter it has been argued that patriotism is a compound concept containing three important unresolved dimensions: first, 'local emotive identification'. This is often given the title 'love of country'. Nineteenth and twentieth century usage of patriotism, which originates from the late medieval period, contains an unwitting if powerful hangover of religious language. The use of the word 'love' is supposed to make it a cognitively 'reasonable' or civilized emotion.[31] However, what actually happened is that a Christianized conception of love took over the 'love of country' dimension. This is the 'love' which we know in state patriotism (*pro patria mori*) and it is not the same as the Greek conception. Nationalism shares this emotive dimension, although it is far more a creature of modernism and secularism. Modernity often translates patriotism into nationalism, but the etymological and 'meaning traces' of the two concepts are distinct.

Second, there is the aspect of 'abstract legal entitlement' attached to patriotism. This is the usage which has close connections with the Roman republican use of the term. Roman thought introduced a notion of legal citizenship and abstract entitlement (*legalis homo*). *Patria* not only had particular local identification, but also more abstract legal connections to wider frameworks, like the *res publica*. It is the law which makes the person. In fact, the more abstracted juridical Roman notion of citizenship has the same root as this legalistic conception of patriotism. Patriotism, as it developed in the medieval, early modern and modern periods, retains this juristic dimension, but it also blends it with moral and religious themes. Citizens do not normally die for an abstract legal norm. Nationalism again, qua nationality law, has a similar usage to patriotism, although the juristic character is not so clear or obvious. Patriotism thus has a definite juristic dimension which is missing within much nationalist discussion.

Third, patriotism is always 'politically defined', as in the American and French revolutions – neither of which was initially nationalist in intent. It also links closely with the development of the state from the late medieval period. The state is in fact the key issue. Patriotism, with its strong statist, religious and emotive connotations, meshes closely here with the doctrine of 'reason of state'. Reason of state blends seamlessly both with the religious interest in *patria*, and with the survival and continuity of the state. Work for *patria* is *opus divinum*. Reason of state *is* patriotism in action. Nationalism does not have such an articulate statist content. It also has no necessary close or overt connections with religious or reason of state language. Patriotism, despite what its republican defenders might try to suggest, has no necessary connection at all with democracy. In fact, patriotism has little necessary connection with republicanism. The separation between patriotism and nationalism is thus true, but patriotism is a concept and practice that we should also be deeply suspicious about. It is not an intrinsically civilizing concept. The positive valorization of patriotism (qua republicanism) in recent years is thus a false dawn, a new myth to replace the older ones.

6   Communitarianism

Patriotism, as we have seen in the previous chapter, has been canvassed as an alternative to nationalism, enabling, for some of its republican proponents, a philosophical link to be made between the particular and the universal. Yet, there is a language resonant with nationalism – which also comes under the same critical scrutiny from some republican patriotic discourse – and that is communitarianism. Some contemporary communitarians have indeed claimed their beliefs as both republican and patriotic. Yet, for many other civic republicans, both nationalists and communitarians are tarred with the same particularistic brush. One might therefore expect that communitarianism would share a great deal with nationalism. Both appear, *prima facie*, very much alike. Consequently, a sophisticated contemporary nationalist commentator, David Miller, notes, without any hesitation, that 'nations are the only possible form in which overall community can be realized in modern societies' (Miller 1992, 93 and Miller 1994, 245). Modern communitarianism can, at first glance, virtually become another face of modern nationalism. Despite the fact that it is generally recognized that nationalism trades upon, or at least, has a close relation with communitarianism, a number of puzzling questions still remain. Is communitarianism really the same as, or a broader phenomenon than, nationalism? Or, alternatively, is nationalism the moral and intellectual basis for communitarianism?

Communitarianism has spawned a large body of literature since the 1980s. This present chapter will not deal with this literature in any great depth. The focus is rather on one specific question: what is the relation between nationalism and communitarianism? Despite some overt particularistic affinities between these two doctrines, there is also a paucity of reflection on their precise relation (O'Neill 1994, Archard 1996 and Vincent 1997b). This chapter analyses the relation, taking cognisance of both the affinities and differences. In one sense, the discussion is a ground clearing or clarifying exercise. However, another undercurrent runs through the latter part of the discussion, namely, an underlying unease that both doctrines fail to address adequately another issue of late modernity – pluralism. Minimally, however, it is possible to examine communitarianism as embodying an ambiguous transitional vision, an uneasy *via media* between two distinct particularisms – nationalism and multiculturalism. On the one hand, it still retains a nostalgia for the universal, on the other hand, it moves into a more unsettled, fragmented vision than nationalism.

After some introductory remarks concerning the concepts of community and communitarianism, the second section considers five basic affinities between contemporary communitarianism and nationalism. These form the basic groundwork for any immediate judgement we might make concerning the relation between these doctrines. The third section turns to divergences between the doctrines. In the fourth section, two of these divergences are focused on more intensively. The first examines the communitarian nostalgia for a form of universalism. The second focuses on the more equivocal fragmentation of communities.

Communities

This first section considers the following questions: who are the communitarians? Second, what is meant by the term community? Third, what do nationalists and communitarians think about their apparent relation?

The first question focuses on the innocuous issue of identification: who are the proponents of communitarianism. At first glance, communitarianism appeared in 1980s academic political theory. It derived much of its initial sustenance from a negative reaction to a more procedural version of liberalism. It was thus initially a philosophical movement associated with the work of Michael Sandel, Charles Taylor, Michael Walzer and Alasdair MacIntyre. By the 1990s, it began, for some, to mature into a political and more policy-orientated movement, appealing across the political spectrum, and attracting some supportive verbal interest from the Clinton and Gore Democrat administration in North America and the New Labour administration in Britain, amongst others. It also has some fugitive connections with the late 1990s interest in third way politics in Europe and North America.

When political theorists use the term communitarianism, what they usually have in mind is the *oeuvres* of the above four thinkers. The oddity of this point is that none of the above want to be associated with communitarianism. MacIntyre, for example, has quite clearly repudiated the label.[1] Amitai Etzioni, the leading light in recent North American communitarianism, identifies MacIntyre as a distinct category – a 'moderate social conservative' (Etzioni 1997, 15). He also notes that Sandel, Taylor and Walzer have all 'been uncomfortable with the label "communitarian"' (Etzioni 1997, 40). Walzer, for example, is ambivalent, but is content to see his work as a 'periodic communitarian correction'

(Walzer 1990). Sandel, in his most recent book, *Democracy's Discontents* (1996), does not mention it. Charles Taylor has also expressed his deep unease with the term as an identification for his work (Taylor 1994, 250 and 256). Minimally, we are faced with an odd scenario here. A very large body of secondary literature is associated with these four philosophical mentors – and overtly trades upon them as committed communitarians – yet only one of them is prepared to indirectly and hesitantly subscribe to the term, and the majority appear hostile or indifferent. Admittedly, it is still possible to override their views and argue that all the above theorists still subscribe, wittingly or not, to a number of theses which are recognisably communitarian. This is admittedly more convenient and easier for the critical commentator. However, the above autobiographical points should make us at least pause. At what point can we say that a philosophical movement exists?

The other dimension of communitarianism, which most political theorists do not usually focus on, is the more practical-minded or policy-orientated movement, which developed in the 1990s. These are the individuals who have no problems with the label. They proudly proclaim it. In North America the most well known are the Communitarian Network and Center for Communitarian Policy Studies. Its key spokesman and chair (of the latter organization) is Amitai Etzioni. 1990s communitarians have developed their own organizations, journals, web site and also cultivated some minimal political appeal. In Britain, the United Kingdom Communitarian Forum (set up in 1995) is less voluble than its American counterpart. One of its recent spokesmen and chair is Henry Tam (Tam 1998).[2] In terms of the literature, Etzioni has contributed a number of more popular texts, like *The Spirit of Community* and *The New Golden Rule*; however, Robert Bellah, and the group who co-wrote *Habits of the Heart*, catch the more practical and heartfelt moral appeal of this communitarianism. The opening sentence of the book sets the tone of the ongoing discussion 'How ought we to live? ... Who are we, as Americans?' (Bellah *et al* 1996, vii). The bulk of the book is taken up with very earnest, practical, policy-orientated discussions on families, education, crime, policing, local communities, and so forth. The practical anxiety is premised on the judgement that 'most Americans agree that things are seriously amiss in our society – that we are not, as the poll questions often put it, "headed in the right direction"' (Bellah *et al* 1996, xxii).[3] In the context of the above discussion there is, therefore, some difficulty in identifying who are the communitarians. The secondary political theory literature, almost totally, concentrates on a small group of four philosophers, who repudiate the label. Those who overtly write, campaign and advocate it are largely ignored.

The second issue focuses on what is meant by the term community? This will be returned to again later in the discussion. Historically, the concept community, and its place in political discussion, is comparatively recent. Spectres of the coherent, consensual community have haunted European social and political thinkers over the past two centuries. Eighteenth and nineteenth century commentators identified the concept of community as a special category. Characteristically, it usually appears in terms of a contrast between two forms of group: a more artificial form and a more 'natural' or 'organic' entity. G. W. F. Hegel, for example, characteristically set the idea of an ethical communal state against a rootless and fragmented civil society. Edmund Burke distinguished a hierarchical, organic, traditional and stable community from an anomic, democratically levelled and individualistically orientated conception. Samuel Taylor Coleridge held similar views to Burke, namely, a division between a commercially orientated individualistic society and traditional organic, pastoral communities. This was also reflected again in the twentieth century political writings of T. S. Eliot, Charles Maurras and Christopher Dawson. Henry Maine distinguished status and contract-based societies. In Herbert Spencer, it was the militant as against the naturally evolved organic industrial society and in Wilhelm Wundt, natural and cultural groups. At the close of the nineteenth and beginning of the twentieth century, the most famous rendition of the distinction was Ferdinand Tönnies' contrast between community and association – *Gemeinschaft* and *Gesellschaft* – also echoed in R. M. MacIver's distinction between communal and associated groups, Otto von Gierke's *Genossenschaft* and *Herrschaft* groups and Émile Durkheim's mechanical and organic solidarity. The same kind of contrasts have gone on appearing in mid to late twentieth century theories. The social and psychological theories of, for example, Abraham Maslow, Herbert Marcuse and Erich Fromm are also punctuated by these familiar contrasts.[4] In all these contrasts, community usually, though not always, appears as more natural, consensual, familiar, organic and coherent.[5]

However, community language has also suffered from its cryptic mid-twentieth century association with movements like fascism, national socialism and corporatist authoritarianism. In fact, communitarianism was absorbed into a more general suspicion of mid-twentieth century nationalism – nationalism being an exemplar of the communitarian impulse. Sociological and political thinkers, such as Ralph Dahrendorf and Friedrich Hayek, tended to view all communitarian ideas as potentially illiberal, reactionary and disturbing (Plant 1976, 33–4). Vigorous critiques by political theorists, such as Stephen Holmes in the 1990s, have traded quite openly upon this liberal suspicion of communitarianism as a single problematic category, linking, for example, MacIntyre directly with a tradition including ultramontanist conservatives, such as Joseph de Maistre, and national socialists *manqué*, such as Carl Schmitt (Holmes 1993). However, when one examines the literary output of

Sandel, MacIntyre, Walzer or Taylor, or the more policy-orientated work of Bellah or Etzioni, terms such as moderate, republican and liberal are surely more appropriate.

Despite the above liberal suspicion, in the closing two decades of the twentieth century, the older eighteenth and nineteenth century images of the ethical, coherent community once again gained intellectual currency. Why this took place is debatable. In one reading, increasing mobility, globalization, the unpredictable effects of market-based liberal policies, rampant atomized individualism and consumerism, rapid technological change, social disruption, changing employment patterns, and the like, have led to a subtle but worrying loss of social cohesion. Deindustrialization has led to the creation of a large anomic underclass in most industrialized societies. Social capital – defined as networks of norms within institutions that facilitate cooperation and mutual benefit – has also been seen to wane (Bellah *et al*, 1996, xvi). For communitarians, there has been a consequent weakening of civic consciousness and civic engagement. For Robert Bellah and his fellow authors, 'we have moved from the local life of the nineteenth century – in which economic and social relationships were visible and, however imperfectly, morally interpreted as parts of a larger common life – to a society vastly more interrelated and integrated economically, technically and functionally. Yet this is a society in which the individual can only rarely and with difficulty understand himself and his activities as interrelated in morally meaningful ways' (Bellah *et al*, 1996, 50). In recent literature, this fragmentation has now acquired the dubious appellation 'detraditionalization' (Heelas *et al*, 1996). Ironically, postmodern, poststructuralist, some multiculturalists and difference theorists see such processes as inevitable and in fact desirable. For communitarians, however, they are a matter of anxiety.

Overall, community is a non-specific term. It connotes broadly a manner of social being that purportedly is more natural. It usually implies some form of fellowship and intimacy. In a community, individuals find, apparently, a deeper collective identity and purpose. However, there are three overlapping cautionary points to note. First, community, *per se*, has no distinctive ideological complexion. It can be found in the mildest of left anarchisms and the most virulent of fascisms. It is an open concept. Communitarians themselves occasionally make a dubious virtue of this, suggesting that their appeal is across the political spectrum (Tam 1998). Secondly, there is a wide recognition that the term 'natural' is misleading and ambiguous. Many now recognize the artifice of both community and nation. The term 'natural' is added to provide gravitas and moral lustre to a human construction. Thirdly, there are clearly stronger and weaker senses of communitarianism. The stronger sense is usually premised on a belief in a more objective, political, moral or cultural order. The kind of society envisaged is more directly homo-geneous. The individual self, in this stronger sense, is merged into the social structure. Such a notion, for its detractors, is difficult to uphold in an advanced industrial scenario with rapid social, political and economic change and mobility (Plant, Lesser and Taylor-Gooby (eds) 1980, 243). In addition, there is a sense that the stronger order can either be foolishly nostalgic or just deeply reactionary. Exponents of a weaker community have often limited its application to encouraging active citizenship and generalized commitments to a common culture. In this sense there are direct parallels with the weaker understanding of both republicanism and liberal nationalism. The individual self is not totally submerged in the community in this scenario and can retain other allegiances, although the overall community is still of prior and overarching im-portance. Most of the recent expositions of communitarianism, in the philosophical and practical arenas, have tended to adopt the 'weaker' format. Critics, on the other hand, usually assume that the stronger variant is at issue.

Third, what do nationalists and communitarians think about their relation? For the sake of argument, I will take both the philosophers and more policy-orientated practitioners as communitarian. One general point can be made here, namely, that there is still a background in-difference to this question amongst many writers. Thus, many take the affinity between nationalism and communitarianism for granted. This would certainly be the case on the nationalist side of the equation. David Miller, for example, comments in his 1995 book *On Nationality*, that 'liberalism versus nationalism may be a specific instance of what is frequently now regarded as a more general contest between liberals and communitarians. It turns out that, if there is a contest here at all, it occurs at the level of justifying theory rather than at the level of political principle: most "communitarians" adopt recognizably liberal political positions'. In other words, nationalism (or 'nationality' as Miller prefers) translates directly and unproblematically into the language of communi-tarianism. Similarly, Yael Tamir also notes that her 1993 book, *Liberal Nationalism*, 'takes liberal theory as its starting point, it attempts to "translate" nationalist arguments into liberal language. In so doing it relies on the current terms of communitarian discourse, which is akin to the nationalist one in its content' (Miller 1995b, 193; Tamir 1993, 14).

The case is slightly different for conservative and fascist nationalists, but the same indifference is present. It is taken as self-evident that the only viable community *is* the nation. However, the concept of community is premised on a belief in a prepolitical objective natural order. It cannot be invented or imposed. This idea of being pre-established and un-available to 'reasoned alteration' is central to conservative thought. In this sense, we encounter a very strong reading of community. The community of the nation is considered organically. The organic analogy conveys the idea that society is a mutually dependent interrelation of parts. Each individual has a place in the organism. This implies, for most conservatives, a natural hierarchy and inequality of status. The organic analogy also indicates an insular sense of community, which looks outward fearfully and suspiciously. The conservative political theorist Roger Scruton argues, for example, for the necessity of deep-rooted prejudice to maintain a community.[6] Recent communitarians are consequently criticized by him for being lukewarm and weak-minded over community. Thus, apparently, 'none of them is prepared to accept the real price of community: which is sanctity, intolerance, exclusion, and a sense that life's meaning depends upon obedience, and also on vigilance against the enemy' (Scruton 1990, 310). Strong communal identity also forms a crucial motif in fascist and national socialist ideology in the twentieth century. No humans, *per se*, exist, only Germans, Frenchmen or Italians, and so forth.[7] This more insular and xenophobic use of community is already integral to some conservative theories. Further, as in conservatism, true identity is found in the community of the nation and the nation is prior to the individual and any rights they might possess.[8]

However, what do communitarians think about nationalism? The case here is not so clear.[9] There is undoubtedly some sensitivity to this question, although it is an oddly muted and unfocused concern. However, if one examines some of the well-known synoptic texts and discussions of philosophical communitarianism during the 1980s, it is significant that there is very little or no reference to nationalism in this first enthusiastic flush.[10] In the late 1990s, the case changed slightly. My own view is that in some cases there was an hypostasized identification of community and nation. This can be clearly observed in MacIntyre's discussion of patriotism, in 'Is Patriotism a Virtue?' (1984), where patriotism, nationalism and community are all elided. In others, there appears to be a different understanding of the concept of community, which is never really spelt out – thus enhancing the overall ambiguity of the issue. In the more policy-orientated communitarians, the issue also remains puzzling. Etzioni, for example, in contending that MacIntyre should be considered as a social conservative, goes on to argue that 'nationalism has long been a powerful, often overpowering, source of secular conservatives' ideologies'. In an effort to clearly distinguish social conservatism from communitarianism, Etzioni therefore suggests that social conservatives want to force virtue on a population, whereas genuine communitarians emphasize education and reasonable persuasion – relying on what he refers to as 'the moral voice of the community'.[11] Thus, Etzioni suggests that nationalism is a factor within social and authoritarian conservatism, not communitarianism. Etzioni's argument is supported, in part, by a later claim – which will be taken up again – that actual communities are more internally diverse and this again does not gel with nationalism.[12]

However, this is not a wholly consistent picture. The *Habits of the Heart* book presents a different reading. For the authors, the politics of the nation is viewed positively in America, as part of a more complex vision incorporating local consensual and interest-based politics. The authors admit that the nation-idea is experienced symbolically and 'less in the practices of everyday life', yet, 'the sense of being part of a living national community colors the meaning of life' (Bellah *et al*, 1996, 201–2). Earlier in the book, this politics of the nation is directly associated with a 'community of memory'. For the authors, there is a national community of memory 'defined by its history and by the character of its representative leaders from John Winthrop to Martin Luther King Jr. Americans identify with their national community because there is little else that we can all share in common'.[13] In a later chapter the national idea is also equated with a sense of a 'public good' and 'public virtue', thus, 'because we share a common tradition, certain habits of the heart, we can work together'. However, the authors also contend that there is an ongoing unresolved tension in American society between private interest and public good. The fear behind their book is that the private is beginning to swallow up the public – 'the citizen has been swallowed up in "economic man"' – public virtue and the national have to be recovered and managed with the private interest (Bellah *et al*, 1996, ch. 10, especially 251–2, 254–5, 256, 260ff). In sum, the nation is a positive republican and virtue-based idea which embodies a positive collective memory. Community is thus associated with the nation, but, for the authors, it is also associated with small town politics. Nation is not, qua Etzioni, associated with conservative politics.

Affinities

In summary of the previous section: first, there are deep ambiguities as to who we associate with communitarianism. Second, the terms community and communitarianism are indeterminate. Minimally, weaker and stronger variants should be distinguished, but even this distinction does not encapsulate the complexity. Third, the relation between 'nation' and 'community' remains contested and enigmatic, even amongst nationalists and communitarians. It is, however, less problematic for the bulk of nationalist theorists who tend to see the only adequate overall community as the nation; but for communitarians the whole issue is much more muddled.

Why is it therefore that many often see a synonymity between national-ism and communitarianism? The answer is relatively straightforward. It relies upon an underlying particularist ontology, which pays little atten-tion to variations. Thus, at first glance, there are quite definite philo-sophical resonances between nationalism and communitarianism which might make the doctrines look synonymous. Five formal themes can be identified: the embeddedness of human nature; a mutual anxiety about a particular species of liberalism; a thesis concerning the role of pre-understandings in human judgement; the demand to respect com-munities as valuable entities; and, finally, the claim that ethics – par-ticularistic ethics – can be found in both. Many of these themes will be reviewed quickly since they have already been touched upon in previous chapters.

First, the structural embeddedness theme asserts that humans are intrinsically social beings. These social beings find their idiosyncratic roles, values and beliefs from within nations *or* communities, which are the most fundamental social units. The outcomes of such social agency might be very diverse, since different nations' and communities' units will give rise to different value systems, but the conditions within which humans establish their differences are nonetheless common to the species. Humans are – to use the favoured terminology – 'constituted' by com-munities. For modern communitarians it is therefore a core thesis (which they share with nationalists) that the self is embedded in the com-munity. In Michael Sandel's phraseology, there are no 'unencumbered selves' standing outside a community frame. There is no sense, therefore, that one could speak of human nature outside of a community. Thus, for Sandel, we cannot adopt the stance of the early Rawlsian original position, because it makes the unwarranted metaphysical assumption of the unencumbered self. There is no Archimedean point.[14] If we cannot accept this unanchored insubstantial Rawlsian self, then it follows that we have no grounds for accepting the two principles of justice. Thus, in the Sandelian view, Rawls presupposes an implausible account of the moral subject, which is the logical prerequisite for the impartiality of justice. Life in the polis and citizenship precede any sense we might have of our unique human individuality. Liberal politics, in the Rawlsian mode (or even more so in the Nozickian mode), lacks any coherent communal underpinning. This argument is also echoed in Alisdair MacIntyre's central theme of a narrative conception of the self, a self which is consti-tuted, in part, from the history and telos of the community (MacIntyre 1981). In *After Virtue*, MacIntyre looks to a modernized Aristotle for diagnoses of the sickness in liberal society. For him, virtue rests on character and character rests on the shared embedded understandings of a community.

Nationalist writers also place a very heavy emphasis on this embedded claim. All humans are 'encumbered' by their nations. Neil MacCormick, consequently, advocates a social, embedded or contextual individualism, as against an atomistic individualism. In fact, he suggests that the more atomistic liberal concept, which allows individuals to form their own sense of the good life, is deeply implausible.[15] He states: 'The truth about human beings is that they can only become individuals – acquire a sense of their own individuality – as a result of their social experiences within human communities' (MacCormick 1982, 247). In David Miller, similarly, national identity also forms an essential part of personal identity. Miller, as already noted, explicitly associates his embedded thesis with communitarianism, noting approvingly that Rawls' 'failure to investigate the sense of community that his principles of justice presuppose forms the basis for Michael Sandel's critique' (Miller 1995b, 94, n. 18). However, it is clear that Miller, for one, wishes to dissociate himself from the stronger communitarianism of conservatism and fascism. Yet, he is still keen to assert that nationality is 'constituted by mutual belief, extended in history, active in character, connected with a particular territory, and thought to be marked off from other communities by its members' distinct traits [these] … serve to distinguish nationality from other collective sources of personal identity' (Miller in Brown (ed.) 1994, 141).

A second comparative theme is a general worry about liberalism, although we should qualify this immediately and speak of a particular species of liberalism. It is not liberalism, *per se*, which is condemned.[16] This latter point should already be clear from earlier chapters, since both the modern communitarianism and nationalism, which are being addressed in this chapter, have liberal dimensions. Thus, in the case of the work of Charles Taylor, Michael Walzer, David Miller and Yael Tamir the liberalism criticized is what Taylor has referred to as a 'procedural' liberalism. Others have called this classical or atomistic liberalism. Rawls, in his own reassessment, in *Political Liberalism*, has called this version 'comprehensive', as opposed to political liberalism (Taylor in Gutman (ed.) 1994, 60).[17] Such a procedural liberalism is seen to offer an implausible view of the self, often ignoring and undermining local and cultural communities, is ethnocentric (in an unwitting manner) and makes erroneous claims about neutrality and universal rights.[18]

A third theme concerns the notion of 'pre-understandings'. Communitarians and nationalists both assume that there are shared moral and customary resources, which are not always clearly open to critical examination, but rather form a backdrop to discussion. In this reading, communities or nations are constituted by such 'pre-understandings' – which form a body of internal standards. The particularity of historical communities is set against the claims of deontic ahistorical universality. The community or nation forms the basis for practical reason, value and political judgement. In this sense, communitarians and nationalists are sceptical about certain aspects of the Enlightenment – and are also indirectly or directly sympathetic to the romantic and expressivist movements of the late eighteenth and early nineteenth century – concerning the ability of abstract universal reasoning to stand apart from social and moral traditions. Reason is substantive and situated within communities. For David Miller, for example, 'nationality is the identity we have in common, an identity in large measure inherited from the past, and not fully open to rational scrutiny' (Miller 1989b, 70). This body of shared 'attitudes, ritual observances and so forth', beyond rational scrutiny, are essential for any community (Miller 1989a, 244). Such a belief system is not conjured out of thin air. It is a deeply rooted pre-understanding.

A fourth theme is an implicit egalitarian potential in both nationalism and communitarianism – particularly in the weaker variants. Each community or nation is to be recognized equally as having a unique identity which should be respected. There is a pattern of argument here, focusing on the complex linkage between 'recognition' and 'identity', which Charles Taylor has called the 'politics of recognition'.[19] The basic idea is that identity is something which needs to be recognized in order to maintain itself. Isolated individuality does not exist, it rather develops through recognition. Denying recognition is thus a form of oppression, since it denies basic identity. We might recognize this immediately in the rights of the human individual. However, in eighteenth century writers such as Herder, the notion of identity was also linked with the *Volk* (or more loosely public culture). Being true to oneself meant being true to one's originality, which, in turn, was both a uniquely personal *and* cultural phenomenon. Herder is thus often linked to the origins of nationalist and communitarian thought. It follows that denying recognition to cultures is also oppression of identity.

One important formulation of the above argument, in relation to nations, would go as follows: individual identity is deserving of respect, since national culture or community is constitutive of individual identity (as argued in the embedded claim), national culture and communities are therefore equally deserving of respect. Constituents of individual identity which are valued, if promoted by the national culture or communities, add substance to the case for respect for communal identity. Institutional arrangements which foster such an identity and maximize the conditions of individual self-development are also deserving of respect. In addition, to fail to recognize the identity (thus the capacity for self-determination and sovereignty) of the nation is to act oppressively. There are admittedly problems here concerning communities which act illiberally.

However, the liberal nationalist and communitarian answer to this is fairly straightforward, namely, that liberalism lays down certain limits to nationalities concerning how far they can internally harm or deny basic liberties to their members. Respect would be premised on these minimal conditions being fulfilled. This constitutes the baseline to a thin communitarian universalism – which will be examined later.

Fifth, there is a strong theme concerning the ethics of nationalism and communitarianism. Both advocate a particularistic ethics which is counterposed to ethical universalism. Thus, communitarians argue that political and moral goods cannot be determined by abstract reasoning *sub specie aeternitatis*. Such 'goods' arise from particular historical communities. There are no absolute external rational foundations for ethics or the good life. There is no theory which stands totally apart from a social context. Morality is neither invented nor discovered, but interpreted as already existent. As David Miller notes, 'ethical particularism ... allows existing commitments and loyalties a fundamental place in ethical reasoning' (Miller 1989b, 68). Michael Walzer also comments that 'what we do when we argue is to give an account of the actual existing morality' (Walzer 1987, 21). For Walzer, as connected critics 'we read off an existing tradition of discourse. The community becomes the locus of the good. We do not need external theoretical foundations for a practical life, rather we draw upon the interpretations of a tradition or form of life. We cannot totally step back to assess communities, morality or justice with a view from nowhere, although we can criticize them from within using internal standards of rationality'.[20] A national culture does not, though, for Miller, have to be monolithic. It is rather a 'set of understandings about how a group of people is to conduct its life together'. Yet, for Miller, our obligations are always deeply coloured by the local ethos. Ethics can still, though, be shaped by rational debate. In the best case scenario, national identity flows from this rational reflection. However, it is still our prior obligations and loyalties which give substance to citizenship and justice concerns.[21]

Divergences

The above themes constitute a baseline for reading nationalism and communitarianism as synonymous. Despite the definite philosophical resonances between nationalism and communitarianism, the comparison cannot be taken too far. Some communitarians – rather than nationalists – are particularly uneasy with the resonance. The first point to take on board is the views of apparent communitarians in the 1990s. Second, there is the question of the manner in which both doctrines are publicly understood and read. Thirdly, there is a question concerning the theory and practice of both doctrines. Fourth, there are certain definitional divergences in the use of communitarian and nationalist language.

First, on the biographical front, it is clear from the earlier discussion that there is an ambivalence about the nation amongst communitarians. Charles Taylor, for one, writing in the early 1990s, comments that nationalism always implies a stultifying uniformity. It encourages the belief that 'unity' requires total harmony. This alone has been the major stumbling block of Canadian politics. Of course, a liberal nationalist, such as David Miller, would not agree with this portrayal of nationalism, which, for him, can accommodate plurality (Miller 1995b, 130ff). Taylor obviously does not see it this way. He describes the idea that Canada is a nation as 'our great historical misunderstanding' (Taylor quoted in Laforest 1994, 206). He continues that 'we all too easily tend to think that national unity has to be maintained against ... diversity'. Reflecting on the affinities (in some minds) between communitarianism and nationalism, Taylor notes that 'I'm unhappy with the term "communitarianism". It sounds like the critics of liberalism wanted to substitute some other all-embracing principle [like the nation]'. (Taylor in Tully (ed.) 1994, 250 and 256). Thus, if Taylor is to be classed as communitarian (and that is questionable), he clearly does not want to be equated with nationalism. Deep unease is felt about the 'over-arching' character of the nationalist 'common good'. The same basic point is made by Michael Sandel, and from a liberal and indirect communitarian standpoint, by Will Kymlicka.[22]

Second, in the bulk of the literature on nationalism – certainly in the post-1945 era – there has been, up to very recently, more unease and scepticism on the precise role of substantive nationalist discourse within political debate. Unlike communitarianism, nationalism has been regarded with both awe, for its manifest capacity to motivate whole populations, but also with profound misgiving, for its capacity for pogrom and other assorted horrors, in the name of some overarching national ethos. Scholars have thus often been more concerned to explain the pathology of the phenomenon of nationalism, rather than to engage with its substantive ideas. Modern communitarianism has not, as yet, been parsed as a pathology. Where the ideas of nationalism have been taken seriously, they are regarded as more heterogeneous than communitarianism. It is widely accepted in the literature that the ideological complexion of nationalism is both diverse and fickle. Most scholars of nationalism do not hesitate to divide it up into markedly distinct forms, for example, as in this chapter, between fascist, conservative and liberal nationalisms.[23] On the other hand, the modern communitarian movement, since its inception, has characteristically had a much more benign liberal reputation. Critics seem less able to differentiate diverse species of communitarianism.[24]

Third, the relation between theory and practice in both these doctrines remains puzzling. Whereas, on the one hand, communitarianism has, up to recently, been a movement predominantly *in* academic social science and political theory, nationalism, on the other hand, has been deeply immersed – in a very bloody and messy manner – in political practice for, minimally, two centuries. There is nothing polite, cosy or restrained about nationalism. There are, however, two further qualifications to be made here. First, there are clearly exceptions to this within recent communitarianism, although they are still, in comparison to nationalism, minuscule. Charles Taylor's active involvement in Canadian and Quebec politics, and the debates over the Meech Lake constitutional debate, have utilized communitarian theory in a somewhat idiosyncratic format.[25] Robert Bellah's (and his compatriots') detailed empirically orientated communitarian studies in *Habits of the Heart* have a strong practical aim. Sandel's more recent public sentiments concerning the recovery of communities, families and the rights of religious minorities have also been a subject of some debate. Most significantly, the work of Etzioni, mentioned earlier, and particularly the communitarian journal, *The Responsive Community*, has quite self-consciously tried to bridge the gap between communitarian theory and political practice (Etzioni 1994). Members of the latter journal's editorial team and board include William Galston, Martha Nussbaum, Mary Ann Glendon, Benjamin Barber and Nathan Glazer. The central aim of the journal is to make 'restoration of civility and commitment to the commons its core theme' (Eztioni in Walzer (ed.) 1995, 100). The main preoccupations of this journal, like Bellah's work, have been to change the moral climate of America, to encourage citizens to shoulder more responsibilities – which reaches down to very basic things such as encouraging a 'designated driver' policy to combat drunken driving, national service to 'enhance the education for and the practice of service for and to the public', sobriety checkpoints on public highways, drug testing on select groups, strengthening family life by making divorce more difficult and providing legislation to assist with education in parenting, encouraging rational political participation at all levels and shifting political discussion from rights to duties and responsibilities.[26]

A second qualification is that nationalism and communitarianism might be said to work at different theoretical levels. Thus, from one perspective, communitarianism should not be understood as a normative theory at all. It works at an interpretative and epistemological level, citing the philosophical conditions for the use of concepts such as the self and human rationality.[27] Communitarian theory is thus neither an instrumental adaptation of politics, nor an adjustment to an external reality; rather, it has a constitutive and interpretative role to play. There are no brute facts which are not permeated with interpretative assumptions and beliefs. From this perspective it is a category mistake to see communitarianism as recommending a particular substantive view of society. Communitarian political theory rather provides an articulate rendering of the unarticulated beliefs of any community. Nationalism, on the other hand, works at *both* the interpretative *and* recommendatory normative levels. Yet, against this, it would be foolhardy to suggest that communitarianism only works on an interpretative level; witness the previous point in this argument (and the still ambiguous relationship between nationalism and communitarianism). Certain studies might be said to work on an interpretative or hermeneutic level, thus ignoring the question of normative recommendation, for example, Sandel's early critique of Rawls. However, this can by no means be made as a generalization about all communitarianism. However, again, in reply to this latter point, the one small element of purchase in the distinction between nationalism and communitarian methods is the point that modern communitarian argument (unlike nationalism) does have an unmistakable Hegelian texture. Characteristically, one problem in Hegelian thought is precisely its 'normative' character. The Hegelian Owl of Minerva flies at twilight and philosophical theory always paints its grey on grey.[28] If communitarianism is interpreting the social world, can it then move into the sphere of normative recommendation? The answer would seem to be – rather like latter day Hegelianism of both left and right – that it is not philosophically warranted, but occasionally it can and does engage in normativism.

Fourthly, there are a number of definitional themes which figure urgently in nationalist discourse, which appear only marginally of interest to contemporary communitarians. Thus, nationhood is often strongly identified with a geographical territory, sovereignty and boundaries. In fact, boundaries take on very particular significance for most nationalist writers. This is the basis for arguments about legal jurisdiction and citizenship. Nations must also be free, independent and secure from external threat if peace and justice are to prevail in the international order. Further, the nation is a deep source of power (Canovan 1996). It is the ground for internal and external legitimacy. Loyalty to a nation overrides other allegiances, although the strength of this claim varies with the type of nationalism. In addition, nationalists, particularly recent liberal nationalists, have been keen to deploy arguments about self-determination. The basic argument is that if the individual has a *right* to self-determination and the constituents of the embedded individual are made up from elements from national culture, then the nation also has a right of self-determination in the international sphere. The nation is therefore an active identity.

In sum, nationalist discussion, unlike communitarianism, is permeated with the statist language of self-determination, sovereignty, citizenship, legal jurisdiction, territory and boundaries. However, it is worth noting here that some communitarians retain an ambiguous attitude to the state. As Michael Walzer has remarked 'while not explicitly statist in character, its [communitarian] defenders are (mostly) committed to celebrating those common convictions and commitments that make us citizens of the state ... The relevant community is the political community' (Walzer introduction to Walzer (ed.) 1995, 3). This would certainly be true of the writers of *Habits of the Heart*. However, there are further reasons as to why communitarians remain equivocal over the issue of the state, which will become apparent in the final section.

Pluralism and community

This section continues with two further divergences between nationalism and communitarianism. The first explores the communitarian nostalgia for a form of universalism. The second focuses on the more equivocal fragmentation of communities into sub-communities.

In most of the philosophers associated with communitarianism, it is noticeable that there is a strong urge to avoid the charge of relativism. The basic problem is that if the human is defined through the rules of a community, then the foreigner can literally become the inhuman. The twentieth century alone provides numerous examples of this strategy. Theorists, such as Richard Rorty, have accepted aspects of this contingency (see Rorty 1998). Rorty's view resonates with many nationalists, with the equivocal exception of recent liberal nationalists. Others have tried to find ways to avoid such exclusions. Cosmopolitanism – searching for a transhistorical conception of human nature – is one response. Communitarians also try to avoid this contingency. For example, in works such as *Interpretation and Social Criticism* and *Thick and Thin*, Walzer suggests that there is a transcultural minimal code of morality and even a minimal content to universal human rights (Walzer 1987, 24–5, 1994 and 1977). To some extent this idea is already prefaced in his earlier books, *Just and Unjust Wars* and *Spheres of Justice*. The minimalist code is seen to emerge from trial and error. He thus conceives of it as a reiterative universalism, as opposed to a covering law universalism – which gives supremacy to a way of life as uniquely and universally right. The latter might be redescribed as a strong universalism. Under the rubric of reiterative universalism are included the expectation not to be deceived, treated with gross cruelty or murdered (Walzer 1988, 22). He, in fact, posits the idea of an international society premised on such ideas. The reiterative universalism is still a distillation from the 'thicker' communal particularist moralities. It emphasizes that, subject to thin universal constraints, there are many different ways of life that have equal rights to prosper and deserve equal respect (Walzer 1990).

There is, however, another dimension to Walzer's thin universalism. Walzer suggests that in any theory about cultures we should not engage in any ranking. Yet, this very contention implies that theories which do rank (which most do in fact) are, by definition, all inferior or wrong. All 'ought' therefore to adopt Walzer's theoretical stance. This implies an implicit metatheory lurking in Walzer's position. Further, Walzer's notion of the 'connected critic', scrutinizing the standards of her own society, also implies some degree of freedom of expression and public rationality for that critic, in whatever society you may find her. Again, this has metatheoretical implications. Walzer clearly wants pluralism and difference within a thin universalistic framework. This thin universal theme is also partly intimated in the work of Taylor, MacIntyre and Sandel. None wish to be associated with pure relativism, whereas many nationalists (with the exception of liberal nationalists) have been relatively unfazed by the charge.[29]

The same preoccupations appear in the work of Etzioni, for whom the communitarian quest is a way 'to blend elements of tradition (order based on virtues) with elements of modernity (well-protected autonomy). This, in turn, entails finding an equilibrium between universal individual rights and the common good (too often viewed as incompatible concepts)' (Etzioni 1997, xviii).[30] Thus, for Etzioni, communitarians should encourage and facilitate cross-cultural dialogues, which 'build on substantive global values that lay a claim on all and are not particular to any one community' (Etzioni 1997, 240). The universalism and particularism divide 'stands in the way of developing a solid paradigm, and recognizing the merit of combination'. Thus, he continues, 'it is not only possible but highly necessary to combine some universal principles with particularistic ones to form a full communitarian normative account' (Etzioni 1997, 248). Consequently, for many contemporary communitarians there are compelling moral universals. For Etzioni it is not enough that such moral universals have been established in a community by democratic accountability. The moral values need to be self-evident universal truths which transcend communities (Etzioni 1997, 241–2). This whole argument is suspect from within a communitarian position.

However, before leaving this equivocal point about thin universals, it is worth bearing in mind Clifford Geertz's response to such issues, emphasizing in his case a strong communitarian particularism. For Geertz, thin universals in Walzer and Etzioni constitute 'fake universals'. He remarks, for example, 'that everywhere people mate and produce children, have some sense of mine and thine, and protect themselves in

one fashion or another from rain and sun, are neither false nor, ...
unimportant; but they are hardly very much help in drawing a portrait of
man that will be a true and honest likeness and not an untenanted ...
cartoon'. He continues, 'Is the fact that "marriage" is universal (if it
is) as penetrating a comment on what we are as the facts concerning
Himalayan polyandry ... or the elaborate bride-price systems of Bantu
Africa?'. Geertz concludes that there is a generic fear of cultural particularity and a retreat to bloodless universals in such attempts at thin
universalism (Geertz 1993, 43). Certainly many nationalist writers would
have some sympathy with this line of criticism.

The second issue concerns the fragmentation question. This is the
most interesting dimension of communitarian thought which, in my
reading, begins to make communitarianism into a transitional or intermediate category. It also constitutes one further important divergence
between communitarianism and nationalism. The central question is
what is the actual substance of community? The background point here
concerns the empirical existence, within most larger states, of many
different types of cultural, ethnic, work-based, gender-based, indigenous,
neighbourhood, kinship and even nationality groups. There is a recognition within some recent political theory that most societies are characterized by a complex underlying group life. In fact, societies have always
been so characterized, but it simply has not figured a great deal in
political theory, except at the margins. As Will Kymlicka notes, 'Most
organized political communities throughout recorded history have been
multi ethnic ... Yet most Western political theorists have operated with an
idealized model of the polis in which fellow citizens share a common
descent, language and culture' (Kymlicka 1995a, 2).[31]

Both nationalism and communitarianism are aware of the problem
of sub-groups. Nationalism has an immediate rough and ready answer.
In variants of nationalism during the twentieth century, sub-groups,
minorities or sub-cultures have been dealt with through strict immigration, assimilation policies, or, at the extreme end, via pogrom, forced
migration or ethnic cleansing. For example, the conservative writer,
Roger Scruton, argues that a nation depends for its very existence upon
'sanctity, intolerance, exclusion' (Scruton 1990, 305 and 310).[32] This
leads Scruton to an intense distaste for multiculturalism (Scruton 1990,
325). However, for David Miller, national identities should not be all-
embracing. Harmless pluralism is tolerable. For Miller, Scruton moves
from a valid premise – that a well-functioning state needs a 'pre-political
sense of common nationality' – to a false conclusion, 'that this sense of
common nationality can be preserved only by protecting the present
sense of national identity' (Miller 1995b, 129). Yet, Miller is also profoundly sceptical of Habermas' idea of 'constitutional patriotism' as just

too weak (Habermas 1992 and Miller 1995b, 163–4). Adherence to a legal constitution does not provide a strong enough unifying identity and does not explain the importance of boundaries. Miller calls for a thicker form of national identity, but not as thick as Scruton's. Miller's view is still monolithic, but also more tolerant and responsive.

Miller's attitude to immigration catches the last point neatly. Immigration is no problem, 'provided only that the immigrants come to share in a common national identity, to which they may contribute their own distinctive ingredients' (Miller 1995b, 26).[33] People need a national story to root their identity – specifically the immigrants.[34] This point also does not stop Miller from 'nationalizing' groups via education. Political education, he says, must 'try to shape cultural identities in the direction of common citizenship. It must try to present an interpretation of, let us say, Indian culture in Britain that makes it possible for members of the Indian community to feel at home in, and loyal to, the British state' (Miller 1988a, 253). In this sense, Miller also expresses unease with multiculturalism, which rests on a spurious neutrality. Apparently, for Miller, the average British citizen (of whatever ethnic background) should be able to imagine themselves 'filling the breach at Harfleur or reading the signal at Trafalgar' (Miller 1995b, 23). Miller is not alone in this kind of judgement. His mentor, J. S. Mill, also remarked, with disdain, that it was better for a Scottish Highlander to be part of Britain or a Basque to be part of France 'than to sulk on his rocks, the half-savage relic of past times, revolving in his own little mental orbit, without participation or interest in the general movement of the world' (Mill 1972, 363–4). Mazzini, an important figure in liberal nationalism in the nineteenth century, also placed severe limits on who should form nations and thus how some minorities should be content to be absorbed into larger nation states – a view shared by President Woodrow Wilson in 1918.

On the question of 'multiculturalism', Miller finds nothing to complain about in Joseph Raz's quite innocuous liberal use of the term, which 'affirms that in the circumstances of contemporary industrial or post-industrial societies, a political attitude of fostering and encouraging the prosperity, cultural and material, of cultural groups within a society, and respecting their identity is justified by considerations of freedom and human dignity' (Raz 1994, 78). On the other hand, more radical multiculturalism for Miller is a challenge to nationality. It allows each member of society to define their own identity and demands the state respond to such claims. Each group is seen to have an equal validity. Radical multiculturalism (or radical pluralism) rejects nationality as too homogeneous and oppressive. For Miller, though, something needs to mediate between the various cross-cutting groups; something needs to establish trust between groups and only nationality can achieve this. Liberal nationality should neither be imposed on cultures nor should it evaporate into separate cultures.

The communitarian picture on sub-groups is more hesitant and often more muddled. First, communitarians – despite the central role played by groups – often seem oblivious to the complexity, hazards and awkward character of group life. Apart from Walzer's work on complex communities and complex equality, communitarians appear overly relaxed about the whole issue of groups. Embeddedness is far more perplexing than many communitarians seem aware. Part of the reason for this is that communitarianism does not really offer a clear account as to what community *is* sociologically and psychologically. It rests its laurels on an assumed beneficial normative consensus – either on a national or local level. It does not explain how the self is constituted by often diverse, overlapping and conflicting groups, loyalties and associations.

Second, whereas the nationalist associates the national community with something more directly monolithic, communitarians have often stressed decentralization within states – focusing on subnational groups and associations, such as families, neighbourhoods, religious communities etc., all of which are, of course, markedly different in character. They show some mistrust of the idea of an overarching national culture. They thus share with 'new social movement' theory an awareness that civil society is both densely constituted and often transcends states. As Michael Walzer notes 'There is today an international civil society, the very existence of which raises questions about the usefulness of the state' (Walzer introduction to Walzer (ed.) 1995, 3). Thus, many communitarians appear to be sceptical about the nation state.

One does not have to look hard for the communitarian interest in decentralization. As one writer has noted '[Communitarianism] proposes a general strategy of devolution or decentralization, designed to end the dominance of large organizations and to remodel our institutions on a human scale' (Lasch in Reynolds and Norman (eds) 1988, 174). Charles Taylor also comments that 'If our aim is to combat, rather than adjust to, the trends to growth, concentration and mobility, and the attendant bureaucratic capacity and rigidity of representative democracy, then some measures of decentralization are indispensable, with the consequent strengthening of more localized, smaller-scale units of self-rule'. Taylor's vision is informed by the Canadian context and he thus looks to forms of provincial government (Taylor 1986, 221–2, 229, n. 37). Michael Sandel, on the other hand, favours New England small-scale communities.[35] Sandel, in point, gives a highly structured historical reading of both the loss and yearning for the recovery of small groups. He notes that, from Jefferson to the populists, 'the party of democracy in American political debate had been ... the party of the provinces, of decentralized power, of small town'. However, with industrial growth and a vast growing economy, a 'nationalizing project' began in the USA and grew until the New Deal. By the time of the New Deal, liberalism had reconciled itself to concentrated *national* power. This power required a strong form of unity and the 'national republic' was the answer. For Sandel, this project faltered in the mid to late twentieth century. Except in moments of war 'the nation proved too vast' (Sandel in Avineri and De-Shalit (eds) 1992, 26). Thus, a shift took place from the public philosophy of the national republic to the procedural republic. It is this procedural republic which forms the focus of Sandel's critique. The future appears to be a modern recovery of the small-scale virtuous republic, not the nation state.

The communitarian writer, Daniel Bell, offers a *via media* here. He argues that communitarians are attached both to the public national state and to the small-scale group, which is not an uncommon attitude amongst contemporary policy-orientated communitarians.[36] One of the main characters in his 'dialogue-based' book (presumably speaking the author's mind) thus notes: 'I don't think it should be an either/or choice between politics which involves face to face interaction at the local level and the politics of the nation-state. The communitarians ... are responding to a widespread sense that national political institutions appear too distant from our ordinary concerns, a feeling that we're at the mercy of the political forces that govern our lives ... Hence political decentralization in some areas, particularly in social and cultural affairs, is necessary if we're to establish our full status as citizens'. Despite sounding a little like right-wing American militia rhetoric, Bell rules out complete decentralization. Practical reasons of defence, economic planning, taxation etc. require national government. Smaller units would always be hampered by lack of resources (Bell 1993, 136 and 137). This point is echoed by Walzer who warns against some 'anti-political' tendencies within some communitarians and radical pluralists, maintaining that the 'network of association ... cannot dispense with, the agencies of state power' (Walzer in Walzer (ed.) 1995, 22). However, not all are as sanguine as Bell or Walzer. MacIntyre, Taylor and Sandel, for example, still appear to be suspicious of the centralized national state.

Conclusions

Thus, communitarians clearly do feel uneasy about monolithic views of community. This marks out a definite shift from nationalism. It is quite clear to most communitarians that there are diverse communities within most states and humans are constituted within these communities. They are, consequently, more than uneasy with the overarching 'common good' of nationalism. However, this unease with monolithic nationalism, at the same moment as it directs them to diversity, also alerts them to the problem of unity *between* diverse communities. Communitarians seem to be playing a continuous game of cat and mouse here with their readership. When diversity is in the offing, they either allow the chimera of a 'national political community' to arise (and certainly that is how nationalists such as Tamir, MacCormick and Miller read them). The only really unifying overall community is therefore the nation. In this sense, there is an equivocal similarity between liberal nationalism and communitarianism. Yet, on the other hand, when the spectre of a monolithic national community appears in the offing, communitarians leap up to stress their deep mistrust of the 'national project' and emphasize subnationality, small virtuous republics, spheres of good and a complex group life. This is certainly the direction that Charles Taylor has drifted towards with his multicultural reflections on Canada, abandonment of neutrality and emphasis on the inevitability of 'deep diversity'. Overall, this is a more disordered account than one finds in nationalists; yet, it also, ironically, draws them much closer to other problems in late modernity concerning pluralism.

At this point, a crucial question arises: if it is the case – sociologically, politically and ontologically – that diverse groups do exist, undermining any secure notion of the common good, then how does one proceed politically? This, at the present moment, is a central problematic of contemporary politics and the ground for poststructuralism, difference theory, detraditionalization and radical pluralism. However, neither nationalism nor communitarianism appears to offer much clarification or any resolution to this problem of late modernity. Nationalism offers a simpler, but unpalatable solution, namely, forcing (by ethnic cleansing or public education) a unity. This is usually the path favoured in political practice and it undoubtedly can be effective. Communitarianism drifts (by the logic of its arguments rather than by direct intention) to the recognition of diverse group life, but, with notable exceptions, is unable to move much further, except to speak with glowing nostalgia of virtuous republics, family life, decent civic behaviour and helpful neighbourhoods. Communitarians are thus both attracted and repelled, on the one hand, by the unity of the state, and, on the other hand, by the sheer complexity and restless conflictual variety of group life.

Radical pluralists, such as William Connolly, have thus made it plain that they consider Taylor's 'deep diversity' (and the like) has still not gone far enough. Taylor's more recent work is still seen to embrace a limited 'enclave multiculturalism' which 'only speaks to a couple of the pressing issues of diversification today' (Connolly 1996, 62). For David Miller, in complete contrast, the radical pluralist divergence between cultural groups (as more natural) and nationality (as an imposed artifice) is utterly false. Cultural group identity can also be pure artifice and force-fully imposed – even gay pride, gender or aboriginal identity. There is no sense, for Miller, 'that identities in the first group are "better" or more "genuine" than those in the second'. For Miller, Connolly and many communitarians, both utterly fail 'to recognize the importance of secure national identities to minority groups themselves' (Miller 1995b, 135). In sum, the present discussion is not suggesting that any of the above positions are correct, but conversely that communitarians have generally failed to address this issue of fragmentation and sub-groups adequately, and when they do address it, it is with an equivocal and hesitant voice.

In conclusion, this chapter has examined the puzzling relationship between contemporary nationalism and communitarianism. It has analysed both the affinities and divergences between the two doctrines. In addition, it has opened up the question whether both movements – communitarianism and nationalism – are able to adequately grasp a key problem of late modernity, namely, the growing awareness of difference and pluralism. Nationalists, because of their attachment to an older statist vocabulary of boundaries, jurisdictions and particularly sovereignty, are less hamstrung by doubts about group life; however, that, at the same time, makes them less responsive to the problems of late modernity. Conversely, communitarians appear to be hampered by their profoundly ambiguous attitude to both the state and sub-groups *and* their relations. In this sense, both nationalism and communitarianism appear, in dif-ferent ways, anachronistic for more radical pluralists. All these move-ments exemplify gradations of particularism. Nationalism represents a revolt of the particular against the universal of cosmopolitanism. Com-munitarianism is often a particularist revolt against the universal of the nation. Pluralism and multiculturalism represent a revolt of another particular against the universalism of nationalism and communitarianism.

7 Multiculturalism

The conclusion to the previous chapter on nationalism and communitarianism maintained that both the latter doctrines appear indifferent to or unable to deal with the problems of pluralism and difference in modern civil society. For many pluralist critics, therefore, both doctrines are anachronistic, given the real gravity of particularism. However, paradoxically, the ethical and ontological appeal of both the latter movements is still premised upon their commitment to particularity. For the pluralist critics, however, the real significance of particularism leads necessarily to the inevitability and moral desirability of group difference. This recognition leads inexorably to the doctrine of multiculturalism.

Despite often being contrasted to nationalism, or seen as a preferable alternative, nonetheless multiculturalism shares a common underlying pattern of argument with nationalism. Its particularistic aims and intellectual *modus operandi* are held in common with nationalism. In this sense, nationalist language – reduced in scale and dimension – paradoxically accounts for much of the appeal and moral impetus of multiculturalism.[1] The structural parallels between multiculturalism and nationalism lie in two interlinked arguments, which will be traced and reviewed in the latter part of this chapter. The first argument focuses on the link between *identity* and *recognition*, the second concerns the significance of *culture* to *identity*.

This chapter will firstly review both the terminology and development of multiculturalism. This will entail primarily an analysis of the concepts of groups and cultures and then an examination of types of multiculturalism. Second, the relation between nationalism and multiculturalism will be explored in the context of the above two arguments concerning recognition, identity and culture.

Terminology

Most commentators agree that multiculturalism is a comparatively recent topic of political debate. However, in terms of its social and legal acceptance in developed societies, it has made significant inroads over the last three decades. It made its first hesitant appearance in Australia, New Zealand and Canada during the 1970s, particularly with changes in immigration laws.[2] It is not surprising in this context that much of the initial enthused theorizing about the idea arose particularly from Canadian and Australian academics.[3] Second, it then appeared in the early 1980s as a significant and often tense oppositional issue within United States politics. Although often discussed in the context of North American liberalism and communitarianism, it has also figured as a critical component within racial, feminist, minority, postmodern and postcolonial political theories. Nathan Glazer, for example, thinks that multiculturalism is, characteristically, a North American concept (linked to a strong rights-based tradition with deep immigrant and racial divisions in society) and consequently has no real connection with European politics (Glazer in Joppke and Lukes (eds) 1999, 183–4). Third, multiculturalism did begin to make a critical appearance in European public policy debate, particularly in France, Germany and Britain, during the 1990s. However, whether this is the same idea as appears in North America or Australia is a contentious point. Some, however, still see the lifetime of *effectual* multicultural and group rights debate as much shorter. For Glazer, it is a product (largely in educational circles) of the last twenty years. For Kymlicka, it has only been effectively present over the last decade (Kymlicka in Joppke and Lukes (eds) 1999, 112).[4]

Why the interest in multiculturalism? Briefly, the 1990s particularly saw the end of the cold war, the opening up of markets and societies, considerable growth of international population movement, acceleration of trade, communication and capital flows across the globe, coupled with the rediscovery of older idiosyncratic nationality, ethnic and religious affiliations. The fortuitous combination of globalizing forces and the mixing of populations, together with the renewed interest in ethnicity and culture, has underpinned interest in multiculturalism. Yet, one important point to mention here is that it is far from clear that multiculturalism is a consistent or coherent phenomenon. Whether the European experience of multiculturalism has anything to learn from or to teach North American, New Zealand or Australian forms remains unclear and un-resolved. In each case, multiculturalism appears to be a contextual res-ponse to events (see Glazer in Joppke and Lukes (eds) 1999 and Glazer 1997).[5] Even within states, such as Australia, it appears to be a deeply contested idea. As Homi Bhabha notes, multiculturalism is a 'port-manteau term for anything from minority discourse to postcolonial critique'; in consequence it has become 'the most charged sign for des-cribing the scattered social contingencies that characterise contemporary *Kulturkritik*' (Bhabha in Bennett (ed.) 1998, 31).

The prefix 'multi' conventionally arises in the context of groups, not individuals. Conventionally, because of its promotion of particular groups, it tends to be placed in opposition to both liberalism and universalism. How opposed it is to liberalism remains to be discussed. In broad overview, multiculturalism views society as composed of groups, each constituted by its own culture. Culture refers loosely to the beliefs, symbols and values of the *group*.[6] This is one solid reference point for any theorizing on multiculturalism. However, the questions what a group is *and* whether it qualifies for a culture, and, in addition, what a culture is, remain open. Further, the concept multicultural – as opposed to less used terms such as unicultural or monocultural – has family resemblances with a number of cognate terms. Concepts such as pluralism, difference, diversity, multi-national, multi or polyethnic, *can* function in a similar conceptual manner or synonymously with 'multicultural'. Those who follow late twentieth century French thought, usually focus on neologisms such as *différance* (Derrida) or *differend* (Lyotard) to convey the same basic idea – although this emphasis is usually anglicized into the term 'difference' or, more grandly, 'difference theory'. It is, ironically, also often laicized, within some literature, into the Anglophone community. Thus, conventional liberal pluralism can be redescribed as 'difference theory', which would no doubt surprise more conventional liberals.

One problem with this terminology is that each term – difference, polyethnicity, multi-national, and the like – has become a rallying point for heated debate. Usually more heat than light is generated by such debates, since there is little clarity as to their precise reference or meaning. Yet, it is important in dealing with multiculturalism, to get some handle on this internal conceptual complexity. The terminological issues which need clarification are: first, what is a group; second, what is meant by culture and do all groups possess it; third, are there different forms of multiculturalism?

What is a group?

As mentioned, multiculturalism always refers to groups. There is though an ambiguity built into most multicultural arguments insofar as they trade on the empirical existence of different groups. The link between multicultural debate and current cultural anthropology becomes more obvious here. The term multiculturalism can, on one level, simply be recording or describing the empirical *fact* of diversity. Most multiculturalists, however, do want to go beyond this to make a normative case for the *value* of such group diversity. This opens up a number of logical problems, not least whether the sociological or anthropological fact of group difference or culture is morally significant in any way, namely, can the fact of group difference entail a moral case for diversity? This is a logical point which will have to be left to one side.

Conventionally, in juristic, sociological and political literature over the last two centuries, groups have been classified in different ways. There is a long-standing tradition here. Crowds and mobs are usually kept distinct from associated groups. Further, groups have conventionally been seen to have some form of collective purpose. They are not just unstructured collections or aggregations. In addition, within the associated group category, standard distinctions have been made between types of group. The better known of such older distinctions are *societas* and *universitas* (used by Michael Oakeshott), *Gemeinschaft* and *Gesellschaft* (Ferdinand Tönnies) or *Genossenschaft* and *Herrschaft* (Otto von Gierke).[7] Groups were either seen to be associations organized for an explicit purpose, often by broader authorities such as states, or, alternatively, they were self-constituting groups. The basic ideas being fostered here are still reflected in the literature in, for example, distinctions between 'communities' and 'associations', 'communities' and 'social aggregates', 'self-collecting' and 'other-collecting', or 'voluntary' and 'involuntary' groups.[8]

One recent example of this type of distinction is Iris Young's contrast between voluntary and involuntary groups. For Young, what constitutes involuntary 'groupness' is a 'social process of interaction' whereby people come to have an affinity for one another. Affinity means sharing assumptions and possessing an affective sense of bonding. Membership is not about satisfying some objective criteria or purpose, but rather a subjective affirmation of affinity. For Young, the involuntary group therefore implies a 'particular sense of history' and 'understanding of social relations' and a common sense of oppression. A voluntary group, qua club, corporation, church, or trade union, is something with which one consciously associates for a defined purpose. An involuntary group, however, has the character of what Young calls 'thrownness'. One finds oneself in such a group.[9] Young however doubts whether there is any substantive or essential identity to such affinity groups.

Whether all involuntary relational groups are 'oppressed' – as suggested by Young – is open to doubt. There are clearly powerful minority groups in all societies, such as company directors or the wealthy, who are not oppressed. Further, there are innumerable examples of 'thrown' minority privileged groups – such as ethnic elites, ruling family dynasties, dominant clans or hereditary aristocracies – who also cannot figure in this oppressed category. Young therefore can only be focusing on a more modest niche within the category of 'involuntary affinity groups'. Thus, for Young, within this latter category are groups which qualify for multiculturalism. It is also worth noting that this concept of the group has *no* intrinsic connection with ethnicity or nationality.

For Will Kymlicka, however, the focus changes to a different concept of the group. He is concerned either with the incorporation of 'previously self-governing, territorially concentrated cultures [indigenous national minorities] into a larger state', or, immigrants entering a state who typically wish to integrate into a larger society. These two categories constitute multi-national states (arising from immigration, as in the USA) and polyethnic states (with indigenous populations, such as Canada, where some will want to integrate, some wish for respect for their culture and some to secede) (Kymlicka 1995b, 10–11). Kymlicka complains that the above terms often get bundled indiscriminately together with other types of grouping under the rubric of multiculturalism. This leads to serious confusion and misunderstandings. He therefore protests against theorists – such as Young – who use multiculturalism in what he regards as an overly broad manner to 'encompass a wide range of non-ethnic social groups which have ... been marginalized' (Kymlicka 1995b, 17–18).

Kymlicka has, in fact, a comparatively restricted understanding of groups focusing on ethnic and national groups. This diminishes, in turn, the range of multicultural claimants. He consequently has no interest in Young's group category. Women, religious groups, neighbourhoods or gays have no place. He notes that Young's 'oppressed groups' in the United States would seem to include eighty per cent of the population, virtually everyone but 'relatively well-off, relatively young, able-bodied, heterosexual white males'. He therefore suggests that Young's analysis moves a long way from genuine multicultural groups, although Kymlicka is prepared to admit that there are analogies between the claims of justice made by these social movements and the claims of ethnic groups (see Kymlicka 1995b, 145 and Young 1990, 40). However, Kymlicka's criticism of Young is slightly skewed, but not for obvious reasons. Young's relational involuntary groups rule out all forms of voluntarist moral or legal groupings from multiculturalism. To conform to Young's relational criteria might, in fact, be impossible, even for many new social movements. Many blacks, lesbians or gays are affluent or educated enough not to consider themselves 'thrown' involuntarily into groups and in fact to find such an idea offensive. Young's group category may thus potentially be much narrower than Kymlicka's. Further, in the context of Young's anti-essentialism and relational overlapping emphasis, 'thrownness' itself becomes suspect (and logically contradictory) as a form of veiled essentialism.

Further, there is an ambiguity built into Kymlicka's conception of groups. *Prima facie*, they appear to fit loosely into the involuntary group category. One therefore finds oneself within an ethnicity. Yet, unlike Young, such groups do have a substantive cultural essence which can be identified. However, paradoxically Kymlicka's group members, although involuntarily 'thrown', also have voluntaristic individual rights of autonomy and exit. For Kymlicka, one can therefore choose not to be within an ethnicity or nation. Further, nationality or ethnicity are indeterminate as regards corporate identification. Some ethnic or national groups can be painfully sensitive to questions of cultural or corporate identity (whether immigrant or indigenous), others are utterly indifferent.

My central complaint here is that a clear typology and definition of groups is crucial for multiculturalism. It lays down parameters for discussion. However, such accounts of groups that do exist remain inconclusive, confusing and inchoate. When, for example, Young discusses groups (qua multiculturalism), she is neither thinking of legal associations, nor the multifarious types of 'voluntary' groups – many of which have distinct and intelligible 'cultures'. She is also not focused on ethnic or national groups. She is *only* interested in one niche or dimension of the abstruse category – 'involuntary affinity groups'. Similarly, when Kymlicka discusses the concept of multicultural groups, he has, again, something quite specific in mind. He focuses on immigrant and indigenous groups – largely territorially rooted minorities, each with an 'essential culture'. For Kymlicka, such groups, ironically, have the character of 'national cultures'. In this sense, multiculturalism has hardly moved at all from the particularity of nationalism. As he remarks, 'The capacity and motivation to form and maintain such a distinct culture is characteristic of "nations" or "peoples" (i.e culturally distinct geographically concentrated, and institutionally complex societies)'. (Kymlicka 1995b, 80).[10]

The question therefore still remains here as to what groups are appropriate for multiculturalism? Crowds or aggregates are too loosely structured. A change in an aggregate's membership can change the nature of the group. Voluntary groups – such as clubs, unions, associations or corporations – do not change in the same way. Voluntary groups are still usually responsible for their corporate actions, even if their membership changes. Corporate groupings characteristically absorb individuals as parts.[11] Some voluntary groups are organized and constituted by larger authorities (such as states), others are self-constituting. All such voluntary groups have cultures (of sorts). However, none of the above types of group fit prevailing discussions of multiculturalism. The generic category of group which appears to be important is the involuntary group. Broadly, this would include families (of all types), kinship, clans, tribes, ethnicities, possibly even gender and sexual orientation. Both Kymlicka and Young are though remarkably selective within this involuntary category. Suffice it to say that both theorists rule out an enormous range of groups from multicultural discussion. Thus the nature of groups within contemporary multiculturalism remains vague and confusing.

What is culture and who has it?

The above issue – as to what a group is and what kind of groups we are thinking of qua multiculturalism – reappears again when we raise the questions: what is a culture and who has it? The basic argument of this section is that culture – which is central to multiculturalism – again remains obscure and contested. This obscurity extends into multiculturalism's relation with nationalism.

Quite unexpectedly, there appears to be little sensitivity within the domain of multicultural theory to the genealogy of the concept of 'culture'. There are three important senses of culture which appear in the literature. Multicultural theory tends to play unwittingly between them. First, the oldest usage refers, in a strong normative sense, to both artistic and intellectual work. It also has connotations of 'being civilized'. There is a groundwork here for deep-rooted respect for culture, 'civilized' conceptually implying some degree of respect. This is the culture which makes life meaningful and rich. When Kymlicka or Joseph Raz, for example, speaks of culture as the context of choice, some of their readership could consider this conception of culture as a significant civilizing practice. However, this would be mistaken. Kymlicka quite clearly does not mean this. The second sense of culture refers to the spread or democratization of the normative conception of culture. This can mean two things: either the diffusion of high culture (qua cultured), or, alternatively, that all immanent belief systems within a society are valuable. In other words, there can be legitimate popular culture. This latter idea is one foundation for the late twentieth century development of 'cultural studies'. The third sense of culture refers to the total system of beliefs and way of life of a community, which can be studied empirically. This has a significant anthropological and sociological dimension.

The first sense of culture is revealed in cognate words such as *cultured* or *cultivated*. These imply education, learning, urbanity, appreciation of the arts; in essence, being civilized. This usage also connects up with the German terms *Kultur* and *Bildung*, which had profound effects on nineteenth century European thought. *Kultur* directly implied civilization. *Bildung* could be translated as education, but it also implies a much deeper and more complex notion of cultivation, or, the all-round creative development of the individual. Both terms figured heavily in German romantic thought, particularly in writers such as Friedrich Schlegel, Adam Müller and Friedrich Novalis, many of whose ideas were derived from a particular interpretation of the writings of Gottfried Herder and J. G. Fichte. Schlegel and Novalis, particularly, identified culture with purity of language, art and mythology. Each culture possessed a unique spirit, will or soul, expressed in language, myths and customs – one indirect link with twentieth century multicultural theory. Languages took on a particularly strong role in this reading. The interest in particular folk art, poetry and music from the mid to late nineteenth century had its roots in the same soil. This interest also entered deeply into the educational curricula, festivals, and even the architecture and monuments of nineteenth century states (see also Eade (ed.) 1983).

Many such writings also expressed unease with the Enlightenment. Enlightenment thought was equated with materialism and rational artifice. Culture, on the other hand, was spiritual, organic, shaped by history, prior to any individuals and possessing its own moral uniqueness. Many scholars of the time, committed to these ideas, devoted themselves to the task of uncovering the antiquity of culture within language and folklore. The philosophies of language developed by Herder, Grimm, Fichte, Schlegel, and later Humboldt, formed much of the intellectual backdrop to this scholarly concern. At the time, some of the above theorists were also reacting to French cultural hegemony within German states. Fichte's *Addresses to the German Nation* was the best known of such reactions. This gave rise, in turn, to the idea of the *Kulturnation*. Culture, uniquely identifying a particular people or folk (*Volk*), preceded and was then expressed in the 'aesthetic state'. The *Volkstaat* took on a sacred creative role, demanding the right to express its own cultural uniqueness. In Fichte, other themes also came to the fore, particularly the idea of superiority and inferiority in cultures. However, this hierarchical idea of culture did not follow necessarily from the romantic perspective.

Apart from the direct attention that was given to 'culture' qua the 'nation' – *Kulturnation* – another direct implication of the perceived importance of 'culture' was the (initially mainly German) academic interest in the 'cultural sciences', *Geisteswissenschaften*, embodying what we might now think of as both the humanities and social science. This term was often used in contrast to the positivistic natural sciences (*Naturwissenschaften*). This distinction became a leitmotif within idealist and hermeneutic traditions, from G. W. F. Hegel to Wilhelm Dilthey and Hans Georg Gadamer. In many such thinkers, there was an assumption of a division between empirical positivistic study and the world of culture (or mind). *Bildung*, in this context, referred to the cultivation of mind. Thus, culture, in thinkers such as Dilthey or Ernst Cassirer, was *synonymous* with the mind and its development. Living culture was the cooperation of minds. In fact, Dilthey, nearer the end of his life, recast his understanding of *Geisteswissenschaften* as *Kulturwissenschaften*, as a clearer indication of his arguments. Dilthey's and Cassirer's conception of the humanistic disciplines, as cultural sciences, basically continued, more explicitly, a tradition from Herder, Goethe, Schiller, Humboldt and Hegel. However, *Kultur* was also universalistic. It focused ultimately on the 'education of the human race'. The conceptual ambiguity here is that 'culture' referred both to *particularity*, namely, the particular 'folk ways' of a community, and, at the same time, it also connoted *Bildung*, implying universalistic cultivation of the person. This later theme has left an unusual legacy within nationalism and multiculturalism. Both doctrines have aspired to link universality with their own particulars.

In nineteenth century and early twentieth century British thought there was less awareness of these broader European debates. Matthew Arnold's *Culture and Anarchy* (1869) does reflect (probably via his acquaintance with the writings of Wilhelm von Humboldt) some grasp of the *Bildung* and culture argument. The basic theme of Arnold's book is that the mass of working people in Britain were being given new democratic freedoms and rights, but *laissez-faire* liberalism had nothing to offer to 'civilize' the masses. Without culture there would be anarchy – culture meaning cultured and cultivation. Liberalism, as simply providing negative freedom, was a social danger. Arnold's answer to this dilemma was the wider diffusion of educated values (culture) through civil society. To gain culture therefore was to be in contact with the most civilized thought that the world had to offer. Culture involved both an appreciation of beauty and truth. As Arnold stated, 'The whole scope of this essay is to recommend culture as the great help out of our present difficulties; culture being a pursuit of our total perfection by means of getting to know, ... the best which has been thought and said; ... More and more he who examines himself will find the difference it makes to him, at the end of any given day' (Arnold 1971, 6). The *Bildung* theme also comes out strongly here. Arnold echoes Humboldt directly in commenting that 'culture, which is the study of perfection, leads us, ... to conceive of true human perfection as a harmonious perfection, developing all sides of our humanity' (Arnold 1971, 11). The educated person is a 'finely-tempered nature'. This theme was also tied directly to Arnold's involvement in the practical reform of British education in the mid-nineteenth century.

However, something strange happens to the concept of culture in this context. A profound tension is introduced into the argument by the second broad sense of the term, namely, its democratization and diffusion. As argued, one sense of culture refers to civilization, qua cultivation. Given its rarefied aspect it does not gel easily with the popularism of mass democracy. The masses for many nineteenth and twentieth century thinkers cannot be cultured, by definition. Culture means refinement and inevitable elitism. Culture is essentially an aristocratic not a democratic value. In one way, this view explains the manner in which a number of writers, in the nineteenth and twentieth centuries, interpreted the term. Writers as diverse as Ezra Pound. T. S. Eliot, George Gissing,

H. G. Wells, George Bernard Shaw, D. H. Lawrence, Beatrice Webb, George Orwell, Thomas Hardy, Virginia Woolf and Clive Bell regarded culture as a 'high' and demanding calling.[12] Modern poetry, for Eliot, for example, had to be difficult by definition. The masses were regarded with fear, amusement, loathing or suspicion. This is reflected in T. S. Eliot's use in *Notes Towards the Definition of Culture* (1948).[13] It is also echoed in Ortega y Gasset's *The Revolt of the Masses* and *The Dehumanization of Art* and the large cult of admiration for Friedrich Nietzsche during the early twentieth century. For Ortega (like Eliot or Pound) 'the characteristic of the hour is that the commonplace mind, knowing itself to be commonplace, has the assurance to proclaim the rights of the commonplace and to impose them wherever it will' (Ortega y Gasset 1961, 14).

The tension in this argument over culture arose from the fact that many others (extending Arnold's view) suggested that culture could and should be diffused and democratized amongst the people to 'raise them up' to appreciate civilized values. This was a common theme amongst a number of social reformers into the twentieth century – neatly encapsulated in T. H. Marshall's call in the 1950s for social citizenship, which implied, amongst other things, the right of all citizens to a substantial civilizing education.[14] The opposition to this line of thought also had a long ancestry back into nineteenth century thought. For example, Henry Maine and W. E. H. Lecky followed Alexis de Tocqueville and J. S. Mill in believing that democracy and cultural liberty were fundamentally at odds. Egalitarian democratic pressures resulted in mass uniformity. Although a defender of democracy, J. S. Mill's attitude was also tempered by a deep misgiving about the power of mass public opinion consequent upon the rise of democracy. Mill perceived individual cultivation as having become subdued under the weight of mass opinion. The individual for Mill, far from being the focus of democracy, is the elevated cultured intellect standing against egalitarianism.

In the same way, Ortega y Gasset and Eliot both feared that once culture had become democratic it would lose all its refinements. As Eliot remarked cryptically on the education reforms of the twentieth century (although exactly the same point has been made again in 2000), 'there is no doubt that in our headlong rush to educate everybody, we are lowering our standards, and more and more abandoning the study of those subjects by which the essentials of our culture ... are transmitted; destroying our ancient edifices to make ready the ground upon which the barbarian nomads of the future will encamp in their mechanized caravans' (Eliot 1948, 108). The masses do not read Plato, listen to Mozart or look at pictures by Rembrandt (except rarely in potted or distilled versions on television). Culture becomes easy, thinned down, mere entertainment. For Eliot, it no longer equates with the arduous path of becoming civilized.

The 'diffusion of culture' argument however appeared in two formats in the twentieth century. The first presentation goes as follows: culture can be democratized and this does not involve any thinning of content. The thinning of content argument is essentially a warped elitist 'high culture' judgement. In one sense, the notion of culture being distributed amongst the people was successfully attempted in the extension of twentieth century education systems. Thus, culture is normatively compatible with its wider diffusion in democracy. The second presentation of the argument can be found in writers such as Raymond Williams. It basically undermines the conception of high and low culture. Culture is viewed as self-consciously ordinary – the lived common experiences of any group. In this sense, culture is *immanent* within all groups. Working class culture, for example, could therefore be rich, varied and qualitatively equal to any other culture. Each person's 'lived experience' is valuable. Culture is, consequently, wrested from its privileged position. Each group is seen to have its own distinctive cultural character. Culture refers, in this usage, to a 'way of life'.

Fortuitously, culture as a way of life links unwittingly with the third broad sense of culture, viewed through the eyes of empirical sociology and anthropology. The origin of this use dates back to the developments of anthropology and sociology in the nineteenth century, in figures such as E. B. Tylor, in his book *Primitive Culture* (1871). The main lines of development of this conception are often encompassed under the rubric cultural anthropology. In the twentieth century this latter discipline developed significantly in the work of Talcott Parsons. The Parsonian conception of culture also impacted upon political science in the 1960s and 1970s. In the well-known text, *The Civic Culture* (1963), by Gabriel Almond and Sidney Verba, culture is defined as the 'attitudes towards the political system and its various parts, and attitudes towards the role of the self in the system'. Having completed comparative field-work studies of the United States, Britain, Germany, Italy and Mexico, the authors drew conclusions about the empirical 'cultural' conditions underpinning democratic stability. Culture is thus incorporated under an empirical description.[15] It encompasses, in effect, the whole gamut of everyday beliefs into which citizens are socialized.

Where does multiculturalism fit into the above discussion? At first glance, one might conclude that culture would be equivalent to any and all groups' 'lived experience' or 'belief structures'. But this judgement would be false. Recent theorists of multiculturalism are fastidious about who does or does not have a culture. Kymlicka, conscious of definitional problems, rules out, for example, the first sense of culture (discussed above), remarking that 'if culture refers to the "civilization" of a people, then virtually all modern societies share the same culture'. Thus, purportedly multicultural countries such as Australia, which share a common culture, qua cultured or civilized, would not be multicultural in this sense. Kymlicka does not read civilization here as being normatively 'civilized', rather, civilization means (for him) descriptively 'modern, urban, secular, industrialized'. This definition uses an empirical sociological and anthropological perspective on culture.

However, the second sense of culture – *vis-a-vis* the diffusion and democratization of culture – is also rejected by Kymlicka. He is prepared to admit that many groups could be said to have some kind of culture, qua discrete conventions and practices.[16] Thus, 'working class culture', 'gay culture' or 'bureaucratic culture' make sense, at a very limited level. Yet he also suggests that these are overly 'localized meanings' of the term. Taken too far, every group, down to the local fishing club or stamp-collecting society, has a culture, and, as Kymlicka points out, in this context, even a relatively homogeneous state such as Iceland would be astoundingly multicultural.

Kymlicka, consequently, seeks to limit the term 'culture' to one form of the involuntary type of group, namely, the nation (and ethnicity). He remarks, 'my focus will be on the sort of "multiculturalism" which arises from the national and ethnic differences ... I am using "a culture" as synonymous with "a nation"'. Consequently, a society is multicultural if and only if 'its members either belong to different nations (a multination state), or have emigrated from different nations (a polyethnic state), and if this fact is an important aspect of personal identity and political life'.[17]

Because of his focus on national societal culture, Seyla Benhabib accuses Kymlicka (with some justification) of falling into the trap of cultural essentialism and ultimately relativism. If culture forms our horizon, then there is no way of deciding between cultures. Each culture becomes necessarily essentialist and myopic. Kymlicka also assumes that cultures – as nations – are homogeneous. Benhabib also finds this objectionable. She contends that there are no societal cultures as such (Benhabib in Joppke and Lukes (eds) 1999, 55). This is not just an argument showing that each state contains many ethnicities or nations; conversely, it is suggesting that each apparent singular culture embodies an internal polyvocity. She thus makes a plea 'for the recognition of the radical hybridity and polyvocity of all cultures: cultures and societies are polyvocal, multi-layered, decentered, and fractures systems of action and signification' (Benhabib in Joppke and Lukes (eds) 1999, 45).

This latter argument has also been adopted by a number of recent multicultural theories. For example, Iris Young, despite her more essentialist-inclined interest in involuntary affinity groups, also tries unconvincingly to argue an anti-essentialist line. Further, James Tully also sees multiculturalism, qua Kymlicka, as tending to falsely essentialize cultures. For Tully, there are no 'internally homogeneous' cultures. Each culture is continually 'contested, imagined and re-imagined, transformed and negotiated ... The identity, and so the meaning, of any culture is thus aspectival' (Tully 1995, 11). He therefore suggests that societies should be considered as 'intercultural' rather than 'multicultural'. Although interculturalism does not have quite the attractive ring for oppressed groups as multiculturalism.

There is though a practical point to this intercultural anti-essentialist claim. Accepting a singular sense of a group culture assumes, firstly, that there is a consensual internal agreement about the practices of the group. Second, it supposes that the history or tradition of that group culture is uncontested, *within* that group. Who, for example, actually defines or articulates what the traditions and history of a group are? Power, domination, personal interest, economic wealth, fear or coercion may account for many pervasive internal definitions of a group culture. Third, it assumes that the dominant element within a group, who define a cultural practice, are defining it uncontroversially and universally; whereas the definition itself may be a temporary and contingent moment within the life of that group, reflecting a very transitory configuration of power. Thus, the definition of marriage, women's and men's roles, the bringing up of children, and so forth, may be internally contested within the group. Kymlicka's, and others', tolerance and respect for intra-group practices may thus be a misleading path to follow. However, it is important to realize here that this critical appraisal of multiculturalism's essentialism of groups may not eventuate in interculturalism. The above critical points are just as likely to underpin a reaffirmation of the need for a common liberal citizenship (with all the panoply of rights implied) and a denial of the significance of any cultural claims.[18]

However, there are also major problems with interculturalism. If something is intercultural, how would one know what a culture is or was, or, what was worth maintaining or jettisoning? Further, how would one differentiate between cultures? The indigenous or aboriginal would overflow and overlap with all other cultural forms. Culture, in the intercultural mode, would become an amorphous lump – a night where all the cultures are black. Alternatively, if one follows Kymlicka's logic, amongst others, then what becomes of the rich diversity of groups – neighbourhoods, families, religions, unions, clubs and the like? All of these are blanked out in the demand for an essentialist, constrained and stipulative definition of culture.

In summary, first, culture can imply the cultivation and civilized development of the person. Multiculturalists totally reject this usage. Second, some have believed that genuine high culture can be diffused to civilize the masses. This again is discarded by multiculturalists. In addition, some have argued that culture is immanent in most groups, implying *any* valued way of life. This led to the proliferation of cultures. Multiculturalism again standardly rejects this interpretation. Third, culture entails a total belief structure of a society or group. In this context, culture is generally taken, in anthropology and sociology, to be any conventional patterns of thought and behaviour, including values, beliefs, rules of conduct and the like. Whereas culture was initially seen as a more conscious rational creation, in the later twentieth century the more structural, functionalist and psychologically determinist aspects of culture have come to the fore. Intellect and rationality have been seen to be constituted *by* culture and its symbolic structures. Multicultural theories – though often drawing upon anthropological evidence – also largely ignore this dimension of culture.

Consequently, multicultural theory has never worked out precisely where it fits in cultural terms. Most multiculturalists focus loosely on culture as a way of life, with accompanying beliefs, but this is not any way of life. For Kymlicka, it has to be ethnic or national; for Young it is associated (confusingly) with non-essentialist involuntary groups; for Tully we should avoid any essentialism of culture (whatever that may be). There is therefore no coherent argument within multicultural theory concerning either what culture means or where it is located.

Forms of multiculturalism

Having interrogated the concepts of both 'the group' and 'culture', the argument now turns to an analysis of the concept of multiculturalism itself. This section examines the forms in which multiculturalism appears in contemporary discussion.

It is now fairly common in the literature to find distinctions being drawn between weak and strong variants of multiculturalism (Miller 1995b, 133, also Shachar 2000, 67–8).[19] Lukes and Joppke, for example, distinguish between 'hodgepodge' and 'mosaic' forms. The former implies intermingling and fusion. The latter idea – whose foremost spokesman they see as Kymlicka – implies that individuals are linked to the larger society through the prior membership of cultural groups (Joppke and Lukes (ed.) 1999, 9–11). They express their own qualified sympathy for the 'hodgepodge' idea on the basis that 'cultures are not windowless boxes'. Rather than debate the respective merits of these broad types, the discussion focuses on a more complex classification which better summarizes the present state of multicultural theory.

Three generic forms of theorizing arise under the rubric multicultural. Firstly, there is liberal multiculturalism. Second, there is an uneasy communitarian reading. Third, there is difference theory, which moves from a moderate expression of liberal difference – hardly distinguishable from variants of liberal pluralism – through anti-essentialist difference theory and ultimately to forms of radical difference.

Firstly, as regards liberalism: on the one hand, multiculturalists often standardly see liberalism as unable to cope with diverse cultures, the suggestion being that liberalism wishes to assimilate or integrate groups within its own perspective. On the other hand, liberalism has historically been wholly concerned with the diversity and plurality of beliefs. As Anne Phillips remarks, 'difference is not something we have only just noticed' (Phillips in Benhabib (ed.) 1996, 140). Similarly, many have noted that democracy itself is another important way of coping with diversity and pluralism. Thus, liberal democracy could be said to presuppose diversity and difference.

The liberal response however is not uniform. This is partly recognized in the literature, in the context of an awareness of differing liberal accounts, even amongst multicultural theorists. There is a common distinction made between two varieties of liberalism, for example, autonomy and tolerance-based liberalisms (Kymlicka), comprehensive and political liberalisms (Rawls), procedural and non-procedural liberalisms (Taylor) and autonomist and integrationist liberalisms (Walzer). In the present account, four basic liberal responses to cultural diversity are considered. The first emphasizes tolerance and non-discriminatory individual rights, the second emphasizes, less positively and more fearfully, a political liberalism which is still premised on rights, the third collapses into the tragedy of value pluralism and the fourth positively embraces cultures and value pluralism.

One multicultural suggestion, already canvassed, is that the older Enlightenment universalist liberalism – comprehensive, procedural, tolerant and rights-based – is incapable of dealing with group difference, partly because it remains neutrally indifferent and presupposes the hegemony of liberal reason. Other liberals, however, make a virtue of this neutral indifference. The origins of this latter argument – which is rights and tolerance-based – go back to the complex sixteenth and seventeenth century constitutional arguments over how to deal with religious civil war. The perspective can however be conceptualized positively or negatively. Thus, Chandran Kukathas adopts a positive view which begins and ends with individual rights and constructive indifference. Classical liberalism thus does not actually have to change its spots. Kukathas' view is individualist, egalitarian and universalist. The rights envisaged are generally non-discriminatory, universal and negative, implying duties of forbearance. Groups *per se* are not special, but liberal institutions should be neutral and should uphold the rights of individual agents to participate actively in groups. No group should have any specific cultural rights or privileges. Culture should neither be supported nor penalized. Kukathas remarks that 'liberalism puts concern for minorities at the forefront. Its very emphasis on *individual rights* or *individual liberty* bespeaks not hostility to the interests of communities but wariness of the power of the majority over the minority'.[20] Thus, groups have no distinctive rights in themselves and have no claim on the support of society, but they have the freedom to flourish.

The second liberal perspective holds onto the rights and neutrality, but in a more negative format. John Rawls adopts this more pessimistic reading. He offers a brief historical sketch map of the problem, which explains his pessimism. Older societies did not have our modern problem of pluralism, although this is highly questionable. Ancient Greek religions were, for example, civic and collective. Even within later Greek thought, when philosophy became the exercise of free disciplined reason, reasoning took place largely within the civic domain of the polis (See Rawls 1993a, xxi–xxii). For Rawls, Christianity, on the other hand, unlike the older civic religions, tended to be authoritarian and politically absolutist. It was often focused, in a potentially uncivic manner, on personal salvation. It was also doctrinal and premised on the idea that people must believe the credal structure. Christianity was also an expansionist religion, recognizing no territorial limits.

For Rawls, this conception of Christianity might have remained relatively unproblematic but for one event – the Reformation. The authoritarian, doctrinal, expansionist aspects of Christianity essentially fragmented. Each Reformation sect now knew the truth. Believers were not in any doubt about the highest good, but, they were divided. Persecution – read ethnic cleansing – was one way to deal with groups. However, in many situations this was not practical, especially for religious minorities. For Rawls, this basic pluralism of belief created the need for political liberalism. Although many Christians were in despair over such an idea, Rawls adds that, 'to see reasonable pluralism as a disaster is to see the exercize of reason under condition of freedom itself as a disaster. Indeed, the sources of liberal constitutionalism came as a discovery of a new social possibility: the possibility of a reasonably harmonious and stable pluralist society' (Rawls 1993a, xxiv–xxv). Thus, Rawls remarks, 'the historical origin of political liberalism ... is the Reformation and its aftermath' (Rawls 1993a, xxiv; see also Larmore 1990, 339). Political liberalism, qua Judith Shklar, is a response to the fears generated by wars of religion, following the Reformation (Shklar 1984). For Rawls, religious civil war 'profoundly affects the requirements of a workable conception of political justice: such a conception must allow for a diversity of doctrines and the plurality of conflicting, and indeed incommensurable, conceptions of the good affirmed by members of existing democratic societies'.[21] Rawls' main problem, therefore, is not freedom, *per se*, but the negative containment of pluralism (Rawls in Tracy Strong (ed.) 1993, 96).[22] Rawls' pluralism is one where reasonable citizens, accepting the basic structures of a liberal democratic constitutional state, nonetheless diverge on substantive questions of the good. Rawls thinks this divergence inevitable. Reason does not unify. In summary, Rawls' vision of liberalism is pessimistic, minimalist, constrained, protective and negative. He envisions his own version of liberalism as one arising out of 'fear', explicitly using Judith Shklar's thesis on liberalism to characterize his position.

The third liberal view is not focused on the political and legal structures of liberalism in the face of diversity. It is more concerned with the immediate personal and public tragedy which faces us with cultural diversity. The mood is quasi-romantic, Stoic and politically passive. This is the counter-Enlightenment liberalism of Isaiah Berlin, which, consciously or not, contrasts itself to the ebullient confidence of Enlightenment liberalism. As Berlin stated, 'if, as I believe, the ends of men are many, and not all of them are in principles compatible with each other, then the possibility of conflict – and of tragedy – can never wholly be eliminated from human life, either personal or social' (Berlin 1997, 239). Society is punctuated by numerous opposing values and cultures which cannot be amicably combined in an individual life or society. There is thus no uniquely right solution. As Berlin put it, 'forms of life differ. Ends, moral principles, are many' (Berlin quoted in Ignatieff 1998, 285). Theorists such as Stuart Hampshire and Bernard Williams link up with this perspective, arguing that there are, in effect, no single truths in morality. No ultimate commensurability is possible. This conception of liberal value pluralism thus emphasizes the tragic incompatibility and contingency of values. This might be described as the 'politics of undecidability'.

The fourth liberal view recovers the optimistic spirit, although unlike Kukathas, it focuses intensely on culture. In fact, as in chapter three, it can be called cultural liberalism.[23] For Kymlicka, both Rawls and Kukathas – in their different ways – place too much emphasis on individual rights. Communities and cultures have no substantive moral existence within their theories. Kymlicka therefore defends cultural rights within the framework of liberalism. Yet, survival of cultures is neither about preserving communities nor maintaining a coherent way of life, rather it is a way of safeguarding core principles around which the society is organized. Liberal societies should protect minorities, not because they form a defensible community, but rather because cultures are a *necessary* condition for autonomy. In other words, there is a universal core within a cultural particular identity. Liberal societies have a duty to support minority cultures, because they provide a context for choice. This does not mean we abandon rights; however, we should have a more flexible response to rights.[24]

The second major theoretical formulation of cultural diversity arises within communitarianism – although it is a cryptic formulation. This is concerned with the survival of communities qua cultures. As discussed in chapter six, communitarianism adheres to a number of general theses. Humans are embedded in communal cultures and the self is constituted through a community. Political and moral goods arise from particular historical communities. One implication for many communitarians is that each society should have a dominant culture. Many communities within one society would cause fatal fragmentation. Further, communitarianism is sceptical about the ability of abstract reasoning to stand apart from social or political traditions. Reason is situated within communities. Communitarians assume that there are shared communal resources and traditions which can be drawn upon.

The dilemma for communitarianism is that all communities deserve protection and respect because they provide the basis of identity. Yet any community needs a common core of values for a stable identity. These two propositions leave communitarianism with a contradiction. Communitarians, who espouse nationalism, have a common core ready to hand. However, there is also an implicit logic in the communitarian argument which is conditioned to acknowledge any cultural identity. Consequently, in complex modern democracies it is inevitable that communitarians will stray beyond the nation into multicultural territory. Consequently, communitarians are led, kicking and struggling in some cases, by the logic of their own arguments to some recognition of diversity.

The discomfiture within communitarianism can be observed in Charles Taylor's writings over the last two decades. For many, during the 1980s, Taylor was the bespoke representative (with Sandel) of communitarian thought. More recently, however, Taylor has expressed embarrassment at being cast in this role, since he is also associated so strongly (in Canada) with what he calls deep diversity and multi-culturalism. It is in this strained context, that Taylor has expressed critical anxiety over nationalism. Communitarianism, like nationalism, can often connote a monocultural structure, which is unacceptable to one who propounds 'deep diversity'. Thus, for Taylor, there is no national identity within Canada. The idea of a national consensus is what Taylor describes as 'our great historical misunderstanding' (Taylor in Tully (ed.) 1994, 206). Nationalism is too exclusionist. For Taylor, 'the insistent demand for common traits, goals or purposes – not in itself, because plainly these have their importance, but as the only basis for Canadian unity – has the effect of delegitimating, and hence further weakening what is in fact an essential element of this unity' (Taylor in Tully (ed.) 1994, 255).

The problem here is that communitarianism functions as an overly general term. Thus, nationalism might even be described as one species within communitarianism. However, there is also a sense in which communitarian theorists are trying to say something quite distinctive on a normative level – although the message still remains opaque. Communitarianism contains arguments for both a general overarching community and the authentic need of diverse groups to develop their own moral framework. In this sense, communitarianism is caught in a double bind. Although philosophically inclined to be receptive to diverse cultures, the phenomena of multi-nationalism, polyethnicity and multiculturalism also generate anxiety amongst communitarians. Communitarianism is thus caught between distinct particularities.

The third main theoretical formulation of multiculturalism is difference theory. However, it is important to realize that for some difference is not so much a doctrine as just a tool of analysis; although this is clearly not a view shared by all (see Benhabib introduction to Benhabib (ed.) 1996, 12). Difference is conventionally contrasted to identity or homogeneity – and thus involves an implicit, if cryptic, rejection of communitarianism. Homogeneity is also seen by some as 'sustaining a complex of unequal and oppressive relations' (Phillips in Kymlicka (ed.) 1995, 288). In this context, difference theory is often corralled into the emancipating teleology of feminism and post-Marxian socialism. Heterogeneity becomes, by default, an emancipating value. The problems of this argument are, first, an internal ambiguity concerning the concept of difference; second, whether it is, *in toto*, really so different to liberalism.

There are three current gradations of difference. The first is barely distinguishable from liberalism. In fact, some would say that difference is liberal pluralism in another guise. The second focuses on a more extensive social movements perspective, which still incorporates limitations. The distinctive point raised here is whether multiculturalism serves any clear purpose any longer and should be replaced by interculturalism. The third embodies the strange idea of 'complete difference'. It is hard to find clear representatives of this latter concern, although it is commonly referred to by difference theorists.

Part of the heterogeneous character of difference theory is due to its genealogy. First, a number of current difference theorists come from a transformed feminist difference perspective, which originated in the 1960s and 1970s. Contemporary feminist difference, however, tends to regard the earlier feminist difference arguments as mistakenly essentializing woman's difference. Second, postmodern and poststructural arguments have also had a profound effect, often blending in writers such as Judith Butler with feminist difference. In the context of postmodern theory, Derrida's critique of the 'metaphysics of presence',

Michel Foucault's exploration of the genealogy of the self and Jean-François Lyotard's analysis of the *differend* are of background significance. Theoretical reduction to any unity of substance is seen to repress difference (see Young 1990, 8–9).[25] This theme also blends in with the earlier critical theory of Adorno and Horkheimer and their attack on the 'logic of identity' in Enlightenment thought. Third, democratic theory has been given close attention in much difference theory, particularly in theorists such as Young and Chantal Mouffe. Fourth, post-Wittgensteinian linguistic philosophy, which stresses the multiplicity of 'language games' and 'forms of life', is also manifest in some difference theory, particularly the writings of Lyotard and Tully. Fifth, older movements, such as expressivist romantic nationalism, where authenticity and uniqueness are tied to diverse cultures, also form a background valorization of distinct cultures. Finally, psychoanalytic theory has also had a role to play here, particularly the work of Lacan. Again, one should not expect much coherence here. All the above are fortuitously part of an ontological drift.

The first gradation of difference overlaps with many liberal writings. Indeed some work now being done explicitly uses the word 'difference' as a synonym for 'liberal pluralism' (Walzer in Benhabib (ed.) 1996). Thus, Berlin or Kymlicka, *et al*, can and have been viewed as liberal difference theorists. Usually the tenor of the argument maintains, first, that most radical difference theorists have misunderstood the complexity of liberalism and have neither taken on board the counter-Enlightenment nor the community-sensitive variants, which are more sympathetic to difference. Second, in a broader vein, liberalism has been historically well able to cope with difference. In fact, it was founded on the problems of difference.

The 'liberal communitarian' theorist who has self-described his work as 'difference orientated', and is most sympathetically considered by more radical difference theorists, is Michael Walzer, particularly in terms of his conceptions of complex equality and spheres of justice. It is thus quite possible to read Walzer as enthusiastically fostering difference and a decentralized democratic society. Walzer's role is thus acknowledged in more mainstream difference theory. Iris Young, for example, comments that 'Walzer's analysis ... has resonance with my concern to focus primarily on the social structures and processes that produce distributions'. However, she continues that he still addresses us in a reified liberal language (Young 1990, 18). Such language assumes an impartial conception of reason and a unitary public realm, which disconnects us from particularity. Young describes this 'neutral reason' as a 'normative gaze' which 'expresses a logic of identity that seeks to reduce differences to unity' (Young 1990, 11 and 97). Consequently she sees impartiality as an 'idealist fiction' (Young 1990, 100 and 104).[26] Impartiality supports the liberal ideology of the neutral state, which is the groundwork for distributive justice. It legitimates bureaucratic authority, defusing calls for democratic decision-making and upholding a privileged liberal elite. Liberalism, overall, is a politics of 'indifference'. Unlike Kukathas, Young uses 'indifference' in a derogatory manner (see Kukathas in Vincent (ed.) 1997). In liberalism, persons can affiliate with whatever they choose. But they still adhere to emancipation from groups. Thus, liberalism is still indirectly assimilationist. The communitarian dimension, within Walzer, is equally suspect for Young. Community suppresses difference and masks the particular in the name of communal consensus. For Young, the public realm, as such, does not need a consensus. Public consensus is anathema in a group-based society. Conversely, the public realm needs to be 'open and accessible'. No social practice should be excluded (Young 1990, 119).

Liberation, in the difference context, is not emancipation from difference. Rather, it is an embrace *of* difference. In this reading, blindness to difference perpetuates cultural imperialism. Thus, 'justice in a group differentiated society demands social equality of groups and mutual recognition and affirmation of group differences' (Young 1990, 191). Formal liberal equality or justice are not however necessarily group sensitive, since 'universally formulated standards and norms ... often presume as the norm capacities, values, and cognitive and behavioural styles typical of dominant groups, thus disadvantaging others' (Young 1990, 173). Ageism, sexism, homophobia, racism, and so forth, are therefore often rendered invisible within formal justice and equality theory.

However, Young adds the qualification (discussed earlier) that group difference should *not* itself be essentialized. She comments that difference theory 'does not posit a social group as having an essential nature composed of a set of attributes defining only that group. Rather, a social group exists and is defined as a specific group only in social and interactive relation to others' (Young in Kymlicka (ed.) 1995, 161). Young's own version is thus what she calls 'relational difference', or concerned with 'intersecting voices'. This conception repudiates the idea that difference has to be concerned with total otherness or essentialism.[27] Relational difference indicates that people can be 'together in difference'. She posits her own version of democracy – communicative democracy – to deal with this phenomenon. Difference thus embraces both heterogeneity and interdependence. Young contrasts this perspective with visions of either assimilation or separation – associating assimilation with both liberalism and communism and separation with communitarianism, which freezes separate identities.

The third formulation of difference is radical difference. Young, for example, refers in critical terms to what she calls 'complete difference', which she finds totally unacceptable, on a parallel with her objection to communitarianism. Complete difference, in effect, essentializes difference. Chantal Mouffe is also insistent that difference should not be associated with what she calls 'extreme difference' (see Young 1997 and Mouffe in Benhabib (ed.) 1996, 246). Extreme difference, for Mouffe, is an impediment to any form of genuine democracy. It neglects the dimension of power and rests, in a quietist manner, with multiplicity.

Complete difference, as such, focuses on total fragmentation, conceiving each culture to be uniquely particular. This is one possible implication of some postmodern theory, emphasizing strong theses of 'incommensurability' and 'untranslatability', for example, in the epistemological relativism of Lyotard. For Lyotard genres of discourse are not only plural, but also heterogeneous and irreducible to any common vocabulary. This is what he calls the *differend*, namely, an irresolvable conflict. However, there is a sense in which Young's and Mouffe's judgements of radical difference (qua Lyotard) are quite correct. Radical difference does undermine itself in the same way that thorough-going scepticism undermines itself as soon as it makes any claim about the truth of scepticism. The thesis of radical untranslatability or incommensurability is incoherent. If cultures are so distinct we would, by definition, have no common lexicon to even circumscribe them as cultures. The argument thus falls at the first hurdle.

There is though one further idiosyncratic perspective on difference which extends it inwards. Bonnie Honig has suggested that not only is there difference within society, but also difference within *all* identity (Honig in Benhabib (ed.) 1996, 258ff). Each human being becomes a psychological multiplicity. She rather awkwardly calls this 'agentic fragmentation' (Honig in Benhabib (ed.) 1996, 260).[28] Difference, in this sense, is much deeper than many of its social proponents suggest. Young and Tully do not take this step. Honig is though insistent that difference is not just another word for social pluralism. Difference is not an *adjective* of identity, it is about the *substance* of all identity. For Honig, making difference an adjective makes it safe. She is thus deeply critical of the pluralism of Berlin, Stuart Hampshire and Bernard Williams, which she argues is premised on undecidability, but does not take the concept of difference with full seriousness. She complains, for example, that Bernard Williams tries to 'relocate' the dilemma of difference 'from the inside of subjectivity to its outside'. Presumably she would want to extend this argument to Young, Mouffe and Tully amongst others, since none of them appear to acknowledge the 'inward' character of the difference argument.

Honig describes her own difference conception as 'agonism', which sees difference as ineradicable from any identity. She suggests that there are advantages in grasping real difference, insofar as it empowers and equates with 'more coalitional variants of social-democratic organization' (Honig in Benhabib (ed.) 1996, 260 and 270–1). Honig's theory relates closely to the work of William Connolly who also embraces agentic difference and rejects all closure.[29] Connolly exposes and celebrates paradox. He also suggests that liberals always try to shield society from strong identities, whereas he, like Honig, wants a future society to encompass them.[30] The crisis of society is not one of fragmentation, but rather the attempt to fix and close identities. Connolly's and Honig's vision of society is thus an 'agonistic democracy'.[31]

Nationalism and multiculturalism

In summary of the discussion so far: first, as argued, there is a distinctly fuzzy conception of groups within multicultural theory. If multiculturalism arises in European discussion, it is often in the context of religious minorities, for example, Catholics in Northern Ireland or Muslims in France or Britain. Yet, under Kymlicka's, Young's and Tully's rubric this is *not* a significant multicultural issue unless tagged with racial or ethnic criteria.[32] Second, the concept of culture also remains inchoate. Theorists usually get round this problem with arbitrary stipulative definitions. Kymlicka, for example, provides a neat solution by just stipulating that he will use culture qua national groups. This might seem to end the problem – apart from the fact that there is no reason given other than convenience for his argument. However, on another level, this is where problems begin rather than end. It is as though the invocation of the concept of nation solves a problem. If we refocus for a moment and consider the extensive amount of literature devoted to trying to make sense of the concepts 'nation' or 'ethnicity', then Kymlicka's solution to the issue of culture looks bizarre. In fact, it is no solution at all.

It might be suggested that nationalism has had very little role to play so far in the discussion. However, it has been necessary to engage in a more extended critical analysis of the complex internal structure of the concept of multiculturalism in order to make some sense of its complex relation with nationalism. In effect, multiculturalism, because it has no adequate account of either groups or culture, tends to trade unwittingly on an older and more established pattern of argument which links it at a deeper level with nationalism. My major contention therefore is that there are deep resonances between nationalism and multiculturalism focusing on a logic of particularity. In fact, in lay terms, the observer might be forgiven for seeing 'multi' cultural identities as simply *smaller* nationalisms, either residues of nationalisms or ethnicities, or, micro-nationalisms in waiting. Both concepts function with the concepts of identity and culture – although identity is a more uncertain term in *some* difference theory. Thus, a multicultural society might be translated, in some minds, quite legitimately, into a multi-national society, which is, in substance, Kymlicka's thesis. Thus, Kymlicka's or Raz's conception of liberal multiculturalism works with culture and identity, understood in the context of nation or ethnicity. This view is resisted by some of the difference theorists, such as Young and Tully. The nagging doubt here is that culture is a broader (or possibly, for some, narrower) term than nationalism or ethnicity. As argued earlier, culture, *per se*, remains vague and contested here.

However, there is one much deeper resonance between nationalism and multiculturalism which focuses on the concept of identity. In most of the nationalist and multicultural arguments, which stress the importance of culture to identity, there is a consistent patterning of argument which focuses on the linkage between 'recognition' and 'identity'. The idea that identity is shaped by recognition has a complex genealogy in European thought from the eighteenth century. The basic idea is that identity is something which needs to be recognized and acknowledged in order to maintain or become itself. Isolated individuality or identity (qua radical difference) does not make sense; it can only become individual identity through recognition. The difference and particularity of the individual or group therefore arise from their recognition by others.

Hegel, for example, embodies this argument in his account of individuality, at the levels of logic, individual personality, individual groups and states. As he puts it, 'existence as determinate being is in essence being for another' (Hegel 1971, § 71). The same point applies to the human agent, the group or the state. As Hegel states, 'A state is as little an actual individual without relation to other states as an individual [person] is actually a person without rapport with other persons' (Hegel 1971, § 331, *Zusatz*). Thus, the identity of the state and persons presupposes the existence of other states and persons who recognize them as such. To define identity is both to articulate separateness (difference) and interdependence (on the recognition of others). In fact, for Hegel, one cannot even *be* conscious of one's self, unless one is aware of other selves. In the same way, a group or state cannot be aware of itself without the recognition of other groups or states. This awareness enables the individual to recognize what it is to *be* an individual. Recognition, in Hegel, also implies being seen as an independent subject and not an object. Denying recognition might thus be legitimately seen as a denial of individuality and autonomy and consequently a form of oppression –

which links with Hegel's famous master/slave dialectic – since it denies identity. The denial of recognition reduces the agent to an object. This whole argument underpins difference theorists such as Young and Connolly.

However, as indicated, identity is more pervasive than just the human agent. Individuality, in Hegel, is initially a logical term. It implies a comprehensive concrete universal – an identity in difference. Hegel also uses the recognition argument (as mentioned above) to speak of the identity of the group and state. Further, in Hegel, and even more so in Gottfried Herder, identity is linked to the customs, folkways and culture of a people. Being true to one's identity means being true to one's individuality, which, in turn, is both a uniquely personal and cultural phenomenon. Herder's argument for this is deeply influential.[33] It focuses attention on the link between culture, identity and language, as part of our self-definition. It is an argument which is prescient of the links between language, nationalism and identity. Culture here implies *both* a way of life *and* something more spiritually exalted. Culture therefore indicates, in both Herder and Hegel, the most significant dimensions of a 'way of life', as embodied in folk song, poetry, history, philosophy, literature, science and music.

Herder's theory arose almost fortuitously from an abstruse debate concerning the origin of language. Herder was critical of a particular theory of language which he associated with Condillac, Rousseau and Süssmilch (see Aarsleff 1982). The theory he opposed saw language as an instrument of information storage and communication. Words were taken to designate things in the world and thoughts in the mind. Herder adopted a more expressive or constitutive approach to language. Words, for Herder, were 'companions of the dawn of life'. As one Herder scholar remarks, 'the essence of language formation is not the creation of *external* sounds, but the *internal* genesis of word symbols' (Barnard introduction to Herder 1969, 20). Language was integral to the conscious activity and development of human beings. It was essentially, therefore, a form of action. It did not just record or designate external objects, but conversely had a constitutive role. Humans both make and were made within language. Humans perceived nature through the expressive medium of speech and reflection. Natural languages, in the form of primitive cries, are distinct from developed human speech (Herder 1969, 119; see also Aarsleff 1982, 151). Language, as developed human speech, is the essential medium of freedom and consciousness, reflecting the totality of human energies. The human capacity for self-awareness is also formed in language. For Herder, all our conscious states are formed in language. Language is thus first and foremost an 'indispensable requirement for the operation of the human mind, an integral part of thought'. The human being develops through thoughtful self-creation, in which language is an integral part.

For Herder, language thus not only describes, but it also expresses the feelings, emotions, thoughts and will of the person. He frequently warned against considering reason alone as the dominant faculty of human beings, which was, in fact, his basic criticism of Kant's conception of humanity. For Herder, language is built out of sense impressions. Since sense impressions of one's locality form the basis of language, it follows that local conditions – geography, climate and traditions of the community – will stimulate differing responses. As languages develop, so do cultures. Language forms the essential historical continuity of a society and its traditions – traditions not being viewed as static phenomena, but rather as processes in continual flux. Culture is the vehicle of this process. All humans, using language in this context, will therefore form, through dialogue and conversation, distinctive cultures. In other words, each *Volk* forms a distinct language community which is not biological or racial, but rather 'a historical and cultural continuum' (Barnard introduction to Herder 1969, 31). For Herder, it is part of the immense richness of the world that we find such individual language communities and cultures. It follows, therefore, that knowledge of the way humans have used language 'yields the story of changing uses and meanings' (Berlin 1976, 169). Herder was immensely keen on the idea of extending empirical studies of this richly diverse material. One can see here why Herder is so frequently linked to the origins of nationalist and communitarian thought.

In summary, the logic of the above recognition argument implies, firstly, that culture is intimately linked with identity; second, cultural identity implies the existence of other cultural identities (other cultural identities are required both to enable a culture to understand what it is to be a culture, as well as to gain recognition as a culture); third, denying recognition to an individual culture is a form of oppression. It denies identity, freedom and individuality. Fourth, the fact that denial of recognition implies oppression also implies the necessary requirement of respect for cultures, in the same manner as respect is required for autonomous persons.

A common pattern emerges here in both nationalist and multicultural argument in terms of the subtle link between recognition, culture and identity. If human identity is intrinsically connected with group culture, and, if both human agents and group cultures are regarded as unique, autonomous and self-determining entities, it follows that both human agents and group cultures also require recognition and respect for their identity. This argument – concerning self-determination and respect for distinct identity – has figured strongly in all nationalist and multicultural discussion. To fail to recognize the identity – and thus the self-determination and the quasi-sovereignty of the human agent, nation or cultural group – is to act oppressively.

It is worth underscoring this point here that the same logic of recognition applies to the individuality of groups. Yet, which specific groups require such recognition is a movable feast. For nationalists it is an overarching community. For Kymlicka it is internal national groups. Tully allows nationalist, linguistic, ethnic, multi-national, and aboriginal groups, but also adds (what he calls) supra-national, intercultural and women's groups. He also contends that each demands 'cultural recognition' *and* aspires to some form of self-government. Tully therefore calls for a 'multilogue' constitutional discussion which gives each of these elements a voice. A common formal pattern of argument – premised on recognition and identity – underpins all of the above. However, who or what gains recognition – as in the earlier analysis of 'who has a culture' – varies considerably.

One additional qualification that Tully, Young, Connolly and Honig add here is that no group culture can be discrete. This is used, on the one hand, to counter radical difference arguments, and, on the other hand, to bypass the charges of relativism and essentialism. All cultures are thus seen as intrinsically contested. No culture, for Tully, is internally homogeneous. Consequently, for Tully, there is a deep-seated conflict between the 'politics of cultural recognition' (which is dialogic) and the 'politics of modern constitutionalism' (which is monologic). The central dilemma for modern constitutionalism is how the 'proponents of recognition [can] bring forth their claims in a public forum in which their cultures have been excluded or demeaned for centuries' (Tully 1995, 56). There is no overarching or all-comprehending language game or form of life.[34]

Predictably, Tully praises Young's work on difference, but goes on to contend that even she is too pessimistic about the positive possibilities of communication. For Tully, 'the reason it is possible to understand one another in intercultural conversations is because this is what we do all the time in culturally diverse societies' (Tully 1995, 133). He remarks, therefore, in an optimistic tone, that 'If interlocutors from other neighbourhoods and boroughs present their examples of struggles for recognition to complement the limited perspective of mine, as I trust they will, our concept of being guided by the conventions of common constitutionalism will be extended further'. For Tully, this will be an endless open dialogue. He continues, 'in this dialogical way, the citizens of such a republic of words, speaking and listening in turn, could gradually become mutually aware of cultural diversity that ought to be recognized and accommodated in the global family' (Tully 1995, 183). One might respond here, in more upbeat mood, 'and so say all of us';

however, the way Tully presents it retains a sickly sweet character. The more brutal and pessimistic presentations of group behaviour seem far more accurate in contemporary politics. Power, survival, security, stability, public order and crude applications of justice seem more appropriate terms for our present situation.

Within current difference theories there are clearly degrees and types of difference. Difference itself is a contested concept with no settled meaning. This creates the following odd scenario: initially, if one focused *only* on individual rights, then most difference theory would argue that 'real differences' are ignored. Yet, 'real difference' is deceptive. Human individuals, *per se*, are really quite different, but these differences do not appear real to many difference theorists, or, at least, they are insignificant differences. Group culture is the realm of difference, not individuals. The individual rights view – from Young's, Connolly's or Tully's perspectives – denies genuine recognition, and, in consequence, is oppressive and difference blind. This is the key criticism of procedural liberalism. However, individual rights exponents respond, with some justification, that granting groups rights can be equally as oppressive to the idiosyncratic differences of human individuals. Difference theory can therefore also be accused of being 'difference blind' from the perspective of particular individuals. Gay, ethnic or aboriginal groups can all be equally oppressive in not recognizing the genuine real differences between human individuals.

'Real difference' for communitarians and nationalists is different again. Difference works at the level of national cultures. This leads to a negative attitude to stronger multicultural views. David Miller, for example, associates this unacceptable face of multicultural difference with the work of Iris Young. However, again, Young is clearly not offering the strongest version. Lyotard would be a better example for Miller. Primarily though, for Miller, the stronger multiculturalism relies upon a false contrast 'between the allegedly authentic group identities that multicultural politics is supposed to express, and on artificially imposed common national identity' (Miller 1995b, 133). Miller points out that group identities of *any* type can be artificial. There is no sense that national identity or micro-group identity are *more* genuine. Second, strong multiculturalism fails to recognize that secure national identity is the foundation to all micro-identity. Micro-groups are vulnerable without the nation. Third, many of the injustices suffered by group members take place within the confines of the group. This is also the argument that Kymlicka directs at difference theory. Fourth, continuing the latter point, although strong multiculturalists focus on injustices against groups, they do not show how these are to be resolved without some core national unity and communal sense of what justice and fairness require in the whole society. Trust needs some overarching unity. There is little thought in such multiculturalism about how politics really works.

A more apocalyptic formulation of the above point is made by Roger Scruton: 'In the modern world, it is precisely national loyalty that the liberal state requires, and national loyalty cannot emerge in a state where other, tighter, and fiercer loyalties compete with it ... Experience ought to warn us against such a society: experience not only of Lebanon, but also of Cyprus, and India. If we are interested in the survival of the liberal state, then we should be doing our best to preserve the loyalties which sustain the liberal jurisdiction' (Scruton in Clark (ed.) 1990, 81). This is what a recent American political theorist, Jean Cohen, refers to as learning about the dark side of difference and new social movements (Jean Cohen in Benhabib (ed.) 1996, 187).

Strong multiculturalism thus appears to be a definite challenge to more orthodox nationality claims. It allows too much leeway to smaller groups to define their own identity and demands the state respond to such claims. Multiculturalism, in turn, rejects nationality as homogenizing and oppressive. One way round this conundrum would be a thinner, more liberal, variant of both multiculturalism and nationalism, where some special opportunities (or rights) might be granted to minorities. Miller comes down here more on the side of freedoms and opportunities being given to minorities, rather than Kymlicka's special rights (Miller 1995b, 147ff). For Miller, the demand for group rights is really, in essence, a demand for equal treatment and equal citizenship. Nationality, *per se*, tends to favour equal citizenship rather than group fragmentation. Nationality, for Miller, in the final analysis, should not be imposed on groups, but neither should it evaporate into groups (Miller 1995b, 154). Kymlicka thus sees Miller's critique as another version of J. S. Mill's position. He comments 'just as Mill thought that "united public opinion" necessary for the working of liberal institutions is impossible without a common language and national identity, so Miller thinks that the "common purpose" necessary for socialist institutions is only possible in a nation state'. Miller assumes that assimilation is viable and possible for a state. Kymlicka, however, is not clear that this will work – 'if peoples' bonds to their own language and culture are sufficiently deep, then attempting to suppress the cultural identity and self-government of national minorities may simply aggravate the level of alienation and division' (Kymlicka 1995b, 73).

There is no denying the divisions between nationalist, multicultural and difference theories. However, it is also still clear that underpinning all of these is a common argument concerning the value of the particular, its identity and recognition. Consequently, the politics of particular human dignity, the politics of particular communities, the politics of nationality, and the politics of cultural groups are all premised on the logic of identity, recognition and correlative respect. The first focuses on the universality of particular individual humans, the second on the universal particularity of communities, the third on the universality of particular nations, and the fourth on the universal significance of the particularity of fragmented cultures. However, all are spawned by the same core argument.

Conclusion

Thus the central conclusion is that despite surface differences nationalism and multiculturalism arise from a common pattern of particularist argument. Both derive from a theoretical critical engagement with essentialism. Both affirm the value of otherness and heterogeneity. Both are uneasy, on various levels, with unadulterated universalism. Both are equally reconciled to the fragmentation of the political and moral world.

Nationalists and multiculturalists have ways round this dilemma of fragmentation. Liberal nationalists particularly affirm the necessity of a procedural framework, within which difference can be accommodated, tolerated and possibly even explored. Some multiculturalists have also insisted on the avoidance of the essentialism of groups, consequently discrete epistemological group worlds do not exist. These are neat solutions, insofar as they affirm simultaneously the virtues of both difference and universalism. Liberal nationalism has its own set of endemic problems – explored in chapter four. In the case of multiculturalism, the argument against essentialism gives the game away before starting. If the point is to affirm the importance of the significance of groups and their cultures, it is difficult to see how this can be achieved by denying the significance and uniqueness of groups. Interculturalism may work rhetorically, but in practice it is self-defeating. Does it help to tell an oppressed indigenous cultural group that it actually has no real independent distinctive character and that it should engage in continuous self-critical dialogue with a multifarious range of groups to which it is fundamentally opposed?

The problem of fragmentation and diversity has however been a perennial political issue from the time of the Greek polis. Yet, it is important to realize that the nation state itself was viewed, in the late medieval period, with the same suspicion that many *now* view multiculturalism. The older empires had their own ways of coping with the problem of internal diversity. With the consolidation of states in Europe from the sixteenth century, various methods were used to cope with groups. Religious civil wars in the sixteenth century focused most minds on the seriousness of inter-group conflict. One obvious solution was to assert absolute power over what Hobbes memorably called the 'wormes in the entrayles' of the body politic. However, more accommodating paths were taken through diverse forms of constitutional arrangements, for example, separation of powers, federalism, confederalism, legal pluralism, forms of democracy and in this century consociationalism. The list is extensive and rich in constitutional detail. Each structural device has been able to accommodate, for a time, quite large amounts of cultural difference.

In summary, difference has been responded to by states in diverse ways. The most simple way of expressing this point would be in terms of: *exhaustion, resignation, incorporation, indifference, curiosity* and *promotion.* Extensive and debilitating civil war accounts for the first two dimensions, giving rise to a *modus vivendi.* Complex constitutional doctrines, culminating in the ideology of liberalism, give rise to the next two. More recently, the rise of multiculturalism accounts for the last two. All these responses to groups *still* exist within contemporary states. Most developed states hover on the margins of constitutionalism and half-hearted multiculturalism. However, the idea that multiple groups, within contemporary states, should be given comprehensive resources from the public purse, gender or ethnic representational quotas, or extensive veto powers on legislation affecting particular groups, sounds far-fetched and lacks any perspective on the brute configuration of power within most states.

The main conclusion concerning the relation of nationalism and multiculturalism is that the same particularist logic drives both doctrines. They are more intimately linked than most of their proponents would like to admit. Within nationalism the very existence and recognition of secession arguments and the simple fact of multi-national and polyethnic states shake the nationalist argument at its foundations. It is clear that virtually all states contain an internal group life – often linked to demands for group rights. Yet, even within these diverse internal groups are further sub-minorities, which again demand (by the same particularist logic) rights of protection, tolerance and even a right of exit. This point extends to new social movements, multiculturalism and difference theory. We can see here the seeds of further fragmentation, although again, it is important to realize that the logic of the argument for further implosion is the same argument implicit within nationalism. Multiculturalism and difference are not exempt from internal secession and in facing it critically they are always hoist by their own petard.

Humans are unquestionably group-orientated creatures. Yet our dilemma is that we have multiple overlapping belongings, some of which directly conflict with each other. There is no easy answer here. We often exist with continuous tensions between our multiple belongings.

We are a living interstice. It is worth noting though that some groups (including nations) can be profoundly dangerous or destructive for ourselves and others. However, groups also can be the grounds for our freedom and self-development. Political theory has, in its communitarian format, grasped the point that liberal individualism can be intrinsically problematic. It has also realized that nationalism can be an unpredictable and lethal allegiance. However, it has yet to fully renew its acquaintance with the dangers implicit in group life, the diversity of types of group life and the frequently profound internal conflicts between our multiple belongings – all a consequence of the focus on particularity.

8   Cosmopolitanism

This penultimate chapter turns to the issue which has underwritten many of the previous debates in this book. If there is one general theme which runs through contemporary political theory, it is the contrast between *particularist nationality* and *universalist cosmopolitanism*. More recently, it has surfaced, with greatest force, in cultural studies, international relations theory and anthropology. However, the focus of this chapter concerns the structure of the debate surrounding this contrast of cosmopolitanism and nationalism mainly within political theory.

The overt relation of these terms is one of marked difference. Yet, ironically, there is also a sense in which cosmopolitanism is already implied in some formulations of national citizenship, a thesis examined in chapter three. There is a further sense in which many 'liberal nationalists' and 'liberal communitarians' are often closet cosmopolitans, or, at least, have deep yearnings in this direction. For example, the chapter on liberalism argues, in effect, that nationalism can be linked with variants of liberal universalism. This latter tendency can also be observed in chapter five, namely, where the particularism of patriotism is occasionally conflated with the universal of reasonable republicanism. On the other hand, within cosmopolitan theories there is also a deep anxiety concerning the particular or local. There is, in other words, a straining of the various particularisms towards the universal (cosmopolitanism) and an equal pressure for cosmopolitanism to take account of particularism.

The first section of this chapter clarifies the terminology surrounding cosmopolitanism. The next three sections, which form the main body of discussion, examine the relation between nationalism and cosmopolitanism via three structures of argument, which have a pedagogic simplicity. The first considers arguments for the importance of cosmopolitanism over all forms of particularism. The second looks at the case for the particularism of cosmopolitanism. The third perspective examines arguments which try to blend and mediate between particularism and cosmopolitanism. The final section offers a brief critical overview of the problems.

What is cosmopolitanism?

The term cosmopolitan overlaps with aspects of other concepts. Thus, universal and universalism – as in universal human rights – are often taken as archetypal forms of cosmopolitanism. There are also the concepts global, globalism and globalization. Globalization is probably now the more common term. It does not have any immediate moral connotations, its more dominant focus being on economics, communication, transport and demographic change.[1] Then, there is the term international (or internationalism). Internationalism was coined by Jeremy Bentham in the 1780s to name a part of his legal theory which was concerned with the 'law of nations'. Internationalism is now though a more polymorphous word than universal, global or cosmopolitan, appearing in many guises from the Communist International, through international trade to international law or justice. These are the main potential overlaps with cosmopolitanism; however, other terms are now coming into use within the literature, for example, interculturalism, cross-culturalism, transnationalism and postnationalism, which allude to similar overlapping themes.

However, there are problems with this terminological domain. It is, for example, far from clear that the above terms are synonyms. Some meanings appear quite distinct. For some theorists, for example, cosmopolitanism has pejorative connotations as against the positive overtones of internationalism or universalism. Further, one might either believe in international law to regulate warfare, or that globalization of communications and markets is inevitable, but have no sympathy whatsoever with any moral or political case for cosmopolitanism or internationalism. It is a commonplace that one can be a legal cosmopolitan, believing in some form of international law, but have no interest in moral cosmopolitanism. For others, universalism appears antiquated, whereas cosmopolitanism is a product of modernity. Universalism can thus be equated with Christianity, Marxism and liberalism, each being associated with the complex legacy of occidental imperialism. Universalism thus asserts a particular authority over other structures of thought. This can be distinguished from cosmopolitanism which engages creatively with other cultures, eschews imperialism, claims no unique authority and does not presume any necessary commonalities (see Hollinger 1995 and Appadurai 1996). It is therefore worth noting immediately that the concepts universalism, internationalism, globalization and cosmopolitanism are all equally contestable. There is no settled meaning to any of these terms.

Further, each term crosses over a number of areas of intellectual concern. The debates in these various domains, although having structural similarities, do not therefore necessarily communicate. Thus, for example, in law cosmopolitanism appears in the context of debates about the viability of international law, international treaties and human rights. In its older and still relevant format, it appears in a long-standing jurisprudential debate about natural law and legal positivism. In present-day concerns about genocide in Rwanda, Bosnia, Kosovo and East Timor, it also surfaces as the background setting for 'crimes against humanity' and the establishment of international war crimes tribunals. This practical emphasis is also embedded in groups such as Amnesty International and the like.

In contemporary economics, particularly market-based economics, there is an unwitting tendency towards a naturalistic cosmopolitanism. Thus, we cannot help being global consumers. Neither the basic laws of economics, nor the universal demands of *homo economicus*, are respecters of localism. Markets, in the name of profit margins, will always run roughshod over local phenomena. Globalization – qua cosmopolitanism – in economics, thus usually means the globalization of companies, labour, capital, finance, banking, credit, production and trade. Nothing is alien to capital.[2]

In contemporary moral philosophy, cosmopolitanism is one important dimension of a long-standing debate about the nature and scope of morality, that is, are moral beliefs universal or particular? Thus, the characteristic moral systems of Kantianism or utilitarianism, as cosmopolitan, are usually contrasted to the situated, particularistic, communal and conventional (Humean or Hegelian) conceptions of morality. The Kantian categorical imperative or the utilitarian greatest happiness principle, are typical of such universal moral beliefs. Kant's universalistic ethics also often links directly with legal, political and moral theories and policies, as, for example, sketched in Kant's essay *Perpetual Peace*. Kant's essay and his underlying work on practical reason are hardy perennials, usually taken as key examples of authoritative philosophical cosmopolitanism.

In international relations political theory, cosmopolitanism surfaces in forms more familiarly encountered in mainstream political theory. Cosmopolitanism can thus be tacitly observed in distinctions between, for example, 'men' and 'citizens' or 'communitarians' and 'universalists', or 'nation states' and 'international justice', as well as in debates about the ideas of boundaries and sovereignty. However, there is also the more unpredictable empirical dimension of war and weaponry, which provides another bleaker perspective on international relations and cosmopolitanism. The nuclear warhead or Kalashnikov rifle are as much symbols of a kind of realistic cosmopolitanism as Kant's perpetual peace. Nuclear weapons are no respecters of nations or localities. Modern warfare, particularly nuclear, chemical or biological warfare – rather like environmental issues – forces a melancholy cosmopolitanism upon us.

One of the most active domains of anxious theorizing about cosmo-politanism is contemporary anthropology. The anxiety stems from a challenge to the very roots of the discipline of anthropology, as developed from the nineteenth century. It is concerned essentially with the status and capacity of Western social science disciplines to study objectively the particular and local. In other words, is Western social science a universal (cosmopolitan), objective mode of rational discourse and observation, or is it just another form of Western parochialism, colonialism, imperialism or particularism? In this context, cosmopolitanism teeters on the edge of its own idiosyncratic localism or particularism. This has become a prevalent theme in contemporary anthropologists such as James Clifford. In the art world, including architecture, the cosmopolitan perspective has also emerged in the claims for 'international art' (thus International Biennales), as against the particularism of the national-based art. This conflict became a major critical theme in the 1980s, in art journals such as *Modern Painters*, a journal initially (but no longer) devoted to criticizing international art from a heavily particularist and nationalist aesthetic perspective.

Finally, in English studies and cultural studies, the cosmopolitan theme has given rise to heated debates, often leading to disciplinary and institutional mutation. English studies have sometimes literally given up both the literature canon and the discipline, handing themselves lock, stock and barrel to cultural and critical theory. Literature traditionalists, who still focus on canonical literature, are vilified. A postmodern insti-tutional apartheid often takes over. A new postmodern hegemony then prevails with its inner elites, doctrinal imperatives, inquisitions and exemplar authority figures. Cosmopolitanism, qua literature, is then replaced by a surreptitious canon of particularist, gendered, gay, ethnic or postcolonial critics of the cosmopolitan canon of European literature. The old canonical literary figures are either deconstructed or just replaced on the curriculum by the ethnically or gender validated poets or playwrights.

Obviously it is impossible to cover all these various dimensions of cosmopolitan debate; however we should be careful not to over-segmentalize. To simply focus on questions of international justice or ethics, ignoring cognate debates, would seriously limit our grasp of the breadth of the issues involved. The problem remains, however, how to encapsulate this debate in manageable proportions? On one level, it is tempting to think that there is one general underlying problem here which is philosophical in character, but keeps reappearing in different forms. As Thomas Nagel puts it: it is the problem of 'how to combine the perspective of a particular person inside the world with an objective view of that same world, the person and his viewpoint included. It is a problem that faces every creature with the impulse and the capacity to transcend its particular point of view and to conceive of the world as a whole' (Nagel 1986, 3). Cosmopolitanism, at one level, is about that transcendental impulse; however it is not just an issue in the philosophy of mind. Particularism, in its own way, is also manifestly an abstraction and a form of transcendence.

The nationalist/cosmopolitan relation will now be examined through three overlapping questions: is cosmopolitanism universalist? Is cosmopolitanism particular? And, finally, is cosmopolitanism universal and particular?

Is cosmopolitanism universalist?

Why do we try to separate out the claims of nationalism and cosmopolitanism? In political theory cosmopolitanism implies that there is some form of order, systems of values, entitlements, rights or justice which transcends any particular social relations. We encounter it most familiarly in the context of human rights theory. It is also a system of values which provides an external standard through which to evaluate particular political order. Cosmopolitanism implies, at one level, both universal values and the ability to transcend the particular. Cosmopolitan justice would be achieved if one responded to the basic needs of all human beings on a roughly equal basis regardless of nationality, gender, ethnicity or location. It also implies a background conception of individualism (human persons over institution or groups) and a notion of equality. In the context of its stress on formal equality, individualism, the rule of law, justice and human rights it has close links with the ideology of liberalism.

The origins of cosmopolitanism date back to the ancient Greek world. There were two prevalent conceptions of order in the Greek world: the natural (which could be observed and used, for example, in agriculture or navigation); the other order was that found in the organizations of human beings, particularly the polis. *Polis* implies city-state, *polites* a citizen. The community of the polis (*koinoneia*) is distinguished from nature by being under human control and practices. There was always an interest in the link between cosmos and polis (natural and political order). It was first explored by the Stoics. For Stoics, social and natural regularities both exemplified the same cosmic force. Nature reinforced the political order. There was thus a 'wise' natural providence behind social existence. 'Nature' was, in fact, one of the Stoic terms for the spiritual principle. To live according to nature was to live according to a spiritual principle, which, in essence, was a life controlled by 'universal' reason. This was the source of both human happiness and virtue. All human beings were

creatures of the same spiritual substance of reason, therefore it followed
for the Stoics that there was a *universal bond* between all human beings.
The whole universe as such might therefore, for the Stoics, be viewed as
a 'civic community of reason' in which the divine and human were linked
in common world citizenship – *cosmopolis* – a city which was co-extensive
with the whole cosmos. It was in this context that the Stoic, Marcus
Aurelius, invited his readers to consider 'Whether a man's lot be cast in
this place or in that matters nothing, provided that in all places he views
the world as a city and himself its citizen. Give men the chance to see
and know a true man, living by Nature's law' (Aurelius 1967, Bk 10,
no. 15, 157). Cosmopolis therefore implied a universal civic order (which
is natural); a *cosmopolitan* is a world citizen. As yet, we do not have a
universalan or globalitan – although give it time.

For admirers and critics alike, the dominant figure of cosmopolitan
modernity is Kant. This is primarily the Kant of the essay *Perpetual Peace*
and the exponent of practical reason.[3] He has thus frequently been seen
as *the* great theorist of international relations, a harbinger of the League
of Nations and United Nations, European or world peace, human rights,
pacifism, and even, for some, a proponent of world government and
world citizenship. A Kantian scholar has thus described Kant's writings
here as 'startlingly prophetic' (see Wood in Pheng Cheah and Robbins
(eds) 1998). Many such interpretations of Kant miss the central themes
of the above essay. For Kant, cosmopolitan peace is by no means an easy
option. In fact, he appears to take a somewhat mordant and pessimistic
view (see Gallie 1977, 12). However, it would be true to say that Kant
(and neo-Kantianism to the present day) still captures an important
sense of why cosmopolitans are resistant to or uneasy with nationalism.

There are three dimensions to the reading of Kant's argument in
Perpetual Peace: first the legal reading – which comes closest to the constitutional gist of the essay; second, the political dimension of the work –
which encompasses the qualified pessimism and minimalist pragmatism
of Kant's essay; and, third, the moral dimension – which encompasses
much of the interest in Kant from moral and political philosophers and
focuses on the concept of practical reason. In fact, the critique of Kant
which is offered by nationalist, postcolonial and postmodern writers
usually focuses on the Kant of moral philosophy, rather than the legal and
political dimensions. These three dimensions do not necessarily cohere.

Under the legal category, the essay has a more worldly aim, namely,
to indicate that constitutional republican governments are preferable,
insofar as they uphold basic internal legal rights and duties of citizens;
that republican constitutional states are less likely to go to war, since
they would tend to accept, with greater ease, cosmopolitan notions of
right and that some of the constitutional entitlements, already held

by individual citizens within states, could be extended, on an elementary level, to citizens of foreign states. Kant had in mind here facilitating free trade and being hospitable and relatively open to foreigners who travelled through a state's territory.[4] For Kant, republican constitutional states were also less likely to try to solve problems with other states by violence or coercion. Freedom of the will and self-determination work equally at the levels of both individual and state.

Kant is neither aiming at world government, nor the undermining of state sovereignty. Kant's legal cosmopolitanism is thus not radical in our own terms, although given the time it was written, and the dominance of absolutist states, such as Kant's own Prussia, it could be said to be forward-looking. There is, for example, a sincere demand for the rule of law. Yet, Kant's legalistic approach in the domestic sphere is, comparative to later eighteenth and nineteenth century ideas of civil society and basic rights, fairly austere and minimal. However, in the international sphere, such ideas do look much more optimistic. Yet, in a stringent legal sense, Kant's cosmopolitanism can be said to largely now exist in the developed world. However, it is a reality which we would no longer probably see as *strictly* cosmopolitan, which shows how far we have moved from Kant's own time.

The second, 'political', category follows on from the legal. On a very directly practical and immediate historical level, Kant was obviously concerned about the political survival of Republican France.[5] He clearly saw France as a 'role model' and possible leader of a broader republican constitutional government in Europe. He also hoped, in the longer term, for the development of a loose political federation of constitutional – hopefully republican-inclined – states, which would acknowledge minimal common rights and obligations. His appeal was to self-interest and political survival. He envisaged that the only alternative to this was the threat of war and insecurity, which undermined civilization and commerce. Unlike Vattel, Kant did not accept any right to the moderate or limited use of war. Although self-defence was politically inevitable, Kant saw *all* war as intolerable. However, political federations were also difficult things to manage, as the present European Union debates amplify. If federations become too strong then 'supra' state conditions develop; if they are not strong enough, then individual states reassert themselves. Kant was aware that a fine balancing act was at issue. He therefore proposed a federation for very limited 'politically appealing' ends, involving mutual agreements to trade, non-aggression, and relatively free movement.

Kant shared a view common with a number of theorists, such as Adam Smith, over the eighteenth century (and still held by some who look at the positive dimension of globalized commerce), that the 'spirit of commerce', particularly, could gradually replace or undermine the 'spirit of war' (see Hirschman 1977). As yet, Friedrich List was not on the scene; free trade and commerce were seen by Kant to stabilize relations between states. This is a classic political *modus vivendi* form of argument. States will accept a federation and peace because it is in both their short and long term interest. There is also a Humean addition that can be made here. Once states have practised such federation for many years, then they will become habituated or accustomed to it and it will then become conventional practice. This is a slightly more cynical way of speaking of the 'evolution' of human consciousness. We gradually mutate through self-interest onto different platforms of conventional practice. In this context, as Kant noted, with some basic pragmatic agreement, consensual rules and intelligent understanding even a nation of devils could get on (Kant, *Perpetual Peace* in Reiss (ed.) 1991, 112). In the context of the pragmatic approach – which hopes for a conventional and growing *modus vivendi*, acknowledging, at the same time, that humans are, by nature, irretrievably flawed – Kant's views are, as one scholar has put it, 'strongly reminiscent of Augustine' (Williams 1983, 266).

One important caveat here is that Kant's *Perpetual Peace* is historically prior to – although on the cusp of the development of – both genuine capitalist commerce and assertive state-based nationalism. The idea that commerce, qua List or Marx, might not be beneficent and that cosmopolitan free trade might have a downside, does not figure in Kant. Further, Kant's apparent cosmopolitanism is not, in itself, anti- or post-nationalist. Despite Kant's subsequent cosmopolitan reputation, nationalism, in its first European blush (before it had colonized European states), was not perceived to be anti-cosmopolitan. This was something that liberal nationalists, from Mazzini to the present day, have always tried to trade on.

The third dimension of the *Perpetual Peace* argument focuses on *reason*, particularly practical reason. This is the key dimension picked up by twentieth century admirers of Kant and proponents of cosmopolitanism. There are, though, three possible readings of the 'significance of reason' claim which progressively weaken the force of cosmopolitanism. The first argues that reason is the universal theme and a fundamental resource for cosmopolitan morality. Kant thus becomes a 'startlingly prophetic' figure, providing powerful responses to the twentieth century issues of world hunger, human rights and nationalism. This is Kant understood as an unequivocal cosmopolitan theorist, who refused to regard human beings in terms of rank, station, class, sex or race; in other words, the father figure of twentieth century deontology and the constructivist practical reason industry. The second view of reason is more ambiguous and stretched. It employs an early 'evolution of consciousness' theme, implying that reason is severely limited and that we need to evolve slowly and be tutored by states and nature over a very long time span. The third view is even more ambiguous again and focuses on the nature/culture relation. This latter argument moves us in a different direction and will take the discussion into the next section of the chapter.

The first view is the most optimistic reading of Kant. There are two aspects to this argument, the first concerned with the term reason itself, and the second with the impact of reason in terms of cosmopolitan rights and duties.

First, Kant's notion of reason implies unity and system (which links closely with the idea of the ordering of our sense impressions and our understanding of the physical world); second, it implies self-criticism and self-determination (which implies controlling our actions under rules). These two main functions of reason constitute theoretical and practical spheres.[6] One of the powerful implications of the Kantian position on knowledge is therefore to distinguish the spheres of theoretical from practical reason. The distinction, which has ancient roots, in Kant's hands becomes immensely influential. Theoretical pure reason is demonstrable. The categories of thought, intuition, space, time, quality, quantity and causality refer to the interrelation between finite things and objects. Such categories are valid for the natural physical sciences; however, for Kant, they are not appropriate in the sphere of religion, morality or political life. Human beings are finite and their cognition and reason are linked to their finiteness. Infinite categories, such as God, morality or freedom, cannot be demonstrated in finite terms. Kant suggests that the only way out of the impasse is through the postulate of practical reason. For Kant, humans, unlike animals, can have knowledge of themselves and can control themselves and assign themselves obligations. In performing acts of self-legislated duty we raise ourselves above our immediate finiteness. Yet, we can never theoretically know anything above the finite. Religion, morality and politics are linked to practical reason. We can act quite reasonably 'as if' God and morality exist. Practical reason remains though for ever open-ended and uncompleted. It is concerned with trial and error. It is also something which cannot be demonstrated or fully known. Its recognition, for Kant, is apodictic.

The essential message of Christianity is that human beings recognize, implicity or explicitly, the authority of reason. The laws of reason therefore constitute the unity of the human species. Practical reason is universal. To be human is therefore to be rational and, at one level, part of the worldwide commonwealth.[7] It is in this light that Allen Wood comments that 'the unity of Kant's philosophy may ... be viewed as the unity of the *historical* task of the Enlightenment. Looking at it in this way, the project of perpetual peace emerges as the central focus of Kant's critical or enlightenment philosophy. As distinct from the progress of morality in each individual, of knowledge in particular sciences ... perpetual peace is the global or cosmopolitan project in which the human race must unite if it is to advance in its historical vocation, and hence preserve its nature, as a species destined to turn natural discord into rational concord. The three Critiques ... aim at a rational system of thought whose historical actuality is vitally bound to the project of perpetual peace' (Wood in Pheng Cheah and Robbins (eds) 1998, 72). This implies a massively optimistic and unifying task for reason.

Strangely, whereas Kant was, on the above theoretical level, optimistic about the scope and future of reason, *per se*, more recent Kantian-inspired thinkers, such as O'Neill, have been far more cautious and minimalist – although O'Neill claims to be a 'maverick Kantian'. Reason, for O'Neill, implies something quite specific. It must account and allow for a variety of agents (all human agents in fact) and also be able to guide action and discriminate between categories. Thus, for O'Neill, 'practical reasoning begins by requiring us to reject principles which we cannot view as principles for those for whom the reasoning is to count'. In other words, reason must be truly universal – universalizality implying 'holding for all cases'. This is the Kantian vision of reason as 'doubly modal', namely, 'as the *necessity* to adopt principles which we think it *possible* for others to follow' (O'Neill 2000, 24). This is also the nub of her objection to all forms of particularism – nationalism and communitarianism. She continues, 'this rather stringent conception of universalizability [is] ... the core of practical reasoning'. This notion of reason is constructed (not discovered) from 'the demand that anything that is to count as reasoning must be followable by all relevant others' (O'Neill 1996, 4–6).

Practical reason also makes no claims concerning motivations. It is consequently neutral to context and circumstance and any 'idealized', perfectionist or virtue-based notions of agency. It must be non-arbitrary, available to, authoritative for and possible for all human agents. O'Neill is insistent here that we should not confuse idealizations and abstractions. Abstraction is 'giving a general account of some matter – one that literally abstracts from details' (O'Neill 1986, 28). *All* theory abstracts. Idealization (practical reason, virtue or perfectionist-based) involves a substantive ideal or set of beliefs about the content of agency or personhood. This also entails, for O'Neill, rejecting all metaphysical accounts of reason and agency.

Her notion of Kantianism is 'maverick' insofar as it eschews any 'idealizations' of agency and insists on more 'context sensitivity', although precisely where context sensitivity arises from is not clear. She also describes this as a 'stripped-down' conception of Kantian practical reason (O'Neill 1996, 25). This is her attempt to link up abstraction with diversity and particularity. In this context, she thinks she side-steps communitarian criticism, which is, in her estimation, always focused on 'idealized' agency. Thus, her sense of reason is quite self-consciously more minimalist and sparse than Kant's. In fact, she thinks that one has to be much more guarded on this issue than even Rawls or other contemporary minimalist neo-Kantians. Practical reason is action-orientated, not ideal-orientated. An action is reasonable not because it seeks an end or principle, but because it embodies intrinsically certain principles which can be 'abstractly described' (O'Neill 1996, 49ff). A similar argument holds in Alan Gewirth's seminal work *Reason and Morality*.[8] O'Neill is clear that universality does not prescribe uniform actions or ideals. It is also sensitive to difference and particularity, and only insists that, on a formal level, universality means 'holding for all'. It thus works with 'grids of existing categories, but retains the capacity to review and criticize them' (O'Neill 1986, 138). Nonetheless, no matter how abstract, reason must still begin with the 'gritty realities of human life' (O'Neill 1996, 61). As O'Neill remarks in another essay, 'Kant's view accords rather well with certain daily pre-philosophical views, particularly of action, principles and judgement' (O'Neill 2000, 2). This is the premise on which one constructs abstractions which are adoptable, authoritative and followable by all. Again, how 'gritty realities' gel with abstract universals remains puzzling and what precisely the gritty realities are for all humans remains problematic.

Brian Barry uses comparable arguments on the question of justice. In fact, justice, in a purely formal sense, can be defined as treating like cases alike, which is conceptually equivalent to reason as universalizability (see Perelman 1963). For Barry, there is no underlying core of values to be discovered. The constructivist theme is thus activated. There are no 'goods' to be derived from social meanings. He considers all such particularist communitarian claims 'tendentious' and 'grotesque' (Barry 1995a, 5–6). Such claims also exaggerate the incommensurability of cultures and reasons. Reason is concerned with abstract conclusions drawn from premises that everyone accepts. Barry thus believes in the 'possibility of putting forward a universally valid case in favour of liberal egalitarian principles'. Principles of justice capture a notion of equality which is equivalent to reason as universalizability. Thus, he comments that 'the criterion of reasonable acceptability of principles gives some substance to the idea of fundamental equality while at the same time flowing from it. This is, if you like, a circle – but not a vicious one'. They are both 'expressions of the same moral idea' (Barry 1995a, 3 and 8). Reason, justice and a notion of equality are equivalent to impartiality and universalizability. Justice, for Barry, is 'a set of reasons why people (or societies) may have duties' (Barry in Goodin and Pettit (eds) 1997, 528).

However, Barry has more faith than O'Neill, in the notion of reason embedded in Rawls' early work. Unlike O'Neill, he sees nothing idealized or particularist about Rawls' idea of reason.

Barry's crucial difference to particularist theory is that he claims to 'draw upon ordinary beliefs critically and selectively, employing a general theory of justice as a touchstone' (Barry 1995a, 10). Practical reason in Barry thus functions in a similar way to O'Neill's notion of abstraction (qua reason). Barry, also, like O'Neill, wants to draw reason (as justice) distinct from a moral cosmopolitan sense of 'humanity'. Our sense of 'humanity' directs us not to cause suffering and to relieve distress where we can. It is tied to substantive notions of well-being, but it is not directly about justice and reason. This has some parallel with O'Neill's notion of 'idealization'. 'Idealization', like 'humanity', invites consideration of a specific substance to community, agency, and the like, and, consequently, opens the argument up to particularist and interpretative criticism. O'Neill is, however, even more minimalist, or morally abstemious, than Barry, preferring not to entertain *any* idealizations, even the concept of 'humanity'. However, in the final analysis, if push comes to shove, one suspects that O'Neill would agree with Barry that in certain circumstances 'humanity, fidelity, and fair play ... coincide and reinforce each other' (Barry in Goodin and Pettit (eds) 1997, 530). Abstraction, qua O'Neill, also parallels Barry's notion of justice (as impartiality); both side-step problems of cultural plurality and difference, by insisting on justice as concerned with power and distribution, and not with idealizations or substantive monistic moral goods. Both also claim to derive hermeneutically their notion of abstract reason/justice from 'gritty realities' (O'Neill) or 'ordinary beliefs' (Barry), which, again, in appearance, side-steps the charge of being too thin and distant from brute realities (Barry 1989, 8; also Barry 1995a, 10).

However, a recent critique of Barry's work by Daniel Bell accuses him of adopting a deeply 'parochial universalism' (qua practical reason), which takes no account of the sensibilities of Asian cultures. Bell continues that 'This should worry those concerned with promoting human rights in a Chinese context, for Barry's book [*Justice as Impartiality*] can be seized upon as yet another arrogant attempt by Western liberals to push forward a "universal" theory that rides roughshod over the cultural particularities of non-Western societies' (Bell 1998, 568). For Bell, given that Barry draws only very *selectively* on the existing beliefs of one particular culture, in terms of Barry's own previous judgement on communitarianism, his theory is only half 'tendentious' and 'grotesque'. In other words, for Bell, Barry is a communitarian particularist in cosmopolitan clothes.

Despite the abstemious minimalist conception of practical reason in contemporary theorists, when it comes to the question of application there is a paradoxical reversal of roles between Kant and neo-Kantians. Whereas Kant has a thicker and more optimistic vision of reason, his vision of politics is remarkably restrained and conservative. This may partly have been the result of living in an autocratic absolutist regime, partly of his own temperament. Strangely, the opposite happens with neo-Kantians who hold to the minimalist abstemious view of reason. Suddenly, thin abstract reason and justice become thick cosmopolitan social democracy. O'Neill claims, for example, that 'there are abstract and widely comprehensible principles without which the activities even of partially rational beings risk incoherence, which have determinate implications for actions that affect the hungry and destitute' (O'Neill 1986, xiii). No matter how intuitively attractive, exactly how the rich 'determinate implications for actions' come about remains mysterious.

For O'Neill, practical reason, in practice, implies that one should not act unjustly, coerce or deceive. Practical reason is 'agent neutral' and 'universal' (O'Neill 1986, 144). It draws our attention to plurality, finitude and our connection with others. These form the baselines for cosmopolitan ethical consideration. Thus, as O'Neill comments: 'What is assumed for purposes of activity must also be assumed in fixing the scope of ethical consideration' (O'Neill 1996, 106). Practical reason implies a universal obligation to respect all agents – which is possible for all agents. Respecting agents, however, means responding to them as *physical beings*, since materiality constitutes human beings 'as human'. For O'Neill, 'human beings begin by being physically vulnerable. They are damaged by hunger, disease and cold, and coerced by their prospect'. If material needs are not met, then the principles of ethics are too thin. This has direct parallels with Michael Walzer's 'reiterative universalism' and Martha Nussbaum's 'quality of life' contention that, for example, 'we are all born naked and poor; we are all subject to disease and misery ...; finally we are all condemned to death'. For Nussbaum we should therefore 'recognize humanity wherever it occurs, and give its fundamental ingredients, reason and moral capacity, our first allegiance as respect' (see Nussbaum in Cohen (ed.) 1996, 7 and 132).[9] O'Neill consequently notes, in the same vein, that 'a just global economic and political order would ... have to be one designed to meet material needs'. *If* one accepts that 'agent neutral' universal respect implies responding to physical need, *then* such respect would have to be 'embodied in economic and political structures'. Practical reason thus implies respect for 'rationality and autonomy in the vulnerable form in which they are actually found'. A just global order 'would have to consist of institutions and policies whose underlying principles do not neglect human, including material, needs under actual conditions'. A Kantian just world 'would be one whose economic, social and political structures were based on universalizable principles' (O'Neill 1986, 149 and 159). Cosmopolitan justice and rights are thus apparently derived directly from modal practical reasoning. A parallel point is derived from Barry's 'not so thin' notion of justice as impartiality. For Barry, the application of such impartial reason leads us in the direction of international taxation, progressively related to increases in GNP. As he states, 'humanity and justice requires a substantial expansion in the scale of economic transfers from rich countries to poor ones' (Barry in Goodin and Pettit (eds) 1997, 536).

However, the above view of reason in Barry, O'Neill and the early Rawls is inert. Its character, of necessity, is unchanging and ahistorical. Reason has no history. It is either realized or it is not. The alternatives are either/or's. One is either reasonable or unreasonable, either cosmopolitan or nationalist. As Barry mordantly notes, the *only* alternative to his argument on justice 'is a world in which the general presumption is of national autonomy, with countries being treated as units capable of determining the use of those resources to which they were justly entitled. This is the world we now have, and the only modification in the status quo I am arguing for is a redefinition of what justly belongs to a country' (Barry in Goodin and Pettit (eds) 1997, 539). Thus, either one accepts Barry's account and remains reasonable, or, one has doubts about it, and, by definition, one becomes unreasonable. Surely, by any measure, this is an unreasonable argument!

Unexpectedly, a more equivocal use of reason can also be found in Kant, which modifies the above stark either/or perspective. This second view emphasizes, conversely, a slow painful evolution of reason. This reading gives considerably more space to Kant's conception of nature. There are, however, three more definite conceptions of nature in Kant: nature as benign wise providence, nature as blind amoral causality, and nature as potential depravity. All are problematic and reverberate with something of the slow evolution theme. The first has echoes of Stoicism and Judaeo-Christian cosmology. Nature embodies a wise evolving providence; we are pulled, even in the midst of our imperfections, into a path of moral gradualism. There is a hypostasized teleological design within nature for the education of the human race. This has parallels with Adam Smith's 'invisible hand', although Lessing might also have some bearing upon Kant's ideas.

The second view of nature is probably more familiar qua natural science. Thus, Kant's whole epistemology starts from the premise of self-reflective mind, rather than nature (see Boucher 1998, 270). This is essentially his 'Copernican revolution' and the source of his reputation for epistemological dualism. Nature is essentially the realm of blind causality. Reason and morality are *not* deduced from it. Reason is not sought, for example, in anthropology or biology.[10] Free action is uncaused by empirical conditions. It is action by the will according to a self-legislated law – uncaused cause. There is no *empirical* substance other than the will 'willing'.

The third view of nature is captured, in part, in Kant's notion of 'unsocial sociability', also in his idiosyncratic reflections on 'radical evil'. Behind many of Kant's moral reflections is the traditional, Lutheran pietism of his upbringing. Nature represents passions, instincts and chaotic desires. These are forces which are potentially depraved. The purpose of morality, rationality and religion is to ensure that we are not led by these natural passions into depravity. Thus, for Kant, we are not responsible for having natural passions, but we are responsible for wallowing in or indulging them. Humans can and ought to control themselves rationally. Each individual is the 'protestant' governor of their own soul, conscience and relation with God.

Behind all these readings of nature is the idea of a tortuous evolution of human reason. Hypothetically, for Kant, civil association arises gradually from a state of nature. We are lazy, unsocial, self-interested, led by our passions and often lacking in basic civility. Yet, each of us, as Kant notes, 'possesses a greater moral capacity, still dormant at present, to overcome eventually the evil principles within him (for he cannot deny that it exists), and to hope that others do likewise' (Kant, *Perpetual Peace* in Reiss (ed.) 1991, 103).[11] The evil principle appears to be our 'animal or bestial inclinations' and our inclination to depravity. In this context, it is hardly surprising that Kant notes that men, in general, tend to need a master to control and tutor them.[12] War is just a facet of this 'evil principle'. But war, by natural providence and the fear and insecurity it engenders, focuses humans on peace. Practical reason gradually evolves from the deeply unpleasant conditions we surround ourselves with. This reading sounds distinctly Hobbesian or Augustinian, but Kant, unlike Hobbes or Augustine, did not see human relations as immutable. Humans can learn and evolve through commerce, travel and education. Initially, self-interest will lead them in this direction to a *modus vivendi*. They will try to exercise self-control and thus practical reason will very slowly arise. Order, peace and, more particularly, cosmopolitan right will be a painfully slow process.

Is cosmopolitanism particular?

The final Kantian reading of reason moves the discussion into the second major question of this chapter. In the previous analysis, reason is viewed teleologically. Cosmopolitanism is the outcome of a long tortuous evolution of reason. Although universal practical reason is sullied and muddied in practice, it still stands out as a future possibility, no matter how improbable or remote. This connects up with the more politicized and realist reading of *Perpetual Peace*.

However, the third reading of reason, in Kant, marks out a definite transition from an inert ahistorical conception, towards a world of greater uncertainty and contingency. An attempt will be made in this next section to unpack some of the roots of that uncertainty. This analysis will, by default, thus consider the question as to whether cosmopolitanism is particularist. It is, though, a mark of Kant's greatness that he bestrides, however problematically, both questions.

The first intimation of this third reading can be found in writers such as Gottfried Herder. Herder, in criticizing Kant, denies the key status of reason itself as the dominant faculty of the human being. This alone is a fundamental shift. He comments: 'Human reason has been conceived as a novel and quite distinct faculty of the mind, as something that had been added to man to distinguish him from the animals ... destined to be singled out for special consideration. But to speak of reason in this manner is to talk philosophical nonsense, even if the greatest philosophers do the talking' (quoted in Barnard 1965, 41). For Herder, '"reason" approximates to "reasoning"; it is a *process*, not a faculty. Reason, thus conceived, cannot, however, be divorced from the other activities of mind'.[13] This contention opens up reason to blending with other faculties, like emotion. The 'status' of nature, qua mind or reason, becomes deeply problematic here. Second, reasoning is premised on language. For Herder, language is built out of sense impressions. Since sense impressions of locality form the basis of language, it follows that local conditions – geography, climate and traditions of a community – will stimulate differing responses. As languages develop, so do societies and cultures. Reason, with feeling, becomes embedded in language which is situated within culture. Culture is the bearer of this process. All humans using language will therefore form, through dialogue and conversation, distinctive cultures, mythologies and modes of expression. In other words, each *Volk* (people or nation) forms a distinct language community. This approach epitomizes Herder's attitude towards Kant, developed in his *Metakritik* (Barnard 1965, 41–2). The distinction between reason which is situated and Reason with a capital 'R', abstracted from all situations, is central to the particularist case.

However, despite Herder's more culturally based conception of reason, Kant's own moral argumentation contains its own internal puzzles. Reason, in Kant, is envisaged as an invariable, tranquil and neutral faculty, as distinct from the more chaotic faculties of emotion or feeling. Certainly this is the message of one reading of Kant's dualism of reason with passion and feeling. It follows, for Kant (also for O'Neill, Rawls and

Barry), that rights and justice are premised on abstract 'cosmopolitan' reason. Loyalty as feeling for a nation is wholly different. Feelings are elusive, inconstant, partial and lacking in universality. Justice, therefore, cannot arise from particular emotions. Universal or cosmopolitan validity is distinct from sentiment or historical attachment. Social or political conflict is resolved ultimately by reason, justice and rights. We must, in other words, to solve conflict, turn away from particular loyalties towards something more impartial and abstract. Modern-day Kantians, such as Habermas, O'Neill or Rawls, still largely share this general view.

Yet, there are ambiguities in Kant's views. Only the individual can freely choose. Only the self-determining being with 'auto-nomy' (self-giving of laws) can be free. This is the essence of enlightenment to Kant – the individual growing up and becoming mature, reasonable and responsible. Oppression is defined as being prevented, in some manner, from self-direction. But self-direction can be either quietistic, intro-spective and insular or extrovert and confrontational. Anything which enhances my self or alternatively inhibits my self-direction becomes significant. Fichte's ego or Max Stirner's anarchistic *Eigenheit* lurch into view here. The crucial point here is that all values must be '*my* values'. It is the self-ownership and self-authorship which become pivotal. 'I' *construct* my own values. This might be described as the flip side of 'constructivism'. This position still trades ambiguously on Kantian themes, but the implications are different. *My* willing is crucial. The timeless transcendent aspect of the self opens up questions on the self, namely, what constitutes the self? This argument brings us onto familiar territory. Many things can constitute the self. Probably the most obvious constituent of the self, for us, is the particular community, culture or language we were brought up with. In this sense, an internal dimension of Kant's argumentation unwittingly begins to link up with Herder's arguments. This is, of course, also the familiar theme of contemporary communitarian writing. For Walzer and Sandel there is no ultimate tribunal of reason or reasonableness – as in Rawls, Habermas, Barry and O'Neill – standing outside particular communities. The self is formed by and connected with the community.

The term *culture* also figures here with *community*, particularly in the German tradition. However, other 'collective' terms have also been employed, such as nation, race, tribe, army, church and class. Kant, of course, would not have accepted this interpretation. Yet, ironically, the moral significance of the choosing self, fortuitously, can open up the question of the moral significance of the community, by default, that is, once the self is queried and subsumed under some larger community entity such as the culture or nation. Moral values, by definition, qua Kant's dualism, are not constrained by nature or natural conditions.

There are *no* constraints outside of the will. The will 'wills'. Once the will becomes that of the community – as the source of the self – then something quite different arises.[14] Individual autonomy becomes, by default, national or communal autonomy. This is an argument discussed in previous chapters, thus I will not belabour it.

What we are faced with here is a peculiar amalgam of arguments. Kant formulates, for modernity, probably the most precise philosophical and practical account – reformulated in a number of thinkers to the present day – of the cosmopolitan perspective.[15] Kant's Enlightenment voice, however indistinct, speaks to us through much of the twentieth century yearning for cosmopolitanism, international law and political organization. However, in writers such as Montaigne, Hume or Herder, the sense that reason is more situated, ambivalent, enmeshed with custom, embedded in all the anfractuations of human existence, begins to take hold. Paradoxically, Kant unwittingly facilitated the development of this latter argument from within the terms of his own ethical thought. One important implication of this argument is that it can no longer cope with the more pristine assertion of cosmopolitanism. Cosmopolitanism inevitably is viewed through the lens of the particular.

There are three comparatively recent arguments which unpack this latter emphasis on the particularity of reason. Each has a distinctive bearing on the question of cosmopolitanism. The *first* negates cosmopolitanism by insisting on the thesis of humans as communally situated creatures. A *second* argument is more directly reductionist. Rather than denying the existence of cosmopolitanism, it accepts the reality of cosmopolitanism but sees it as a form of particularism in disguise. This argument has been most vociferously presented in some postcolonial theorizing, but it also forms one leitmotif in some of the reflections of the 'new ethnography' and postmodern theorizing. A *third* argument tries to evacuate pure particularity and universalism in favour of the hybrid and discrepant.

The first argument counters cosmopolitanism by affirming the brute reality of the nation or community as the only viable ontologies. The basic ideas of both communitarianism and nationalism obviously loom large here. However, this also links, quite fortuitously, with the 'realist' position in international relations.[16] The communitarian perspective would tend to view justice as the product of particular political communities, at identifiable times. Thus, any accounts of justice should be constructed within the terms of reference dictated by these communities.[17] Cosmopolitanism totally collapses here before the imperative of the nation state. Thus, Gertrude Himmelfarb, a more realist-inclined writer, equates cosmopolitanism with intellectual weak-mindedness and immaturity. Cosmopolitanism is described as a 'perilous illusion'. For her, no universal citizenship or welfare exist. These are all linked to nation state traditions. As she puts it, 'we do not come into the world as free-floating, autonomous individuals' (Himmelfarb in Cohen (ed.) 1996, 77). This argument will not be dwelt on, except tangentially, since it is discussed in previous chapters.

With regard to the second more reductionist argument, postcolonial theory has been described as a 'theoretical resistance to the mystifying amnesia of the colonial aftermath ... a disciplinary project devoted to the academic task of revisiting, remembering and, crucially, interrogating the colonial past' (Gandhi 1998, 4). Postcolonial theory is concerned with the *power* that is embedded in texts and discourse, for example, Edward Said's notion of 'oriental discourse'. Colonialism represents a textual takeover. Postcolonialism is the resistance to this (Gandhi 1998, 143). In effect, the first world of large industrialized Western societies, the ex-colonial powers, is seen to dominate the 'discourse' and 'identity' of the third world ex-colonies. An attempt is therefore made to discard or undermine the identity given to subject peoples by colonizers. Thus, for Gyan Prakash, 'it requires the rejection of those modes of thinking which configure the third world in such irreducible essences as religiosity, underdevelopment, poverty, nationhood, non-Westernness' (Prakash 1990, 384).[18] For Prakash, postcolonial theory wishes to 'undo the Eurocentrism produced by the institution of the West's trajectory, its appropriation of the other as History' (Prakash in Haynes and Prakash (eds) 1992, 8). Cosmopolitan liberalism is taken as an exemplar of Eurocentric theory.

One key area from which postcolonial argument initially developed is subaltern studies – particularly the work of Partha Chatterjee and Ranajit Guha (see Guha 1982, vol. 1). The term 'subaltern' derives from Antonio Gramsci, implying those in an inferior position, as distinct from an elite, for example, in terms of military rank. The roots of this position are Marxist (in fact, Gramscian), rather than postmodernist or poststructuralist, although there are postmodern aspects to some subaltern theorists. In subaltern studies, 'subaltern' becomes a more generic term for 'subordination', in terms of culture, ethnicity, class, gender, age and office. Western imperialist, Marxist and liberal histories are seen to embody Eurocentrism (premised on stark asymmetries of economic power), namely, the tendency to assume that history is European at root and founded upon and 'representable through some identity – individual, class, or structure' (Prakash 1990, 97). The aim of subaltern study is therefore to reinstate the histories of subaltern groups in South East Asia who have, in effect, been silenced, pushed to the margins or expunged by the colonizers and Westernized elites, from the historical record (Gandhi 1998, vii).

The second key influence on postcolonial writing is Edward Said's work, particularly his book *Orientalism*, which was the first of a trilogy (Said 1978).[19] This work is seen as an inspirational text by many post-colonial theorists, even if they are uneasy with some of its argument. The book, in essence, is about unmasking colonial ideology and its complex aftermath. All Western systems of description and interpretation of Asia and the East – particularly in the colonial period – are seen to embody, qua Foucault, 'strategies of power'. For Said, orientalism, in fact, denotes power (over or within knowledge). Essentially, the Western colonial nations are seen to construct the orient. This has the effect of shaping perceptions about (and within) colonized societies. Said draws on both Gramsci and Foucault here. Foucault is central to his account of the power of orientalism as an impersonal force controlling knowledge and cultural claims. Oriental discourse fabricates the object of knowledge and configures representation. The orient is, therefore, a 'discursive orient'. Orientalism represents a 'degradation of knowledge' – that is, a degradation of 'genuine' subaltern knowledge. Gramsci provides the more material end of the argument. Thus, Said conceives of colonialism as both a material domination, as well as a discursive power over knowledge.

One problem here is actually reconciling Foucault and Gramsci. In Foucault, power is not something that can be eradicated. It is impersonal. There is thus a latent pessimism within Foucault's poststructuralism. Gramsci, on the other hand, has all the optimistic teleology of potential emancipation one would expect from a Marxist.[20] Thus, whereas sub-altern studies appear to have a more obvious Marxist ethos, Said tries to bolster this materialist argument with Foucault's poststructuralism. The question is does it work? The two theories (Marxist and poststructural) appear to be directly contradictory. Said's later work in fact expresses his own severe doubts on this very issue.

On the other hand, writers such as Spivak succumb totally to the postmodern perspective (in her case to Derrida) and are consequently deeply uneasy with the Marxist, essentialist and foundational impli-cations of both Said's work and subaltern studies in general. A recent synoptic commentator even defines postcolonialism as 'work which is shaped primarily, or to a significant degree, by methodological affiliations to French "high" theory' (see Moore-Gilbert 1997, 1, and Young 1990). There is thus a quite definite intellectual link between postmodernism, subaltern and postcolonial studies, which can be observed quite clearly in Foucault's critique of Kant. Kant's notion of cosmopolitan reason (and thus Kant's conception of humanity) is seen, by Foucault, as an acci-dental phenomenon, which takes little or no account of the contingencies of human nature. Kant focuses on humanity manifesting 'adult western rationality'. Whereas Kant, and neo-Kantians to the present day, think of rationality as universal and transcending contingency, Foucault considers it a highly specific Eurocentric notion requiring genealogical investigation. Cosmopolitan enlightened reason 'is an event, or set of events and complex historical processes, that is located at a certain point in the development of European societies' (Foucault in Rabinow (ed.) 1984, 85). This notion of reason defines humans in certain ways, namely, according to their possession of this conception of cosmopolitan practical reason. Once humans are defined in this manner it excludes other ways of being human. This gives rise, for Foucault, to the notion of the in-human, namely, conceptions of humanity which do not conform to the cosmopolitan 'rationalist model'. Once the idea of Western adult rationality becomes the measure of being human, then others, for example the colonized or oriental, are viewed as only partly human – irrational, immature and childish.[21] Here we see the postmodern passion for unsettling 'binaries'.

The childlike, irrational or developing character of the colonized groups thus contributes directly to colonialism, namely, to the idea of the progressive civilizing, enlightened mission of colonialism and imperialism. We can see at this point the precise link between Foucaultian poststructural analysis and postcolonial theory. The particular interests of countries are defensible insofar as they are universalizable or conceived as cosmopolitan. Thus, Western colonizers and Kantian rationalists can say, in effect, that their interests are universalizable. Therefore, they move beyond the particular to the universal. For Foucault, however, this is only achieved by sleight of hand. For Foucault, 'Humanity does not progress ... until it arrives at universal reciprocity, where the rule of law finally replaces warfare; [rather] humanity installs each of its violences in a system of rules and thus proceeds from domination to domination' (Foucault in Rabinow (ed.) 1984, 85). For Foucault, it follows that the categories of cosmopolitan liberal thought (with Kant as a prime mover) can no longer be taken for granted, insofar as they have been deployed in the dubious projects aimed at 'civilizing' subjugated peoples and encouraging their 'development'. Thus, postcolonial and subaltern thought, in the language of postmodernism, are seen as forms of marginalized knowledge.

The other more ambiguous aspect of this intellectual resonance between postmodern and postcolonial writing is over the question of identity. Postmodernism is standardly critical of theories of the self and identity. The beginnings of this unease can be found in 'critical theorists', such as Adorno and Horkheimer, who focus on the 'logic of identity' present in Enlightenment thought, and consequently the 'terrorizing unity' implicit in such identity. The unified identity is revealed through what it excludes. Identity is thus indifferent or hostile to difference. In a somewhat far-fetched manner, Adorno and Horkheimer suggest that fascism is a product of Enlightenment desire for unity and the fear of difference (see Adorno and Horkheimer 1992). This latter point also resonates with Derrida's critique of the 'metaphysics of presence' and 'logocentrism', Foucault's whole theoretical *oeuvre* and Iris Young's critical work on justice theory and democracy. For Young, the logic of identity always 'flees sensuous particularity'.[22] Colonialism, for postmodern writers, is motivated by anxieties about difference and alterity. Grand narratives, such as cosmopolitanism, exist to suppress cultural identity and difference.

Strong intellectual resonances with the above views can also be found in current anthropology and ethnography. The general point would be that classical anthropology (for its critics) reinforces the idea of the inferiority and immaturity of the 'studied groups' – often the colonized peoples. The discipline of classical anthropology is seen to be complicit therefore in the history and practices of colonialism. In fact, its growth as an academic discipline largely coincides with the development of Western colonialism over the nineteenth century. Nineteenth and early twentieth century academic anthropologists largely reported from imperial colonial centres commenting on the customs of 'orientals' and the like. The twentieth century carried on this tradition, less obviously, in the subtle contrast between the Western academic social scientific investigator and the studied primitive society. In more recent anthropology, since the 1970s and 1980s, there has been more sensitivity on these questions. Initially, it was a concern in writers, like Clifford Geertz, with the interpretation of other cultures. Yet, with the increasing education of colonized peoples, the subject/object relation looked increasingly strained. The postcolonized subject could now speak (and write) back. In fact, the Western anthropological investigator, with her academic imperatives, conventions and limited audience, is seen to be as much in need of anthropological investigation as the previously studied colonial peoples.

Poststructural theory, particularly, encouraged an awareness of the 'constructed' nature of academic socio-cultural representations. Non-Western ethnography thus developed (often in the context of postcolonial theory and subaltern investigation) and the interrogative gaze of Western anthropology was met by an equally interrogative postcolonial gaze, a kind of 'ethnography in reverse'. A more reflexive anthropology developed in response to these pressures. This new anthropology is marked by a retreat from social science, the adoption of more literary methods of study, more awareness of the constructed nature of ethnographic texts and doubts about their purported authority. The scientific method of more traditional twentieth century anthropologists, such as Malinowksi, were therefore challenged by new anthropologists, such as James Clifford. The concern in Clifford, and others, is consequently to allow the indigenous to speak. The result, for its proponents, is a more decentered, reflexive and dialogic anthropology. Objective commentary is destabilized by self-reference and an awareness of diverse cultural audiences (see, for example, Clifford 1988, Clifford and Marcus (eds) 1986, Geertz 1988, Marcus and Fischer 1986).

A final argument concerns the recent Asian values debate. The central claim of the Asian values argument is that universal or cosmopolitan values, such as human rights, should always be viewed *through* particular cultures. As Abdullah A. An-Na'im argues, 'Like all normative systems, human rights regimes must necessarily be premised on a particular cultural framework'.[23] There are also strong resonances here with the recent attempts to envisage group or cultural rights as human rights. The underlying complaint is that Western human rights exponents are both profoundly ignorant of Asian societies and cultures and of Asian perceptions of the colonial legacy. Western human rights values are the product of particular colonial states. These parochial Western values miraculously become universal 'human values'. Thus, all such claims to human rights should therefore be treated with considerable caution.

Further, Western legal and political theorists usually fail to see their own culture (from which universal values are derived) as just *one* amongst many cultures.[24] They also tend to impose, subtly in this case, their own historical assumptions upon Asia. Thus, Western human rights proponents, for example, would tend to see universal human rights arising from a rejection of both older traditions and strong religious commitments. As Charles Taylor comments, 'To this extent they will tend to think that the path to convergence requires that others too cast off their traditional ideas, that they even reject their religious heritage'. Yet, Asian cultures have not gone through the same historical trajectory.[25] Religion may conventionally be more significant for them in justifying any rights.

This whole debate has been given a high profile by the interventions of Lee Kuan Yew of Singapore and Prime Minister Mahathir Mohamad of Malaysia. They have also reinforced the point that in countries where economic stability and security have already been gained there is not always a clear grasp of the importance it still has in Asia. Consequently, they contend that a curtailment of Western conceptions of human rights in the name of economic development and social harmony is fully justified. Democratization and individual civil freedoms, for example, are irrelevant to economic growth. Universal civil and political rights are thus expendable luxuries. However, they also claim that Asians also have their own very specific conception of what is valuable. It is argued, for example, that they place a very special emphasis upon communitarian values such as stable families and social harmony, as opposed to the West's obsession with individualism.[26]

A brief summary of the thrust of this *second* line of argument is therefore, that, rather than denying the existence of cosmopolitanism, it insists that cosmopolitanism *is* a form of nationalism or particularism in disguise. Postcolonialism privileges the localized and particular over the cosmopolitan or global. Indigenous nationalisms and particularisms, of many and diverse forms, clearly exist for these writers as viable forces, which either flourish or are suppressed. What we encounter in cosmopolitanism is therefore forms of Western particularism, namely, nationalism and imperialism, in the semblance of cosmopolitanism. This is what lies behind the critical accusation of 'Eurocentrism' regularly used by subaltern, postcolonial, postmodern, Asian values and ethnographic theories. The task this latter amalgam of theories sets itself, in a phrase, is essentially to 'provincialize Europe' or 'particularize cosmopolitanism'.

However, there are major problems with the above analyses: first, postcolonial writings are a peculiar, uncoordinated, incoherent amalgam of postmodernism, psychoanalysis, Marxism, feminism and ethnography – particularly in writers such as Edward Said, Homi Bhabha and Gayatri Spivak. Postcolonialism thus remains a deeply unsatisfactory, incoherent blanket term.[27] The relation between Marxism and poststructuralism remains unexplained and contradictory. Further, the relation between the anti-normativism of poststructuralism and the positive normative sentiments about postcolonial nationalisms and localisms remains inexplicable. Finally, many would also see the Asian values arguments as a peculiarly convenient cover for forms of authoritarian rule.

Is cosmopolitanism both universal and particular?

A *third* body of argument, which develops against the backdrop of the second, suggests a reformulation of cosmopolitanism to retain its most promising dimensions and jettison its worrisome aspects. Here we encounter eclectic creatures with titles such as discrepant, situated, rooted, vernacular, first world, third world or critical cosmopolitanisms. There is therefore neither rational cosmopolitanism nor particular nationalisms, but some form of *via media*.

Cosmopolitanism is seen to be closely linked to particularity, but not reducible to it. An internal plurality is discerned within the universal. Paul Rabinow, for example, in this spirit, defines cosmopolitanism as 'an ethos of macro-interdependence, with an acute consciousness (often forced upon people) of the inescapabilities and particularities of places, character, historical trajectories, and fates' (Rabinow in Clifford and Marcus (eds) 1986, 258). The positions being developed here are complicated. To try to provide some structure to this discussion it is important to grasp something of the background of thought to this new phase of argument about cosmopolitanism. The 'new cosmopolitanism' derives from two divergent sources. The first refers to implicit critical themes within the postmodern, postcolonial and ethnographic critique of traditional cosmopolitanism. The second concerns attempts within contemporary liberal theory to come to terms with difference.

One implicit theme within postcolonial, postmodern and ethnographic writings focuses on the importance of internal difference and hybridity. There is a quite unexpected logic at work here. Difference appears often in the same context as hybridity. Thus, a self-conscious valorizing of heterogeneity and difference might appear, *prima facie*, to be linked with hybridity. However, there are two internal strains within this argument. First, hybridity, *per se*, actually weakens the claim for difference; second, to uphold the heterogeneous or different, it is necessary to reutilize and revalorize the despised Eurocentric language of nationalism.

Thus, hybridity is one important aspect of Homi Bhabha's idio-syncratic postcolonial writings. Bhabha maintains, for example, that the 'postcolonial perspective forces a recognition of the more complex cultural and political boundaries that exist on the cusp of those often opposed political spheres' (Bhabha 1994, 175). The colonial mentality, in Bhabha's view, is more incoherent and ambivalent than many post-colonial or postmodern critics will acknowledge. It is far simpler, on one level, to posit a unified colonial perspective exemplifying Eurocentrism, than to take on board difference *within* that perspective. Part of that internal difference is explained by the interweaving of colonized and colonizers' perspectives. Thus, for Bhabha, colonial identity 'lies between colonized and colonizer. It is an ambivalent identification containing both fear and desire' (see Childs and Williams 1997, 125). Hybridity therefore represents the borderline, blending and complex overlap be-tween cultural perspectives. Bhabha, in effect, tries to 'problematize the *authority* of colonial discourse', namely, as something discrete and separate. The key theme here is a more complex, nuanced interweaving of beliefs between colonizer and colonized. This, in turn, problematizes the contrast between cosmopolitanism and postcolonial discourse and thus universalism and particularism.

Two consequences flow from this interweaving: first, it raises doubts about the postcolonial and postmodern critics who 'essentialize' the Eurocentric. Edward Said's, Foucault's, and much subaltern work thus commits the opposite error of the colonial writings they criticize (namely, those writings that 'essentialize' the orient), by assuming an essential occident, which, a moment's thought, let alone postmodernism, will tell one is ludicrous. In addition, with the growth of globalism – economic and otherwise – in practice, there has been an acceleration of hybridity and syncretism.[28] Many have also noted within modernity the massive acceleration of political, educational, technological and telecommunications interdependence, which has geographically compressed the world (see Virilio 1986). The coming together and blending of the histories of colonizers and colonized can also be partly accounted for in terms of complex processes of emigration, demographic movement, diasporas and economic globalization. In this context, to search for clear essentialist cultures (occidental or oriental) becomes an increasingly fruitless, if not futile, exercise.

The second issue concerns the attempt to valorize 'difference' – which has become a tedious mantra within cultural studies. One of the problems difference theorists and postcolonial writers encounter is that their rediscovery of the subaltern or suppressed voice is surreptitiously cast in terms of a Western vocabulary of valuing the particular (nationalism, culture, localism, ethnicity and the like) over the universal. As one commentator notes, 'nationalism, more specifically exemplified by the argument of the subaltern studies scholars of India, ... is an ideological humanism engendered from colonial discourse' (Pheng Cheah in Pheng Cheah and Robbins (eds) 1998, 21).[29] The notion of rediscovering a subaltern, precolonial, ethnic or local identity reeks of Herderian, romantic and communitarian terminology. It exoticizes the local and particular, which is a quite distinctively European motif. The West (whatever that implies) has no patent on this language. However, it is embarrassingly obvious that this kind of language exists through the broad ambit of European theorizing. The recovery of occluded histories of subalterns is expressed through the academicized vocabulary of European communitarian, nationalist or eclectic expressions of neo-Marxian theory.[30] Prioritizing nationalism or localism is thus not necessarily an answer to orientalism or colonial discourse.

Even the more radical postmodern focus on the marginal, by writers such as Derrida, Deleuze and Foucault, can also be viewed as part of the same European pattern of subtle intellectual appropriation. Thus, as one recent commentator notes, 'whether the object of "ethnocentric scorn" is the imperial period, or of "hyperbolic admiration" today, the subaltern's function (and subject-position) remains primarily constituted by the West' (Moore-Gilbert 1997, 90). This is one stock reason why writers such as Gayatri Spivak and Stuart Hall conceive of nationalism as a 'strategic essentialist' language, which serves a contingent political function for a historical moment, and has no essential interest, meaning or relevance beyond that moment. Yet, who would actually believe such postmodern 'strategic nationalism', apart from the small group of privileged intellectuals? There is something deeply intellectually smug about such pronouncements.[31]

Ironically, reflexive anthropology – in its initial rejection of the colonialism of Victorian and early twentieth century anthropology – has also facilitated colonial versions of nationalism. In asserting the importance of the precolonial customs and traditions and the need for 'authentic native voices' with which to engage in genuine dialogue, it not only reaffirms many highly questionable precolonial or ethnic practices, but also formally reasserts, paradoxically, a European-based nationalist vocabulary. It exoticizes and uncritically admires ethnic particularity, no matter what its content (see Ayelet Shachar 2000, 72).[32] It does seem amazingly myopic not to acknowledge this discomforting but obvious truth.

One upshot of the above critiques is the attempt at some kind of retrieval of 'contingent cosmopolitanism'.[33] The argument would be that any such new cosmopolitanism would have to make some distance between itself and the older cosmopolitanism of, say, neo-Kantian thinkers. As one commentator bluntly remarks: 'The history of colonialism has disproven Kant's benign view' (Pheng Cheah in Pheng Cheah and Robbins (eds) 1998, 234). It must now make its case for universalism in the midst of manifest particularity. Judith Butler's work is typical of this view. For her, the cultural conditions for the articulation of universals are not always the same. There is a reflexive logic at work here, which Butler sees as ultimately beneficial for cosmopolitanism. As she comments, 'If standards of universality are historically articulated, then it would seem that exposing the parochial and exclusionary character of a given historical articulation of universality is part of the project of extending and rendering substantive the notion of universality itself'. The cosmopolitan, in an older format, can act as an unwelcome moral censor (presumably in one form through colonialism). Conventions within universality can actually inhibit universalization. Butler thus claims that we need, in fact, to widen our understanding of the universal. There are literally Kantians in *every* culture. One implication of this is that we should avoid an 'idealized' content within the universal (Butler 1994). Butler sees this as exposing the 'alterity within the norm', which in turn 'exposes the failure of the norm to affect universal reach'. The universal thus shifts into a multicultural setting. Consequently, 'the futural articulation of the universal … can happen only if we find ways to effect cultural translations between these various cultural examples in order to see which version of the universal is proposed' (Butler in Cohen (ed.) 1996, 50 and 51). As Butler comments, 'the task that cultural difference sets for us is the articulation of universality through a difficult labor of translation' (Butler in Cohen (ed.) 1996, 47 and 52). In effect, the universal is criticized and made particular *for the sake of* the universal!

Something very similar to Butler, although more weak-minded, appears in Julia Kristeva's *Nations without Nationalism*. She is clearly uneasy with the older variants of cosmopolitanism, but, at the same time is also deeply disturbed by what is happening with particularism and national-ism in Eastern Europe. Unexpectedly – for a postmodern feminist – she unequivocally commits herself to the idea that there is still intellectual mileage in classical cosmopolitanism. She comments that 'It would seem to me that to uphold a universal, transnational principle of Humanity that is distinct from the historical realities of the nation and citizenship constitute, on one hand, a continuant of the Stoic and Augustinian legacy, of that ancient and Christian cosmopolitanism that finds its place among the most valuable assets of our civilization and that we henceforth must go back to and bring up to date. But above all and on the other hand, such upholding of universality appears to me as a rampart against nationalists, regionalists and religious fragmentation' (Kristeva 1993, 26–7). Kristeva thus sees something in the Enlightenment, and even the older classical cosmopolitanism, after all. The idea of a more civic or liberal-orientated nationalism is to be preferred over ethnicity. Countries, such as France or the USA, where patriotism is more overtly universalist in intent, therefore have some broader credence. In this case liberal nationalism drifts once more into view from the postmodern frame of reference.

Commentators on this whole drift of argument often see this re-claiming of a contingent cosmopolitanism as arising *from* hybridity. When the original cosmopolitanism encounters other cultures it inevitably blends with them. The particular cultures of both colonizer and colonized merge into a syncretic indeterminate hybrid. This new contingent com-pound acts as an alternative both to traditionalist local culture and to the original cosmopolitanism. Hybridity and contingent cosmopoli-tanism thus undermine both nationalism and the older cosmopolitanism. Kantians consequently become particularized. Further, hybridity sug-gests that 'if we view culture as something constructed by discourses ... then the subject of culture becomes the site of permanent contestation'. This is favoured by exponents of hybridity because it implies the continual possibility of subversion (Pheng Cheah in Pheng Cheah and Robbins (eds) 1998, 293). Cultural identity to such theorists only exists in discourse. It is the result of complex negotiations within discourse. This is what the anthropologist, James Clifford, refers to as the 'predica-ment of culture', namely, the fluid and negotiated character of all human identity. Clifford thus employs the term 'discrepant cosmopolitanism' to account for this more fluid notion of identity. This is not just a 'tourist' or migrant labour view of other cultures. It is a more 'intellectualist' view.

Another dimension to this 'contingent cosmopolitanism' is provided, as suggested, by current anthropology. This anthropology embodies an empirical recognition of the diverse number of *types* of cosmopolitanism.

Further, cosmopolitanism itself becomes a subject for anthropology. For Bruce Robbins, for example, we possibly should think of cosmopolitanism 'as an area both within and beyond the nation (and yet falling far short of "humanity") that is inhabited by a variety of cosmopolitans'. Cosmopolitanism, for Robbins, represents 'one effort to describe, from within multiculturalism, a name for the genuine striving towards common norms and mutual translatability that is also part of multiculturalism' (Robbins in Pheng Cheah and Robbins (eds) 1998, 12). This is where one finds the term 'multicultural universalism' being coined [sic].

Some critics are justifiably suspicious, however, of hybridity theory, seeing it as confined to a 'metropolitan migrant group' who play down the significance of nation states. The migrant metropolitans who value this hybridity are, in fact, a limited elite group of academics who travel, try to find common norms in the midst of cultural differences, and write about their nomadism reflectively. These are the ones who construct postcolonial theories, postmodern tracts and the new ethnographic material. They are the cultivators of intellectual fashions. There is, in other words, something autobiographical and self-referential about such theories. It is not wholly surprising in this context that culture and cultural mutability become the central themes, not so much of reality, as of the migratory preoccupations of these academics. Culture (and its mutability) become bywords for a certain freedom from national traditions, premised on a Mastercard and subsidized airfares. To be intellectual today is to be, *de rigueur*, 'transnational', even if you earn a living from making an intellectual case for particularity.[34] Yet, how many humans travel in this relaxed and reflective manner between cultures, sensing their own hybridity and reflecting on their enriched contingent cosmopolitanism? Very few, one suspects.

Thus the gist of contingent cosmopolitanism is to reconnect with the idea that all humans *are* important, without at the same time crushing the 'blessed' cultural difference.[35] This avoids what Robbins has termed the 'paranoid fantasy of ubiquity and omniscience' embodied in neo-Kantian senses of cosmopolitanism (Robbins in Pheng Cheah and Robbins (eds) 1998, 260). Contingent cosmopolitanism cannot transcend states. It needs to be more worldly and realistic about what is possible. It is thus seen as an impulse to knowledge that is shared by others, a striving to get beyond partiality, which nonetheless accepts particularity and difference. The contingent cosmopolitan claims therefore to engage in a more incremental and casual manner with other cultures. One author, in fact, labels this 'casual normativity' (Amanda Anderson in Pheng Cheah and Robbins (eds) 1998, 275). This is a cosmopolitanism which lives 'in between', enfolding patriotism in cosmopolitanism within a multi-layered construct.

The above argument has also ironically been compared to Isaiah Berlin's pluralism with added 'bite', although occasionally one senses more the impress of gums in such writings. Berlin leads to another dimension of unease with more orthodox cosmopolitanism, which arises from within liberal theory itself – although it is a tamer variant than that found in ethnographic and postcolonial writing. Some of this area has already been covered in previous chapters and thus will not be dwelt upon. In fact, one precise attempt to get at the 'philosopher's stone' – linking nationalism with a more rooted cosmopolitanism – is liberal nationalism. Rawls' later work on political liberalism also links up with the same underlying logic. Various compounds have proliferated in recent literature, hinting at the same elusive quarry, for example, patriotic cosmopolitanism, rooted cosmopolitanism, civic patriotism, constitutional patriotism, communitarian liberalism, multicultural universalism, civic nationalism, transnational citizenship, even ethical transnationalism (see Cohen 1992 and Ackerman 1994).

The gist of the generic position is to suggest that the pristine classical cosmopolitanism – which insists on the chauvinistic qualities of all nationalism and the consequent importance of common humanity, world citizenship and global ethics – is too abstract, empty and bloodless, even for the modern liberal sensibility. A large number of post-1970s liberals (of various types) are already well disposed – on a moderate level – towards domestic pluralism, qua multiculturalism. Consequently, the idea that we are faced with an international pluralism of cultures is an unsurprising extension of the same argument. There are not now many internationally minded liberal imperialists around any longer, which is a shame.[36] There is also a clear historical recognition amongst liberal writers of hybridization of cultures, increasing nomadism, travel, migration, diasporas and even global intellectual tourism. There is also the clear perception of the enormous expansion of non-governmental agencies, international associations (in law, trade, medicine, science, education and culture). Cosmopolitanism, in this qualified sense, is not seeking for one world culture, but is rather prepared to respect cultures, but at the same time to acknowledge certain common minimal standards for humanity. It is, however, through identity within a cultural tradition that the individual acquires an initial sense of their humanity. The individual is seen to learn about the uniqueness of cultures, through experiencing their own.[37] A civic, constitutional or liberal form of nationalism renders the particular safe and potentially universal. It does not seek homogeneity, but respects the heterogeneous. Patriotism or nationalism may in their extreme ethnic forms provide a pretext for exclusion and violence, but, the addition of the civic, constitutional or reasonable dimension removes that 'pretext' and leaves an indigenous tradition with a special sense of binding, which allows one to look at the world with a sonorous confidence in one's own community. Effective cosmopolitanism would thus be a by-product of moral education within a liberal communal tradition.

One suspects, in the final analysis, the above is what the majority of recent contingent cosmopolitans (of all shades) are after. Walzer, for example, from a liberal communitarian stance, is acutely aware of the dangers of over-emphasizing particularity. As mentioned previously, he therefore posits a minimal code of universal morality, constituting cross-cultural requirements (Walzer in McMurrin (ed.) 1988, 22). One can thus endorse difference whilst subscribing to 'thin universalism'. Walzer sees this as a reiterative universalism (see Walzer 1990). Walzer is aware that if the human being is only defined according to the standards of a community, then the foreigner can literally become 'inhuman'. The twentieth century alone provides multiple examples of this use of the 'inhuman'. Richard Rorty, from a more postmodern difference perspective, on one level, does dispute transhistorical notions of human nature, maintaining that 'the only lesson of either history or anthropology is our extraordinary malleability.' (Rorty 1998, 115). Yet, despite a deep scepticism about universals, he also is still committed to a contingent cosmopolitanism.[38]

Agnosticism with provisos

The debate over cosmopolitanism and nationalism is central to the twenty-first century and marks out the domain of future political theory and practice. Political theorists will go on trying to define human nature in a cosmopolitan universalist manner in order to avoid exclusions of communal contingency and particularity. Communitarians, nationalists, postcolonialists and multiculturalists, and the like, will continue to insist on the significance of particularity.

In the case of nationalism, despite its power and prevalence in contemporary politics, it remains a basically naïve theory which cannot really explain its relation with the majority of political concepts and trades upon its vacuity – as argued in previous chapters. Cosmopolitanism presents a more theoretically sophisticated account, which is also intuitively more persuasive. There is still much to be said for the noble enterprise of classical cosmopolitanism, particularly in the sphere of human rights.[39] However, such cosmopolitan political theory, specifically in the neo-Kantian format, should be careful not to rest too much on its laurels. Norman Geras, for example, asks for the response of contemporary political philosophy (both neo-Kantian and utilitarian) to deep cosmopolitan issues such as the Jewish Holocaust (or Cambodia, Uganda,

Kosovo, and Rwanda, for that matter), observing that 'the political philosopher coming to the study of it may be surprised how little she will find in the way of serious and extended reflection on the subject'. Despite the abundant material on the Holocaust within recent history, theology, drama, film, the novel and poetry, political philosophy has little or nothing to say. For Geras, one reason for this neglect lies in the abstracted, universalistic, 'justice-based' focus of political philosophy, so lauded by neo-Kantians. For Geras, 'theories of rights and justice ... do not seriously measure themselves against the realities of violation – violation of the norms about which they theorize, violation of the lives of human beings – and do not seriously measure themselves against the factors conducive to such violation' (Geras 1998, 24–6). Such normative political theory remains a neutral bystander and consequently partakes in a contract of 'mutual indifference'. For Geras, such a philosophical culture also 'underwrites moral indifference' (Geras 1998, 59).

Most contemporary neo-Kantians would bitterly resist this view. For O'Neill, for example, practical reason is premised on our mutual connection, awareness of plurality and finitude. On a more assertive level, Brian Barry comments that 'justice has certain formal characteristics ... the universal validity of this proposition cannot be challenged by showing that a lot of people in some benighted society think otherwise' (Barry in Miller and Walzer (eds) 1995, 75). This also has direct parallels with Habermas' comment that 'To gain distance from one's own traditions and broaden limited perspectives *is the advantage of Occidental rationalism*' [my italics] (Habermas 1998, 162).

What is not so clear here is the nature of reason itself. Reason is an intrinsically slippery entity. As O'Neill puts it very neatly, 'If reason is the basis of all vindication, how can we vindicate it?' (O'Neill 2000, 11). Leaving aside this reflexive issue, can reason be completely abstracted from sociality? To abstract from all social forms and cultures is unquestionably appealing as a vantage point. Thus, it appears that to reason is to migrate immediately to the universal. In this sense, reflexive reason is virtually synonymous with liberal cosmopolitanism, which takes us full circle back to Nagel's comment quoted at the beginning of the chapter. There are oddities implicit in this conception. There is an assumption here, qua Barry and Habermas, that only occidental culture (whatever that is) uniquely contains this reflexive reason and ability to criticize itself. This surely is far-fetched, if not false. Further, there is a supposition that this notion of reflexive reason is somehow superior to all other forms of reasoning. In addition, reflexive reason is also autonomous from any particular social basis or culture; whereas all other cultures determine the reason of their members. Barry's 'benighted' colonized or oriental subjects might well object to being all viewed as irrational, immature or childish simply because they do not share a particular view of reason. Barry conforms quite well in fact to the time-honoured ideal of liberal imperialism. He is a kind of modern-day Macauley. All these latter claims about reflexive reason, in the cold light of day, are again surely vaguely ridiculous.

Further the precise link between universality (justice and practical reason) and particular policies remains elusive. The necessary conceptual shift from abstract non-ideal reason or justice to practical cosmopolitan policies remains ultimately mysterious. If practical reason means that it is followable by all relevant rational agents, does this imply anything in particular? O'Neill suggests that we are connected, aware of diversity and our finitude, but, again, is there any necessary logical connection between these themes and the notion of 'holding for all'? Further, does it imply anything specific about development or taxation policy? Both O'Neill and Barry wish to retain the element of abstract universality and yet also want substantive things to arise from it. The link, however intuitively appealing, is never clearly established anywhere in their writings.

Putting to one side the moral debates, what is clear is that both cosmopolitanism and nationalism are ductile terms. Both include and exclude, from different perspectives. Both can be either naïve or realistic. Further, what is less obvious in the literature (as in more conventional accounts of nationalism, where benign liberal versions are drawn distinct from more bellicose) is the positive *and* negative dimensions of cosmo-politanism. This becomes more apparent when the cosmopolitan net is widened. One pervasive form of cosmopolitan activity today appears in the economic sphere. Despite Kant's (and others') benign view of liberal commerce, unregulated global capitalism now renders both nationalism (plus all forms of particularism) and legal or moral cosmopolitanism unstable. This might be termed 'predatory cosmopolitanism'. This is probably the most pervasive sense to cosmopolitanism to be encountered by most human beings today and it hardly inspires confidence.

This chapter has examined three very broad bodies of argument concerning the relation between cosmopolitanism (universalism) and nationalism (particularism). The first favours the unsullied universal over the particular – although the case is more muddied than many of its proponents would allow. The second body of argument sees particularity and locality as crucial, although the arguments become too fragmented and directionless to be of much use. Even critics sympathetic to the 'drift to particularity' have seen the need to blend the cosmopolitan and the particular. The third body of argument offers various *via media* positions, trying to situate the universal within the particular or the particular in the universal. It is this last body of argument which seems the most fruitful direction to take, although again there do not appear to be any really persuasive formulations of the argument to date. At the present moment – although it may well be an ephemeral moment – it is largely the latter two themes which have most intellectual currency, although the neo-Kantian and utilitarian themes are remarkably resilient and productive within a small elite of political theorists. However, even contemporary neo-Kantians and utilitarians still feel the strong impulse to link themselves in some manner with particularity, usually in response to the counter pressure from communitarianism or the like.

In one sense, all the arguments outlined are partly caricatures. Kant is read remarkably selectively and optimistically by virtually all contemporary moral and political philosophers. Despite the howls from universalists who see cosmopolitan practical reason in Kant and strong particularists who see Kant's practical reason as contingency personified, Kant himself is altogether more cryptic. In the context of this immensely complex relationship between cosmopolitanism and nationalism it is difficult not to become agnostic, although it is an agnosticism with the important proviso that the impulse to some sense of cosmopolitanism seems inevitable given our common human vulnerability. Faced with international disaster and horrifying pogrom there is a deep impulse to aid beyond borders. However, at the same time, boundaries, languages and cultures curtail us and form deep-rooted side-constraints to our responses.

9   Concluding Particulars

This final chapter will, firstly, situate the whole debate concerning particularity within the discipline of contemporary political theory and review the general lines of critical arguments taken by both universalism and particularism. Second, it will argue that there are certain deep rooted problems in the particularist position which remain unresolved.

The debate between universalists and particularists, which underpins the studies in this book, configures the general parameters of much contemporary political theory debate. One of the main preoccupations of theorists from the 1970s and 1980s has been with various dimensions of justice theory. Justice, in a purely formal sense, can be defined as treating like cases alike, which might be seen as literally equivalent or synonymous with reason and universalizability.[1] The major issue that arises in such arguments is the concern to identify the universal or generic grounds of justice which apply regardless of any particular time or place. The counter tendency within contemporary theory has focused on what might loosely be termed particularist accounts, of which, clearly, there are many types.[2] Nationalism is but one of the more potent of these particularizing vocabularies. The following discussion will initially examine the general character of both universalism and particularism in political theory.

Universality

The first point to note is that there are different universalist accounts. Thus the conflict between universalists and particularists is not quite as straightforward as many of its contenders would make out. A distinction can be drawn between a richer, more substantive metaphysically based universalism and a thinner more translucent account. In the richer universalist accounts the metaphysical dimension looms large. Metaphysics has problematic connotations for many twentieth century political theorists of all persuasions. It usually denotes a comprehensive, perfectionist and transcendental theory, which implies some form of objective standard of ethics and politics. The comprehensive aspect of metaphysics indicates that a metaphysical conception is identifiable in terms of its explanatory breadth. The metaphysical view here is loosely equivalent to a 'world view'. The attempt to examine reality as a whole can be seen to be systematically pursued, for example, in Spinoza's monism, Leibniz's monadology or Hegel's absolute idealism. Many metaphysical systems attempted this by connecting up virtually all the domains of human knowledge. There is also an additional perfectionist element to this conception of metaphysics which imports a value into the total view. This is where metaphysics (for some) can become a surrogate religion. Metaphysics is thus seen as the highest and most perfect form of human knowledge – accounting for the nature and destiny of human beings and possibly the existence of God, freedom and immortality. Metaphysics, in this sense, not only speaks of the reality behind all appearances, but offers the initiate the very essence of reality through which some form of perfection of knowledge and practice can be attained. This form of knowledge is only available to those able to receive it, who have the capacity to move and breathe in this realm. The grasp of metaphysics thus moves apace with personal virtue and character. Another aspect to metaphysics is the transcendent dimension. The sense of transcendence, which most antagonizes anti-metaphysicians, is the idea that metaphysical resources lie outside the empirical or experiential realm altogether, namely, in some form of luminous transcendent reality. Metaphysics is concerned to identify certain universal, suprasensible or transcendental foundations. Thus, the transcendent non-empirical things help us (in particular times or circumstances) to account for the world being one way rather than another. The divine craftsman of Plato's *Timaeus*, the unmoved mover of Aristotle, the neo-Platonic Demiurge, the Augustinian or Thomistic God, Hegel's *Geist* or even, possibly, Heidegger's *Being*. This is the rich view of the world, expressed from a transcendental nowhere – a god's eye view, *sub specie aeternitatis*, from the rim of the world, spectating on human doing. It would be well nigh impossible to understand, for example, Plato's, Augustine's, Aquinas' or Hegel's conceptions of politics without grasping the underpinning universalist metaphysics.

However, this metaphysical universalism is far too rich a diet for the generation of late twentieth century universalists, where the main aim is to jettison the metaphysics, without abandoning universality, and provide, as one recent theorist puts it, a 'rigorous conception of reasoning about action ... without the need to establish any metaphysics of the person, or of the Good' (O'Neill 1996, 6). This thin gruel of universalism is to be found in neo-Kantians, contractualists and contemporary consequentialists and utilitarians. In this latter perspective, the common task is to seek for a non-metaphysical and non-foundational 'view from nowhere'. For example, within contemporary utilitarian theories, particularly theories of government, there is no room for any metaphysical baggage, let alone any conception of particular histories, loyalties or communal conceptions of the good. Most utilitarians would in fact express total indifference to any metaphysical argument, despite being committed universalists. Similarly, for neo-Kantians, universalist metaphysics is not a good ground for social or political cooperation. As John Rawls notes, for example, 'philosophy as the search for truth about an independent metaphysical and moral order cannot ... provide a workable and shared basis for a political conception of justice'. The task of political philosophy is consequently a thinned down Kantianism, namely, to 'examine whether some underlying basis of agreement can be uncovered and a mutually acceptable way of resolving these questions publicly established' (Rawls in Strong (ed.) 1992, 97). The aim of political philosophy is consequently to examine rigorously the basic principles which underpin or regulate reasonable cooperation. Justice is premised upon reasonable, widely shared intuitions and values, which can be developed, transmuted and tested in a theoretical construction. Consequently, for Rawls, 'the public conception of justice should be so far as possible, independent of controversial philosophical and religious doctrines ... the public conception of justice is to be political, not metaphysical' (Rawls in Strong (ed.) 1992, 95).

With no metaphysics available, reasonable social and moral coordination becomes an issue. In modern neo-Kantians this is where we find public reason taking on an extra heavy philosophical load, as in the writings of Jürgen Habermas, Brian Barry or Alan Gewirth, amongst many others. In fact, some variation of universal practical reason fills the void left by the death or decline of traditional universalist metaphysics. The term constructivism also usually arises here in neo-Kantian thinkers. In essence, it is a form of foundational self-recovery kit. Constructivism implies that one reasons 'with all possible solidity from available beginnings, using available and followable methods to reach attainable and sustainable conclusions for relevant audiences' (O'Neill 1996, 63). Constructivism does not simply invent; it rather builds – virtually hermeneutically – upon what is present in reason. The neo-Kantian thinker Onora O'Neill's conception of constructed practical reason is thus, in her view, neither end-orientated nor norm-orientated. Reason coordinates in the sense of providing a negative internal authority. It must account and allow for a variety of agents – all human agents in fact – and also be able to guide action and discriminate between categories. Thus, for O'Neill, 'practical reasoning begins by requiring us to reject principles which we cannot view as principles for those for whom the reasoning is to count'. In other words, reason must be truly universal –

universalizability implying 'holding for all cases'. This is the nub of her objection to all forms of particularism. This conception of universalizability is the essence of practical reasoning.[3] Practical reason is neither purely formalistic nor idealized. Further, it neither assumes any idealized (metaphysical) conceptions of persons, reason or action, nor roots itself in any particular human lives. Yet, for O'Neill, although abstract, this conception of reason always begins with the 'gritty realities of human life' (O'Neill 1996, 61).[4] It tries to draw out from the principles embodied in the ordinary 'real' processes of reasoning a basic normative pattern. The end result may be abstract, but it is not an idealized view of what ought to be. It is rather based on existing practical reason and is attainable by all.

Similarly, in Brian Barry, justice as impartiality captures a kind of equality which is also embodied in forms of practical reason. Yet, this notion of impartiality and reason arises from, what Barry calls, the most 'earthy ethics' imaginable. It draws upon the 'ordinary beliefs' of human beings (Barry 1995a, 10 and 1989, 8). Further, in Habermas, there is a clear attempt to recover the universal conditions of any possible reasonable understanding, conditions which are implicit within all forms of communication. For Habermas, there is, in other words, a universal telos implicit within our reasonable communicative actions that is orientated to mutual understanding. This telos transcends systematically distorting particularistic communication. Habermas even implies that that this could constitute the core of a constitutional patriotism (Habermas in Gutman (ed.) 1994).

However, O'Neill, for one, does admit that stray elements of metaphysics do linger in many apparently non-foundational universalist arguments. Notions like motivation, reason, impartiality, rational choice all contain metaphysical traces. Thus, she comments, 'It is an open question whether universalists who invoke these sorts of ideals can substantiate the principles for which they variously argue without establishing accounts of the metaphysics of the person' (O'Neill 1996, 12). It might be suggested, to take one step beyond O'Neill's views here, that every political or moral judgement involves some ontological or metaphysical component – no matter how sublimated or hidden. At most, therefore, one could describe the attempts of Rawls, O'Neill, Gewirth, Habermas or Brian Barry as a form of metaphysical minimalism.

In addition, those in the postmodern frame of contemporary theory take the above point one step further, again, arguing that even this apparently non-foundational minimalism requires rigorous genealogical analysis. This analysis is usually done in the spirit of Friedrich Nietzsche's anti-metaphysical philosophy. As William Connolly comments, paraphrasing Michel Foucault, 'every dialogue invokes a set of prejudgements and pre-understandings not susceptible to exhaustive formulation within its frame'. Connolly describes this more radical genealogical critique as an awakening of *all* philosophical thought from its 'anthropological sleep' (see Connolly 1995, 10–12). This critique searches out metaphysics and ontology in all the remote and hidden corners of political theory. This genealogical inquisition usually finds particularism implicit within all the claims to universalism.

Particularity

The other major dimension of contemporary political theory is particularism or particularity. As suggested, a great deal of political theory, in the last two to three decades, has drifted in this direction, specifically into the substantive domains of groups and collectivities. Particularism, like thin universalism, also premises itself on a rejection of the richer variant of metaphysical universalism, although it rejects it for different reasons to those of the thin universalists. Further, the bulk of particularism, with some exceptions, is critical of thin universalism. However, particularism also embodies an amalgam of theories, which are far more extensive than those covered in this book. Thus, communitarianism, neo-Aristotelianism, historicism, nationalism, multiculturalism, postmodernism, essential contestability theory and difference theories, in all their diverse epistemological shapes, focus on the value of particularity. One of the more politically and historically pervasive of these has been nationalism. Unlike most other particularist theories, nationalism has tended to suffuse both theory and political practice. It has thus been used as a linking strategic motif and comparator throughout the book.[5]

In academic political theory, up until the early 1990s, the most characteristic expression of particularism was the communitarian perspective. It traded upon its status as a more acceptable or congenial expression of particularity. The formal tenets of contemporary communitarian thinking (as discussed in chapter six) are though deeply characteristic of many of the facets of particularist arguments in general: first, the communitarian perspective suggests that political and moral goods cannot be determined by abstract reasoning. Such 'goods' arise from particular historical communities at particular contingent moments. There are no universalist premises, such as 'cosmopolitan human rights' or 'abstract reason'. There is no moral Esperanto. We cannot step back to assess communities with a view from nowhere. We always have a view from somewhere. Thus, when, for example, we argue about democracy, we must give an account from *within* the existing practices of a particular community. Reason, democracy, justice or rights, in this context, cannot be used as an external universal standard of assessment.

Either a society embodies a notion of reason, democracy, justice and rights, or it does not.

Second, the community forms the basis for practical reason. Communitarianism is therefore sceptical about aspects of the Enlightenment and more sympathetic intrinsically to the romantic and expressivist movements of the late eighteenth and early nineteenth century. Reason is situated within communities. Communitarians assume that there are shared communal resources and traditions which can be drawn upon. In other words, the community is constituted by internal pre-understandings. Thus, democracy, in this reading, reflects pre-existing traditions. In this hermeneutic perspective, it is difficult for communitarianism to offer any normative account of reason, democracy, justice or rights which could be universally applicable.

Third, the human self is constituted through a community. Thus, for Michael Sandel, for example, we cannot espouse the early form of the Rawlsian original position because it makes the unjustifiable conjecture of the unencumbered self (standing outside a communal framework). If we cannot accept this Rawlsian self, then it follows that we have no basis for accepting the two principles of justice which are premised, for Sandel, upon the unencumbered self. Rawls, thus, presupposes an improbable account of the moral subject, which is the logical prerequisite for the impartiality of justice. For Sandel, however, this improbable self generates an implausible theory of justice. Life within the community precedes any conceptions of justice, rights or democracy.

However, not everyone considers communitarianism or nationalism as the primary form of particularism. Idiosyncratically, O'Neill takes the philosophical work of the late Wittgenstein as exemplifying particularity, as she puts it, 'with a vengeance', namely, that we learn all our words, concepts and values in particular contexts or forms of life (O'Neill 1996, 12).[6] Particularity is thus embedded in language games and forms of life. Each particular form of life contains its own conception of reality.[7] Overall, for O'Neill, particularists hope to 'orient ethical reasoning without appeal to universal principles of inclusive scope, or are generally without claims about what would be good, or right, or obligatory'. Consequently, they try to anchor ethics in particular practices or forms of life (see O'Neill 1996, 13). Thus, for O'Neill, the real division between universalists and particularists is 'over the *extent of the domains* across which certain principles hold, over the *content of ethical principles* and over the *degree to which* they prescribe uniform or differentiated action within their domains' (O'Neill 1996, 77). She does, however, draw a further distinction between 'moderate historicizing particularists' (Hans Georg Gadamer and Alisdair MacIntyre) and 'radical particularists' (Wittgenstein). Historicist particularists are interested in the particularity of tradition, community and social practices. Radical particularists focus on 'sensibilities, attachments, commitments' in particular situations. However, both forms of particularism share a basic deep critical unease with all accounts of universalism. Minimally, universalism ignores the situatedness of individuals. It consequently contains an implausible account of the person or self. Further, universalism overlooks cultural difference for the sake of abstract reason. In addition, without metaphysical appeals, universalism usually fails. The modern foundations are too thin to bear the weight put upon them.

The above analysis, although primarily a brief account of universalism and particularism, is also indirectly an overview of recent debates in political theory. There are three points which can been drawn out from this synopsis. First, the notion of the universal, specifically the idea of a rich metaphysical universal, has clearly fallen on hard times. It has been under assault not only from an assorted band of Wittgensteinians, communitarians, hermeneuticists, neo-Aristotelians, civic republicans, Nietzscheans, and postmodernists, but also by a large grouping of uneasy non-foundational minimalist universalists (neo-Kantians, contractarians and utilitarians). The minimalist universalists share a vigorous critique of the older metaphysically rich universalism with the various forms of overt particularism. Thus, ontological minimalism, anti-essentialism, fallibilism and non-foundationalism appear now to be *de rigueur*. This form of critique has all been premised, in one shape or another, on the importance of particularity.[8] The second point is that a loose consensus has developed over the importance of particularity. Although thin universalists have been vigorously fighting their corner, by and large, it is now more favourable to be seen as a particularist.[9] Third, one of the oddities of the stronger metaphysical universalist account – as it appeared primarily in nineteenth and early twentieth century liberal theories – is that the human 'individual' is accorded a very fundamental moral status. Natural and then human rights theories, for example, have traditionally accorded a very deep central metaphysical role for the 'individual person'.[10] The oddity of this point is that if one were searching for a self-evidently 'idiosyncratic particular', then the human individual appears to be a prime example. Individual is a synonym of the particular. Each individual is unique. This unique human individual is, in fact, also the metaphysical core of an older form of liberal universalism (and in fact anarchism), vestiges of which remain in Rawlsian and other forms of twentieth century liberalism. In this sense, the sovereign individual is often the prime example, for many, of particularity.

The extreme counter argument to this thesis can be found in postmodern theories, which, as mentioned, are keen to tease out the metaphysical and universalist underpinnings, even within the thinnest of universalisms. This teasing out process is redundant in terms of liberal thinkers, such as T. H. Green, where the enriched metaphysics is overt and unashamed. However, late twentieth century renditions of liberalism, as argued, shied away from metaphysics. For postmodern critics, however, even the individual of non-metaphysical liberalism, in O'Neill, Brian Barry or Gewirth, becomes suspect, as obscuring an implicit and deadening universalism. For example, as already seen in the major discussions of this book, for Iris Marion Young, liberal individualism expresses 'a logic of identity that seeks to reduce differences to unity' (Young 1990, 97). Thus, treating particular human individuals with equal respect may well be a way of *refusing* to acknowledge their real difference and particularity (Young 1990, 11). Such action *abstracts* the notion of individuality from particularity and reduces the plurality of moral subjects to one unifying notion of individuality (Young 1990, 100).[11] This is the key reason as to why there is a resistance in some quarters to taking the liberal individual as the significant particular. William Connolly argues, in the same vein, that liberal individualism actually crushes individuality. He remarks that liberal individualists 'insinuate a dense set of standards, conventions, and expectations into the identity of the normal individual by failing to identify or contest a constellation of normal/abnormal dualities already inscribed in the culture they idealize' (Connolly 1991, 74). Liberal individualism, in short, evades the paradox of difference. It is 'not merely a benign perspective that does not go far enough. It is an anachronism'. Thus, a 'mere *ethic* of individuality evades an encounter with the Foucaultian world of discipline and normalization'. Liberal individualism treats 'an ethic of individuality as if it were a political theory of identity/difference' (Connolly 1991, 85–7). Young and Connolly both suggest that emancipation can only take place *through* recognition and respect for difference and particularity. Many recent like-minded political theorists link this argument (somewhat obscurely) with an implausible conception of radical democratic pluralism and new social movements.

However, it is important to stress here that individuality is clearly not unimportant to Young, Connolly and other such difference and postmodern theorists. Postmodern individuals are real particulars, as opposed to bogus particulars.[12] Connolly, following Foucault and Nietzsche, thus continually tries to destabilize the liberal understanding of the individual. Recent difference theory, in general, is thus largely concerned about the recognition and emancipation of real particulars. They wish for emancipation from the bogus notion of the liberal human individual, which is always, they argue, used by liberals in an unwittingly disciplinary manner. The liberal individual is a creature established by exclusion. Power plays the key role here, since the definition of the individual and otherness is a way of disciplining and controlling knowledge. What exactly any release from such discipline and power, if it is even possible, would look like, is anyone's guess. Possibly to speculate on it is rather like Marx speculating on the details of communism. If one followed out this point, though, we would need to make a further distinction between the liberal individual (which is a bogus particular shielding an underlying disciplinary universal) and a postmodern individual (which is a real particular manifesting difference and contingency). The ideal of emancipation implicit in this perspective is closest to Nietzsche's ideal of self-overcoming, with all that this implies regarding the loss of the self that has been overcome. This forms a central, if vague and unexplained, theme in much postmodern theory.

However, one other aspect of the postmodern and critical theory response to the value accorded to difference is that difference is usually located with marginal groups, more recently under the rubric of new social movements. Although this latter point is not always made wholly clear. Difference theory, in contemporary parlance, therefore links closely with debates over multiculturalism and marginalized groups or cultures.[13] This latter focus – qua new social movements, marginalized or affinity-based groups – is one important, if ambiguous, subtext in Connolly's idea of pluralization and the major premise of Young's work.[14] Difference, for Young, implies what she calls 'affinity groups'. Yet, where and how do such affinity groups derive their value? One answer is that these groups are regarded as individual and unique, in other words, they are the really significant particulars. Some might even suggest that groups have a distinct moral or legal personality, although this would be one step too far for some. However, there is a fine line here between particularity, individuality and personality.

The problem here is that the registering of value in 'group entities', that is, indigenous cultures, nations or ethnicities, is often a way of finding an alternative to liberal individualism. The rallying cry for such argument is often the importance of difference, cultural distinctiveness, cultural identity – in a phrase the *value of group particularity*. Thus, the particular group is seen as an alternative to both liberal individualism and universalism. Yet, the human individual (even liberal individualism, despite Connolly's and Young's fulminations) is still persistently, for many, a prime exemplification of the ontological shape of particularity. Further, the manner in which the cultural, ethnic or national group is drawn distinct and made a locus of value – as particular – still surreptitiously relies upon the *value* of individuality and particularity. Groups, states, cultures, ethnicities, and the like, are frequently described as particular, different, self-determining, unique and individual. They might, under the same rubric, be described as legal or moral persons. There is clearly a shifting location for particularity.

In summary, particularity frequently mutates in front of our eyes. What is particular and unique for one theorist becomes a mode of unifying universalist oppression for another. What is universal for one is an exemplification of particularity for others. Yet, oddly, across this shifting field, subtly, the value of particularity and individuality still carries faint echoes of the human individual.[15]

Particular problems

Universalists usually respond to particularist criticism by pointing out the inherent dangers of irresponsibility and relativism implicit in all forms of particularity – specifically the potential nihilism implicit in the more extreme versions. For universalists, particularists also make themselves intellectually redundant in terms of trying to formulate *any* general statements about other cultures or belief systems. Cross-cultural reasoning and multiculturalism can become insurmountable problems for any particularist. Even if communal standards are appealed to by particularists, they can give no good reason why these norms are in any way authoritative for other cultures. If communal norms are constitutive of identity, then one cannot go behind them. Further, if there is a consensus in a community, there is no guarantee that it will not be a wholly iniquitous one. Even if particular communities or forms of life embody internal modes of criticism, the basic problems are not solved, but only put back one step.

For many particularists, however, moral and cultural problems simply cannot, in the final analysis, be resolved. It is a universalist daydream to think that they can offer any solutions. We live in an agonistic age. Humans do not improve. There is no observable sequential development of human nature and no possibility of any growing consensus, consequently scepticism and negativity are inevitable. It is simply mistaken to try to find a universal moral theory that could serve as a justification or foundation for any loyalty. No general or universalizable theory exists.

However, are all forms of universalism rejected by particularists? Two points need to be underscored here. Firstly, the majority of the particularist arguments, reviewed in this book, rest on a form of conventionalist argument – that is the very general assertion that the nation, state, culture, subaltern culture, ethnos, or community, are the *conventional mediums* through which values are recognized, articulated and legitimized. The logic of the particularist case is basically that the convention (that is, the cultural, ethnic or national beliefs) is *primary* and the value claim is *derivative*. The alternative universalist scenario is where the value is articulated independently of any conventional attachments. For many critics, the conventional or particular character of universal claims is a *fait accompli*.

If this were the key position taken by all particularists, then this might well be the end of the matter. We would be waiting, possibly, for a 'god to save us' or a new St. Benedict. But, if one carefully examines particularist writings, then one can observe a subtle but significant slippage on the question of universals. This has already been noted in passing in earlier chapters of this book; it is now taken up more systematically. Thus, not all particularist thinkers are wholly critical of universalism. There is, what might be termed, a softer, slightly more ambivalent sense of particularism, as well as a harder-edged form.

The distinction between hard and soft particularity underpins all particularist arguments. The softer variant can be brought to the surface if we focus on a specific example, such as human rights. The question which is crucial here is: are universal human rights simply expressions of particular cultures or states, or do they contain any universal components? The hard-edged particularist would have a very direct response, namely, that human rights are always the reflection of the concerns of particular states or groups. The idea that they could be universal is treated with derision. However, the softer rendition of particularism is not so certain.

To take but one example of the softer rendition: Michael Walzer, from within an initially clear particularist perspective, has drawn a distinction between thick and thin moralities, or, what he also refers to as minimal and maximal values, or reiterative and covering law universalism. The reiterative universal is a minimal universal code, constituting cross-cultural requirements which have become commonly accepted by all groups and states (Walzer in McMurrin (ed.) 1988, 22). Walzer suggests that this 'minimal morality consists in the rules of engagement that binds all the speakers' (Walzer 1994a, 12). Minimal (reiterative) claims are, he argues, ultimately distilled down from maximal moralities (qua covering law universalism). He identifies these minimums as: the expectation not to be deceived, treated with gross cruelty or murdered, tortured, grossly oppressed, tyrannized over, or treated with manifest injustice. These might be thought of as 'limit conditions' – concerning conditions of birth, death, child rearing and the like – which every human culture must engage with. He consequently posits these as a minimal content for universal human rights (see Walzer 1977). For Walzer, 'minimalism makes for a certain limited, though important and heartening solidarity'. However, he adds, that 'It does not make for a full-blooded universal doctrine' (Walzer 1994a, 11).

The minimum is therefore distinct from the rich maximal moralities of different cultures. The thin universalism, as reiterative, acknowledges that, subject to these minimal universal constraints, there are many different and valuable ways of life that have equal rights to flourish in their respective locations and deserve equal respect (Walzer in McMurrin (ed.) 1988, 22). Walzer therefore essentially holds onto the conventionalist claim of cultural or communal difference, while at the same time adhering to a 'thin universalism', which upholds universal human rights.[16]

A similar thesis is suggested, more indirectly, by Richard Rorty, from a postmodern perspective. He argues, for example, that the notion of 'we' or 'us' (co-nationality) is central to the concept of obligation. Yet, this can also lead to excessive particularity and potential inhumanity. Thus, for Rorty, we do tend to narrate sad sentimental stories about universal human rights to each other (see Rorty 1998). We also tend universally to abhor cruelty and affirm the minimum of human solidarity, even if it is in a detheologized language. There may be no substantive universal truths, only worn out metaphors; however, Rorty still acknowledges the importance of some minimal universals in the way we conduct ourselves. We may not be able to justify these ideas by reason or rule-governed moral theory, but we still adhere to an underlying ethic of care. Thus, a *sotto voce* universalism reappears within postmodern-inclined political theory. There are, in other words, for many particularist theorists, limit conditions which constitute minimal cross-cultural conditions underpinning the most basic of human rights.

My criticisms here have both a general and a more specific focus. The former are directed at particularist logic. The latter criticisms are directed at particularists who focus on specific religious, customary or communal conventions as a basis for understanding human rights.

Under the more general criticism: first, one major problem with the hard-edged case for particularism is that it does tend to undermine itself. If meaning and value lie totally in particular groups, cultures or states, there would literally be no possibility of any communication. There would be an ongoing complete incomprehension. This is clearly absurd and flies in the face of what we do know. Cross-cultural communication is difficult but not impossible and can occasionally be fruitful. Further, even to try to communicate the meaning or importance of the hard-edged conventionalism commits one to the contradictory assumption that others will understand your reasoning and ideas. This is the classic logical dilemma of trying to assert the universal truth of relativism. Even the deployment by particularists of common rules of reasoning for understanding arguments commits the same basic error.

If the harder-edged position is self-refuting, the softer particularist position also has some awkward problems. Thus, if basic minimums for all human existence are exempt and regarded as universal, then it implies that there are apparently non-conventional universal truths about humanity, which all cultures acknowledge. If this is the case, what is the non-conventional *justification* for such rights for conventionalist critics? The problem here is that the potential candidates for justification of human rights – utilitarianism, neo-Kantianism and contractualism – are all noteworthy for their universalism. Furthermore, as we have seen, the majority of particularists reject these latter arguments at the outset. The problem then for the soft particularists is that, in acknowledging that the most basic human rights minimums are exempt from the particularist logic, they appear then to be admitting that universal claims have some validity *regardless* of conventions. However, the key question is: where do they go next to find a justification for why, for example, we abhor cruelty, or find starvation, extreme racial discrimination and torture universally unacceptable? There seems to be a large hole in the particularist argument here over the issue of human right minimums.

There are two possible particularist responses to this line of criticism. The first would assert that we should separate out the *mode of justification* from the *legal or institutional form* of the human right. Thus, the legal or public form of the right (which acknowledges basic minimums) is not logically dependent on the normative background.[17] It free floats. Thus, if the particularist only stresses the legal form, then it does not really matter too much what the underlying mode of justification is. Consequently, a minimum human right would hold regardless of the justification – that is, whether it is universalist or particularist.

The central weakness here is that not many soft particularist critics of human rights would want to say this – specifically the more recent culturally orientated critics. If the critic were a Muslim, for example, and she accepted human right minimums, it is more than likely that she would want such human rights to be justifiable, in some way, from the *Qur'an*, unless I am very mistaken. This would also be the case for most nationalists, communitarians and indigenous cultures. Thus, the distinction between 'legal form' and 'mode of justification' looks distinctly shaky.

However, a second soft particularist response to the above criticism could argue that the minimum actually *is* (at root) a cultural convention, which just happens to be 'widely accepted' across cultures and communities. Thus, there is a purely fortuitous coincidence between the conventions of different cultures. This is what Walzer refers to as a reiterative universalism. One can therefore retain the credibility of both the particularist and the universalist logic. There is some validity to this point. However, there are two weaknesses in the argument. Primarily, if one tracks across thick cultures and thick moralities, the minimum would clearly not be accepted for the *same* reasons. Thus, Muslim, Hindu or Confucian 'thick' reasoning about minimums is likely to be very different. This touches, again, upon the argument concerning the first response. My question is, can one really distinguish clearly between the acceptance of a human right minimum and the reasons for holding to it?

Further, the universalist critic could also argue that the particularist position simply does not hold water, since the universal acceptance of the minimum is due to the fact either, that the minimum actually is a universal 'grounding experience' or 'limit condition' for all human beings, outside of any cultural reasons, or, that universal practical reason actually leads one to view it as universal. Both points would be generally unacceptable to the particularist position.

However, if one does accept that reasons are integral to conventional belief structures, then another problem arises. If human rights minimums are integrated with conventional belief structures, then, why single out universal minimums in the first place, as exempt and different from maximal morality? One way of articulating this issue is to suggest that the distinction between minimal and maximal morality is too unwieldy. The argument would be that human rights minimums are already deeply integrated within conventional belief systems. Thus, the religious texts, communities and cultures already contain implicitly *all* the authoritative basic human rights minimums. The believer may have to search in the authoritative texts or communal value system, but they are nonetheless present. This is, however, a deeply contentious argument, which would need detailed comparative study to confirm one way or the other. The argument suggests a deep underlying global ecumenism in all world cultures and religions. At first glance, given of what we know of religious and cultural conflict, this does not sound particularly convincing.

A related problem to the above point is that if one justifies human rights minimums through the distinct cultures or conventions, those justifications are not articulating isolated or discrete values. A belief about the family or women's roles in society in, for example, Confucianism or an aboriginal culture is not a wholly discrete value, which can simply be amputated from the body of less or more comfortable Confucian or aboriginal beliefs. Values are a part of systems of values, as words are part of languages. They cannot simply be cut off at will to suit a syncretic modern universalist convenience. In other words, can the idea and reasons for a minimum human right be separated from the whole structure of conventional reasoning? Can a right to life, for example, be separated from the conventional norms which make the right, literally, come to life for a proponent? One response to this is to suggest, again, that we should distinguish the maximal and minimal values and the background justifications from the legal forms. However, again, my query is: does this actually make sense to a communitarian, Islamic, Buddhist or nationalist proponent of human rights?[18]

An additional problem here is that for some soft particularist theorists the traditional Western approach to human rights frequently entails actually abandoning or bracketing out religious and cultural beliefs.

As Charles Taylor comments, Western human rights exponents will often 'tend to think that the path to convergence requires that others too cast off their traditional ideas, that they even reject their religious heritage'. Yet, for Taylor, other cultures have not gone through the same historical trajectory as the West. This, for Taylor, handicaps the manner in which the West views culturally embedded claims about humanity (Taylor in Bauer and Bell (eds) 1999, 143–4). However, again, there is something distinctly odd in this soft particularist argument. One of the key reasons for asserting the human rights minimums (for even soft particularists) is that it allows one to bypass or bracket out religious, moral or political beliefs, in a similar manner to the proceduralism favoured by many contractual theorists. To take those beliefs on board as integral to the minimum does not solve any problems, it surely only exacerbates them.

Finally, if, qua Taylor, one does view human rights minimums through the refracting lens of conventions, then it seems that there are *no* neutral starting points to critically assess them. This even seems to be the implication of the bulk of softer particularist arguments. For Walzer, for example, minimums are fundamentally important, but they are still culturally mediated. He comments that 'minimalism … is less the product of persuasion than of mutual recognition among the protagonists of different fully developed moral cultures'. Thus, for Walzer, 'the minimum is not the foundation of the maximum, only a piece of it' (Walzer 1994a, 17). In this context, the minimum does not offer a standard for criticism. The only critique which is possible is 'internal critique' from within a particular perspective. Thus, if one had reservations about the treatment of women, family customs or forms of punishment, the only way to address these would be to work from within the particular cultural or religious norms and try to point out internal inconsistencies within that particular value system. Debate about human rights would be a deliberation about how to interpret religious or cultural beliefs. Human rights theory and political philosophy would then become a branch of ethnography or comparative religious and cultural studies. Human rights minimums would be in danger of losing all their critical universal edge. This would be as worrying to soft particularists as to universalists.

In sum, the particularist case is caught in a profound dilemma. If it holds to a hard-edged particularism, it becomes self-refuting. On the other hand, if it is prepared (qua soft particularism) to accept the minimal claim that torture or starvation, and the like, are universally unacceptable for all cultures, then the question arises as to the relation between particularist logic and the actual justification of the universal minimums. Thus, the concept of the minimum human right opens up a deep chasm in the whole particularist position. Particularist critics who exempt the human rights minimum are committed to a contradiction.

They assume (that, is the universal minimum) what they appear to
deny (via their particularist argument). Further, if one interprets human
rights from say an Islamic, nationalist, communitarian or Confucian
perspective, what actually comes prior in the argument, the minimal
requirements or the religious or normative justificatory reason? Can the
normative justification be separated conceptually from the idea and
practice of the human rights minimums?

Conclusion

The above critique of particularism – through the concept of human
rights minimums – is not intended as a direct argument for universalism
or cosmopolitanism, except negatively. Particularism is still regarded
throughout this book as an extremely powerful and pervasive aspect of
contemporary political argument. But, at the same time, it is also considered to be a deeply complex, internally divisive, often incoherent and
conceptually suspect structure of argument. In other words, this book
advocates treating all forms of particularism, specifically nationalism,
with extreme caution and scepticism. This should not be taken, though,
as an automatic defence of undiluted universalism. Many of the arguments of particularism have considerable merit and cogency. Universalism should not therefore rest on its laurels, but neither should it
despair. Part of its case has already been implicitly and somewhat
duplicitously acknowledged by soft particularists.

In conclusion, each of the preceding chapters has involved a detailed
critical discussion of a specific concept and its relation with nationalism.
These two components – the critical analysis of the concept and the
intersection with nationalism – have formed a major theme of the book.
All the concepts discussed figure as significant components of contemporary political dialogue. The intersection with nationalism has acted
as an anchor for the whole discussion, providing an overlapping and
resonant range of issues and debates. Nationalism has thus been
employed throughout as a strategic device. The main argument of this
critical study is that the character of nationalism and its relation with
these concepts is much more enigmatic and complex than is usually
acknowledged in most current political theory debates. The second major
theme, which underpins all the studies in the book, is the 'drift to
particularity' in contemporary politics and political theory. This theme
contends that, over the last two to three decades, there has been a
strongly sympathetic movement towards group particularity. On a substantive level, the particulars which have been the major focus of this
book have been groups and collective conceptions. There is, however, no
coherence between any of these articulations of particularity. In fact, in

some cases, there are profound antagonisms between them. Finally, particularism, as promulgated in contemporary political theory, is seen as a flawed and an internally contradictory perspective. In many ways, the time has come for a new agenda for political theory which tries to move beyond the contrast between universality and particularity. Perhaps, though, as yet, we do not quite have the conceptual vocabulary to express this aspiration.

Notes

INTRODUCTION: THE DRIFT TO PARTICULARITY

1 This would specifically be the case if one viewed the nation as a form of enlarged tribe.
2 This is what may be termed an ontological premise.
3 The term liberal is complex. However, it is analysed in a number of the chapters in this volume, therefore I leave it at this stage unexplained.
4 This is also an ontological premise, which contains many subtle variations.

1 SOVEREIGN PARTICULARS

1 The only point to note here is Jacques Maritain's warning 'the words *principatus* and *suprema potestas* are often translated by "sovereignty" ... this is a misleading translation, which muddles the issue from the start. *Principatus* ("principality") and *suprema potestas* ("supreme power") simply means "highest ruling authority," not "sovereignty" ... Conversely, "sovereignty" was rendered at that moment by "majestas"', Maritain 'The Concept of Sovereignty' in W. J. Stankiewicz (ed.) 1969, 43.
2 Black indeed sees sovereignty (like the state) pre-existing its use as a word in the European political vocabulary, see Black 1993, 113 and 188ff.
3 For example, F. W. Maitland remarked: 'While we are speaking of this matter of sovereignty, it will be well to remember that our modern theories run counter to the deepest convictions of the Middle Ages – to their whole manner of regarding the relation between church and state. Though they may consist of the same units, though every man may have his place in both organisms, these two bodies are distinct ... That the church is in any sense below the state no one will maintain, that the state is below the church is a more plausible doctrine; but the general conviction is that the two are independent, that neither derives its authority from the other. Obviously, when men think thus, while they more or less consistently act upon this theory, they have no sovereign in Austin's sense; before the Reformation Austin's doctrine was impossible', see Maitland 1908, 101–2. This lack of a proper grasp of sovereignty was also commented on by Otto von Gierke, see Gierke 1939, 150–1.
4 Anthony Black sees Bartolus of Sassoferato (1314–57) as the first theorist or jurist to develop a thorough-going account of state sovereignty. He ascribed to the *civitas* all the legal powers previously ascribed to the emperor (and certain kings). If such a *civitas* had recognition of its legislation by the

242

people and other states. This put a legal imprimatur on a *de facto* sovereignty that already existed, see Black 1993, 115–6.

5 For Carl Schmitt 'All significant concepts of the modern theory of the state are secularised theological concepts, not only because of their historical development ... but also because of their systematic structure' (Schmitt 1985, 36). The same point was made by A. P. D'Entreves 1951, ch. 5.

6 Lon Fuller, in fact, calls Hobbes the 'father of legal positivism', in Fuller 1966, 19; see also Quentin Skinner 1978, vol. 2, 289.

7 Sovereignty is often seen rather differently by lawyers and political theorists than by sociologists and political economists.

8 The sovereign state could thus be viewed as an insurrection of the particular.

9 Although other commentators, such as Anthony Black, see Ullman (Black's own teacher) as too much under the influence of Gierke, overdoing the 'cellular' and 'ascending thesis of government' and consequently misreading the nature of medieval political life, see Black, introduction to Otto von Gierke 1990, xxv and xxix.

10 'Nowhere can one discern a direct impact of the Italian model on the internal development of the other states of Europe. The little Italian states were hardly the shapers of international politics. The world of the Italian Renaissance states is a freak', Hans Ritter in H. Lubasz (ed.) 1964, 20.

11 For Black, 'In the Ciceronian and Aristotelian languages of the humanists and philosophers, the legal self-sufficiency of the *civitas* required no justification. Jurists were aware of the empire. Cities and kingdoms may have certain powers, but not simply to make law willy-nilly on their own authority', see Black 1993, 114.

12 For Ullman, the concept state was not available before the 1300s and was not present in practice until the 1500s, see also Walter Ullman 1975,137, H. C. Dowdall, 1923, 100, Ernst Cassirer 1946, 134, F. Meinecke 1957, W. F. Church 1972; J. H. Hexter 1973; F. L. Cheyette 1978, Q. Skinner 1978, vol. 2, 354–5, K. H. F. Dyson 1980, 28; Andrew Vincent 1987, p. 18ff. Black's views seem to be in the minority on this issue.

13 Austin's thesis on sovereignty has closest ties with Bentham's theories. He was seeking a tidy logical account which would clarify the legal process and wipe out its archaisms. Like Bentham's desire for codification of law, Austin wanted to know precisely how and by whom positive law is promulgated and enforced. He wanted to cut through the baggage of natural, constitutional and customary law into the utilitarian essence of legal rules. He would have had no interest in the intellectual context of Bodin's idea or even Hobbes' for that matter.

14 Most seventeenth century sovereigns increasingly relied, of necessity, upon a complex and growing bureaucracy. These were part of the sovereign, therefore, by definition, they were part of the state. The abstraction of the personality of the state was accelerated in these various developments. There is a complex and unexplored relation between the 'state as monarchical sovereign or sovereign institution', the 'monarchical sovereign or assembly as *servants* of the state', the 'office or offices of the sovereign as servants of the state' and the 'personality of the legal state standing above assemblies and offices'.

15 Thus in the vocabulary of the time, 'The conception of sovereignty begins its career as the inherent attribute of the prince; the state is scarcely

distinguishable from the monarch ... With the passing of absolute sovereignty the attribute is detached; it becomes a wandering adjective seeking a substantive ... In the end there is no solution except to permit the adjective to set up as a substantive on its own account. Sovereignty inheres only in the state, and the state is merely a personification of sovereignty. The personality of the state is exhausted in the attribute since the state-person has no reality except as a juristic or political entity', see Krabbe 1930, introduction, xxxii.

16 Kant in fact addresses the state in comparable terms. He remarks, for example, that a state is 'a society of men, which no-one other than itself can command or dispose of. Like a tree, it has its own roots, and to graft it on to another state as if it were a shoot is to terminate its existence as a *moral personality* [my italics]' in Kant, 'Perpetual Peace: A Philosophical Sketch' in Hans Reiss (ed.) 1991, 94.

17 And thus the ground for the development of administrative law.

18 It is not surprising in this context that some nineteenth century writers, such as Ratzel, even thought of boundaries like skins of bodies.

19 For example, Liah Greenfeld in an immensely detailed and scholarly book focuses on nationalism as an elite phenomenon which arose in England in the early sixteenth century in the reign of Henry VIII. In France, Russia, and Germany it also predated industrialization and modernization, see Greenfeld 1992.

20 On the nationalist dimension, it is important to emphasize that these themes are purely formal and empty. Any nationalist, from the most liberal to the most extreme fascist, could interpret them from within their own perspective.

21 It has been argued that Roman law anticipates some of the idea of popular sovereignty in the doctrine of *lex regia*. The people were seen to confer authority. Some canonist teaching in the Catholic church, reinforced by conciliarist debates, also saw the whole church embodying authority rather than the Pope.

22 The term 'people' remains very vague here.

23 General Assembly Resolution 1514, United Nations Declaration on the Granting of Independence to Colonial Peoples and Countries.

24 'Nationalism and democracy were in their origin contemporary movements, and in many respects sprang from similar conditions', Kohn 1945, 191–2.

25 As Hobsbawm remarks on the development of such democracies by the end of the nineteenth century, 'Its tragic paradox was that ... it helped to plunge them willingly into the mutual massacre of World War One', Hobsbawm 1992, 89.

26 Again, in the twentieth century, with the use of ideas such as the popular mandate, representative democracy has drawn somewhat closer to the popular conception.

27 It might be replied here that the notion of the state being deployed here is very *ancien regime*-like, that is, just focused on law and a specific institutional structure. This criticism evinces a profound historical ignorance about the development of state theory. Undoubtedly, as Foucault has argued, power has changed and is more contingent, impersonal and diffused in the modern era, but, nonetheless, the old ways of state sovereignty are still with us, as Foucault was clearly aware, and it is these old ways that are still with us in nationalism.

2 NATION STATE

1 Amongst the nations created during the nineteenth and early twentieth centuries: 1830 Greece; 1831 Belgium; 1861 Italy; 1871 Germany; 1878 Romania, Serbia and Montenegro; 1905 Norway; 1908 Bulgaria; 1913 Albania; 1917 Finland; 1918 Poland, Czechoslovakia, Estonia, Latvia, Lithuania; 1922 Ireland. The League of Nations founded in 1920 had forty-two members, the United Nations, founded in 1945, had fifty-one, by 1969 eighty-two, by 1973 one hundred and thirty-five, and by 1988 one hundred and fifty-nine and the list will no doubt keep growing in the new century.

2 The first nation states grew out of the model of the original west European absolutist and semi-absolutists states, like France and England. There then followed the more culturally inclined nation states in central and southern Europe, and particularly unificatory nation states, like Germany and Italy. Finally, secession nation states expanded in number, and led to the consequent disintegration of multi-national states. 'The entire band of states stretching from Finland in the North, via the Baltic states to Poland and Czechoslovakia, and on to Albania, Romania and Greece in the South are the products of political secession'; secession also occurred elsewhere, as in Belgium breaking from the United Netherlands (1831), Norway from Sweden (1814); Southern Ireland from Britain (1922); Iceland from Denmark (1944), see Alter 1989, 99. This pattern would need to be extended to include the large number of post-1945 postcolonial nationalisms in Africa and Asia, as well as the break-up of the Soviet Union.

3 There is a more than fortuitous coincidence between the rise of universities – and the development of historical, literary, legal, and political curricula – and the interest in nation states, for example, in terms of the nation state involvement in the history curriculum, see Soffer 1994, also Berger, Donovan and Passmore (eds) 1999. The concluding chapter of the latter book, entitled 'Historians and the nation-state: some conclusions', is a clear survey of this issue.

4 For German historiography and the nation state, see also Georg Iggers, 'Nationalism and Historiography 1789–1996: The German example in historical perspective' in Berger, Donovan and Passmore (eds) 1999, 15–29. This edited book includes other examples of such writing across Europe.

5 However, as Smith remarks, in a later piece, the state 'refers exclusively to public institutions, differentiated from, and autonomous of, other social institutions and exercising a monopoly of coercion ... The nation, on the other hand, signifies a cultural and political bond, united in a single political community', Smith 1991, 14–15.

6 This might be a slight misreading of Walzer's view, or alternatively possibly he has not made up his own mind. Walzer obviously believes that most states that make up international society are 'nation states' and they have a dominant group, but still, as he remarks elsewhere, 'homogeneity is rare, if non-existent, in the world today', see Walzer, 'The Politics of Difference' in R. McKim and J. McMahan (eds) 1997, 249.

7 David Archard in Noel O'Sullivan (ed.) 2000, 156. In the same volume, Paul Hirst, in 'Globalization, the nation-state and political theory', also sees the nation state, with some qualifications, as 'pivotal', 178.

8 In acknowledging the distinction between state and nation the theorist could be arguing for cosmopolitanism, for statism without nationalism, or a better appreciation of both nations and states.

9 This was not, of course, a normative argument for the state-nation relation, it was more of an empirical premise.

10 In MacCormick's analysis the future of Scottish nationalism lies in a regional policy within Europe, not in a state.

11 'Nations do not make states ... but the other way round', Hobsbawm 1992, 10; see also Peter Sugar, 'From Ethnicity to Nationalism and Back Again' in Palumbo and Shanahan (eds) 1981, 81.

12 Some of these accounts are dependent upon the terminology used. Anthony Smith's work is typical of this point. He initially draws ethnic communities (ethnie) distinct from nationalism, with the major qualification that ethnie are still embodied in and carry over into nationalism. Thus although nationalism, as a movement and an ideology, might legitimately be regarded as a fairly modern idea and practice, nonetheless ethnie are ancient units, which are as old as human cooperation, see Smith 1986.

13 The faculty of arts of many medieval universities was divided administratively into 'nations' for voting purposes, according to place of birth, see Louis Snyder 1954, 29; Boyd C. Schafer 1972, 14.

14 See Smith 1979, 1; Kohn 1945, 3, although Kohn does see strong elements of what he calls an 'unconscious nationalism', predating the French Revolution; Snyder 1954, 29; Kedourie also places a strong emphasis on the French Revolution in conjunction with certain crucial philosophical ideas, in Kedourie 1974, 12; A. H. Birch 1989, 4; James Mayall 1990, 43; E. Kamenka, introduction to Kamenka (ed.) 1976, 4; I. Berlin, 1990, 244.

15 'Even the casual observer of European history since the French Revolution can see that the multitude of ethnic variations and distinctions make it to all and practical intents and purposes impossible for cultural nation and state perfectly to overlap ... In terms of universal history, nation-states are the exception even in the present and past centuries; multi-national states are the rule of historical reality. They still exist in present day Europe, even after two hundred years of wrestling with national and nationalist issues', Alter 1989, 111–12. See also Hobsbawm 1992, 17, for similar reflections.

16 Unless one conceded that there are 'official nationalisms' fostered by states, which are distinct from ethnic or popular nationalisms. However such official nationalisms are quite clearly more obviously artificial than ethnically based ones.

17 The right of the German *Volk* under the national socialists, or any other such autocratic regime, also becomes legitimized by self-determination. In this latter context, individuals participate or identify their selves with the national policies. In other words, there is little place in this latter perspective for orthodox individual liberty or representative democracy, in the liberal or social democratic mode. In fact it is literally very difficult to see how pure individual self-determination could be reconciled with national self-determination. The two appear to be potentially at odds, depending upon exactly how one interprets the relation of the individual to the nation.

18 This is Michael Walzer disputing Ernest Nagel's point, namely, that we all speak from 'somewhere' not 'nowhere', see Walzer 1987, 6–7.

19 As Miller comments, 'Social justice will always be easier to achieve with strong national identities and without internal communal divisions. Belgium, Canada and Switzerland work as they do partly because they are *not* simply multinational, but have cultivated common national identities alongside communal ones', Miller 1995b, 96.

20 Often in the form of legal obligations, or strictly defined organizational norms, but also often in the form of conventional or moral claims arising in the context of our participation in a social practice.

21 William Connolly suggests, for example, that the liberal and communitarian visions are all located in the same exclusionary Enlightenment frame, see W. E. Connolly 1991, 29.

22 Connolly's case corresponds to the story told by Bauman, who sees the early growth of nations marked out by a merciless war against the local, irregular and spontaneous. He notes that 'Earnest efforts were made throughout the modern era to replace manifold communal gettings-together, in their much needed function of replenishing the reservoirs of sacred unity, with a centrally designed and controlled calendar of festivities'. The new religion was nationalism. Communities gradually dissipated into masses. The masses, even though deprived of worth in their locality, could still bask in the eternal sun of the nation's glory. Morality was subordinated to politics – the collective conscience. However, in the postmodern era, for Bauman, the nation state is letting go. There is no more need for such spiritual leadership. With the globalization of the economy, the state has lost many of it original roles and mass participation is no longer crucially necessary. Self-formation becomes privatized. In this context we see, for Bauman, the proliferation of spontaneous rudimentary groups, which he calls 'neo-tribes'. They do not last any longer than their membership. They are episodic, often single-issue and inconsequential. They are eruptions of sociality, 'unplanned expeditions into the world beyond moral reach', Bauman 1993, 135 and 141.

23 For Canovan, patriotism is not an acceptable alternative to nationalism, a point which I have considerable, if slightly oblique, sympathy with. See the chapter on patriotism.

24 The nation might *officially* coincide with the state because state institutions publicly construct it that way.

25 As one of the older post-1945 political theory university texts put it 'It seems strange ... that a type of association so ill-defined as the nation could be considered of such enormous importance in modern politics', Benn and Peters 1969, 247.

26 John Hoffman provides a different perspective on this question. He views the state as incoherent as the nation, partly because the state is a logical contradiction. The logical contradiction, for Hoffman, lies at the heart of the state (qua the Weberian definition). Basically the state asserts a monopoly of legitimate force which it cannot have. This monopoly is only raised in the context of being challenged. If it was not challenged it would not need to be a monopoly of force. The state therefore, for Hoffman, is a logically contradictory identity. The contradiction of the state identity leads to a contradictory identity in the nation, Hoffman 1995, 66–7.

27 'The number of *intergovernmental* international organizations grew from 123 in 1951 through 280 in 1972 to 365 in 1984; the number of international

non-governmental organizations from 832 through 2,173 in 1972, more than
doubling to 4,615 in the next twelve years', Hobsbawm 1992, 181.

28 Each gives rise to a different range of demands. Some will want to integrate;
some just respect or autonomy (civil rights movements or non-discrimin-
ation); some greater autonomy from the centre, that is self-determination
within the state (consociational or federal model); some to secede.

3 CITIZENSHIP

1 The manner of approach in this chapter may appear counter-intuitive at first
glance. To begin with cosmopolitanism and only later to come to the idea of
citizenship within the state may appear slightly odd. A critic might think that
it is more sensible to begin with the state. Further, most liberals do remain
committed to a conception of universalism within a state structure. Thus,
it is arguable, that 'universalism within the state' should be kept distinct
from 'universalism outside the state'. My argument is that it is precisely the
'universalism within the state' – from a liberal moral and political perspective
– which is *arbitrarily* linked to the idea of boundaries. That is to say, the
structure and values implicit within the liberal concept of citizenship contain
no logical constraints, such as to confine it to the state. The notion of a
boundary thus becomes arbitrary. It follows therefore that the distinction
drawn between 'universality within' and 'universality outside' the state is
itself arbitrary. The distinction may be politically and legally the case, but it is
still unreasonable and illogical from the perspective of liberal citizenship.
Liberal citizenship, in this sense, provides the rational groundwork for human
rights doctrine.

2 The major critical point against cosmopolitan citizenship – say in Kant – is
that citizenship, in whatever form it appears, is tied to a state or a particular
political structure. Andrew Dobson remarks here that 'Those who talk of
cosmopolitan citizenship in today's globalized world are open to the same
objection, and they would probably meet it by pointing to incipient regional
and global political entities such as the European Union and the United
Nations through which the ideas of transnational citizenship can be
exercised', Andrew Dobson, 'Ecological Citizenship: A Disruptive Influence?'
in S. Pierson and Simon Tormey (eds) 2000, 45.

3 Kant argued for the moral autonomy of states within a voluntary league of
states committed to maintain peace. Liberal constitutional republics would
thus be inclined, in his view, to international peace. Liberal theory, qua Kant,
conceives of citizenship in terms of contract and consent. The citizen comes
to the state ideally or actually with entitlements. The citizen will agree to
limitations for the common good. Liberal citizenship is thus a bearer or
vehicle of rights within the state. This whole cosmopolitan perspective will
be focused on more rigorously in the penultimate chapter of this volume.

4 Thomas Pogge sees two forms in practice: institutional and moral cosmopolitanism. Institutional cosmopolitanism assigns responsibility to institutional
schemes. It is dependent upon the existence and maintenance of human
rights through institutions. Some argue, in this scenario, for supra-national
statelike institutions to be set up. Ethical cosmopolitanism assigns responsibility to individual or collective agencies. Each person is equally a subject of

moral concern. There is no necessary link here between the institutional and ethical types. One could believe therefore in the institutional conception and not adhere to moral cosmopolitanism. Equally, one could be a moral cosmopolitan and not believe in an institutional setting, or, at least, a central world state. Therefore, even if one rejects world government, it does not lead to a rejection of moral cosmopolitanism, see Thomas Pogge 1994, 89–122.

5 A parallel tension to civil and social rights can be observed in those who conceive of human rights as either universal and generic liberties, or, alternatively, particular or special substantive economic and social rights.

6 This is close to Michael Sandel's use of the term 'procedural republic' for this form of liberalism, see Sandel 1992.

7 For Taylor, the *procedural* view is best encapsulated in Ronald Dworkin's 'Liberalism' paper in Hampshire (ed.) 1980, 113–43; see Taylor 'The Politics of Recognition' in Gutman (ed.) 1994, 56.

8 The term 'new liberal' or 'social liberal' is immensely complex and contested. I have not attempted to examine the term, but have largely taken it for granted in this chapter that we can speak of its ideology and social theory. This is by no means an uncontested position. My own attempt to summarize and assess some of the diverse accounts of the new liberalism can be found in Vincent 1990, 388–405, see also Vincent and Plant 1984, ch. 5; Vincent 2000, ch. 2; Michael Freeden 1978.

9 This latter argument will be examined in chapters 6 and 8.

10 Dominique Schnapper has suggested (somewhat mischievously) that German interest in constitutional patriotism and reform of citizenship may well be a belated discovery of the French idea of nationhood and citizenship, see Schnapper 1994, 182.

11 'The legal nationality conferred by the state and the ethnocultural nationality invoked by the "principle of nationality" are of course different things; the former may be conferred in utter disregard of the latter. Yet the thrust of the principle of nationality was precisely to connect the two – not directly ... but indirectly via the redrawing of political boundaries so as to make legal and ethnocultural nationality converge', Brubaker 1994, 99.

12 All quotations from Tom Paine's translation of the 'Declaration of the Rights of Man and of Citizens' by the National Assembly of France (1789) in D. G. Ritchie 1954, 291–2.

13 Debates about both nationality and citizenship are also closely associated with distinct state traditions, although this is an even bigger issue.

14 A number of current thinkers appear to want to address this dilemma. Bruce Ackerman, for example, has consequently described himself as a 'rooted cosmopolitan'. Liberal universalism is seen to be virtually implicit within the particular United States Constitution. Consequently, Ackerman is provisionally persuaded to 'embrace the American Constitution'. A more cynical appraisal of this same point would see such universalism as 'Kantianism in one country'. However, for Ackerman, the poor Europeans would be condemned to be 'rootless cosmopolitans'. This sounds like a new form of Addresses to the American Nation. There is a problem in Ackerman's view of the precise character of the national mission, in relation to liberal universalism. There are a number of liberal states where global citizenship can be seen as an extension of their own rights structures. Yet, different

interpretations of both liberalism and cosmopolitanism are inevitable. North Americans might well embrace generic liberal rights (on a civil level), but not widespread distributive (social) rights, let alone special cultural rights. Some might see social rights as a logical extension of the generic human rights to life. If this was accepted it would imply large transfers of wealth across the globe. However, since this latter conception has been, to date, reliant upon social liberal or social democratic sovereign states, it is an unlikely international scenario. France, on the other hand, would give full legal rights within its Republican notion of citizenship. These would *include* civil, political and social rights. But, this would not necessarily allow any special or cultural rights. On rooted cosmopolitanism, see Bruce Ackerman 1994.

15 Another, possibly simpler way, of framing this dilemma is through Veit Bader's thoughts on transnational citizenship. Bader, reflecting on procedural and cultural liberalism, remarks that procedural liberalism 'has underestimated the importance of communities and cultures'. But, cultural liberalism, which he describes as 'communitarian liberalism', has actively taken culture and nation on board, but for Bader, it has 'not yet fully addressed the exclusionary effects of communities and cultures', see Bader 1997, 772.

4 LIBERALISM

1 The theme of the book contends that 'the liberal tradition, with its respect for personal autonomy, reflection and choice, and the national tradition, with its emphasis on belonging, loyalty and solidarity ... Can indeed accommodate one another', see Tamir 1993, 6 and 10.

2 One of the more popular theories, which is widely quoted in the recent literature, is by Miroslav Hroch. He sees three definite phases. First, nationalism is embodied in nineteenth century folklore, custom and the like. This is essentially a cultural idea, fostered by the middle and upper classes, with little or no political implication. Secondly, nationalism is pursued as a political campaign. It is usually connected with and fostered by political parties. Finally, nationalism becomes translated into mass support and mass movements. Each of these phases is linked by Hroch to economic and cultural changes, see Miroslav Hroch 1985.

3 Lord Acton in the nineteenth century distinguished between two forms – French and English, see Lord (J. E. E. D.) Acton 1948, 183–4. The earliest and most influential twofold classification was Hans Kohn's Western and Eastern nationalisms, see Kohn 1945; John Plamenatz follows roughly in the same path in 'Two Types of Nationalism' in E. Kamenka (ed.) 1976. Friedrich Meinecke distinguished *Staatsnation* and *Kulturnation*, see Meinecke 1970; see also Minogue 1969, 13; also Anthony Smith distinguishes 'territorial' from 'ethnic' nations in Smith 1986, 134–8. In many of the twofold classifications there is usually a fierce desire to keep Western, more liberal-minded nationalism distinct from the nationalism associated with fascism and national socialism, see Kohn 1945, 351; Tamir 1993, 90; Smith 1971, 7 and 1979, 83–5. This twofold classification will form the key theme of this chapter. There are threefold typologies in Kellas who distinguishes ethnic, social and official nationalism, Kellas 1991, 52; Peter Alter's *Risorgimento*, integral and reform nationalisms, Alter 1989. There are

fourfold classifications via historical shifts: integrative nationalism; disruptive nationalism; aggressive nationalism; and finally, 1945 to the present, the worldwide diffusion of nationalism, see Louis Snyder 1954, ch. 5. Carlton Hayes uses a fivefold classification: Jacobin; liberal; traditionalist; economic protectionist; and integral totalitarian, see Hayes 1926 and 1949.

4 My own favoured typology reflects the way in which nationalism crosses over the territory of other ideologies. The first type is liberal nationalism; secondly, there is a more traditionalist conservative nationalism. Thirdly, there is integral nationalism, which is the form most closely associated with fascism and national socialism. There are also other possible variants, such as socialist nationalism and anti-colonial nationalism. Romantic nationalism has strayed across all these forms. However, in my reading, all of these latter categories either overlap or form sub-aspects within the major categories above. For expansion on these points see Vincent 2000, ch. 9.

5 The distinction itself is extremely questionable for a start, but it would take a more historically based enquiry to justify this point. As Andrzej Walicki remarks, 'It would not be too difficult for a critic of Kohn's theory to demonstrate that all the characteristics which he regards as specific to Central and Eastern European nationalism could also be found in Western Europe', see Walicki 1989, p. 5ff. The other point to note here is that Eastern (ethnic) nationalism is occasionally also associated with the notion of cultural nationalism. Yet both the ethnic (or Eastern) nationalism and civic liberal nationalism have cultural components. Also the ethnic or Eastern nationalism is often seen to be inward-looking, excluding immigrants. Yet it is clear that groups such as the Québécois or Flemish, despite their strong cultural and ethnic emphasis, are prepared to accept immigrants, as long as they learn the language and culture. Similarly the USA requires immigrants to learn English and American history in schools.

6 'International *Risorgimento* nationalism had no blue-print to hand for avoiding the growing number of situations in which the competing aims of different nationalisms were hopelessly at loggerheads', Alter 1989, 33.

7 Erica Benner 1997, 202. I am grateful to a series of Georgios Varouxakis' scholarly articles on the issue of Mill and nationalism, namely, for drawing my attention to the complexity of this issue. Varouxakis makes the point that my own earlier work on this question of liberal nationalism – which argues a pragmatic case – might well be said to sum up Mill's own position, qua nationalism. Thus, Mill, and other such liberals, should not simply be lumped with the contemporary arguments. I find his arguments compelling, see G. Varouxakis 1998c, 1998b, 375–91 and 1998a. My own earlier article, from which this present chapter is adapted, is Vincent 1997a.

8 In fact a similar distinction appears in many other writers of the same period such as Isaiah Berlin. As one commentator remarks on Berlin, 'It is important to stress that Berlin's sympathy with nationalism is sympathy with the nationalism of the Risorgimento and with the European revolutionaries of 1848; it is sympathy with the nationalism of Verdi and Clemenceau, not with the nationalism of Treitschke and Barrès', Stuart Hampshire in Edna and Avishai Margalit (eds) 1991, 132.

9 MacCormick, despite writing about nationalism in the early 1980s, also claims to have been influenced by Yael Tamir's work (as well as Plamenatz's

writings) whilst examining her doctoral thesis in 1989. Tamir's doctoral thesis was transformed into the 1993 book *Liberal Nationalism*, see Neil MacCormick 1990, 12. Tamir's views are thus equally instructive on liberal nationalism, on very similar grounds to MacCormick.

10 He says in another piece, 'The truth about human individuals is that they – we – are social products, not independent atoms capable of constituting society through a voluntary coming together', MacCormick 1990, 14.

11 As Miller states: 'a belief that belongs together with the rest; that this association is neither transitory nor merely instrumental, but stems from a long history of living together which (it is hoped and expected) will continue into the future; that the community is marked off from other communities by its members' distinctive characteristics', Miller 1989a, 238.

12 An unease that he shares with the conservative writer Roger Scruton, see 'In Defence of the Nation' in Scruton 1990, 325. There are also some parallel sentiments (without the nationalist emphasis) developed from a more classical liberal perspective, by Chandran Kukathas in Kukathas (ed.) 1993, 29–30.

13 'All evidence suggests that people give greater weight to [the principle of distribution according to need as a requirement of social justice] to the extent that they see themselves as bound to the beneficiaries of the principle by common ties. The more communal the relationship, the more need displaces merit (in particular) as a criterion of justice. Thus the kind of underpinning for a welfare state that socialists will look for can only be provided through a widespread sense of common membership throughout the society in question … It is … worth stressing that this common identity must exist at the national level', see Miller in Mendus (ed.) 1988a, 243.

14 See I. Kant 1974, Part 2, 'Anthropological Characterizations'. See MacCormick 1982, 261. See also Vincent 1995, 35–50.

15 As in MacCormick, for Tamir the justification of national self-determination is that membership of a nation is a 'constitutive factor of personal identity'. In addition, peoples should be able to protect their identity. There should be, in other words, a right to preserve national identity which would allow groups the opportunity 'to express this identity, both privately and publicly'. All such expressions of identity, for Tamir, 'however restricted, merit respect and support'. There is a need for a shared public space for 'ensuring the preservation of a nation as a vital and active community'. National self-determination implies a domain for both individual interests and communal identity; thus 'The ability to conceive of certain social and political institutions as representing a particular culture and as carriers of the national identity is at the heart of the yearning for national self-determination'. Finally, the right to national self-determination 'can be fully realised only if the national group is recognised by both members and non-members as an autonomous source of human action and creativity, and if this recognition is followed by political arrangements enabling members of the nation to develop their national life with as little external interference as possible', see Tamir 1993, 73–4.

16 'Self-determination in a dual sense meaning that there has to be scope both for individual self-determination inside a political community and for collective self-determination of the community without external domination', MacCormick 1990, 16.

17 MacCormick also thinks that 'liberty in a free country requires schemes of redistribution, welfare provision and educational support', MacCormick, 1990, 15. See also Tamir 1993, 16–17.

18 He remarks elsewhere that 'some form of democratic self-determination has to be considered both justifiable and valuable ... Some form of collective self-constitution, some kind of active participation in shaping and sustaining the institutions of social or communal government whose aim is to advance liberty and autonomy, seems to be a necessary part of the whole ensemble of conditions in which the autonomy of the contextual individual could be genuinely constituted and upheld', see MacCormick 1990, 15.

19 Tamir also sees some hope in the Lijphart's model of consociational democracy, Tamir 1993, 156.

20 I find myself perplexed by Miller's somewhat easy distinction between ethnic and national allegiance. Some scholars see ethnicity as a very old idea rooted in kinship, and nationalism is just another way of speaking about such ethnic identity. In this context, even liberal nationalism would be ethnically based. In other words, nationalism and ethnicity are virtually identical as premodern forms of natural allegiance. As one recent socio-biologically influenced writer remarks, 'we have in nationalism a combination of biological ethnocentrism, psychological ingroup/outgroup hostile propensities, and cultural and political differences', Kellas 1991, 13; see also V. Reynolds *et al*, 1987. Other scholars (such as Ernest Gellner and Benedict Anderson) are adamant modernists who see nationalism (and ethnicity to some degree) as distinctly modern inventions. Alternatively, ethnicity will sometimes be seen as more 'natural' as opposed to the invented artifice of nationalism. Anthony Smith takes a *via media* position; although seeing ethnicity and nationalism as distinct; nonetheless, he argues that all nationalism is traceable back to ethnic communities. He identifies his position as intermediate between the modernists and primordialists. He remarks that 'Nationalism, both as an ideology and movement, is a wholly modern phenomenon, even if, ... the "modern nation" in practice incorporates several features of pre-modern *ethnie* and owes much to the general model of ethnicity', Smith 1986, 18. Thus Miller's deployment of the distinction between nationalism and ethnicity, as though it were obvious, looks highly questionable.

21 'Our sense of identity arises from our experience of belonging within significant communities, such as families, schools, workplace communities, religious communities ... and also nations, conceived as cultural communities endowed with political relevance', MacCormick 1990, 17.

22 '... nations are quite real and quite identifiable as some among the types of community constitutive of people', MacCormick 1990, 17.

23 I am not denying that it is possible to make an argument for ranking; however as yet it remains undeveloped by liberal nationalist writers.

24 Admittedly MacCormick and Tamir do not favour this association. It is also important to note here that my arguments here are not directed at the state, but rather the 'nation state'.

25 Unless, of course, one presupposed a distinction between 'ethnie' and 'nationals', then one could link nationalism with the state and reduce everyone else to ethnie. However, such a strategy is presupposed upon a

profoundly dubious distinction between ethnicity and nationalism and also assumes that 'a' substantive nationalism can be clearly identified.

26 This argument can be found stated in Bob Goodin's notion of the 'assigned responsibility model', see Goodin 1988, 678ff. Goodin's argument hangs on the Hartian distinction between general and special duties. The purportedly classical nationalist argument denies general duties and emphasizes the place of special duties to our conationals. Goodin doubts the significance of special duties in practice, arguing, alternatively, for the idea of special duties as 'distributed general duties'. Thus special duties are viewed as 'merely devices whereby the moral community's general duties get assigned to particular agents' (p. 678). Special duties thus derive their moral force from universal general duties (underpinned in Goodin's case by utilitarianism). Goodin concludes from this that special duties – read national imperatives – can be overridden by general duties. Goodin therefore suggests that our fellow countrymen 'are not so very special after all' (p. 679). It also leads him to doubt the significance of nationalism, discrete state-orientated citizenship, state boundaries and presumably state independence or sovereignty. Goodin thus remarks, somewhat alarmingly, 'If some states prove incapable of discharging their responsibilities effectively, then they should either be reconstituted or assisted' (p. 685).

27 'Sovereignty' has always been regarded as a tricky issue by liberals particularly; however this is primarily due to its association with the absolutist tradition on sovereignty. The idea that sovereignty could be shared has thus always been a puzzle within this perspective, which identifies sovereignty with unitary absolute power.

28 For List, liberalism, as a consequence of its blindness to commercial history, neglected the fact that it rested upon the pre-existence of the nation. There was always therefore a residual suppressed statism and nationalism implicit in all liberal thought. States and nations formed the essential backdrop to successful liberal markets. The framework of national law, national defence, national well-being, national aims and the national state was the secure, virtually unconscious background for the market, see Friedrich List 1966. As Hobsbawm more recently remarked '... no economist of even the most extreme liberal persuasion could overlook or fail to take account of the national economy. Only liberal economists did not like to, or quite know how to, talk about it', Hobsbawm 1992, 28.

29 As indeed has already been stressed from another angle in the previous chapter.

30 To some extent the liberal nationalist 'embedded' claim can be read, ironically, through the dimensions of Goodin's argument mentioned in note 26. The national culture, for liberal nationalists, is acceptable insofar as it embodies commitments to autonomy and self-determination by individuals. This allows them to demand that respect for national identity is intimately connected to the personal identity. Thus – reading this through Goodin's spectacles – the special duties that we owe and feel towards our conationals are really general duties that humanity owes to itself in totality. General duties of respect for human autonomy, for example, are embedded in the supposedly special duties of those who live in liberal nation states. Ironically, whereas Goodin uses this argument to provide succour for a denial of the

significance of nationalism and particularism, the liberal nationalists use it to provide salvation for nationalism. Both, of course, ultimately desire justice across boundaries – although Goodin is undoubtedly more convinced of this than liberal nationalists, who see more obstacles. Goodin achieves his aim by emphasizing the generality of the duty and undermining the local character of circumstances. Liberal nationalists achieve it by downplaying the general duties when they wish to emphasize the particularity and the converse when they wish to stress the salve of more universal commitments. If anyone is being more duplicitous here it looks like the liberal nationalist. However, it is clear from this discussion that the argument from embeddedness certainly does not necessarily aid the case for liberal nationalism. On the other hand, Goodin's position can be questioned again by reversing the argument, namely, by asking from whence the distinction between general and special duties, and the arguments for the universality of, say, liberal utilitarianism, derive? It would be fairly easy to show that such a distinction derives from a historically situated or embedded liberalism. Liberalism does not stand god-like with a view from nowhere assessing the political scene. Thus liberal nationalism could easily be seen as the socially embedded premise from which such interesting distinctions (such as general and special duties) derive. Special duties and nationalist concerns never have a chance of a look in from the beginning of the argument.

31 A similar logical conundrum could be traced out in terms of 'self-reflective critical agency', which is an important facet of liberal theory. Is self-reflective agency itself the product of a particular liberal national community or is it something than can transcend any particular community? See Buttle 2000.

32 He states in another work: 'a sense of nationality is for many people constitutive in part of their sense of identity and even of selfhood, then respect for this aspect of their selfhood is as incumbent as respect for any other, up to a certain point', MacCormick 1990, 18. The 'point' that MacCormick notes is where nationalist practices become destructive of others. However there is a dilemma here, from a nationalist perspective, as to how one would recognize 'destructive' practices. What 'objective' criteria could be adopted to condemn a practice as destructive – surely nationalist argument *per se* appears to intrinsically limit any clear judgement on this issue? It is not clear at what point respect stops and condemnation begins. Also, does this 'destructiveness' include internal destructiveness or does it only imply external destructiveness, i.e. if cruelty is being exercised only upon a domestic population, is this cruelty to be respected, or is it only when one nationalism attempts to destroy another? This whole area appears remarkably blurred.

33 That is unless one were to argue a Gierke 'Germanist' type of thesis about groups and associations in relation to the law and the state, see, for example, Vincent 1989.

34 The principle of subsidiarity states that in 'areas which do not fall within its exclusive competence, the Community shall take action, in accordance with the principle of subsidiarity, only if and in so far as the objectives of the proposed action cannot be sufficiently achieved by the Member States and can therefore, by reason of the scale or effects of the proposed action, be better achieved by the Community', see Art 3b, Treaty of the European Union.

35 Some thus see subsidiarity 'as meaningless and misleading gobbledegook designed to disguise the actual increase in central powers at the expense of national rights ... Indeed it is seen by some as a spur to "centralizing federalism" and not a barrier to it. Other Articles, such as 5 and 235, are held to rob it of real effect', Church and Phinnemore, 1994, 68.

36 The 1992 Edinburgh agreement, amongst other things, more explicitly linked decision-making to local subnational levels. However it has also 'compounded [Maastricht's] contradictions by making [subsidiarity] a matter of democracy as well as of federal balance and execution of power', Church and Phinnemore 1994, 74.

37 'National self-determination and individual self-determination were declared part of the historical self-deliverance of mankind from ignorance and tyranny', M. Keens-Soper 1989, 702.

38 Some critics find the idea of 'self' totally mythical in this sense, see Richard T. DeGeorge in Twining (ed.) 1991, 1–4. Other theorists appear quite unfussed by the moral rights of nation states to be self-determining entities, see Michael Walzer 1977.

39 Yet if one adopted arguments about self-determination by the 'higher self' or more 'communally orientated self', then the salve of democracy might well lose its efficacy. Individuals could still identify themselves with national policies, but it would not necessarily imply representative liberal democracy. In other words, there are no necessary grounds for adopting orthodox liberal individual liberty or representative democracy.

40 Singapore, for one, in recent years has made a point of denying the significance of democracy and individual rights to the development of their nation. In fact they have taken to lecturing other states, such as Australia, on the virtues of this position for a healthy economy.

41 I should emphasize, that this is not an argument against representative democracy.

42 One response to this could be that if there is no ethical argument involved in nationalism how could one limit or criticize it in any way? Surely my argument cuts away the ground from any rational assessment of nationalism? How could one therefore ensure that it corresponds with liberal intuitions? My response to this is to argue firstly that this chapter is, in itself, a critical commentary on the inchoate character of liberal nationalist argument. It is an argument which denies the ethical character of nationalism. It is this sceptical stance which should be adopted to all nationalist claims. It is accepted though that nationalism is a pragmatic fact. Moderate nationalism, which corresponds with liberal intuitions, is even socially tolerable. However, conversely giving an ethical gloss to nationalism should be avoided because of its inchoateness, brutal history and political unpredictability.

5 PATRIOTISM

1 The much later doctrine of patriarchalism has an important root in this idea.

2 The link of *pays* to land is more obvious in the French word for peasant – paysan – defined as a 'personne de la campagne'.

3 David Miller thus gives an encyclopaedia definition of patriotism as 'really a sentiment rather than a political idea', see item on 'Patriotism' in D. Miller *et al* 1987, 369.

4 It is not fortuitous, for my subsequent argument, that Machiavelli should be regarded as a founding father. He embodies the ambiguous legacy of patriotism as emotive, moralistic and virtue-laden, but also orientated to the abstracted power of the state.

5 'With the rise of classical utilitarianism in the eighteenth century, and with the use of utilitarian principles to underpin so much of the liberal state in the century following, the theory of free states fell increasingly into disrepute, and eventually slipped almost wholly out of sight', Skinner 1998, x and 96.

6 As one writer notes, patriotism 'has existed as long as there have been communities. Though the word was seldom used before the eighteenth century, the thing itself was old and familiar under other names, such as "love of country" or "loyalty to one's people"', Plamenatz in Kamenka (ed.) 1976, 24.

7 Skinner has been chairman of the European Science Foundation network entitled *Republicanism: A Shared European Heritage*.

8 Anthony Black, for example, contends that medieval republicanism developed in the context of monarchy, but monarchy was a movable feast between 300 and 1500. It did not mean absolutism. He comments that regimes 'described by medieval and renaissance people as monarchical might be described as republican today', see Black 1998, 919, also 1997.

9 It is possible to draw a distinction between patriot and patriotism: patriot (and *patria*) being a much older usage and 'patriotism' being a neologism of the eighteenth century. Whether anything fundamental can be made of this distinction is open to question.

10 See chapter 6.

11 Dietz actually deeply regrets the blurring of patriotism and nationalism. This blurring she thinks means that 'we have literally lost touch with history'. In consequence, the republican citizen is, she notes, 'nearly lost to us', Dietz 1989, 191. I would say that the republican citizen is lost, despite all the fabrications and soul-searchings.

12 Nussbaum comments that 'By conceding that a morally arbitrary boundary such as the boundary of the nation has a deep and formative role in our deliberations, we seem to deprive ourselves of any principled way of persuading citizens they should in fact join hands across these other barriers', Nussbaum 1996, 14. Nussbaum's whole opening essay rests on the assumed synonymity of these terms.

13 In rooted cosmopolitanism it would be more accurate to say that universality has been saved for particularity.

14 Although this would also rule Rousseau out of the whole republican perspective.

15 In effect there are two competing notions of citizenship here for Habermas. One is participatory self-rule, which he associates with Taylor and communitarian writings (which he sees as linked with republicanism). The other model sees citizenship in terms of the power to retrieve rights and ensure equal treatment. This latter theme sounds like Roman citizenship.

16 'Instead of polishing or retrieving the ethnocultural oneness, one should devise political changes able to educate democratic citizens. And the political means to be used are those suggested by republican patriots: good government and well-ordered participation ... Democratic politics do not need ethnocultural unity; they need citizens committed to the way of life of the republic', Viroli 1995, 176.

17 This goes against the views of David Miller's liberal nationalism and Roger Scruton's conservative nationalism.

18 'The transfer of the Rome or Empire ideologies to the territorial monarchies was hardly less momentous than the applications of religious thought', Kantorowicz 1957, 267.

19 As the Bishop of Caerleon stated to the soldiers, about to fight a Saxon army, 'Fight for your *patria* and suffer even death for her ... Death itself is Victory and is a means of saving the soul. For whoever suffers death for his brothers, offers himself a living host to God, and unambiguously follows Christ', quoted in Kantorowicz 1957, 241.

20 As Coluccio Salutati stated (without a hint of irony) 'Thou knowest not how sweet is the *amor patriae*: if such would be the expedient for the fatherland's protection or enlargement, it would seem neither burdensome and difficult nor a crime to thrust the axe into one's father's head, ... to deliver from the womb of one's wife the premature child with the sword', quoted in Kantorowicz 1957, 245.

21 'War for the king, war for France, war for justice, war for culture and education, war for the Church, war for the Christian faith – all these were interrelated, interdependent arguments', Kantorowicz 1957, 255. In an earlier discussion he remarked 'The Christian martyr ... who had offered himself up for the invisible polity and had died for his divine Lord *pro fide*, was to remain – actually until the twentieth century – the genuine model of civic self-sacrifice', Kantorowicz 1957, 234–5.

22 For the neo-Platonic view see Plotinus 1969. In the Fifth Tractate, III, 5, Plotinus describes love as 'like a goad; it is without resource in itself; even winning its end, it is poor again. It cannot be satisfied ... true satisfaction is only for what has its plenitude in its own being', Plotinus 1969, 197ff.

23 'Christianity did come into the field with a very definite, indeed quite unique view of love, which ... was radically different from all the Greek notions', Armstrong and Markus 1964, 78.

24 'English speakers, like French and German speakers, quite commonly assert that they love their dogs, their cars, their golf games ... They treat their love of these things as simply a more developed form of liking them, and believe, presumably, that "liking" and "loving" overlap', Robert Brown 1987, 18.

25 For Viroli, as quoted earlier, 'modern citizens ... can love their republic, if the republic loves them', Viroli 1995, 184.

26 There was a deep theological issue between Augustinian and Thomist views on *patria* – the Thomist view adapted Greek views of the *patria* to the Christian world, the Augustinian view abandoned the world altogether.

27 For Carl Schmitt, for example, 'All significant concepts of the modern theory of the state are secularized theological concepts, not only because of their historical development ... but also because of their systematic structure', see Schmitt 1985, 36.

28 This doctrine became more fully formed in absolutist theory. One important exponent of reason of state was Cardinal Richelieu. As one scholar on Richelieu remarked, 'A majority of the writers who supported the Cardinal therefore sought to develop a concept of Reason of State that was grounded upon the religious nature and purposes of the French State and attempted to demonstrate that one of the objectives of royal policy was the benefit of

universal Christendom ... Far from divorcing the interests of the state from organized religion, they defined the aims and ends of official policy partially in religious terms', Church 1972, 44.

29 Unless, of course, one considered patriotism a neologism from the eighteenth century.

30 This oscillation is also reflected in the chapters of citizenship and liberalism.

31 Love is quite often regarded as a civilizing force moving the individual from egoism to altruism, see, for example, Freud 1953, 103.

6 COMMUNITARIANISM

1 Amitai Etzioni quotes a correspondence from MacIntyre to the communitarian journal *Responsive Community*, 1, no. 3 (1991), 91–2 indicating this point, see Etzioni 1997, 261, n. 20. See also A. MacIntyre 1995, 35. See also Daniel Bell 1993.

2 Tam has Etzioni on his advisory panel for the UK group.

3 Etzioni, although a key exponent of the communitarian ideal, has found himself somewhat swamped in the USA by a clamouring crowd of community-minded groups, climbing on the same civic bandwagon. The idea of 'renewing community' in America has attracted a number of extremely wealthy philanthropic foundations, such as the Boston-based Institute for Civil Society, The Pew Charitable Trusts and the more venerable Brookings Institute. The National Commission on Civic Renewal and National Commission on Society, Culture and Community, set up in the late 1990s, have also started to plough the same communitarian furrow, see, for example, the article by Melissa Healey 1997, 6–7.

4 For example, Fromm's contrast between a 'having' society and a 'being' community, see Erich Fromm 1976, Herbert Marcuse 1968 or Abraham Maslow 1968.

5 In Tönnies, Durkheim and MacIver, for example, this is more of a disinterested sociological observation. In Spencer and Maine, also, the more consensual groups (status and militant) are not seen as the preferred option.

6 'Choice must start somewhere: and even if this starting point is later described, from the point of view of reason, as mere prejudice, this is not to condemn it, but on the contrary, to show the indispensability of prejudice in the make-up of a rational agent', Scruton, 'In Defence of the Nation', in Roger Scruton 1990, 303.

7 The direct echo here is Joseph de Maistre's remark ' I have seen Frenchmen, Italians, Russians, etc.; thanks to Montesquieu, I even know that *one can be Persian*. But as for *man*, I declare I have never in my life met him; if he exists, he is unknown to me', Maistre 1974, 97.

8 As the Italian fascist Charter of Labour stated, 'The Italian nation is an organic whole having life, purposes and means of action superior in power and duration to those of individuals ... of which it is composed', 'Charter of Labour' in Oakeshott (ed.) 1953, 184.

9 This particular point will be examined in more detail later in the discussion.

10 For example, Stephen Mulhall's and Adam Swift's *Liberals and Communitarians* has no discussion or index reference to nation, nationalism or patriotism. This is not very surprising on one level. If one examines some of

the key texts which generated the 1980s communitarian debate: Michael Sandel's *Liberalism and the Limits of Justice*, Alasdair MacIntyre's *After Virtue: A Study in Moral Theory or Whose Justice? Which Rationality?*, Charles Taylor's *Sources of the Self: The Making of Modern Identity*, there are no substantive discussions or any index references at all to nationalism or nation. Walzer is the only exception to this list, although his views on nationalism remain unclear, especially in relation to his earlier work *Spheres of Justice*. Some of the above authors, subsequently, in the 1990s, raised the issue, but, initially, there was obviously little awareness of any problem. Also, in Schlomo Avineri's and Avner de-Shalit's edited book *Communitarianism and Individualism* the bulk of the brief index references to nationality or nationalism are to an essay by David Miller – a committed nationalist theorist. Sandel, in his essay in the above text, does mention nationalism briefly, but it is only in the passing context of it being too vast 'to cultivate the shared understandings necessary to community'. Thus, for Sandel, 'politics is therefore displaced from smaller forms of association and relocated at the most universal form – in our case, the nation', Sandel 1992, 26–7. In addition, this gap is reflected in a recent encyclopaedic text, summarizing the state of political theory, Goodin and Pettit's (eds) *A Companion to Contemporary Political Philosophy* (1996), which has no chapter on 'nationalism', but an extensive chapter on 'Community', by Will Kymlicka. In the introduction to the book, the reason for this absence is that 'nationalism ... does not figure, on the grounds that it hardly counts as a principled way of thinking about things' (Goodin and Pettit, 3). Interestingly, the 'Community' chapter does have a final page on community and nationalism. Kymlicka raises it under the rubric of national self-determination. He complains that 'one looks in vain to contemporary liberal and communitarian authors for a discussion of this principle of community' (Kymlicka, 376). This is not national self-determination though, qua 'the nation state', but national self-determination 'within' states. Kymlicka sees this as a major gap in the literature on community. Still, the odd underlying assumption here is that nation and community are more complex than previously assumed by nationalists, communitarians and liberals, but *still* nation and community are synonymous. It is not quite clear what Kymlicka means here, but he still seems to assume that community resolves itself into nation, at the micro level.

11 Social conservatism is also drawn distinct from authoritarian conservatism. The latter tends to foster conformity in theocratic forms, Etzioni 1997, 16ff.

12 'In effect, the more individuals are active in multiple and cross-cutting groups ... the more likely the communitarian nature of society will persist. The more individuals are monopolized by any one group, the less communitarian a society will be', Etzioni 1997, 208. However, Etzioni is not altogether consistent here. In elucidating the communitarian notion of identity, he cites approvingly David Miller's nationalist definition of the issue, see Etzioni 1997, 93.

13 In order not to forget a past 'a community is involved in retelling its story, its constitutive narrative, and in so doing, it offers examples of the men and women who have embodied and exemplified the meaning of the community', Bellah *et al* 1996, 153.

14 'For justice to be the first virtue, certain things must be true of us. We must be creatures of a certain kind, related to human circumstances in a certain way. We must stand at a certain distance from our circumstances, whether as transcendental subject in the case of Kant, or as essentially unencumbered subject of possession in the case of Rawls. Either way, we must regard ourselves as independent; independent from the interests and attachments we may have at any moment', Sandel 1982, 175.

15 Neil MacCormick in Twining (ed.) 1991, 13. He says in another piece, 'The truth about human individuals is that they – we – are social products, not independent atoms capable of constituting society through a voluntary coming together', MacCormick 1990, 14.

16 Although, it is worth noting that in stronger versions of conservative and fascist communitarianism, it is liberalism, in general, which is condemned.

17 For Miller's rejection of the more atomistic liberalism see Miller 1989a, ch. 3, also Rawls 1993a.

18 I am not suggesting that Rawls shares all these criticisms.

19 There is an implicit egalitarianism in this process. The collapse of social hierarchies and the growth of democracy helped usher in this perspective.

20 Michael Walzer is disputing Ernest Nagel's contention, namely, we all speak from 'somewhere', see Walzer 1987, 6–7.

21 As Miller comments 'Social justice will always be easier to achieve with strong national identities and without internal communal divisions. Belgium, Canada and Switzerland work as they do partly because they are *not* simply multinational, but have cultivated common national identities alongside communal ones', Miller 1995b, 96.

22 'The nation proved too vast a scale across which to cultivate the shared self-understandings necessary to community', Michael Sandel, in Avineri and De-Shalit (eds) 1992), 26. From a different perspective, which is moderately hostile to the communitarian case, Will Kymlicka 1995, 92–3. Equally, from a more neo-Aristotelian, quasi-Straussian and communitarian view, Ronald Beiner notes depressingly: 'that participation in political community is a real human good. But if such participation is to be meaningful, it must be upheld by a source of enduring commitment. What is to sustain that commitment? ... Modernity *has* offered an answer to this puzzle about citizenship, but I must confess that this answer – nationalism – makes me feel uncomfortable', Beiner 1992, 123.

23 Some writers have observed this point on communitarianism. Yet the 'meaning variance' is usually between liberal and anti-liberal. This is both questionable (as regards modern communitarians) and even if true, far less dense and layered than nationalism. Further, it is often denied in the literature that nationalism has much theoretical sophistication. In fact, a great deal of the literature on nationalism, in history, sociology and political science, pays little if no heed to the ideas or theories of nationalists. There is far more interest in the empirical phenomenon of nations. The academic literature on nations is also both enormous and remarkably diverse, certainly in comparison to contemporary communitarian theory. For a general discussion see Vincent 2000, ch. 9.

24 Even Holmes is prepared to see much of the modern communitarian output as relatively harmless, see Holmes 1993, xiii. Admittedly, some have made

distinctions. For example, Richard Bellamy does distinguish anti-liberal communitarianism, relativist communitarianism and rationalist communitarianism, see Bellamy 1992.

25 The Canadian Meech Lake constitutional accord, made in 1987, was an attempt to reconcile Quebec's distinct cultural and political needs with the interests of all other Canadian provinces.

26 For these and other proposals see Etzioni in Walzer (ed.) 1995, 101–5 also Etzioni 1994.

27 It concerns 'the factors you will invoke to account for social life', Taylor in Rosenblum (ed.) 1989, 159.

28 F. H. Bradley puts this Hegelian view rather well, 'All philosophy has to do is "to understand what is", and moral philosophy has to understand morals which exist, not to make them or give directions for making them. Philosophy in general has not to anticipate the discoveries of the particular sciences nor the evolution of history; the philosophy of religion has not to make a new religion ... political philosophy has not to play tricks with the state, but to understand it; and ethics has not to make the world moral', Bradley 1962, 193.

29 For Taylor it is clear, for example, that 'recognising difference ... requires a horizon of significance, in this case a shared one', Taylor 1992, 52. In MacIntyre and Sandel there is also an unwillingness to be associated with relativism.

30 He also notes later 'The community provides one with a normative foundation, a starting point, culture and tradition, fellowship, and place for moral dialogue, but is not the ultimate arbitrator. The members are.' Etzioni 1997, 257.

31 Kymlicka is, though, a mere faint echo of a long-standing European tradition, see, for example, discussion in Black 1984, Vincent 1987, ch. 6, or Vincent 1989.

32 It is worth reminding ourselves that this position, in the post-1945 era alone, has been the cause of untold suffering. In the Indian sub-continent partition of 1947, around half a million deaths and eleven million refugees; one million deaths in the Nigerian civil war (1967–70); Idi Amin's ethnic cleansing (1971–9) saw several hundred thousand fatalities; six hundred thousand displaced persons (and rising) in the Sri Lankan civil war; well over 2.5 million displaced and unknown thousands of deaths in former Yugoslavia; well over a hundred thousand deaths in the ethnic cleansing in Rwanda, and the list goes on. Scruton's 'foreigner' goes on being excluded and killed across the globe. For these and more depressing figures see Diamond and Plattner (eds) 1994, xvi–xvii.

33 Kymlicka notes that Miller's position assumes that 'assimilation is a viable option – that is, that the state has the capacity to promote a common national identity amongst all citizens which will displace or take precedence over the existing identity', Kymlicka 1995, 73.

34 Kymlicka disagrees sharply with Miller on this point, arguing that Miller's vision will only 'aggravate the level of alienation and division' of certain groups, Kymlicka 1995, 73.

35 Given Sandel's comments on New England communities, it is no wonder that Amy Gutman remarks that 'communitarians ... want us to live in Salem, but not to believe in witches', in Gutman 1985, 319.

36 Etzioni thus sees society as a *layered concept*, where 'social and moral communities are not freestanding; they are often parts of more encompassing
social entities. This is the case because members of any one community,
especially a modern one, have memberships and bonds in other communities;
because the values held by one community affect the moral voices of the
others; because the reach of one's moral commitments ranges beyond the
membership of one's own community (for instance, our humanitarian
concerns about hunger or civil wars in other societies); and because unless
communities are bound socially and morally into more encompassing entities
they may war with one another'. Thus, 'In effect, the more individuals are
active in multiple and crosscutting groups … the more likely the communitarian nature of society will persist. The more individuals are monopolized by
any one group, the less communitarian a society will be', Etzioni 1997, 188
and 208. Further, for Henry Tam, the nation state is just one community, 'In
terms of opportunities for influence and participation, it is far less significant
than local authority areas – and more power should for this reason alone be
devolved to more local units of government. In terms of macroeconomic
issues, it is not just the nation-state, but also transnational political institutions and multinational corporations that affect societies – and more
involvement by citizens in the deliberations of such bodies needs to be promoted'. Consequently, for Tam, 'no communitarian theory can be sustained
on the basis of a single overriding community which commands the exclusive
allegiance of its members. The need for association and interaction with
others simply cannot be satisfied in this arbitrary manner. Furthermore, the
task of developing communal association among the multiplicity of communities is becoming more urgent as the process of globalisation takes out
the option of communities existing in splendid isolation from one another',
Tam 1998, 226. For the same sentiments, see Bellah *et al* 1996, xxix.

7 MULTICULTURALISM

1 The relation of multiculturalism to nationalism also resonates with the
relation between nations and empires. Nations argued, from their inception,
that empires took too little account of the significance of particular cultures
and customs.

2 'Interestingly, official multiculturalism was instituted in post-colonial
societies that lacked independent nation-founding myths and clear breaks
with their colonial past', introduction to Joppke and Lukes (eds) 1999, 3.

3 Nathan Glazer noticed, in researching his book *We are All Multiculturalists
Now* (1997), that in Harvard University Library every item containing the
word 'multiculturalism' in the 1970s and 1980s originated in either Australia
or Canada. See also David Bennett, introduction (ed.) 1998, 1ff.

4 He does see though certain specific waves of argument affecting the debates,
see Kymlicka in Joppke and Lukes (eds) 1999, 113.

5 Glazer concludes that North America has very little to teach or learn from
the European experience of multiculturalism, see Glazer in Joppke and Lukes
(eds) 1999, 192. The editors of this latter volume (Lukes and Joppke), in
their introduction, broadly agree with Glazer's assessment. They conclude
that there is no multiculturalism *toute court*, see introduction by Joppke and

Lukes, 17. Multiculturalism is seen to be wholly context-dependent. This chapter would have benefited from a close reading of Brian Barry's book *Culture and Equality* (2001) which only came into my hands very late in the writing process.

6 The concept culture will be discussed in a later section.

7 For Gierke, for example, *Herrschaft* emphasized the role of central authority (state) in constituting groups. *Genossenschaft*, however, stressed the self-constituting character of other groups, such as clans, tribes, or early free associations (medieval guilds). These groups, for Gierke, predated central authority. The legal act which brought such groups into a legal frame was declaratory not constitutive. This distinction kept the power, reality and existence of groups apart from the legal statute of incorporation. Further, when the corporate group acts it is, in subtle ways, different from the individuals that constitute it. This latter point is an old argument in European thought. Basically, it is a form of value collectivism or methodological holism, as opposed to value individualism or methodological individualism. Corporate (as opposed to aggregate) groups are seen as prior to individuals. For discussion of this tradition, see Vincent 1989.

8 One can view these distinctions through the vocabulary of rights. Thus, if you view a group as a legally constituted *aggregate*, then the action and rights of the group are often reduced to the activity of the individual members. Rights remain largely individual, unless the association is given a fictional legal status by the state. However, if you view groups as 'self-collecting' corporate entities, then it is possible to see them as *more* than the sum of their parts. The contention here is that groups can have an interest *as* groups – an interest which is not reducible to its individual interests. Thus, when the group acts it is qualitatively distinct from the individuals that constitute it. There is some form of internal principle of action within it. The group might thus be said to have a purpose which it acts upon. Thus, the group might be viewed as an agent, or, alternatively, it might be viewed as *person*. Some, however, who view groups in this latter form would not always wish to speak in the vocabulary of rights.

9 Thus, 'a person's identity is defined in relation to how others identify him or her', Iris Marion Young in Beiner (ed.) 1999, 186ff.

10 Seyla Benhabib comments here that 'With this admission, Kymlicka's multicultural liberalism comes to resemble varieties of nineteenth century nationalism, in that he is compelled by the logic of his own argument to confuse *societal culture* with the *dominant culture*, and to pleas for the preservation of such cultures', Benhabib in Joppke and Lukes (eds) 1999, 55.

11 This notion has had a perennial appeal to organicist theorists and methodological holists such as Émile Durkheim.

12 John Carey, for example, has explored the deep echoes of this theme in British and some European intellectuals up to the 1930s and beyond, see Carey 1992.

13 Eliot's essay is a more complex, dialectical and nuanced discussion than just a defence of 'high' culture. However, as Eliot remarks in the conclusion 'if only', as he says, 'to relieve the feelings of the writer and perhaps a few of his more sympathetic readers' that 'the culture of Europe has deteriorated

visibly within the memory of many who are by no means the oldest among us', Eliot 1948, 108.

14 The argument for the 1960s expansion of universities in Britain and elsewhere was one consequence of this same theme.

15 The term culture thus focused on the 'psychological orientations toward social objects'. It was 'internalized in the cognitions, feelings, and evaluations of citizens'. The orientations were cognitive, affective and evaluational: the first referred to 'knowledge of and belief about the political system', the second to 'feelings about the political system', and the third to 'a combination of value standards ... with information and feelings', Almond and Verba 1963, 13–15.

16 It does not have to mean this. Democratization of culture could mean that everyone (say in the working class) has a distinctive culture.

17 He complains though that a distinction between ethnic and national is often ignored by theorists. For all references see Kymlicka 1995, 18. Yet, given that culture and nation become synonyms in his account, it makes the older term 'cultural nation' (*Kulturnation*) into a pleonasm. Further the term 'cultural nation' has not had a particularly good press in the twentieth century, although Kymlicka offers relief for this anxiety, by insisting that the majority of political communities are multi-national.

18 For the development of this argument in relation to multiculturalism, see Ayelet Shachar 2000, 70ff.

19 Kymlicka is taken by Shachar as the key spokesman of the weak variant.

20 Kukathas does though accept group internal restrictions, see Kukathas' essay in Kymlicka (ed) 1995, 230.

21 The historical origins of this in liberal ideas 'is the Reformation and its consequences. Until the Wars of Religion in the sixteenth and seventeenth centuries, the fair terms of social cooperation were narrowly drawn ... one of the historical roots of liberalism was the development of various doctrines urging religious toleration.', Rawls in Tracy Strong (ed.) 1992, 115.

22 There are two stark dimensions to this problem of pluralism, which might be called radical and reasonable pluralism. The first concerns extremes of difference. The second concerns reasonable difference which can be negotiated through reason. Some postmodern writers are exercized by the first form of difference. For Connolly, for example, a postmodern position rejects *all* closure. Connolly celebrates strong identities and difference. Where liberals try to shield society from strong identities, Connolly wants a future society to encompass them, see Connolly 1991, 29. Rawls is only concerned with the reasonable pluralism.

23 One might also describe it as a form of liberal communitarianism.

24 It is in this context that Kymlicka argues for his three types of groups of differentiated rights, Kymlicka 1995.

25 Young notes 'Difference, as I understand it, names both the play of concrete events and the shifting differentiation on which signification depends. Reason, discourse, is always inserted in a plural, heterogeneous world that outruns totalizing comprehension', Young 1990, 98.

26 Equal respect is also ambiguous. It implies that one can treat individuals with respect, yet not address or acknowledge their difference.

27 This has direct links to Tully's notion of interculturalism, see Tully 1995.

28 It would also raise the question: which Bonnie Honig is addressing us?

29 Connolly suggests, for example, that the liberal and communitarian visions are all located in the same exclusionary Enlightenment frame, see Connolly 1991, 29.

30 Further, where communitarians offer a harmony of communal pre-understandings, Connolly wants real differences exposed to the full. He suggests that no argument is offered by communitarians for consensual pre-understandings, rather 'textual tropes that presuppose [harmonization's] availability'. For Connolly, the 'rhetoric of harmonization must be ambiguated and coarsened by those who have not had its faith breathed into their souls, particularly those moved by nontheistic reverence for the rich ambiguity of existence', Connolly 1991, 90.

31 Connolly's and Honig's case partially corresponds to the story told by Baumann who sees the early growth of nations marked out by a merciless war against the local, irregular and spontaneous, Bauman 1993, 135 and 141.

32 For Young, religious minorities are voluntary groups, and, for Kymlicka, such groups are neither ethnic nor national.

33 Charles Taylor's early interest in Herder is symptomatic of this argument. The fact that he was also supervised by Isaiah Berlin for his doctoral work in Oxford is also significant. Berlin's counter-Enlightenment liberalism (and his own interest in Herder) have often made him attractive to milder difference or particularist theorists.

34 Tully utilizes Wittgenstein's later philosophy to make this claim.

8 COSMOPOLITANISM

1 Although the term 'global ethics' is now being used much more commonly.

2 Benjamin Barber's *Jihad vs McWorld* opens with a quote from the chairman of the large American corporation, Gillette, which neatly captures this perspective. The Gillette chairman commented, 'I do not find foreign countries foreign'. Barber adds – referring to a central thesis of his book – 'welcome to McWorld', Benjamin Barber 1995, 1.

3 Kant was obviously not alone in his interests in cosmopolitan ideas, particularly in the German context, see Kleingel 1999.

4 This 'facilitation' point is also investigated in the chapter on citizenship, namely, that there is a 'cosmopolitan intuition' embedded within the notion of citizenship. This intuition implies that citizenship has been used within states to equalize, generalize and regularize treatment – thus preventing exclusionary or unfair practices. If citizenship, within the state, is used *against* exclusionary practices, what is the reason for not extending it beyond state boundaries or to foreign citizens? What is significant about boundaries?

5 The essay *Perpetual Peace* was written after the Treaty of Basel which ended the war between Prussia and Republican France.

6 Kant often claimed that it was Rousseau who taught him the importance of practical reason in the social and moral spheres.

7 It is a 'moral ideal which, given the nature of men, appears unattainable [but] does not absolve mankind of the duty of trying to achieve it', Williams 1983, 265.

8 'The main thesis of this book is that every agent, by the fact of engaging in [any] action, is logically committed to accept a supreme moral principle having a certain determinate normative content. Because any agent who denies or violates this principle contradicts himself, the principle stands unchallenged as a criterion of moral rightness, and conformity with its requirements is categorically obligatory', Gewirth 1978, 48.

9 See also Martha Nussbaum (1992), where she calls for 'thick universals' to be recognized. Although, exactly how Nussbaum reconciles her neo-Kantian-inspired arguments with her Aristotelianism remains unclear.

10 This point shows why O'Neill would regard herself as a 'maverick Kantian'. Her own Kantianism relies upon 'existing' (empirical: anthropological and biological?) conditions giving rise to, or internally manifesting, the demands of practical reason. It is O'Neill's way of trying to bridge the dualism implicit in Kant's position.

11 Later in the same discussion Kant notes 'man's inclination to defy the law and antagonize his fellows', Kant in Reiss (ed.) 1991, 105.

12 'Man is *an animal who needs a master*. For he certainly abuses his freedom in relation to others of his own kind. And even although, as a rational creature, he desires a law to impose limits on the freedom of all, he is still misled by his self-seeking animal inclinations', Kant, *Idea for a Universal History with a Cosmopolitan Purpose*, in Reiss (ed.) 1991, 46; Kant also discusses Herder's critical remarks on this point in a 'Review of Herder's *Ideas on the Philosophy of the History of Mankind*', in Reiss (ed.) 1991, 219.

13 Herder remarks that: 'When in our thoughts and words we single out reason from among the other (mental) energies (*Kräfte*) of our nature we do so for a specific (conceptual) purpose; but in doing so we must never forget that in actual fact it cannot subsist in isolation apart from the other mental energies. It is one and the same mind that thinks and wills, that understands and perceives, that seeks reason and applies it. All these tendencies or energies of the mind are so close to one another, so intertwined and interacting, not only in practical application, but even in their origin and development, that we must never presume that in naming any one operation of these energies we are actually naming a distinct faculty in a substantive sense. For by the act of naming we do not erect compartments in our mind; we do not sub-divide it. All we are doing is to classify its operations, the application of its energies', quoted in Barnard 1965, 41.

14 This argument might be recognized in a more familiar way in terms of the state. The state maintains a common way of life which it guards against outside interference. If it fulfils this purpose as a state, it might be said to be worthy of moral status. This entails the state itself acquiring a persona and bearing the same rights of life and liberty against other states, who might without adequate constraints attempt to impose their collective ways of life. States have value and worth, not because they are like individuals, but because they provide collectively for the pursuit of individuals' purposes. If states possess rights, as individuals do, then it is possible to envisage a society of states, just as there are societies comprised of individuals.

15 That cosmopolitan perspective is also present in Marx, but in a different format.

16 Realist argument obviously adopts this position for different reasons to communitarianism.

17 Further, within any society, particularly liberal societies, there will be a variety of social goods whose distribution is governed by different criteria in their respective spheres of activity, see Michael Walzer 1983. Walzer suggests 'another way of doing philosophy is to interpret to one's fellow citizens the world of meanings that we share. Justice and equality can conceivably be worked out as philosophical artefacts, but a just or egalitarian society cannot be. If such a society isn't already here – hidden as it were, in our concepts and categories – we shall never know it concretely or realize it in fact', see Walzer 1983, xv and xiv.

18 The attempt to force a rethink of the underpinnings and use of rationality in argument has strong parallels with some of the feminist criticisms of Western rationality.

19 His subsequent books have effected a partial *volte face*. Said thus questions his own approach in *Culture and Imperialism* (1994).

20 Spivak asked here with what kind of voice and system of representations do the subalterns actually speak? Taking the angle of poststructuralism and postmodernism, she suggests they cannot speak. Spivak takes subaltern theorists to task for their 'impossible (and essentialist) objects such as know-ledge of subaltern consciousness'. She suggests that the subaltern possibly might not be able to speak, partly because the subaltern subject could be said to be an inscription of colonial discourse. Spivak is one of the postcolonial theorists who sees poststructuralism as the potential way forward, see Spivak 1987, 205. Spivak is the translator of J. Derrida's *Grammatology* (1977).

21 Brian Barry's views on reason conform neatly to this form of judgement.

22 Identity abstracts from particularity in order to generate the universal. The reduction to a single unified substance represses difference denying the uniqueness or character of the 'different'. For Young, 'difference ... names both the play of concrete events and the shifting differentiation on which signification depends'. She continues that 'reason ... is always inserted in a plural, heterogeneous world that outruns totalizing comprehension', Iris Marion Young 1990, 97–9.

23 'Because cultural context is integral to the formulation and implementation of all state policies, including those that have clear human rights conse-quences, [thus] detailed and credible knowledge of local cultures is essential for the effective promotion and protection of human rights in any society', see Abdullah A. An-Na'im in Bauer and Bell (eds) 1999, 147.

24 As Charles Taylor comments, 'An obstacle in the path to ... mutual under-standing comes from the inability of many Westerners to see their culture as one amongst many', see Taylor in Bauer and Bell (eds) 1999, 143.

25 Consequently, Taylor continues, 'Only if we in the West can recapture a more adequate view of our own history, can we learn to understand better the spiritual ideas that have been interwoven in our development and hence be prepared to understand sympathetically the spiritual paths of others', see Taylor in Bauer and Bell (ed.) 1999, 143–4.

26 There are various perspectives on the relation of Asian values to human rights. Some see human rights as just alien. Others see human rights already present within authoritative value traditions or texts, like Confucius'

Analects or the Islamic *Qur'an*. Thus, human rights can be seen as distinctively Asian. Others see a space for active internal religious and legal reform. In the latter two, the crucial contention is that human rights need to be reconsidered and redrafted through the medium of Asian values. The ASEAN Bangkok declaration of 1997 (which recast universal human rights in the light of Asian values) is characteristic of this general process. Further, priority is given to social and economic rights over political and civil human rights. Some of the initial enthusiasm of this debate was dampened by the Asian finance crisis (1997–8).

27 As Terry Eagleton comments, with his usual esprit, postcolonialism signifies 'a whole gamut of doctrine and pieties which are far from historically or politically innocent'. The doctrine, overall, belongs 'for the most part (not exclusively) to a rampant lefty culturalism, by which I mean an implausibly excessive emphasis on what is constructed or conventional or differently constituted about human animals, rather than what they have in common ... Such culturalism is just as reductive as the economism or biologism or essentialism to which it is a mildly panic-stricken over-reaction. Anyway, why "colonialism" in the first place, even if one adds a "post" or "neo" for good measure? For the term suggests, traditionally, a form of (intended permanent) settlement which is in one sense the last way to describe the relation of the transnational corporations to their client terrains. And why define a whole social order in terms of what it comes after, which – since that condition is itself cast in bleakly negative terms – then entails a sort of double displacement', Eagleton in David Bennett (ed.) 1998, 126.

28 Which, as a recent text notes, 'promote both the liberating, pleasurable aspect of miscegenation, interrelationships and cultural difference', Childs and Williams 1997, 210.

29 It should be stressed that the author, Pheng Cheah, views this judgement critically.

30 It is a well-observed historical pattern in Europe and elsewhere that externally imposed rule generates an internal cohesiveness expressed through ideas such as nationalism.

31 My own use of the term 'strategic' in this book, qua nationalism, is simply pedagogic, namely, a way of analysing and contrasting different forms of particularity. It implies nothing about the substantive political usage of the term, which I take to be what Spivak and Hall are addressing.

32 For discussion of this point see the previous chapter of this book.

33 One can take a very much more cynical view of this development, a cynicism which has its charms, for example, that 'The left academy, camped as it has been in the forests of multiculturalism, the cultural studies suburbs, or the postcolonial city, seems to be mobilizing itself for another look at the monism that was meant to be buried by *Grammatology*', Scott Malcomsen, 'The Varieties of Cosmopolitan Experience' in Pheng Cheah and Robbins (eds) 1998, 234.

34 Bruce Robbins, 'Comparative Cosmopolitanism' in Pheng Cheah and Robbins (eds) 1998, 248. This also leads to an unease with writers such as Salman Rushdie, V. S. Naipaul, Edward Said and Homi Bhabha who are seen as metropolitan academicized cosmopolitans, trading on their 'apparent' exile

or partial homelessness and reflecting on the postcolonial nations for rapt Western audiences.

35 'Instead of renouncing cosmopolitanism as a false universal, one can embrace it as an impulse to knowledge that is itself partial, but no more so than the similar cognitive strivings of many diverse peoples', Robbins in Pheng Cheah and Robbins (eds) 1998, 259, see also Bruce Robbins 1993. In this context, Robbins seeks more self-awareness of 'an unembarrassed acceptance of professional self-interest' in cosmopolitan claims by academics, see Robbins 1993, 181.

36 Although there is a long and honourable tradition of liberal imperialism, see H. C. J. Matthews 1973 or Andrew Vincent and Raymond Plant 1984, 87–90.

37 As Benjamin Barber puts it, we require initially 'healthy, democratic forms of local community and civic patriotism' not 'abstract universalism and the thin gruel of contract', Barber in Cohen (ed.) 1996, 31.

38 Rorty is thus concerned to *include* others in 'us' or 'we', in terms of the capacity to experience pain and humiliation, to grieve or cherish loved ones, thus paralleling Walzer's reiterative universalism.

39 This point is developed in the final chapter.

9 CONCLUDING PARTICULARS

1 Chaim Perelman (1963) is a prime exemplification of this idea.

2 Many of the more recent arguments, specifically in multiculturalist discussion, have focused on particular marginalized groups. Nations and cultures can, of course, be marginal, but they can also be dominant within a particular boundary.

3 For O'Neill, this notion of reason is constructed (not discovered) from 'the demand that anything that is to count as reasoning must be followable by all relevant others'. See O'Neill 1996, 4–6.

4 She comments later: 'Principles indeed abstract from differences: but it does not follow that they must assume idealized accounts of human agents that not only bracket but deny human particularities and differences. Universal principles indeed apply across a plurality of differing cases, but need not prescribe or proscribe, recommend or reject uniformity of action or entitlement', O'Neill 1996, 77.

5 The term 'strategic' is being used in a purely pedagogic manner, that is, as a convenient way of articulating different senses of particularity.

6 As regards Aristotle, she sees both particularist and universalist readings of his work in contemporary interpreters. O'Neill's sense that Wittgenstein embodies 'particularism with a vengeance' is partly borne out if one considers the use made of him by political theorists like James Tully 1995.

7 In terms of contemporary political theory, the essential contestability thesis is the most obvious particularist candidate for developing the Wittgensteinian position (see Gallie 1964).

8 Marginal groups and cultures, for example, now often, paradoxically, claim the moral high ground.

9 Although no doubt the fashion will change again.

10 As John Dunn comments 'from Samuel Pufendorf's seventeenth century *De Officio Hominis et Civis* through the American Declaration of Independence

of 1776 and the French Declaration of the Rights of Man and of the Citizen of 1789 to the United Nations Charter of our own day are intractably universalist. All of them take the individual human beings, more or less as they are, as the fundamental ethical units and assess the legitimacy of possible or political arrangements in terms of the axiomatically identical rights that such human beings are presumed to possess', John Dunn 1979, 57.

11 This is utilizing Adorno's critique of the 'logic of identity' and Derrida's critique of 'metaphysics of presence'. This is reminiscent of the old quip: 'everyone stand up now and say together, after me, "I am an individual"'.

12 In Young's case the particularity moves into the realm of 'group particulars'.

13 The idea of the 'marginalized group' is another popular term in the more recent particularist vocabulary.

14 For Connolly, 'What is needed politically … is a series of cross-national, non-statist movements organized across state lines, mobilized around specific issues of global significance', Connolly 1995, 24.

15 Again it is important to emphasize here that this is not an argument for the centrality of the human individual. It is rather a phenomenological registering of the way the concept is deployed in arguments.

16 There are parallels between Walzer's minimums and Herbert Hart's earlier suggestions concerning a 'minimal good sense to natural law'. Hart provides a neat rendition in his five truisms about the minimums of human existence. These are: the fact of *human vulnerability* (this does not imply active service, rather forbearance and negative prohibitions on violence or bodily harm); an *approximate equality* (in other words, no individual is so much more powerful than others therefore one needs mutual forbearance); a *limited altruism* (humans are neither devils nor totally self-interested, but we do need rules to prevent temptations); further, there are only *limited resources* available to us. Food, clothing and shelter are relatively scarce. They have to be created by toil, and this implies the need for basic property to be secured and defended. In this context, minimal forbearances on property need to be guaranteed. Finally, most humans have a *limited understanding and strength of will*. Each 'truism' for Hart provides an 'internal reason' as to why it should be recognized. Without recognition of these universal truisms, humans would have no reason for even minimum cooperation. These truisms can be read as roughly comparable to Walzer's limit conditions, see H. L. A. Hart 1961, 189ff.

17 In fact, this could be extended, thus the *experience*, the *normative justification* and the *legal form* of the right can be drawn distinct.

18 This point however does not imply that these religious or cultural beliefs could not be internally reformed or adjusted. Neither does it take full account of the diversity of sects within these categories, some of which might well be more conducive to the universal minimums.

Bibliography

Aarsleff, Hans (1982) *From Locke to Saussure: Essays on the Study of Language and Intellectual History* (Minneapolis, University of Minnesota).

Ackerman, Bruce (1994) 'Rooted Cosmopolitanism', *Ethics*, 104.

Acton, Lord (J. E. E. D.) (1948) *Essays on Freedom and Power* (Boston, Beacon Press).

Acton, Lord (J. E. E. D.) (1907) 'Nationality', in Acton, *History of Freedom and Other Essays* (London, Macmillan).

Adorno, Theodor and Horkheimer, Max (1992) *The Dialectic of the Enlightenment* (London and New York, Verso).

Almond, G. A. and Verba, S. (1963) *The Civic Culture: Political Attitudes and Democracy in Five Nations* (Princeton, N.J., Princeton University Press).

Alter, P. (1989) *Nationalism* (London, Edward Arnold).

Althusius, J. (1995) trans. F. S. Carney, *Politica* (Indianapolis, Liberty Classics).

Anderson, Amanda (1998) 'Cosmopolitanism, Universalism and the Divided Legacies of Modernity', in Pheng Cheah and Robbins (eds) *Cosmopolitics*.

Anderson, Benedict (1983) *Imagined Communities: Reflections on the Origin and Spread of Nationalism* (London, Verso).

An-Na'im, Abdullah A. (1999) 'The Cultural Mediation of Human Rights: The Al-Arqam Case in Malaysia', in Bauer and Bell (eds) *The East Asian Challenge for Human Rights*.

Appadurai, Arjun (1996) *Modernity at Large* (Minneapolis, University of Minnesota Press).

Archard, David (1996) 'Should Nationalists be Communitarian?', *Journal of Applied Philosophy*, 13, 2.

Archard, David (2000) 'Nationalism and Political Theory', in Noel O'Sullivan (ed.) *Political Theory in Transition* (London, Routledge).

Armstrong, A. H. and Markus, R. A. (1964) *Christian Faith and Greek Philosophy* (London, Darton, Longman and Todd).

Arnold, Matthew (1971) *Culture and Anarchy* (Cambridge, Cambridge University Press).

Aurelius, Marcus (1967) *Meditations*, trans. M. Staniforth (Middlesex, Penguin).

Austin, J. (1880) *Lectures on Jurisprudence* (London, John Murray).

Avineri, Schlomo and De-Shalit, Avner (eds) (1992) *Communitarianism and Individualism* (Oxford, Clarendon Press).

Bader, Veit (1997) 'Transnational Citizenship', *Political Theory*, 25, 6.

Barber, Benjamin (1995) *Jihad vs McWorld: How Globalism and Tribalism are Reshaping the World* (New York, Ballantine).

Barker, Ernest (1927) *National Character and the Factors in its Formation*, 4th edition (London, Methuen).

Barnard, F. M. (1965) *Herder's Social and Political Thought: From Enlightenment to Nationalism* (Oxford, Clarendon Press).

Baron, Hans (1966) *The Crisis of the Early Italian Renaissance*, 2nd edition (Princeton, N.J., Princeton University Press).

Barry, Brian (1983) 'Self-Government Revisited', in David Miller and Larry Seidentop (eds) *The Nature of Political Theory* (Oxford, Clarendon Press).

Barry, Brian (1989) *Theories of Justice* (London, Harvester Wheatsheaf).

Barry, Brian (1993) 'Humanity in Global Perspective', in Goodin and Pettit (eds) *A Companion to Contemporary Political Philosophy*.

Barry, Brian (1995a) *Justice as Impartiality* (Oxford, Clarendon Press).

Barry, Brian (1995b) 'Spherical justice and Global justice', in David Miller and Michael Walzer (eds) *Pluralism, Justice and Equality*.

Barry, Brian (2001) *Culture and Equality* (Cambridge, Polity).

Bartelson, Jens (1995) *The Genealogy of Sovereignty* (Cambridge, Cambridge University Press).

Bauer, J. R. and Bell, Daniel (eds) (1999) *The East Asian Challenge for Human Rights* (Cambridge, Cambridge University Press).

Bauman, Z. (1993) *Postmodern Ethics* (Oxford, Blackwell).

Beiner, R. (1992) *What's the Matter with Liberalism?* (Berkeley, University of California Press).

Beiner, R. (ed.) (1999) *Theorizing Nationalism* (New York, State University of New York Press).

Bell, Daniel (1993) *Liberalism and Communitarianism* (Oxford, Clarendon Press).

Bell, Daniel (1998) 'The Limits of Liberal Justice', *Political Theory*, 26, 4.

Bellah, Robert *et al* (eds) (1996) *Habits of the Heart: Individualism and Commitment in American Life*, updated edition (Berkeley, University of California Press)

Bellamy, R. (1992) *Liberalism and Modern Society* (Cambridge, Polity).

Benhabib, S. (ed.) (1996) *Democracy and Difference: Contesting the Boundaries of the Political* (Princeton, N.J., Princeton University Press).

Benhabib, S. (1999) '"Nous" et "les Autres": The Politics of Complex Cultural Dialogue in Global Civilization' in Joppke and Lukes (eds) *Multicultural Questions*.

Benn, S. I. and Peters, R. S. (1969) *Social Principles and the Democratic State* (London, Allen and Unwin).

Benner, Erica (1997) 'Nationality without Nationalism', *Journal of Political Ideologies*, 2, 2.

Bennett, David (ed.) (1998) *Multicultural State: Rethinking Difference and Identity* (London, Routledge).

Berger, S., Donovan, M. and Passmore, K. (eds) (1999) *Writing National Histories* (London, Routledge).

Berlin, I. (1976) *Vico and Herder: Two Studies in the History of Ideas* (London, Hogarth Press).

Berlin, I. (1990) *The Crooked Timber of Humanity* (London, John Murray).

Berlin, I. (1997) *The Proper Study of Mankind* (eds) H. Hardy and R. Hausheer (London, Chatto and Windus).

Bhabha, Homi (1994) *The Location of Culture* (London, Routledge).

Bhabha, Homi (1998) 'Cultures in Between' in Bennett (ed.) *Multicultural State*.

Billig, Michael (1995) *Banal Nationalism* (London, Sage).

Birch, A. H. (1989) *Nationalism and National Integration* (London, Unwin Hyman).

Black, Anthony (1984) *Guilds and Civil Society* (London, Methuen).

Black, Anthony (1993) *Political Thought in Europe 1250–1450* (Cambridge, Cambridge University Press).

Black, Anthony (1997) 'Christianity and Republicanism: From St. Cyprian to Rousseau', *American Political Science Review*, 91.

Black, Anthony (1998) 'Christianity and Republicanism: A response to Nederman', *American Political Science Review*, 92.

Bodin, Jean (1962) *The Six Bookes of the Commonweale*, reprint of the translation by R. Knolles in 1606, edited by K. D. McRae (Cambridge, Mass., Harvard University Press).

Bosanquet, Bernard (1899) *Philosophical Theory of the State* (London, Macmillan).

Boucher, David (1998) *Political Theories of International Relations* (Oxford, Clarendon Press).

Bradley, F. H. (1962) *Ethical Studies* (Oxford, Clarendon Press).

Brown, C. (ed.) (1994) *Political Restructuring in Europe: Ethical Perspectives* (London, Routledge).

Brown, Robert (1987) *Analyzing Love* (Cambridge, Cambridge University Press).

Brubaker, R. (1994) *Citizenship and Nationhood in France and Germany* (Cambridge, Mass., Harvard University Press).

Brugger, Bill (1999) *Republican Theory in Political Thought: Virtuous or Virtual?* (London, Macmillan).

Bull, Hedley (1977) *The Anarchical Society* (London, Macmillan).

Butler, Judith (1994) 'Kantians in every Culture', *Boston Review*, 19, 5.

Buttle, Nicholas (2000) 'Critical Nationalism: a Liberal Prescription', *Nations and Nationalism*, 6, 1.

Canovan, Margaret (1996) *Nationalism and Political Theory* (London, Edward Elgar).

Carey, John (1992) *The Intellectuals and the Masses: Pride and Prejudice among the Literary Intelligentsia 1880–1939* (London, Faber and Faber).

Cassirer, E. (1946) *The Myth of the State* (New Haven, Yale University Press).

Cheyette, F. L. (1978) 'The Invention of the State', in Bede Karl Lackner and K. R. Philp (eds) *Essays on Medieval Civilization: The Walter Prescott Webb Memorial Lectures* (Austin, University of Texas).

Childs, P. and Williams, P. (1997) *An Introduction to Post-Colonial Theory* (London and New York, Prentice Hall, Harvester Wheatsheaf).

Church, Clive and and Phinnemore, David (1994) *European Union and European Community: A Handbook and Commentary on the Post-Maastricht Treaties* (New York and London, Harvester Wheatsheaf).

Church, W. F. (1941) *Constitutional Thought in Sixteenth Century France* (Cambridge, Mass., Harvard University Press).

Church, W. F. (1972) *Richelieu and Reason of State* (Princeton, N.J., Princeton University Press).

Clark, J. C. D (ed.) (1990) *Ideas and Politics in Modern Britain* (London, Macmillan).

Clifford, James (1988) *The Predicament of Culture* (Cambridge, Mass., Harvard University Press).

Clifford, James and Marcus, G. E. (eds) (1986) *Writing Culture: The Poetics and Politics of Ethnography* (Berkeley, University of California Press).

Cohen J. (ed.) (1996) *For Love of Country* (Boston, Beacon Press).

Cohen, J. L. (1996) 'Democracy, Difference and the Right of Privacy', in Benhabib (ed.) *Democracy and Difference.*

Cohen, M. (1992) 'Rooted Cosmopolitanism', *Dissent* (Fall).

Coker, F. W. (1910) *Organismic Theories of the State* (New York, Columbia University Press).

Connolly, William E. (1991) *Identity/Difference: Democratic Negotiations of Political Paradox* (Ithaca, NY, Cornell University Press).

Connolly, William E. (1995) *The Ethos of Pluralization* (Minneapolis, University of Minnesota Press).

Connolly, William E. (1996) 'Pluralism, Multiculturalism and the Nation-State', *Journal of Political Ideologies*, 1, 1.

Constant, Benjamin (1988) 'The Liberty of the Ancients Compared with that of the Moderns', in Constant, *Political Writings*, trans. B. Fontana (Cambridge, Cambridge University Press).

D'Entreves, A. P. (1939) *The Medieval Contribution to Political Thought* (Oxford, Oxford University Press).

D'Entreves, A. P. (1951) *Natural Law* (London, Hutchinson).

Dahrendorf, R. (1974) 'Citizenship and Beyond: The Social Dynamics of an Idea', *Social Research*, 41.

DeGeorge Richard T. (1991) 'The Myth of the Right of Collective Self-Determination', in Twining (ed.) *Self-Determination.*

Dehousse, R. (1995) 'Community Competences: Are there Limits to Growth?', in S. Bronitt, F. Burns and D. Kinley, *Principles of European Law: Commentary and Materials* (Sydney, Law Book Company Ltd).

Diamond, L. and Plattner, M. F. (1994) *Nationalism, Ethnic Conflict, and Democracy* (Baltimore and London, Johns Hopkins University Press).

Dietz, Mary (1989) 'Patriotism', in T. Ball, J. Farr and R. L. Hanson (eds) *Political Innovation and Conceptual Change* (Cambridge, Cambridge University Press).

Dobson, Andrew (2000) 'Ecological Citizenship: A Disruptive Influence?', in S. Pierson and Simon Tormey (eds) *Politics at the Edge* (London, Macmillan).

Dowdall, H. C. (1923) 'The Word State', *Law Quarterly Review*, 34.

Dunn, John (1979) *Western Political Theory in the Face of the Future* (Cambridge, Cambridge University Press).

Dworkin R. (1980) 'Liberalism', in S. Hampshire (ed.) *Public and Private Morality* (Cambridge, Cambridge University Press).

Dyson, K. H. F. (1980) *The State Tradition in Western Europe: A Study of an Idea and Institution* (Oxford, Martin Robertson).

Eade, J. C. (ed.) (1983) *Romantic Nationalism in Europe* (Canberra, Australian National University Press).

Eagleton, Terry (1998) 'Postcolonialism: The Case of Ireland', in David Bennett (ed.) *Multicultural Questions.*

Eliot, T. S. (1948) *Notes Towards the Definition of Culture* (London, Faber and Faber).

Ergang, R. R. (1931) *Herder and the Foundation of German Nationalism* (New York, Columbia University Press).

Etzioni, A.(1994) *The Spirit of Community* (New York, Crown).

Etzioni, A. (1995) 'Too Many Rights, Too Few Responsibilities', in Michael Walzer (ed.) *Towards a Global Civil Society*.

Etzioni, A. (1997) *The New Golden Rule: Community and Morality in a Democratic Society* (London, Profile Books).

Fichte, J. G. (1979) trans. R. F. Jones and G. H. Turnbull, *Addresses to the German Nation* (Westport, Conn., Greenwood Press).

Figgis, J. N. (1914) *Churches in the Modern State* (London, Longman, Green and Co).

Figgis, J. N. (1922) *The Divine Right of Kings* (Cambridge, Cambridge University Press).

Forsyth, Murray (1987) *Reason and Revolution: The Political Thought of Abbé Sieyes* (Leicester, Leicester University Press).

Foucault, Michel (1980) 'Truth and Power', in Foucault, *Power and Knowledge: Selected Interviews and other Writings 1972–1977* (Sussex, Harvester Wheatsheaf).

Foucault, Michel (1984) 'What is Enlightenment?', in Paul Rabinow (ed.) *The Foucault Reader* (Middlesex, Penguin).

Franklin, J. H. (1973) *Jean Bodin and the Rise of Absolutism* (Cambridge, Cambridge University Press).

Freeden, Michael (1978) *The New Liberalism: An Ideology of Social Reform* (Oxford, Clarendon Press).

Freeden, Michael (ed.) (2001) *Reassessing Political Ideologies: The Durability of Dissent* (London, Routledge).

Freud, Sigmund (1953) 'Group Psychology and the Analysis of the Ego', in *The Standard Edition of the Complete Works of Sigmund Freud*, vol. 28, trans. J. Stachey (London, Hogarth Press).

Fromm, Erich (1976) *To Have or To Be* (London, Sphere Books).

Fuller, Lon (1966) *The Law in Quest of Itself* (Boston, Beacon Press).

Gallie, W. B. (1964) *Philosophy and Historical Understanding* (London, Chatto and Windus).

Gallie, W. B. (1977) *Philosophers of War and Peace* (Cambridge, Cambridge University Press).

Gandhi, Leela (1998) *Postcolonial Theory: A Critical Introduction* (Edinburgh, Edinburgh University Press).

Gasset, Ortega y (1961) *The Revolt of the Masses* (London, Allen and Unwin).

Geertz, Clifford (1988) *Works and Lives* (Stanford, Stanford University Press).

Geertz, Clifford (1993) *The Interpretation of Cultures* (London, Harper Collins).

Gellner, E.(1983) *Nations and Nationalism* (Oxford, Blackwell).

Geras, N. (1998) *The Contract of Mutual Indifference: Political Philosophy after the Holocaust* (London, Verso).

Gewirth, Alan (1978) *Reason and Morality* (Chicago, Chicago University Press).

Gierke, Otto von (1900), trans. F. W. Maitland, *Political Theories of the Middle Ages* (Cambridge, Cambridge University Press).

Gierke, Otto von (1939) *The Development of Political Theory* (London, George Allen and Unwin).

Gierke, Otto von (1990), introduction by Anthony Black, *Community in Historical Perspective* (Cambridge, Cambridge University Press).

Glazer, N. (1997) *We are All Multiculturalists Now* (Cambridge, Mass., Harvard University Press).

Glazer, N. (1999) 'What can Europe Learn from North America?', in Joppke and Lukes (eds) *Multicultural Questions*.

Goodin, Robert (1988) 'What is so Special about Our Fellow Countrymen?', *Ethics*, 98.

Goodin, Robert and Pettit, Philip (eds) (1997) *Contemporary Political Philosophy: An Anthology* (Oxford, Blackwell).

Greenfeld, Liah (1992) *Nationalism: Five Roads to Modernity* (Cambridge, Mass., Harvard University Press).

Guha, R. (1982) *Subaltern Studies*, vol. 1 (Delhi, Oxford University Press).

Gutman, Amy (1985) 'Communitarian Critics of Liberalism', *Philosophy and Public Affairs*, 14.

Gutman, Amy (ed.) (1994) *Multiculturalism: Examining the Politics of Recognition* (Princeton, N.J., Princeton University Press).

Habermas, J. (1992) 'Citizenship and National Identity: Some Reflections on the Future of Europe', *Praxis International*, 12, 1.

Habermas, J. (1994) 'Struggles for Recognition in the Democratic Constitutional State', in Gutman (ed.) *Multiculturalism*.

Habermas, J. (1998) 'Remarks on Legitimation', in *Philosophy and Social Criticism*, 24, 2/3.

Hampshire, S. (1980) *Public and Private Morality* (Cambridge, Cambridge University Press).

Hampshire, S. (1991) 'Nationalism', in Edna and Avishai Margalit (eds) *Isaiah Berlin: A Celebration* (London, Hogarth Press).

Hart, H. L. A. (1961) *The Concept of Law* (Oxford, Clarendon Press).

Hayes, Carlton (1926) *Essays on Nationalism* (New York, Macmillan).

Hayes, Carlton (1949) *The Historical Evolution of Modern Nationalism* (New York, Macmillan).

Haynes, D. and Prakash, G. (eds) (1992) *Contesting Power* (Berkeley, University of California Press).

Healey, Melissa (1997) 'New Money, Old Values', *Guardian*, Wednesday, January 8th, 6–7.

Heater, Derek (1990) *Citizenship: The Civic Ideal in World History, Politics and Education* (London, Longman).

Heelas, P., Lash, Scott and Morris, P. (eds) (1996) *Detraditionalization* (Oxford, Blackwell).

Hegel, G. W. F. (1971) *Philosophy of Right*, trans. T. M. Knox (Oxford, Oxford University Press).

Hegel, G. W. F. (1979) *The Phenomenology of Spirit*, trans. A. V. Miller (Oxford, Clarendon Press).

Herder, J. G. (1969), introduction by F. M. Barnard, *J. G. Herder on Social and Political Culture* (Cambridge, Cambridge University Press).

Hexter, J. H. (1973) *The Vision of Politics on the Eve of the Reformation* (London, Allen Lane).

Himmelfarb, G. (1996) 'The Illusion of Cosmopolitanism', in Cohen (ed.) *For Love of Country*.

Hirschman, Albert (1977) *The Passions and the Interests: Political Arguments for Capitalism before its Triumph* (Princeton, N.J., Princeton University Press).

Hirst, Paul (2000) 'Globalization, the nation-state and political theory', in Noel O'Sullivan (ed.) *Political Theory in Transition*.

Hobbes, Thomas (1968) *Leviathan* (Middlesex, Penguin).

Hobbes, Thomas (1990) *Behemoth*, F. Tönnies (ed.) (Chicago, Chicago University Press).

Hobsbawm, E. J. (1992) *Nations and Nationalism since 1780: Programme, Myth and Reality*, 2nd edition (Cambridge, Cambridge University Press).

Hoffman, J. (1995) *Beyond the State* (Cambridge, Polity Press).

Hollinger, David (1995) *Post Ethnic America* (New York, Basic Books).

Holmes, Stephen (1993) *The Anatomy of Anti-Liberalism* (Cambridge, Mass., Harvard University Press).

Honig, B. (1996) 'Difference, Dilemmas, and the Politics of Home', in Benhabib (ed.) *Democracy and Difference*.

Hroch, Miroslav (1985) *Social Preconditions of National Revival in Europe: A Comparative Analysis of the Social Composition of Patriotic Groups among Smaller European Nations* (Cambridge, Cambridge University Press).

Hume, David (1994) 'Of National Characters', in Knud Haakonssen's edition of *Hume's Political Essays* (Cambridge, Cambridge University Press).

Ignatieff, Michael (1993) *Blood and Belonging: Journeys into the New Nationalism* (New York, Farrar, Straus and Giroux).

Ignatieff, Michael (1998) *Isaiah Berlin: A Life* (London and New York, Metropolitan Books).

Ingram, Attracta (1996) 'Constitutional Patriotism', *Philosophy and Social Criticism*, 22.

Jackson, Robert (1999) 'Sovereignty at the Millennium', special issue of *Political Studies*, edited by Robert Jackson, 47, 3.

Jackson, Robert (1999) 'Sovereignty in World Politics: A Glance at the Conceptual and Historical Landscape', in Jackson (ed.) 'Sovereignty at the Millennium', *Political Studies*.

Joppke C. and Lukes, S. (eds) (1999) *Multicultural Questions* (Oxford, Oxford University Press).

Kamenka, E. (ed.) (1976) *Nationalism: The Nature and Evolution of an Idea* (London, Edward Arnold).

Kant, I. (1974) *Anthropology from a Pragmatic View*, trans. Mary J. Gregor (The Hague, Martinus Nijhoff).

Kant, I. (1991) 'Review of Herder's *Ideas on the Philosophy of the History of Mankind*', in Reiss (ed.) *Kant's Political Writings*.

Kant, I. (1991) Hans Reiss (ed.) *Kant's Political Writings* (Cambridge, Cambridge University Press).

Kant, I. (1991) 'Idea for a Universal History with a Cosmopolitan Purpose', in Reiss (ed.) *Kant's Political Writings*.

Kant, I. (1991) 'Perpetual Peace: A Philosophical Sketch', in Reiss (ed.) *Kant's Political Writings*.

Kantorowicz, Ernst (1957) *The King's Two Bodies: A Study in Medieval Political Theology* (Princeton, N.J., Princeton University Press).

Kedourie, E. (1974) *Nationalism*, 2nd edition (London, Hutchinson University Library).

Keens-Soper, M. (1989) 'The Liberal State and Nationalism in Post-War Europe', *History of European Ideas*, 10, 6.

Kellas, J. G. (1991) *The Politics of Nationalism and Ethnicity* (New York, St. Martins Press).

Kelly, G. A. (1999) 'Who Needs a Theory of Citizenship?', in R. Beiner (ed.) *Theorizing Nationalism*.

Kelsen, Hans (1969) 'Sovereignty and International Law', in Stankiewicz (ed.) *Defence of Sovereignty*.

Kleingel, P. (1999) 'Six Varieties of Cosmopolitanism in Late Eighteenth Century Germany', *Journal of History of Ideas*, 60, 3.

Kohn, Hans (1945) *The Idea of Nationalism: A Study in its Origins and Background* (New York, Macmillan).

Krabbe, H. (1930) *The Modern Idea of the State*, trans. G. H. Sabine and W. J. Shepherd (New York, D. Appelton and Co).

Kristeva, J. (1993) *Nations without Nationalism* (New York, Columbia University Press).

Kukathas, C. (ed.) (1993) *Multicultural Citizens: The Philosophy and Politics of Identity* (Canberra, The Centre for Independent Studies Readings 9).

Kukathas, C. (1997) 'Liberalism, Multiculturalism and Oppression', in Andrew Vincent (ed.) *Political Theory: Tradition and Diversity*.

Kymlicka, Will (1991) *Liberalism, Community and Culture* (Oxford, Clarendon Press).

Kymlicka, Will (ed.) (1995a) *The Rights of Minority Cultures* (Oxford, Clarendon Press).

Kymlicka, Will (1995b) *Multicultural Citizenship: A Liberal Theory of Minority Rights* (Oxford, Clarendon Press).

Kymlicka, Will (1996) 'Community' in Goodin and Pettit (eds) *A Companion to Contemporary Political Philosophy*.

Kymlicka, Will (1999) 'Comments on Shachar and Spinner-Halev: An Update from the Multicultural Wars', in Joppke and Lukes (eds) *Multicultural Questions*.

Laforest, Guy (1994) 'Philosophy in a Multinational Federation', in Tully (ed.) *Philosophy in an Age of Pluralism*.

Larmore, Charles (1990) 'Political Liberalism', *Political Theory*, 18, 3.

Lasch, C. (1988) 'The Communitarian Critique of Liberalism', in Charles Reynolds and Ralph Norman (eds) *Community in America: The Challenge of Habits of the Heart* (Berkeley, University of California Press).

Lichtheim, G. (1971) *Imperialism* (Middlesex, Harmondsworth).

Linklater, Andrew (1992) 'What is a Good International Citizen?', in P. Keal (ed.) *Ethics and Foreign Policy* (St. Leonards, NSW, Allen and Unwin).

List, Friedrich (1966) *The National System of Political Economy* (New York, Augustus M. Kelley).

Lubasz, H. (ed.) (1964) *The Development of the Modern State* (New York, Macmillan).

MacCormick, N. (1982) *Legal Rights and Social Democracy: Essays in Legal and Political Philosophy* (Oxford, Clarendon Press).

MacCormick, N. (1990) 'Of Self-Determination and other Things', in *Bulletin of the Australian Society of Legal Philosophy*, 15.

MacCormick, N. (1991) 'Is Nationalism Philosophically Credible?', in Twining (ed.) *Issues in Self-Determination*.

MacIntyre, A. (1981) *After Virtue: A Study in Moral Theory* (London, Duckworth).

MacIntyre, A. (1984) 'Is Patriotism a Virtue?' (Kansas, Kansas University Press).

MacIntyre, A. (1988) *Whose Justice? Which Rationality?* (London, Duckworth).

MacIntyre, A. (1995) 'The Spectre of Communitarianism', *Radical Philosophy*, 70 (March/April).

Maistre, Joseph de (1974) *Considerations on France*, originally published in 1797 (Montreal and London, McGill-Queens University Press).

Maitland, F. W. (1908) edited by H. A. L. Fisher, *The Constitutional History of England* (Cambridge, Cambridge University Press).

Malcomsen, Scott (1998) 'The Varieties of Cosmopolitan Experience', in Pheng Cheah and Robbins (eds) *Cosmopolitics*.

Marcus, George and Fischer, M. M. J. (1986) *Anthropology as Cultural Critique* (Chicago, Chicago University Press).

Marcuse, Herbert (1968) *One-Dimensional Man* (London, Sphere Books).

Margalit, G. and Raz, J. (1995) 'National Self-Determination', in W. Kymlicka (ed.) *The Rights of Minority Cultures*.

Maritain, J. (1969) 'The Concept of Sovereignty', in W. J. Stankiewicz (ed.) *In Defence of Sovereignty*.

Maslow, A. (1968) *Towards a Psychology of Being* (New York, Van Nostrand).

Matthews, H. C. J. (1973) *The Liberal Imperialists: The Ideas and Politics of a post-Gladstonian Elite* (Oxford, Clarendon Press).

Mayall, James (1990) *Nationalism and International Society* (Cambridge, Cambridge University Press).

Mayall, James (1999) 'Sovereignty, Nationalism and Self-Determination', in Jackson (ed.) 'Sovereignty at the Millennium', *Political Studies*.

McIlwain, Charles (1910) *The High Court of Parliament and its Supremacy* (New Haven, Conn., Yale University Press).

McKim, R. and McMahan, J. (eds) (1997) *The Morality of Nationalism* (Oxford, Oxford University Press).

McMurrin, S. M. (ed.) (1988) *The Tanner Lectures on Human Values*, VII (Salt Lake City, University of Utah Press).

Meinecke, F. (1957) *Machiavellianism: The Doctrine of Raison D'Etat and its place in modern history*, trans. Douglas Scott (London, Routledge and Kegan Paul).

Meinecke, F. (1970) *Cosmopolitanism and the Nation State* (Princeton, N.J., Princeton University Press).

Merriam, C. E. (1900) *History of the Theory of Sovereignty since Rousseau* (New York, Columbia University Press).

Mill, J. S. (1972) *Considerations on Representative Government* (London, Dent).

Miller, David (1987) 'Patriotism', in D. Miller *et al*, *The Blackwell Encyclopaedia of Political Thought* (Oxford, Blackwell).

Miller, David (1988a) 'Socialism and Toleration', in Susan Mendus (ed.) *Justifying Toleration* (Cambridge, Cambridge University Press).

Miller, David (1988b) 'The Ethical Significance of Nationalism', *Ethics*, 98.

Miller, David (1989a) *Market State and Community: Theoretical Foundations of Market Socialism* (Oxford, Clarendon Press).

Miller, David (1989b) 'In what sense must socialism be communitarian?', in E. F. Paul, F. D. Miller and J. Paul (eds) *Socialism* (Oxford, Blackwell).

Miller, David (1992) 'Community and Citizenship', in Schlomo Avineri and Avner De-Shalit (eds) *Communitarianism and Individualism*.

Miller, David (1994) 'Nation-State: A Modest Defence', in Chris Brown (ed.) *Political Restructuring in Europe: Ethical Perspectives*.

Miller, David (1995a) 'Citizenship and Pluralism', *Political Studies*, XLII.

Miller, David (1995b) *On Nationality* (Oxford, Clarendon Press).

Miller, David and Seidentop, Larry (eds) (1983) *The Nature of Political Theory* (Oxford, Clarendon Press).

Miller, David and Walzer, Michael (eds) (1995) *Pluralism, Justice and Equality* (Oxford, Clarendon Press).

Minogue, Ken (1969) *Nationalism* (London, Batsford).

Moore-Gilbert, Bart (1997) *Postcolonial Theory: Contexts, Practices, Politics* (London, Verso).

Moruzzi, Norma C. (1994) 'A Problem with Headscarves: Contemporary Complexities of Political and Social Identity', *Political Theory*, 22.

Mouffe, Chantal (1996) 'Democracy, Power and the Political', in Benhabib (ed.) *Democracy and Difference*.

Mulhall, Stephen and Swift, Adam (1996) *Liberals and Communitarians*, 2nd edition (Oxford, Blackwell).

Nagel, T. (1986) *The View from Nowhere* (Oxford, Oxford University Press).

Nathason, S. (1989) 'In Defence of "Moderate Patriotism"', *Ethics*, 99.

Nathason, S. (1993) *Patriotism, Morality and Peace* (Lanham, Rowman and Littlefield).

Nodia, G. (1994) 'Nationalism and Democracy', in Diamond and Plattner (eds) *Nationalism, Ethnic Conflict and Democracy*.

Nussbaum, Martha (1992) 'Human Functioning and Social Justice: In Defence of Aristotelian Essentialism', *Political Theory*, 2.

Nussbaum, Martha (1996) 'Patriotism and Cosmopolitanism', in Cohen (ed.) *For Love of Country*.

Nygren, Anders (1982) *Agape and Eros* (London, SPCK).

O'Neill, John (1994) 'Should Communitarians be Nationalists?', *Journal of Applied Philosophy*, 11, 2.

O'Neill, Onora (1986) *Faces of Hunger* (London, George Allen and Unwin).

O'Neill, Onora (1996) *Towards Justice and Virtue: A Constructive Account of Practical Reasoning* (Cambridge, Cambridge University Press).

O'Neill, Onora (2000) *Bounds of Justice* (Cambridge, Cambridge University Press).

Oakeshott, Michael (ed.) (1953) *The Social and Political Doctrines of Contemporary Europe* (New York and Cambridge, Cambridge University Press).

Oldfield, Adrian (1990) *Citizenship and Community: Civic Republicanism and the Modern World* (London, Routledge).

Palumbo, M. and Shanahan, W. O. (eds) (1981) *Nationalism: Essays in Honour of Louis L. Snyder* (Westport, Conn., and London, Greenwood Press).

Paul, E. F., Miller, F. D. and Paul, J. (eds) (1989) *Socialism* (Oxford, Blackwell).

Perelman, Chaim (1963) *The Idea of Justice and the Problem of Argument* (London, Routledge and Kegan Paul).

Pettit, Philip (1997) *Republicanism: A Theory of Freedom* (Oxford, Clarendon Press).

Pheng Cheah (1998) 'Given Culture: Rethinking Cosmopolital Freedom and Transnationalism', in Pheng Cheah and Robbins (eds) *Cosmopolitics*.

Pheng Cheah and Bruce Robbins (eds) (1998) *Cosmopolitics* (Minneapolis, London, University of Minnesota Press).

Pheng Cheah (1998) 'The Cosmopolitical – Today', in Pheng Cheah and Robbins (eds) *Cosmopolitics*.

Phillips, Anne (1996) 'Dealing with Difference: A Politics of Ideas, or a Politics of Presence?' in Benhabib (ed.) *Democracy and Difference*.

Phillips, Anne (1996) 'Democracy and Difference: Some Problems for Feminist Theory', in Kymlicka (ed.) *The Rights of Minority Cultures*.

Philpott, Daniel (1999) 'Westphalia, Authority and International Society', in Jackson (ed.) 'Sovereignty at the Millennium', *Political Studies*.

Plamenatz, J. (1976) 'Two Types of Nationalism', in E. Kamenka (ed.) *Nationalism: The Evolution of an Idea*.

Plant, R. (1976) *Community and Ideology: An Essay in Applied Social Philosophy* (London, Routledge).

Plant, R., Lesser, H. and Taylor-Gooby, P. (1980) *Political Philosophy and Social Welfare* (London, Routledge and Kegan Paul).

Plato (1971) *The Symposium*, trans. W. Hamilton (Harmondsworth, Penguin Books).

Plotinus (1969) *The Enneads*, trans. S. MacKenna (London, Faber and Faber).

Pocock, J. G. A. (1975) *The Machiavellian Moment: Florentine Political Thought and the Atlantic Republican Tradition* (Princeton, N.J., Princeton University Press).

Pogge, Thomas (1994) 'Cosmopolitanism and Sovereignty', in Brown (ed.) *Political Restructuring in Europe*.

Post, Gaines (1964) *Studies in Medieval Legal Thought: Public Law and the State 1100–1322* (Princeton, N.J., Princeton University Press).

Prakash, Gyan (1990) *Bounded Histories: Genealogies of Labor Servitude in Colonial India* (Cambridge, Cambridge University Press).

Pufendorf, Samuel Freiherr von (1991) *On the Duties of Man and Citizen*, trans. Michael Silverstone, ed. James Tully (Cambridge, Cambridge University Press).

Rabinow, Paul (1986) 'Representations are Social Facts', in J. Clifford and G. E. Marcus (eds) *Writing Culture: The Poetics and Politics of Ethnography*.

Rawls, J. (1993a) *Political Liberalism* (New York, Columbia University Press).

Rawls, J. (1993b) 'Justice as Fairness: Political not Metaphysical', in Tracy B. Strong (ed.) *The Self and the Political Order*.

Raz, J. (1994) 'Multiculturalism: A Liberal Perspective', *Dissent*, 41.

Responsive Community (Journal) (1991), 1, 3.

Reynolds, V. *et al* (1987) *The Sociobiology of Ethnocentrism: Evolutionary Dimensions of Xenophobia, Discrimination, Racism and Nationalism* (London, Croom Helm).

Ritchie, D. G. (1954) *Natural Rights* (London, George Allen and Unwin).

Robbins, B. (1993) *Secular Vocations: Intellectuals, Professionalism, Culture* (London, Verso).

Robbins, B. (1998a) 'Actual Existing Cosmopolitanism', in Pheng Cheah and Robbins (eds) *Cosmopolitics*.

Robbins, Bruce (1998b) 'Comparative Cosmopolitanism', in Pheng Cheah and Robbins (eds) *Cosmopolitics*.

Rorty, Richard (1989) *Contingency, Irony, and Solidarity* (Cambridge, Cambridge University Press).

Rorty, Richard (1998) 'Human Rights, Rationality and Sentimentality', in *Truth and Progress: Philosophical Papers*, vol. 3 (Cambridge, Cambridge University Press).

Rosen, Fred (1997) 'Nationalism and Early British Liberal Thought', *Journal of Political Ideologies*, 2, 2.

Said, Edward (1978) *Orientalism* (London, Routledge and Kegan Paul).

Said, Edward (1994) *Culture and Imperialism* (New York, Vintage Books).

Sandel, M. (1982) *Liberalism and the Limits of Justice* (Cambridge, Cambridge University Press).

Sandel, M. (1992) 'The Procedural Republic and the Unencumbered Self', in Tracy Strong (ed.) *The Self and the Political Order*. Reprinted in Schlomo Avinieri and Avner De-Shalit (eds) *Communitarianism and Individualism*.

Schafer, Boyd C. (1972) *Faces of Nationalism: New Realities Old Myths* (New York, Harcourt Brace Jovanovich).

Schmitt, C. (1985) *Political Theology: Four Chapters on the Concept Sovereignty* (Cambridge, Mass., MIT Press).

Schnapper, D. (1994) *La Communauté des Citoyens: Sur L'Idée Moderne de Nation* (Paris, Gallimard).

Scruton, Roger (1990) 'In Defence of the Nation', in *The Philosopher on Dover Beach* (London, Carcanet). Reprinted in Clark (ed.) *Ideas and Politics in Modern Britain*.

Scruton, Roger (1999) 'First Person Plural', in R. Beiner (ed.) *Theorizing Nationalism*.

Shachar, Ayelet (2000) 'On Citizenship and Multicultural Vulnerability', *Political Theory*, 28, 1.

Shklar, Judith (1984) *Ordinary Vices* (Cambridge, Mass. and London, Belknap Press of the Harvard University Press).

Skinner, Q. (1978) *The Foundations of Modern Political Thought*, 2 vols (Cambridge, Cambridge University Press).

Skinner, Q. (1998) *Liberty before Liberalism* (Cambridge, Cambridge University Press).

Smith, Anthony (1971) *Theories of Nationalism* (London and New York, Torchbook Library).

Smith, Anthony (1979) *Nationalism in the Twentieth Century* (Canberra, Australian National University Press).

Smith, Anthony (1986) *Ethnic Origins of Nations* (Oxford, Clarendon Press).

Smith, Anthony (1991) *National Identity* (Harmondsworth, Penguin).

Snyder, Louis (1954) *The Meaning of Nationalism* (New Brunswick and New Jersey, Rutgers University Press).

Soffer, Reba (1994) *Discipline and Power: The University and the Making of an English Elite 1870–1930* (Stanford, Stanford University Press).

Spivak, G. (1987) 'Subaltern Studies: Deconstructing Historiography', in Spivak, *In Other Worlds* (London, Methuen).

Stankiewicz, W. J. (ed.) (1969) *In Defence of Sovereignty* (Oxford, Oxford University Press).

Strong, Tracy B. (ed.) (1992) *The Self and the Political Order* (Oxford, Blackwell).

Sugar, Peter (1981) 'From Ethnicity to Nationalism and Back Again', in Palumbo and Shanahan (eds) *Nationalism: Essays in Honour of Louis L. Snyder*.

Tam, Henry (1998) *Communitarianism: A New Agenda for Politics and Citizenship* (London, Macmillan).

Tamir, Yael (1993) *Liberal Nationalism* (Princeton, N.J., Princeton University Press).

Tamir, Yael (1999) 'Theoretical Difficulties in the Study of Nationalism', in Beiner (ed.) *Theorizing Nationalism*.

Taylor, Charles (1986) 'Alternative Futures', in Taylor, *Legitimacy, Identity and Alienation in Late Twentieth Century Canada* (Toronto, Knopff and Morton).

Taylor, Charles (1989a) 'Cross Purposes: the Liberal-Communitarian Debate', in Nancy Rosenblum (ed.) *Liberalism and the Moral Life* (Cambridge, Mass., Harvard University Press).

Taylor, Charles (1989b) *Sources of the Self: The Making of Modern Identity* (Cambridge, Cambridge University Press).

Taylor, Charles (1992) *The Ethics of Authenticity* (Cambridge, Mass., Harvard University Press).

Taylor, Charles (1994) 'Reply and Re-articulation', in James Tully (ed.) *Philosophy in an Age of Pluralism*.

Taylor, Charles (1997) 'Nationalism and Modernity', in Robert McKim and Jeff McMahan (eds) *The Morality of Nationalism*.

Taylor, Charles (1999) 'Conditions of an Unforced Consensus on Human Rights', in Bauer and Bell (eds) *The East Asian Challenge for Human Rights*.

Tilley, Charles (ed.) (1975) *The Formation of National States in Western Europe* (Princeton, N.J., Princeton University Press).

Tolstoy, Leo (1974) 'Christianity and Patriotism' (originally published in 1893), in Tolstoy, *The Kingdom of God and Peace Essays* (London, Oxford University Press).

Tully, James (1995) *Strange Multiplicity* (Cambridge, Cambridge University Press).

Tully, James (ed.) (1994) *Philosophy in an Age of Pluralism: the Philosophy of Charles Taylor in question*, with the assistance of Daniel M. Weinstock (Cambridge, Cambridge University Press).

Twining, W. (ed.) (1991) *Issues in Self-Determination* (Aberdeen, Aberdeen University Press).

Ullman, W. (1975) *Medieval Political Thought* (Middlesex, Penguin)

Valery, Paul (1963) 'America: A Projection of the European Mind', in Paul Valery, *History and Politics* from *Collected Work of Paul Valery* (ed.) J. Mathews (London, Routledge and Kegan Paul).

Varouxakis G. (1998a) 'John Stuart Mill on Race', *Utilitas*, 10, 1.

Varouxakis G. (1998b) 'National Character in John Stuart Mill's Thought', *History of European Ideas*, 24, 6.

Varouxakis, G. (1998c) 'Nations and Nationalism: Theory, Ethics and Policy', *Contemporary Political Studies*, vol. 11 (Political Studies Association).

Vincent, Andrew (1987) *Theories of the State* (Oxford, Blackwell).

Vincent, Andrew (1989) 'Can Groups be Persons?', *Review of Metaphysics*, 42.

Vincent, Andrew (1990) 'The New Liberalism in Britain 1880–1914', *The Australian Journal of Politics and History*, 36, 3.

Vincent, Andrew (1995) 'Kant's Humanity', *Political Theory Newsletter*, 7, 2.

Vincent, Andrew (1997a) 'Liberal Nationalism: An Irresponsible Compound?', *Political Studies*, 45, 2.

Vincent, Andrew (1997b) 'Liberal Nationalism and Communitarianism: An Ambiguous Association', *The Australian Journal of Politics and History*, 3, 1.

Vincent, Andrew (2000) *Modern Political Ideologies*, 2nd edition (Oxford, Blackwell).

Vincent, Andrew (2001) 'Power and Vacuity: Nationalist Ideology in the Twentieth Century', in Michael Freeden (ed.) *Reassessing Political Ideologies*.

Vincent, Andrew (ed.) (1997) *Political Theory: Tradition and Diversity* (Cambridge, Cambridge University Press).

Vincent, Andrew and Plant, Raymond (1984) *Philosophy Politics and Citizenship* (Oxford, Blackwell).

Vincent, Andrew and Boucher, D. (2000) *British Idealism and Political Theory* (Edinburgh, Edinburgh University Press).

Virilio, Paul (1986) *Speed and Politics*, trans. Mark Polizzotti (New York, Semiotexte).

Viroli, M. (1995) *For Love of Country* (Oxford, Clarendon Press).

Walicki, Andrzej (1989) *Enlightenment and the Birth of Modern Nationhood: Polish Political Thought from Noble Republicanism to Tadeusz Kosciuszko* (Notre Dame, Indiana, University of Notre Dame Press).

Walzer, Michael (1977) *Just and Unjust Wars* (New York, Basic Books).

Walzer, Michael (1983) *Spheres of Justice: A Defence of Pluralism and Equality* (Oxford, Martin Robertson).

Walzer, Michael (1985) 'The Moral Standing of States' in Charles Beitz *et al* (eds) *International Ethics* (Princeton, N.J., Princeton University Press).

Walzer, Michael (1987) *Interpretation and Social Criticism* (Cambridge, Mass., Harvard University Press).

Walzer, Michael (1988) 'Interpretation and Social Criticism', in S. M. McMurrin (ed.) *The Tanner Lectures on Human Values*, VII (Salt Lake City, University of Utah Press).

Walzer, Michael (1990) 'The Communitarian Critique of Liberalism', *Political Theory*, 18, 1.

Walzer, Michael (1992) 'Reply to James B. Rule', *Dissent*, Fall.

Walzer, Michael (1994a) *Thick and Thin: Moral Arguments at Home and Abroad* (Notre Dame, Indiana, University of Notre Dame Press).

Walzer, Michael (1994b) 'Comment', in A. Gutman (ed.) *Multiculturalism*.

Walzer, Michael (ed.) (1995) *Towards a Global Civil Society* (Providence and Oxford, Berghahn Books).

Walzer, Michael (1997) 'The Politics of Difference', in R. McKim and J. McMahan (eds) *The Morality of Nationalism*.

Wight, Martin (1977) *Systems of States* (Leicester, Leicester University Press).

Williams, Howard (1983) *Kant's Political Philosophy* (Oxford, Blackwell).

Willoughby, W. W. (1896) *An Examination of the Nature of the State* (London, Macmillan).

Wood, Allen (1998) 'Kant's Project for Perpetual Peace', in Pheng Cheah and Bruce Robbins (eds) *Cosmopolitics*.

Yates, F. A. (1977) *Astraea: The Imperial Theme in the Sixteenth Century* (Middlesex, Penguin).

Young, Iris Marion (1990) *Justice and the Politics of Difference* (Princeton, N.J., Princeton University Press).

Young, Iris Marion (1995) 'Polity and Group Difference: A Critique of the Ideal of Universal Citizenship', in Beiner (ed.) *Theorizing Citizenship*.

Young, Iris Marion (1997) *Intersecting Voices: Dilemmas of Gender, Political Philosophy, and Policy* (Princeton, N.J., Princeton University Press).

Young, Robert (1990) *White Mythologies* (London, Routledge).

Index